NERVOUS EXHAUSTION

A Gen-X Saga of Clergy Abuse, PTSD, & The Path to Acceptance

ED HANRATTY

For Jay. And her patience.

PART 1	XXX
I	XXXI
II	XXXII
III	XXXIII
IV	XXXIV
V	PART 3
VI	XXXV
VII	XXXVI
VIII	XXXVII
IX	XXXVIII
X	XXXIX
XI	XLV
XII	XLVI
XIII	XLII
XIV	XLIII
XV	XLIV
XVI	XLV
XVII	XLVI
XVIII	
XIX	
PART 2	
XX	
XXI	
XXII	
XXIII	
XXIV	
XXV	
XXVI	
XXVII	
XXVIII	
XXIX	

PROLOGUE

"Did you tell Uncle Tommy what you're doing tomorrow?" My mother's voice carried a hint of anticipation, and she had a proud gleam in her eye. It was the first Monday morning of summer vacation after third grade, a pivotal moment that would alter the course of my life and leave an indelible mark on those around me.

"I'm serving my first mass," I replied, echoing with excitement and apprehension. It was a simple declaration, but little did I know how profoundly it would shape my future and influence the relationships I held dear.

Uncle Tommy wasn't my uncle by blood, much like his brother, "Uncle John," who hosted the June 1986 cookout. Yet, in our tight-knit community, familial titles transcended biological ties. It was a common practice to refer to family friends as "Aunt" or "Uncle."

Tommy was an Irish Christian Brother. Which was like a priest, but not entirely. I didn't understand the difference at nine. Prohibited from marrying, they could read the gospel at mass and administer communion—but they weren't officially priests. Come to think of it, I don't understand the difference at forty-seven either.

He was excited to hear about the journey I was about to embark upon on this overcast Sunday afternoon. He gave me pointers on how to light the big ass candles on the altar (I was deathly afraid of matches at the time)—told me about how he had to learn Latin to be an altar boy back in Brooklyn in the postwar era and how the role of an altar boy was much easier now, without golden spatulas to catch falling communion or second languages or the threat of being beaten by the priest for missing an assignment.

I remember the feeling of apprehension being relieved as Uncle Tommy taught me a trick about match lighting—folding the matchbook cover backward to shield your hands from the spark and how always to hold the lit match below the wick since holding it upside down makes the fire spread upwards towards your fingers. He made me excited about the role. And honestly, it was something I had aspired to be since my earliest remembrances of attending Catholic mass. There was something special about being up on the altar.

Of course, there was the priest, but he wasn't the only figure in the liturgy. There were ordinary folks, too, playing crucial roles. Those who read the scriptures guide the congregation through the First and Second Readings or the Responsorial Psalms. The vocalists, their voices soaring, leading us in song. And then there were the laypeople, like my grandmother, who assisted in the solemn communion ritual. Shuffling through the pews with the collection basket, even the hungover men from the local Knights of Columbus held a certain mystique. In a small town, these individuals became our de facto celebrities, especially to a child not yet ten years old. I couldn't help but stare when the mayor and his family graced our mass with their presence; it felt akin to being in the company of political royalty as if Ronald and Nancy Reagan were offering me the sign of peace.

Even at a young and awkward age, I didn't enjoy being on the sidelines. So it was only fitting that I was getting advice on the eve of my headfirst dive into active participation in the Catholic Mass from what you could consider an expert, a decorated veteran. He calmed my fears and my stage fright. He made me feel like I was about to embark on a path that would last my life. Hell, my father and Uncle John were both altar boys, and they were sitting at the same Bergenfield, New Jersey table I was. I was joining a club. At the ripe old age of nine, I was making a rite of passage into the exclusive company —company I looked up to.

But Uncle Tommy didn't tell me—what nobody told me that day—that becoming an altar boy would be the single most impactful decision of my life. I could never comprehend what my life would look like thirty-plus years later if I had chosen otherwise.

And that signing up to serve mass at St. Francis of Assisi would alter the lives of everyone I came to know and love for parts of 5 decades. I have no idea how my life would have been different if I had bypassed serving mass for the comfort of Fruity Pebbles and *The Smurfs* in 1986. And I never will.

PART 1

I

My upbringing adhered to the conventional Irish-Catholic norms of the 1950s. Mom held down the fort during the day while Dad worked. Sundays meant hearty family dinners at my grandparents' place after church, followed by watching whatever my father deemed suitable for our lone television set. It encapsulated the quintessential experiences of a white, middle-class family in the Eisenhower era. Except, of course, I made my debut in 1977, just eight days after President Jimmy Carter's inauguration.

We had contemporary clothes, cars, and haircuts. (A "contemporary" car in the 1980s was usually a 5-year-old used Chevy.) We were never the first family to have new tech, but we were never the last. We kept with the times in most other ways. But in an era when it was becoming less common—when a generation of "Latch Key kids" was emerging—my upbringing would involve a traditional nuclear family, born of two conventional nuclear families.

Mom, a homemaker, tried to run a tight ship. Dad, who worked "in finance," attempted to be the family policeman. And one figure commanded even more respect than they did: God.

This divine entity answered every query of my childhood and every question. Wondering why it was raining? God's tears. Thunder? That was God's angels bowling. Curious about a house move? God was gifting me a brother.

The Almighty explained even the most straightforward anatomical questions. "*Mom, why does dad stand up to go pee-pee, and you sit down?*" Because God gave boys a pecker so they could stand up to pee.

God reigned supreme in my family, providing the absolute answer from an early age. It made sense; kids bombard you with questions. I get it. But how long can you expect an inquisitive, developing human to keep falling for it?

You'd be surprised.

...

My father (and namesake) was born on September 14, 1950, the first of two twins—a few minutes before his brother Robert in Poughkeepsie, New York. Compared to his twin and my eventual godfather, Uncle Bob, Dad was a diminutive newborn and immediately experienced respiratory problems.

My grandmother never hesitated to let us know she didn't expect him to survive long enough to leave the hospital; hence, they named him Edward after his father. (I never really inquired how my grandfather felt about that decision. "*He's probably not going to make it, so let's name him after you.*") My father would always brag that he received the most sacraments out of anyone in the family, with the complications from his birth leading his mother to seek a priest so her child could receive the Anointing of the Sick/Last Rites—giving him six of the seven sacraments recognized by the Catholic Church.

But Dad would have what you could consider an American Baby Boomer Catholic upbringing as one of four kids born between 1946 and 1950. You go through the motions: You observe what you're supposed to observe, get your sacraments, show up Sunday morning, and spend the rest of your Sunday with family.

And you become an altar boy.

I have little intel on my grandfather—he passed away just two months after my parents tied the knot in 1974. My grandmother stuck around well into her eighties, witnessing her grandchildren getting hitched and even welcoming a few great-grandchildren. She embodied the essence of a good American Catholic. She sent all her kids to a Catholic school in The Bronx, served as a Eucharistic Minister (a lay person who dishes out communion at mass), and stuck to the daily mass grind as long as her health allowed.

Father Sean Horrigan, a Hanratty fixture from the parish of St. Phillip Niri, two blocks south of my grandparents' Grand Concourse apartment, was her companion at many family parties, functions, and sacraments. In 1969, Father Horrigan befriended my family in the tumultuous Bronx, married all of Mary's children, and baptized all but one of her grandchildren.

Despite his stubby stature and humble origins in County Cork, Father Horrigan exuded a quiet authority that commanded respect. His slicked-back salt-and-pepper hair framed a face weathered by years of wisdom and experience and not an insignificant amount of Scotch.

While his Irish-countryside accent may have been difficult to decipher, there was no mistaking the reverence with which people regarded him. From my earliest memories, my parents taught us to treat Father Horrigan with the same deference we would offer to God himself. So, whether it was a baptism, communion, confirmation, birthday, graduation, or wake, this Corkman chowing down on a tray of sausage and peppers was Jesus with a mild drinking issue to me.

That's how it was on the Hanratty side of the family. The Priest was a person of honor and reverence. Father Horrigan commanded more respect than my parents or grandparents by that white strip that popped into the collar of their all-black attire.

It was a very New York City Irish Catholic mindset.

•••

The maternal side of my family? It was a very *Irish* Irish Catholic mindset.

Philomena (Phyllis) Anne Reilly was born on June 12, 1950, in the recovering city of London, England—snagging the title of the first daughter in Bill and Rita Reilly's burgeoning family. Despite being born and raised in Dublin, the abundance of postwar rebuilding pulled my grandfather to England when the Irish economy suffered from high prices and unemployment.

When her little sister, my future Godmother Breda, joined the scene two ½ years later, the Reilly family had circled back to their roots in Dublin. And Ireland in the 1950s—like most of its post-Saint-Patrick existence—was soaking in Catholic vibes.

But despite rampant poverty on the Emerald Isle, as clear from Irishmen like my grandfather seeking greener pastures in places like London, Manchester, and Liverpool, every photo from my mother's early years showcased relatives dressed to the nines for Catholic sacraments like baptisms, communions, confirmations, or weddings.

A few months after the Beatles landed at JFK airport in Queens, New York, another quartet from the European islands, the Reillys, arrived. They carried their unwavering devotion to the Roman Catholic Church straight to the shores of northeastern New Jersey.

My mother and aunt swiftly enrolled in Holy Trinity Elementary School in Hackensack, New Jersey. It didn't faze them that the family crammed into a one-room apartment in Bergen County's capital. The priority was tuition to the local Catholic school, and my grandparents hustled to offer more than a run-of-the-mill unscientific education for their two daughters.

Grandpa, a union carpenter at Fairleigh Dickinson University in Teaneck, New Jersey, clocked in 25 years of labor. Meanwhile, Nana navigated the transport realm at Holy Name Hospital in the same town where they eventually acquired a home. Remarkably, neither of them ever wielded a driver's license.

Yet, religious commitment was their forte. Grandpa walked over a mile to church weekly, while Nana took the pious route and did it daily. Catholic iconography adorned their home, a sanctuary where I found unbridled comfort. Holy water fonts graced both entryways and crossing the threshold meant an automatic self-blessing, a ritual for everyone, including yours truly.

Saint Elizabeth Seton's ceramic likeness held court on the mantle, crucifixes adorned every room, and a driveway grotto dedicated to the Blessed Mother stood tall. It was stationed perfectly in sight of the kitchen window, offering Nana a chance to pray while doing the dishes. There was no escaping Jesus or his mom; they watched over you from every angle.

Among the Catholic trinkets, Nana maintained a collection box for the "Children of Saint Joseph," whoever they were. In her defense, only pennies, nickels, and dimes found their way to St. Joe's kids. Quarters, well, those were reserved for the arcade games during our yearly summer getaway to the Jersey Shore, where, yes, she still sought daily mass.

In a twist of fate, these two Irish Catholic worlds collided on a Saturday night in 1972 at the fittingly named Hitching Post in the Bronx, where my parents' story began. Now, I've done my best to suppress the cringe-worthy details of their first date—let's say alcohol and the opposite sex were involved—but there's enough left to craft a vivid picture.

Believe it or not, people danced with each other in the early seventies, and the Hitching Post was a hot spot in the Bronx for those moves. If you've ever endured "Saturday Night Fever," your parents meeting in such a place might turn your stomach.

Two years later, Father Horrigan would marry them. A native Irishman who ran a Bronx parish blessed this union of Old World and New in Holy Trinity Church in Hackensack, New Jersey.

When I was born 2 ½ years later, I didn't stand a chance of avoiding a life painted by the mores and structure of the Roman Catholic Church.

II

I got my baptismal ticket to Catholicism punched as Edward Michael Hanratty III on February 20, 1977, at Holy Trinity in Hackensack—the exact spot where my folks tied the knot three years prior. And indeed, Father Horrigan did the honors three weeks after my late January birth.

Even the stories from my diaper days that survived had a holy twist. My mother loves to share the one about when we were at Holy Trinity for Sunday mass, and I spotted Dr. McAuliffe, my pediatrician, in the pew behind us. Allegedly, I kicked up such a fuss—screaming and crying—that Mom had to escort me out.

As I got older, I attended a special mass for someone in the family. In the Catholic playbook, you can shell out (yes, there's always a fee) for a mass dedicated to a loved one or celebrating a milestone. As a double-Irish-Catholic family, we had our fair share. When the celebrant stepped out to light the altar candles, I burst into a rendition of "Happy Birthday to You." Supposedly, it set off a round of laughter. Not the grandest commotion I'd stir up in the Church, but laughter's good for the soul, so they tell me.

The pivotal part of my toddlerhood had little to do with doctors, candles, or churches. It was a move my parents made—a choice likely fueled by pure economics and the intricacies of public transit.

We crammed into a one-bedroom pad in Hackensack until my "terrible twos"–allegedly epic. This was the same turf my grandparents landed on after their immigration escapades until they upgraded to a place just over the Hackensack River in Teaneck. I can't confirm if I snored back then, like the nocturnal freight train I am now, but I reckon my folks longed for the luxury of their own private bedroom. Sleeping in the same room as me has never been a treat for anyone involved.

Dad worked at an accounting firm in Midtown Manhattan while pursuing a bachelor's degree at Fairleigh Dickinson. Back in those days, when getting a college degree didn't require mortgaging your future, relatives of university employees got sweet tuition discounts. Thanks to my grandfather's gig, Dad paid next to nothing for his college credits.

We only had a hand-me-down Chevy Nova with plaid interior upholstery, so Dad relied on New Jersey Transit to shuttle him to and from work—a tale familiar to many North Jersey dwellers. They set their sights on a village south of Teaneck, just across the river.

The Village of Ridgefield Park traces its founding back to 1685. Known as "RP" to the locals, it nestled near the southern tip of Bergen County, a perennial contender for the country's most affluent counties. Folks from the Big Apple have always eyed the suburbs for family-raising, and in every direction, there was an opportunity for space (and sprawl). South led to Staten

Island or the gateway to the Jersey Shore. North would take you through Manhattan to Westchester County, New York, and to the Hudson River Valley. East, through Queens, lands you on Long Island, which can seem like an eternal drive but has limited space before you hit the Ocean or the Sound. Or you could head west, cross the Lincoln Tunnel or the George Washington Bridge, and find solace in your bucolic suburban haven in minutes.

RP offered adequate but not abundant space, incredible proximity to all areas of work and commerce, and a decidedly middle-class demography. While there were a handful of well-off families up north and low-income housing units on the southern tip of town, the general vibe in RP was what I'd call "baby blue-collar." White-collar families meant middle management corporate types, teachers, salesmen, or small business owners. Blue-collar households housed skilled laborers—union members, independent contractors, cops, and mechanics. Class division wasn't a thing in twentieth-century Ridgefield Park, at least not in the last two decades I called it home.

Most homes were single-lot properties with modest front yards and slightly roomier backyards. Main Street was a bustling hub, offering groceries, flowers, restaurants, shoes, toys, clothes, stationery, bicycles, records, liquor, insurance - anything you could need before the prevalence of shopping malls littered the Bergen County landscape. A gas station and a lone movie theater. Two haircutters. A family-run pharmacy. Three pizzerias, vying for customers with a bunch from nearby towns. For a historical touch, the town post office housed a Depression-Era WPA mural in the lobby, depicting indigenous folks gazing at the Hudson River that separates Manhattan from New Jersey.

It was as "small town USA" as you could get while living less than five miles from the Hudson. I eventually traversed the town on foot for over a thousand miles, biked through every nook and cranny, and even hand-painted every yellow curb in RP. It was an ideal two square miles of land to grow up in—and it emanated from its epicenter.

Primarily a north-to-south town in terms of general traffic flow, RP has its heart cut by the east-to-west Mount Vernon Street. And right smack in the middle stood St. Francis of Assisi Roman Catholic Church. There were about half a dozen other churches in town, mainly Protestant, and one synagogue. But St. Francis, with its attached elementary school, reigned supreme in the RP community. Even if your folks sent you to public school, odds were high they enrolled you in "CCD" (Confraternity of Christian Doctrine)—a weekly after-school crash course in Catholicism, prepping you for childhood sacraments like Reconciliation, First Communion, and if your folks were dead set on it (or your grandparents were still kicking,) Confirmation.

The neo-Gothic structure boasted a bell tower, making it the highest point in town. It was visible for blocks in each direction as it sat at the elevated peak of the town. Standing tall for ninety years, it wasn't unusual in 1980 to find many second-and-third-generation parishioners who had spent their lives in town remaining active in the church.

At the southern end of Teaneck Road, the busiest road in town, the Hanratty family planted their roots in a 2 bedroom basement apartment.

•••

My first vivid memory of Nana and Grandpa's cozy abode in Teaneck dates back to the chilly early hours of January 7, 1980. I found myself there in my pajamas because the little blessing that God gave my mother was ready to enter the world. It was also when I first noticed the Holy Water fountain in their side vestibule. I wasn't entirely sure how to bless myself properly—In the name of The Father, and of The Son, and The Holy Spirit, Amen, while forming the sign of the cross from forehead to chest to left shoulder and right. But from that moment until my last visit to the house in 1999, I instinctively made that sacred gesture.

Later that day, Nana's phone rang, sealing the deal—we were officially a family of four. Sean William Hanratty was born around 3:00, marking one of the most pivotal moments of my life. He would become my constant companion through every significant event and turning point I'd ever encountered, even though I couldn't stand him initially. He cried—a lot. I get it; babies cry, but man, I wasn't prepared for that.

A few months later, we baptized Sean. Father Horrigan naturally officiated the ceremony. This time, however, it happened at our new "home" parish: St. Francis of Assisi.

A year after Sean's arrival, my parents enrolled me in a half-day program at an Episcopal school called "Saint James" nearby. Ostensibly, it was to socialize me. It wasn't daycare or one of those prestigious institutions crucial for Ivy League aspirations. St. James was a blur in my memory, with one classmate rumored to have starred in an Oscar Mayer lunchmeat commercial and another with the last name "Boner." My parents enjoyed teasing me by asking me to repeat her name in front of their friends and siblings.

Regrettably, St. James marked just the beginning of my academic adventure. I had to endure a ten-year stint at a different institution. In the fall of 1981, I ascended a 20-foot concrete staircase into the brick tower that housed St. Francis of Assisi Elementary School, which offered Pre-K through 8.

Pre-K and kindergarten felt like an extension of the playtime I enjoyed at St. James. More blocks, arts and crafts, and naps, but with an added dose of God. Hymns praising God and Jesus dominated our musical repertoire. Christmas tilted more towards the manger than Santa, and Easter was less about bunnies and more about, brace yourself, a man rising from the dead. At that point, death was an abstract concept for me. I knew Grandpa Eddie was "in heaven," but did that mean he could claw his way out of that grave in Monsey, NY, which we visited every summer?

Despite the absurdity of this indoctrination, I fell for it completely. I'd come home proudly declaring God's love for me, sermonizing about Jesus dying for our sins and how it meant we could visit Grandpa Eddie in heaven. My parents enrolled me in the town's recreational soccer league that year, and I'd pray to Jesus before every game, seeking divine help in my athletic pursuits. (Never take an athlete seriously when they thank the Lord. I am living proof that no matter how fervently you pray to Christ for athletic prowess, it just doesn't cut it.)

But for all the early childhood brainwashing, I'll never forget St. Francis' kindergarten, for whom I met more than what I learned.

I still remember our teacher, Mrs. Bowles—with her short, dyed perm that every non-nun at St. Francis seemed to have—leading Jaime Reap into the classroom by her hand and introducing her to the rest of the half-day class. Maybe it was because I had no older siblings or friends in my third year of schooling outside of the ones I had made via my parents, but I immediately found myself drawn to this lanky, shy girl with dirty blonde hair.

I know that "a crush" has a different definition as you move through life. A crush at 12 differs from one at 16, and that's a far cry from a crush at 22. At 5 or 6, though? That's a funny crush. I mean, you aren't getting physically aroused, but there's something magnetic there. I guess you could call it cute. Hell, if I know. But I had a crush on Jaime Reap. It carried into first grade, where we were again placed in the same class.

III

In my memory, St. James Pre-School, St. Francis Pre-K, and Kindergarten melded together. Via hindsight, I learned some valuable cognitive and social skills, but it often felt like a never-ending arts and crafts project. And that May, we even crafted clay ashtrays for our mothers, a surprisingly unquestionable and practical choice for Mother's Day that would probably get you locked up today.

Both school years operated on half-day schedules; kindergarten was little more than glorified babysitting back then, and many stay-at-home moms were able to pick their children up in the middle of the day. However, once we transitioned to 1st grade, everything changed drastically, and it wasn't just about the mandatory uniforms and the extended school day.

The early developmental stages kept us isolated from the rest of the institution. No recess or lunch meant no chance to mingle with older students. Splitting us into morning and afternoon sessions for kindergarten also meant missing out on assemblies and the like. While we were vaguely aware of the church and parish figures, our interactions were limited, mostly confined to our "graduations."

The moment they thrust a baby blue shirt, navy pants, black shoes, and a navy/blue/gold argyle tie on me each day, it became an entirely different paradigm. It was the same brick building but an altogether different school.

The daily structure was more rigid than anything I'd encountered in my short time on earth. Before school started, we had to gather and line up outside, separated not only by gender but also in height order. This made the tallest kid (me) feel awkward, and the shortest one felt inadequate. Great rearing.

The day began with a morning prayer, followed by the pledge of allegiance and a directive to open whatever workbook the lesson dictated. In first grade, the subjects were straightforward: Religion, Math, Phonics, Spelling, and Reading. Every classroom boasted the same standardized clock, its thin red seconds-hand audibly ticking away during periods of silence. And it was quiet—a lot.

But I thrived in it! In first grade, I received an A or 100 mark in every subject, made the biannually published "Honor Roll," and came home from school itching to do my homework. I couldn't wait for Dad to get home to tell him about my day. All I wanted to talk about was school.

In the middle of my first-grade adventures, the Hanratty crew officially expanded to five members, with my first sister, Elizabeth Ann Hanratty, born on the memorable date of February 9, 1984. Just like Sean before her, Elizabeth underwent the sacred ritual of baptism at St. Francis, a ceremony once again presided over by the familiar Irishman, Father Horrigan.

My entire class celebrated her birth, as our teacher assigned all students to make a card—on pink construction paper—welcoming Elizabeth into the world. It was a tremendous, spontaneous art project you could keep repeating. First graders in a Catholic school in a town that was predominantly full of second and third-generation Irish and Italian residents are prime for sibling acquisition. Twenty kids in a class, you could bank on about half of them getting a sibling: that's two weeks of art. I remember making a card for Jaime Reap's third brother just a month before she made one for Elizabeth.

...

Around half of the faculty were nuns, part of the "Sisters of Charity" order. They were still adjusting to the relatively new rule that prohibited them from beating the daylights out of kids. The principal, Sister Katherine, was elderly but not quite decrepit like some of her "sisters." Stern and imposing, she was a broad-shouldered woman whose uniform, from habit to shoes, was as impeccably maintained as a Marine in dress blues. Despite her intimidating demeanor, she emitted an aura of warmth and compassion, a stark contrast to most other convent women. While not precisely humorous, she was approachable and tried to know each student personally, along with their families.

I suspect my fond memories of her might be different had she been the principal when I was an upperclassman, but for a first-grader, she commanded respect without inducing fear.

On the flip side was Sister Virginia, whom I can only categorize as the lunchroom monitor—evil in every sense. A blend of a garden gnome possessed by Vlad the Impaler and the Tasmanian Devil. She was too short to be a jockey but could probably intimidate the 1986 Giants offensive line. Given Ridgefield Park's tight-knit community and St. Francis as its epicenter, tales of Sister Virginia's corporal punishment era still echo well into the 21st century. When we encountered her, she couldn't have been younger than 80, and I wouldn't be shocked if she were a centenarian.

Sister Therese had recently joined the ranks at the St. Francis convent. Though the exact date eluded me, her inaugural third-grade class still roamed through the hallways, placing her arrival within five years of my enrollment. At a sprightly fifty-nine years old, she barely qualified as legal in nun years.

Meanwhile, Sister Rosemary and Sister Maryanne ruled the fifth and eighth grades. Beyond the confines of school, they were an inseparable duo, popping up around town, venturing to malls further out in the county, and even catching matinee movies together. For two mature women sharing the same convent roof, they spent an extraordinary amount of time side by side.

Just a stone's throw south of the convent stood the St. Francis Rectory, presided over by the formidable Father Francis Ignacuinos. Despite his unassuming stature, his reputation as the drill sergeant of St. Francis preceded him. From a young age, a simple mantra was engrained in us—don't fuck with Father Francis, for lack of a better term. Legend had it he could reduce kids to tears with a mere glance if their report cards fell short of his expectations.

The teachers wielded him like a sadistic Santa Claus, threatening to report any classroom misbehavior to him to keep us in line.

Father Francis' trusty sidekick, Father Joseph Vaccaro, cut a stocky figure into middle age. He was an amiable soul, often spotted tossing a tennis ball around the schoolyard. However, he harbored a peculiar fondness for the Blessed Mother, and his coaxing often took on a weird tone as he'd inquire, "What's it going to take to get you to say the Rosary daily? A shot in the arm?"

There was no faith-based exercise worse than the awful repetition of the Rosary. A total of 55 "Hail Marys," plus I think one for good luck, separated ten a clip by an "Our Father." There was some "Glory Be" sprinkled in there, and it fucking took forever to say. Still, some hardcore devotees would show up at 7:00 PM every weeknight to say the Rosary.

The parish had a series of "third priests" during my first five years of schooling at St. Francis. One of them, Father Reyes, had a heavy Spanish accent so thick I could never understand a word he was saying. Naturally, I chose him to receive my First Penance—my second sacrament.

Now referred to as a more affable "First Reconciliation," the sacrament of Penance requires the sinner to confess their sins to a representative of Christ (a priest). You verbalize all of your sins and transgressions. The priest informs you of your penance—usually reciting a few prayers, perhaps making restitution to the offended—you do it, and Voila! You're absolved of sin.

My Jewish friends do this so much better, from my perspective. One day a year, sit in the corner and think about what you've done. The rap sheet gets wiped clean for the following year.

•••

If first grade was an orientation to the parish surroundings, second grade was the initiation into them. By this point, I had already delved into recreational soccer and baseball, acquainting myself with some Ridgefield Park kids beyond the confines of St. Francis. When sacrament season rolled around, our age group saw a noticeable surge with the addition of students from Grant, Roosevelt, or Lincoln public schools at these after-school rehearsals.

It took little time to catch wind of the collective nickname given to us uniform-clad students: "The St. Francis Sissies"–a moniker straightforward and impactful. The nuns didn't exactly ease the intimidation, either. Every day, we were admonished about the supposed loose morals of public school children, painting a picture as if every public school resembled the disciplinary challenges of Joe Clark's Eastside, from *Stand By Me* fame.

First Holy Communion class brought us together with the public schoolers. The girls adorned themselves like child brides, and my mother took me to West New York's garment district to buy a new blue suit for the occasion. Then, we drove to Sears for the requisite commemorative photos.

In the lead-up to the big day, we diligently practiced the intricate choreography of the ceremony. We learned the art of forming lines, the procession down the aisle, the entrance into pews, and the maneuvering out of them to queue up for communion. The intricacies extended to the method of receiving communion—a choice between the mouth and hands. A lingering skepticism toward mouth receivers remains with me to this day. The act of one human feeding another human should be reserved for the infirmed or the excessively romantic.

Our rehearsals also involved a curious ritual of practicing the consumption of wine, albeit the non-alcoholic variety, as the church had made that switch a few years earlier.

The grandeur of the celebration didn't end with the religious proceedings; it continued with a lavish party and a showering of gifts. The attention hoisted upon me was unprecedented, each envelope containing what felt like a small fortune, with $50 or $100 bills. This windfall was entirely alien to me; never had I possessed over twenty bucks on any given birthday.

The "Welcome to the Club" vibe surrounding the event was real. The following Monday in school, we eagerly compared notes and discussed the impressive hauls, collectively astonished by the unexpected loot.

Brimming with the afterglow of First Holy Bounty, the allure of the church continued to pull me in new directions. Throughout my third-grade year, the prospect of becoming an altar boy loomed over my days like a sacred obligation, though it was not considered a sacrament.

The reminders were incessant, whispered in hushed tones during religion class, and subtly woven into conversations about our roles in the church. The school's influence wielded immense pressure as if joining the ranks of altar boys was a rite of passage, an expected progression in our Catholic journey. At home, it seemed like a foregone conclusion. I was going to be an altar boy. All but two Catholic boys in my grade signed up to serve mass.

•••

The St. Francis Altar Boys were organized by Mrs. Kennedy–a tiny, grandmotherly woman in her mid-50s. The youngest of her four children was still in St. Francis, and Mrs. Kennedy had been overseeing the group for about fifteen years by the summer my class joined. She ran the organization with the love of a mother running a household. She remembered birthdays. She organized field trips. She coordinated fundraisers—all with a gentle smile that commanded so much respect. You would hate to disappoint her.

Her "bad cop" was anything but. Mr. James Paddock was a tall, lean senior gentleman well into his seventies. He billed himself as "the world's oldest altar boy," as he was a daily congregant at 7 AM mass (in a full three-piece suit) and would fill in if the scheduled altar boy did not show up.

Together, Mrs. Kennedy and Mr. Paddock fostered a wholesome family environment. Altar boy meetings and events were always different from other general school activities. We left playground tensions or hostilities at the door. A collection of boys between third and eighth grade would routinely remain quiet, attentive, and respectful.

Training seemed daunting. Memorizing what to do throughout a Catholic mass was like memorizing your lines as the lead for a school play. This was heavier learning than Phonics and multiplication flash cards.

In reality, it became second nature before I served my first mass a fortnight later (there wasn't much of an incubation period between sign-up and serving—kind of like Vietnam). The altar boy's duty begins when he walks into the sacristy, the private area connected to the altar.

The St. Francis sacristy was up one flight of stairs from "the rectory entrance," as opposed to the main entrance facing Mount Vernon Street, or the "Side Entrance" on Euclid Avenue—at some point very early in my memory, this became the handicap entrance when the church installed a wheelchair lift.

As you stepped into the sacristy, a sizable, center-island table immediately commanded attention, resembling a bar-top in height and stretching at least 8 feet long by 4 feet wide. On the left, you'd find the altar boy cloaking area, where we hung our cassocks to meet the discerning standards of Mr. Paddock. The availability of suitable garments was a hit-or-miss affair, leaving much to chance. Factor in the unpredictable growth spurts of boys aged nine to fourteen and a laundry system reliant on nuns or volunteers, and my skinny ass either felt like I was wearing a tent or wrapped in cellophane.

A sink and a series of tables were past the center island against the north-facing windows. On one of them was a book where you signed in. This was how Mrs. Kennedy kept attendance—a strict honor system. However, she occasionally attended a weekday mass and was a surefire bet for one of the five Sunday masses: 7:00, 8:30, 10:00, 11:30, and 1:00 PM. Calling up the altar boy you were scheduled to serve with and asking him to sign your name for you wouldn't be unheard of, but doing so meant playing with fire. Mrs. Kennedy wasn't stupid, and 10-year-old boys aren't known for handwriting-duplication skills.

Next to the sign-in desk was a chair. You never sat in the chair. That chair was for the priest's ass only.

Opposite the cloakroom was a closet that ran the size of the entire wall. This held the priestly vestments and the individual chalices—the fancy precious metal wine glasses—each priest possessed. Finally, at the end of the vestment closet was a mini fridge—this held the sacramental wine. Again, it was non-alcoholic and had a twist-off cap.

A horrendous royal-and-navy blue shag carpet blanketed the sacristy. It bled out to cover the complete altar so that the view from the front pews of the church could make you seasick, getting lost in the patterns of the shag. And when you had to kneel on it, you got the whiff of decades' worth of incense, spilled wine, and whatever other elemental remnants a carpet can pick up.

The sacristy and altar appeared to us as they did to the generations of altar boys who served before us. We were the next in line of what we were told was a proud and pious tradition. We were tipped cash for weddings and funerals. What wasn't to love?

...

For all the hype and attention that becoming an altar boy earned us, truth be told, it was the most effortless responsibility I've ever had—at least the official duties were. Before the mass, your job comprised lighting the altar candles and filling the decanters holding the water and wine for the transubstantiation portion of the mass—the minute a wafer becomes a Messiah.

You didn't have to do that much more during mass. You led the priest to the altar—on weekdays, you entered directly from the sacristy. On Sundays, you led from the back of the church up the center aisle, one of you carrying a crucifix scepter.

The mass's most strenuous part occurred right after the opening greeting. You had to bring the prayer book up to the priest and keep it held open as he recited a series of ritualistic blessings (that I knew by heart, so you know he did — holding that damn heavy ass volume was unnecessary.)

After that, you had nothing to do but look holy through the readings, gospel, sermon, and responsorial psalms. When it came time to consecrate the wine and bread, you brought the two decanters to the altar. One altar boy would hold a dish while the other poured water over the priest's fingers.

The priest would whisper, "Lord, wash away my iniquities and cleanse me from my sins."

Just like that, inequities were washed, sins were cleansed, and the priest was in good enough grace to administer the body and blood of Christ.

After that, you were all done until the final blessing, where you once again carried that book boulder up to the top of the altar so the big guy could recite a prayer he'd already recited 10,000 times.

Once mass was over, you would head back into the sacristy, turn, face the priest, kneel, and bow your head as he gave a special blessing to you. In reality, there was nothing special about it. Both Fr. Francis and Fr. Vaccaro would do little more than make the sign of the cross over you.

So, despite the intimidation factor or the pressure of being that close to the action with all eyes on you, I felt very prepared on that cool June morning right after the third grade ended for the year and served my first mass as an Altar Boy. That same morning, I discovered that Father Francis had halitosis and bathed in Old Spice.

For the rest of my life, I would be "discovering" things about my time as an altar boy.

IV

To this day, the pivotal year of 1986 is a defining moment of change and transition in my life. The year brought about seismic shifts within both my family dynamics and the confines of St. Francis School. Among these changes, the most significant was the Hanratty clan's move from our apartment to a one family house. The address, 208 Teaneck Road, was only a mile north of the building we were leaving — a prewar home boasting three bedrooms, a single bath, and a prime location along the busiest north-to-south road in town.

It was an understated house with practical amenities: two driveways, an unfinished basement, and an attic that would later transform into a fourth bedroom. A spacious fenced-in backyard would become the backdrop for family parties and eventually boast a massive above-ground pool.

I wouldn't have my own bedroom yet, but I would have a backyard, and I was okay with that.

I waded into rock 'n' roll waters, insisting that my mom chauffeur me to Bradlee's department store to snag a vinyl copy of Bon Jovi's "Slippery When Wet." Bon Jovi mania was in full swing in the heart of New Jersey, with "Livin' on a Prayer" dominating MTV and Z100 radio rotations. Everywhere you heard it, you overheard someone say, "He's from Jersey, ya know."

Most significant of all domestic changes, however, was the announcement that my mother was pregnant again, ten years, almost precisely after she was carrying me in utero. Hanratty Child #4 was due a mere day after my tenth birthday.

In St. Francis School and Parish, there were massive changes as well. Sister Katherine, the principal, retired from her post, taking three decades of stale, rote Catholic education out the door with her. In her place was a 52-year-old whippersnapper, Sister Patricia Meidhoff. A New Jersey native, Sister Patricia could be a miniature pinscher or a warm, motherly figure, depending on the day. Isn't it strange that we force kids to deal with the multiple personalities of authority figures?

Sister Virginia was gone, called home to Satan over the summer. Her replacement in the lunchroom, Sister Eileen, was as sweet as she was senile.

The most noticeable change in the parish didn't occur in the school or convent, but in the rectory. Following a series of rotating priests that culminated in another confessor struggling with broken English, a new young priest with local roots was assigned to our parish during the significant summer of 1986.

Hurricane Gerry made landfall at St. Francis with the Reverend Gerald E. Sudol arriving between the 3rd and 4th grades. He was a larger-than-life presence, standing tall at over 6'1", commanding attention with a robust frame, conservatively weighing in at 275 lbs. Sporting a crown of thick, black, curly hair that seemed to have a life of its own, exuding an aura of vitality and energy, he was the antithesis of the graying, deteriorating relic of "I Love Lucy" days that St. Francis has devolved into.

His nose, long and distinctive, added character to a face adorned with rosy red cheeks, creating a juxtaposition of strength and warmth. Despite his imposing physical stature, he was remarkably open and affectionate, embodying a rare combination of Father Francis' perceived strength and Father Vacarro's kind gentleness. He moved through the parish in his opening weeks with an embracing spirit, readily offering warmth and camaraderie to everyone he met. His sheer physicality caught your eye, but his genuine, affectionate nature left a lasting impression, turning this formidable figure into an approachable and endearing presence that was so desperately needed in the parish.

He was the parish's first Baby Boomer priest.

Almost overnight, St. Francis morphed from a staid, depressing laughingstock to a hip place on Sundays—even for the public school kids!

•••

I served my first mass with Father Gerry during that summer. It was a Sunday mass, possibly his first. The most noticeable thing was that he never sat in "The chair." Every other priest commanded that chair at least ten minutes before showtime, but I don't recall Gerry seated in the sacristy.

Instead, he would engage in interesting conversation. Did you go on vacation this summer? Do you play any sports? What's your favorite subject? How are your grades? It's hard to understate how important those questions and connections made me feel. The philosophy that children should be seen and not heard governed the first five years of my St. Francis sentence. If you stood out, it probably wasn't for a good reason. Sister Patricia slowly eased that approach in the school. Gerry Sudol blew right through it in the church.

His sermons would reference MTV or Indiana Jones, and he kept the congregation engaged the entire time, no small feat with a parish used to the low-key, low-inspiration mumblings of the existing clergy.

The most noticeable difference, however, took place behind closed doors. When we returned to the sacristy following mass, he halted us from taking our position down on one knee and bowing our heads. Instead, he pulled us in for a hug, one altar boy under one shoulder, the other two under another, and I heard the blessing that would repeat over and over in my head for decades for the first time:

"For all that you are, and for whatever your needs may be, especially any needs that might make you worried, anxious, or afraid, I ask the heavenly father to bless you in the name of the Father, and of the Son, and of the holy spirit, Amen."

We then got pulled in tighter for one last bear hug and left with smiles.

Soon, Sunday mass would take an additional twenty minutes because everybody and their mother wanted to meet and greet Father Gerry outside the main entrance. He appeared to have memorized the name of every parishioner he introduced himself to. Before fourth grade kicked off, it was as if Gerry Sudol had been a part of the St. Francis community for a decade.

It didn't take long before rumors started circulating that he was sent as a pastoral replacement for Father Francis. It was accepted widely, and he would have agreed himself, that Father Vacarro was not pastor material, preferring to peruse the ground, moving his lips as he recited the Rosary and basking in the wonder of the Blessed Mother. Likewise, it was becoming painfully apparent that Father Francis couldn't handle the responsibilities of the parish as he was approaching his seventieth birthday. He was developing a noticeable tremor in his hands, and the bend in his back was becoming quickly more exaggerated.

This breath of fresh air felt like a natural replacement.

Father Francis continued to wield influence over the parish despite the intriguing new principal who had taken charge at the school. However, one individual who should have commanded attention was our fresh fourth-grade teacher, Mrs. Rothbaum.

The compensation at St. Francis was not particularly enticing. During my early years at the school, the absence of a teachers' union and less stringent accreditation standards contributed to a noticeable turnover of laypeople. Mrs. Rothbaum was another one-and-done.

Dealing with nine- and ten-year-old boys is undoubtedly a handful, but our collective mischief in fourth grade surpassed what we had exhibited in third grade or would later exhibit in fifth grade under the guidance of a nun. It felt like a pre-adolescent Rumspringa—like some instinctual switch flipped and told us this was our year to be rambunctious.

Classroom discipline was a constant challenge. We resisted returning to our seats during the poorly implemented "free time" period, leading to stern warnings from other teachers or even Sister Patricia herself, who had to intervene regularly.

Mrs. Rothbaum, being Jewish, had to leave the room daily for Sister Therese to take over and teach our religion lesson. Oddly enough, this lesson did not differ from what Sister Therese had taught us the previous year, and we even used the same Catechism book—The New Saint Joseph Baltimore Catechism Number 2.

That Catechism book, a mind-bending relic from the 1880s revised in the 1940s, persisted into the 1980s. It featured disturbing imagery, like microscopes and statues of Buddha in a "damnation" column for those who worshiped science or other gods. Cartoons of children looking at adult magazines in one frame and burning in hell in the next likewise adorned the pages of this book.

The message was obvious. Almost as straightforward as how we would segregate not only teachers like Mrs. Rothbaum but the two or three non-Catholic students in every grade—students who had to sit a pew behind the rest of the class during weekly or "First Friday" Mass: you're a Catholic, or you're damned.

...

That unruliness and oat-feeling in the fourth grade led to an inexplicable schoolyard phenomenon that we called "Whiskey!". How did you play "Whiskey!"? The rules were pretty complex: when another boy wasn't paying attention, you would sneak up on him, grab his dick, and yell, "Whiskey!"

Because Mrs. Rothbaum couldn't contain our boisterousness, the "game" worked its way from the outdoor spaces of the recess to the confines of the fourth-grade classroom. Someone must have mentioned something to someone—or a certain priest must have discovered it on his own—because all fourth-grade boys were promptly directed to the gymnasium for a meeting with Father Gerry.

While the St. Francis Gymnasium appeared modest to an adult, it unfolded as an expansive wonderland for a child's imagination. Anchored by regulation basketball nets and a standard court, it was the battleground for our youthful athletic aspirations. The grand stage, positioned behind the northern hoop, added a touch of grandeur to our school plays and talent shows. Natural light poured in through windows near the roof, casting a warm glow on the court below.

On the southern end, opposite the stage, stood a counter opening leading to a kitchen. Like a hidden treasure trove, this space promised post-game snacks and secret hideouts during school events. Sister Eileen oversaw it, so it was almost a help-yourself operation.

That day, however, it became my portal into the consciousness of manhood.

At the foot of the stage, Father Gerry sat cross-legged on the floor. He invited us to join him, sitting "Indian style," as was the day's parlance. He began lecturing us why playing "Whiskey" was unsuitable for the playground. There was enough shame and humiliation that it could have stopped right there. A dozen boys in a Catholic school gym being told by a priest not to grab each other's peckers and bellow the name of intoxicating spirits were up there on the mortification chart.

But then things took a bizarre turn.

Father Gerry told us why our penises were sacred and not meant to be played with. Because when a man and a woman decide they love each other and want to have a child, the penis would become erect, and the man would insert that into his partner's vagina. The man's erect penis would then ejaculate and make the woman pregnant. Mind you, there was no talk about ovulation or fertilization. Just get hard, stick it in a girl, cum, and you're a dad.

Like that, the St. Francis Class of '91 boys knew about the Birds and the Bees. Decades later, I finally asked my parents why they consented to this—this strange segue into adulthood from a man who took a vow of "celibacy."

My mother told me that the school never informed the parents of this. I don't know how they knew. I knew there wasn't a stork; maybe they assumed I heard it on the playground. But they never consented to a brand new priest sitting down for a group of nine-year-old and explaining why the penis is holy.

...

The holiday season of 1986 left an indelible mark on my memories, and surprisingly, it had nothing to do with my recent enlightenment about the practical functions of a vagina. It was the first Christmas when the illusion of Santa Claus crumbled, resulting from my relentless questioning about the logistical impossibilities, like the lack of a chimney in our home. Armed with newfound knowledge, courtesy of Gerry's sex talk, I felt like a mature nine-going-on-ten-year-old.

This festive season also marked Gerry's inaugural visit to our residence at 208 Teaneck Road. I adorned my bedroom walls with iconic figures from music magazines—Bon Jovi, Motley Crue, Poison—representing the cream of '86. My mother tried for two years to shield me from the phenomena known as MTV, but by 1986, that prohibition was powerless against my desire to hear and see music. Despite being willing and able to challenge my mother, the fear of disappointing Father Gerry led me to take down all of my posters and magazine cutouts.

During dinner, Dad, in his customary fashion, seized the opportunity to embarrass me, remarking, "Hey Father, did you know Eddie took down all of his music posters when he heard you were coming over?" Gerry chuckled good-naturedly and, recognizing the awkwardness, asked to see the now-bare wall. As he sat me down on the bed, he shared a valuable lesson: not everyone had to appreciate my taste in music, and vice versa. The crucial thing was that the music brought me joy, regardless of the artist or their lyrical content.

He had me hook, line, and sinker. One parent prohibited MTV, and the other mocked me for idolizing Bret Michaels. But Father Gerry saw my perspective. He made me feel seen, like an adult.

Before he left, he took a piece of chalk and wrote a few symbols over the threshold of our front door. It was a Polish blessing of the home, intended to keep evil spirits out. The remnants of that blessing remained for years until my parents renovated the living room.

And I used it as a good luck charm. A month after the holidays, we had Nana, Grandpa, and Aunt Breda over to celebrate my tenth birthday, but all Dad, myself, and seven-year-old Sean could think about was the New York Giants' first Super Bowl appearance later that night.

Mom was about to pop with Hanratty Child Four at any minute. Dad sat anxiously on the couch with the Yellow Pages open to "Taxicab" in case Mom went into labor. He vowed he couldn't go to the hospital until after the game. And I jumped up to touch Father Gerry's Polish blessing marks every time the Giants got the ball.

...

Erin Ann Hanratty did not show up during the exhilarating Super Bowl XXI victory over John Elway and the Broncos or amidst the spectacle of Michael Jackson's memorable halftime show. No, Erin opted for a more understated entrance, allowing the Hanratty family to bask in the championship's glow for a week before her arrival.

When she finally made her debut, our familial lineup was complete: Ed Jr., Phyllis, "Little Eddie" (the moniker differentiating me from "Big Ed" during mom's vocal moments), Sean, Elizabeth, and now Erin. Erin's uniqueness extended beyond completing our family unit; she was the sole member born while we lived in the Teaneck Road family home. Father Horrigan, still alive and kicking, was present and even invited to Erin's baptism.

However, the honor of officiating the ceremony fell into the hands of Father Gerry Sudol.

V

Erin's arrival at 208 Teaneck Road marked the most significant Hanratty event of 1987, but it wasn't the sole addition to our household. Following a year of raucous backyard play, my parents enhanced the yard by installing an above-ground pool. The purchase provided a refreshing aquatic escape on hot summer days, save for early mornings when it stood in the shadow of a large oak tree over the neighbor's fence.

The newfound hydro-entertainment meant bidding farewell to the Ridgefield Park Town Pool, my summer retreat for the past four years. In the sunniest part of town, with next to no tree cover, it was a hotspot for Jersey teens, scantily clad with mullets, high hair, and booming boom-boxes that provided the soundtrack to my summers.

The pool was where I discovered the art of swimming—an athletic feat that miraculously existed despite my otherwise spastic coordination. Those swimming skills became a staple during our annual trips to the Jersey shore, where my grandfather rented a beach house, and we spent our days riding the waves from breakfast to dinner.

Having a pool meant every day was a party. In the summer of 87, my mother hosted lunch dates with other stay-at-home moms (a blossoming term separating them from "working moms") multiple times a week. It didn't matter who was over, how entertaining they were or weren't, or what my mother wanted me to do—I wasn't coming out of my pool. Plus, everybody wanted to be your friend when you had a pool, so I was never lacking for my playmates or entertainment. I had a sudden surge in popularity, beginning uncoincidentally that summer.

Another welcome addition to my summer schedule was Dad's company gaining box seats behind the third base dugout at Yankee Stadium. Dad was advancing at his company, Computer Leasing Incorporated, working as a middleman to bring the latest but expensive technology to businesses of all sizes. While most of the Yankee tickets were for entertaining clients and prospective clients, management had an allotment for personal use. No more upper-deck games for us!

It was almost impossible to realize that eighteen months earlier, I was living in a two-bedroom apartment with four other family members, eating Burger King before tee-ball practice because we were down to one running car—BK was down the block from Dad's job—to a family with a new house, a new pool, and regular access to premium Yankee seats.

•••

Father Gerry purchased a Chevy Astro van that year—a brand-new family mode of transportation. But it was nothing more than the first minivan, which would have a shorter and more shameful lifespan than the station wagon it replaced. But before the minivan takeover, the Astrovan—with seating for eight—was the cooler, newer, modern upgrade to the same station wagon that had dotted the American roadscape since the Kennedy Administration.

Leasing cars was a concept that wouldn't hit the mainstream for a few more years. During the 80s, there just wasn't much turnover in family vehicles. I can probably remember five times a close friend's parents got a new car between 1985 and 1995. It's not as if Astro vans started popping up everywhere. But the one place it showed up was the Rectory garage.

Why would a priest, he who took a vow of celibacy, need the most prominent and newest family vehicle on the road? He provided that answer quicker than anyone could ask by bringing select members of all Ridgefield Park schools' just-graduated 8th-grade classes to his family beach house in Wildwood Crest, New Jersey.

•••

Fifth grade brought a fresh addition to our class: Matthew Baker, a resident who had previously attended a school in the neighboring town. The parish greeted him with open arms, a new face in a stagnant class that had seen minimal change since communion. However, our collective disposition towards him underwent a drastic shift when we realized the special attention Father Gerry seemed to afford him.

As we uncovered Matthew's close relationship with Father Gerry, an abrupt and unsettling change occurred among the boys in our class. The warmth with which we initially embraced Matthew turned into a cold and harsh rejection. The atmosphere became hostile, and Matthew was central to our pre-adolescent fury.

Our tactics of ostracism manifested in various forms. We threw him into the bushes. Two-hand touch football became a platform for our aggression, with Matthew becoming the unwitting target of our pent-up frustrations. Shunning him became a group sport, an unwritten rule that pervaded our interactions in and out of the classroom. And when there was snow on the ground? Forget about it. The question wasn't, "Would we pelt him with snowballs?" it was, "Would he bleed?"

Every minute of the day was a battleground where Matthew was made to feel like an outsider, an unwelcome participant in the daily rituals of our lives. The abuse was so noticeable our teacher would lecture. So did Sister Patricia. And also Father Gerry himself.

He summoned all the altar boys not named Matthew to meet him in the rectory after school. He wanted to know why we were picking on the Baker boy. Then told a tale about how kids bullied him in school and never understood why. The priest said children cast him out at his school. He wanted to know why we were so angry at this kid.

We had no answers—at least not yet. To us, it appeared to be nothing more than territorialism and a dislike of outsiders. We falsely assured Father Gerry that we would try to be better, but we decided Baker would pay for this once we left the rectory.

And by paying for this, all it meant was we would keep doing what we were doing to him: knocking him into statues, tripping him when he walked up to the teacher's desk, crank calling his house—that's an adrenaline rush kids today will never get to feel.

In the days before Caller ID, or even *69, the telephone was an unlimited source of entertainment. One Friday night, during a sleepover, we ordered five pizzas, three calzones, and two orders of chicken parmesan to his house. Monday morning, he was bragging about how his parents sent it back, and the only people hurt were the pizzeria owners. He was right; intentional food waste is one of the gravest sins you can commit. But we didn't care. We just punched him for turning the pizza away.

We were brutal, and we vitriolically called him "a fag". It's unfortunately painfully obvious why we chose such a slur now; it's scary how trauma can impact the brain like that. We determined that if he was that close to Father Gerry, he must be "gay"—use your imagination for what a ten-year-old who just learned about how babies get made thought "gay" meant because I don't remember, other than it had to be cringe-worthy.

...

Not everything at St. Francis of Assisi bore the "new" label. Preparations were in full swing to commemorate the 50th anniversary of Father Francis's ordination to the priesthood. In his early seventies now, his hair had taken on a snow-white hue, yet he steadfastly adhered to the slicked-back style with a Brylcreemed comb-back, likely similar to its style on the day of his ordination. The parish, in turn, was orchestrating quite the spectacle to honor this milestone.

The keystone event of the Jubilee—yes, that's what the Archdiocese calls the celebration of an anniversary, the British royals are the only others I've ever heard use such a silly term—would be the 12:15 Sunday Mass, and Archbishop Theodore McCarrick would officiate it. The mass was to be served by five altar boys; one from each grade in St. Francis. I don't know what the metrics were to choose—probably being a kiss-ass or having an over-involved parent in the school—but yours truly got the honor for the fifth grade.

My mother was over the moon. It was as if I was getting to serve mass with Pope John Paul II (a man McCarrick would eventually choose a successor for in his future role as Cardinal). I remember her excitable instructions on how to speak to him: "You address him as Your Eminence."

Naturally, I had to get on the horn and call both of my grandmothers and tell them at Mom's request. Neither could have been prouder of me, their first grandson, serving mass with the Archbishop of Newark. Both promised to be there for the mass.

I don't think I slept much the night before the mass because I remember being unusually tired for a boy of ten as I entered the sacristy shortly before noon, as the sparsely attended 11:15 mass was ending. It probably had more to do with serving mass with older altar boys than the pressure of meeting someone I didn't know was a celebrity till a hot minute beforehand.

Perhaps it's because I was the oldest child and had no real older connections heading into school, but older children always intimidated me (Conversely, maybe it's because the coked-out teenagers at the town pool in the mid-80s were scary as fuck). In the summer of 1985, my honor roll status earned me a spot on the "Queen's Float"—a decked-out flatbed truck featuring the highest achieving boys and girls at specific grade levels at the annual Ridgefield Park 4th of July Parade (Billed as the longest continuous 4th of July parade in America. Or at least it was till 2020 and the Trump presidency). The school chose me as the male representative for all second graders in town, but I was petrified around the students from grades 4 through 12.

However, when I arrived in the sacristy that day, that anxiety lay to rest when I saw Willie Foster putting his cassock on. Willie was two years older than me and the antithesis of most upperclassmen's intimidating bullying (accurate or feared) personas. He marched to the beat of his drum and didn't appear to be part of any cliques. While he was involved in recreational soccer, his true talent came in dancing, as he was a talented tap dancer and a regular performer in the annual St. Francis talent show that Sister Patricia would begin that year.

While seeing Willie there was disarming, the alert that "Elvis was in the building" sent the sacristy into a tizzy as we got to our places. The priests were lined up closest to the door—Father Beck (a weekend visiting priest who just concluded the 11:15), Father Gerry, Father Vaccaro, and Father Francis, the man of the hour. Then distinguished "church elders"—the kiss-asses that spent all of their free time at the parish organizing, enforcing, and being visible for their personal glory. Finally, the altar boys were bending past the chair and around in front of the cleric's closet along the north wall.

Then the sacristy door opened.

Archbishop Theodore McCarrick was a master of social grace, working a room with the finesse of a seasoned politician. His glad-handing prowess extended to everyone he encountered, each handshake accompanied by a wink and a charming smile. If he didn't already know your name, he repeated it back to you—priest, parishioner, passerby—it didn't matter.

His wardrobe was just as distinctive, with gilded cream vestments adorned with scarlet red and gold that reeked of opulence. Topping off his ensemble was a fuchsia beanie resembling a yarmulke.

Archbishop McCarrick's physical appearance was distinguished. His receding hairline was complemented by silvery strands on the sides. His eyes, a dark and almost black hue, held a depth, conveying a sense of mystery. Despite his average size and build, his presence commanded attention, enhanced by a wry smile that hinted at those complexities.

The mass was the glorious spectacle as planned. It was a con-celebrated mass, which meant that all ordained priests took part in it. (During our WWF-crazed days, we referred to con-celebrated masses as "Tag-Team matches"). The choir loft was full, and the orchestral section in the church's front was to capacity. The mass was standing room only, with the church's nave sporting a healthy collection of congregants unable to see the altar from their vantage point.

And there I was, in the middle of the action, on a jam-packed altar with the Archbishop of Newark and everyone who's anyone at St. Francis. I shook his hand in the sacristy during introductions and during the "Sign of Peace" segment of the Catholic Liturgy.

I was maintaining honor roll status, and Mrs. Kennedy chose me to represent my class at a mass celebrated by the Archbishop. Father Gerry would occasionally have dinner or a midweek dip at our place. I had just begun competitive basketball for St. Francis in the local CYO league. St. Francis was my home away from home, and I felt like I was on the Yellow Brick Road to heaven.

In celebrating something old, I found a new purpose. I was a proud Catholic altar boy. If fourth grade was the year of transitions at St. Francis, fifth grade was when the latest and most modernized parish and school settled into their new normal. I couldn't be prouder to be at its epicenter.

VI

"I was at the game that set the record for the longest game in baseball history between the Mets and the Saint Louis Cardinals in 1974. It lasted 25 innings," Father Gerry said as he wiped his mouth after putting down his fork at Sizzler.

It was the summer of 1988. Eric Carmen's "Make Me Lose Control" seemed to blast from every open car window at every red light. America seemed captivated by the game-changing technology of "Who Framed Roger Rabbit." I sat in a Sizzler restaurant with Father Gerry and two other altar boys, enjoying a pre-game buffet.

It was all my father's idea. The Yankees fielded a competitive team for what would be the last time until my college years, and his company was in its second season of owning a corporate box at Yankee Stadium. Dad offered tickets against the red-hot Oakland A's featuring the Bash Brothers—Jose Canseco and Mark McGwire—to Father Gerry to take "the boys, or whoever you want."

Gerry accepted, and his thank-you was a trip to the place every eleven-year-old with a ferocious appetite wanted to go: Sizzler, with its all-you-can-eat "salad bar" that had chicken wings, French fries, ice cream, and complete nacho makings. Sizzler was the shit—it became a "family birthday" destination choice for Sean and me for a few consecutive Januarys. And despite not serving alcohol, Dad loved it too because the Bronx in him couldn't resist stuffing Ziploc bags with chicken wings for some Saturday night munchies.

Everybody loved Sizzler. I wish I remembered the game as much as the meal. The Yanks got tattooed, and all I remember was perusing the scorecard and talking with the other altar boys about Sizzler.

The ride home was memorable, however. Given where I lived, where the other altar boys lived, and where the St. Francis rectory was, there was no plausible way to enter town from where I wouldn't be the first person dropped off, save for one, where I'd be the second. But I was the third and last.

After the first boy—the one sitting in the passenger seat — was dropped off, Gerry asked who wanted to hop up front and ride with him. I was closest to the passenger side in the luxurious middle row of the Astrovan, so I volunteered and eagerly hopped up front. We dropped off the second kid and drove the five or six blocks to my house.

After pulling into our driveway, Gerry threw the car into park. He folded his hands over his belly, as he often did while delivering a sermon. He looked me in the eye and told me how honored he was that my family offered these tickets.

And then he kissed me.

In all likelihood, that wasn't the first mouth-to-mouth, lip-to-lip, feel-the-stubble kiss Father Gerry planted on me. Around this time at St. Francis, he made the leap from affectionate to uncomfortable. The altar boy blessings now ended with Gerry looking each altar boy in the eye, giving a look and smile that conveyed pride, and planting an extended kiss on our lips.

Though we led him off the altar, he continued to move in the sacristy, where we weren't visible from the main section of the church but couldn't be seen from the glass windowed door to the rectory side of the building.

"For all that you are, and for whatever your needs may be, especially any needs that might make you worried, anxious, or afraid, I ask the heavenly father to bless you in the name of the Father, and of the Son, and of the holy spirit, Amen."

Then he kissed us.

What differentiated these kisses from a gentle peck that inadvertently makes lip contact couldn't have been more explicit: He held our heads in place. One giant paw is over the left ear; the other is over the right. And always on the same spot on the sacristy floor—where you couldn't see him from the rectory-side entrance that passes the glass partitioned door, and you couldn't see us from the front-of-altar perspective.

...

He remained very affectionate in public—overly affectionate, actually. This rubbed some old-timers the wrong way. One of them was my grandpa. They weren't parishioners at St. Francis, but given the age of our four grandchildren and all the Catholic rites of passage and Sacraments, it wasn't unusual for Nana and Grandpa to "get their mass," as they would say, at St. Francis on select Sundays.

But Grandpa never fell for Gerry's charm like his daughter, son-in-law, and grandkids did. In his thick Dublin brogue, he would say, "There's something wrong with that man." And many of his generation agreed.

As popular as Gerry was in the parish, the parish elders, members of the so-called "Greatest Generation," never seemed to invite him over for dinner or collaborate on church programs or initiatives with him. And that was an additional part of his appeal. If the rapidly aging Father Francis—his chin getting closer to his sternum weekly— represented the stoic seniors who run the parish affairs, Father Gerry belonged to the people.

It was a very populist movement, and it led to this charismatic man of the cloth finally harpooning his Great White Whale. After two years of suggestions and discussion, Gerry finally started the St. Francis of Assisi Youth Group, which operated out of the church basement.

The basement was a monument, or better yet, a time capsule to when the parish flourished. After walking down a spiral stone staircase, you advanced further down a stonewalled hallway before coming to the center of the basement—once referred to as "the lower church." It was a chapel with an altar and a sanctuary to hold the Blessed Sacrament (communion, the bread). Due left of the altar was a stage, which presumably held school plays before the "New School" was created with the St. Francis gym.

By the end of the 80s, it was more of a storage facility than anything else. Alcoholics Anonymous held their weekly meetings there, which were about the extent of its practical usage. Gerry Sudol was going to change that.

Half the room would keep folding chairs and a cafeteria table or two. AA would still have gatherings and coffee each week, like any other organization that saw the need. On the other side, farther from the altar, they would remove the chairs and bring in couches, recliners, and love seats to create a more relaxed vibe in the room—a coffee house atmosphere before coffee houses became popular.

The youth group was an instant success. Early meetings were jam-packed. Father Gerry had made it a point to make Catholic students who attended public school feel extra welcome in the organization, extending the membership age well beyond elementary school to eighteen. He did not want it to be an extension of the school. The youth group would have full autonomy and independence. And the parish ate it up.

One of the first initiatives was to organize an overnight ski trip for high school students. How fucking cool! It gave younger members something to look forward to when their time came—a carrot on a stick to maintain active membership. There would also be teenage spiritual retreats that oddly became a hot ticket, though I would never show a hint of interest once I was old enough. Retreats would always strike me as mental detention. They still do.

There was a resentment building inside me towards the public school members who were now lurking around the parish on more than Sundays. Weren't we the "St. Francis Sissies"? Didn't I feel intimidated or insecure at every civic event or sporting activity where we co-mingled because of that? Now, they were invading my turf, my sanctuary, and competing for the attention of my priest.

There were rumblings that Father Gerry wanted public school students eligible to be altar boys. As he would explain, he was once a public school pupil and remembered feeling ostracized by the more popular Catholic school in town. It didn't matter that the paradigm shifted away from parochial schools in the time between Baby Boomer Gerry would have been in school and the era of the "Sissies" we experienced. He was becoming more vocal about it.

Mrs. Kennedy would have none of it. As a mother of children who attended the school that spent over a decade organizing and scheduling altar boys to cater to the parish's needs, she cashed in some of her chips. She insisted that altar boys needed to be on the parish campus because of needs such as funerals, which occurred at 10:30 AM on weekdays.

It was flimsy reasoning at best. Nothing stopped public schoolers from serving Sunday mass or even 7 AM daily mass, as we were expected to. Serving funerals was optional and not a requirement. They were pretty desirous because the funeral directors—referred to as "undertakers"—would "tip" the altar boys $3. Sometimes, especially with Italian funerals, the family would seek us out to "take additional care of us."

Weddings were even more lucrative, with the parish coordinator letting engaged couples know gratuity was expected for altar boys. Inevitably, the Best Man would reach into his breast pocket, go through the sealed envelopes—priest, organist, singer, DJ, bartenders…altar boys—and hand us as much as $20 (usually closer to $10 when the groom wasn't Italian).

As long as Mrs. Kennedy remained in charge, the St. Francis Altar Boys would remain open only to St. Francis students. From the beginning, she maintained the Altar Boys in her reserved, respectful fashion. We would continue to serve the community through activities like our annual Christmas caroling—Mrs. Kennedy was the only person I ever met who could get a couple of dozen elementary school boys who were already insecure about the ribbings we took for being Catholic schoolers and have them excitedly walk around their town singing "Silent Night" and "O Come All, Ye Faithful."

The parish had transformed in the two years since Gerry, and to a lesser degree, Sister Patricia (who was instituting slow modernization initiatives in the school, like music class, because they deemed the recorder more critical than learning Spanish in 1988). Father Francis was a shell of himself; Father Vaccaro remained aloof. The Altar Boys would be a grounding anchor, a slower and more deliberate alternative to the Youth Group, though most altar boys, myself included, belonged to both.

We would also host an annual Smorgasbord dinner fundraiser for the parish. Parents would cook food trays; we would serve them in the St. Francis gym. Mrs. Kennedy saw some proceeds went towards rewarding us for our dedication. She would organize bus trips to see the New Jersey Nets play in The Meadowlands—dads suddenly eager to chaperone. We would visit arcades, pizzerias, movie theaters, and other recreational activities young boys enjoy.

The Nets games were delightful. A bus—usually a school bus, nothing fancy—would pick us up in the school parking lot, where a parent would wait to take us home.

There were no awkward or disturbing goodbye kisses.

VII

Learning to record songs off the radio was a Gen X rite of passage—much like figuring out that you could get a Nintendo game to work by blowing into the cartridge opening. If you didn't mind an overtalkative DJ marring a song's intro, all you needed was a blank cassette and some patience, and any hit song of the day could be yours.

I vividly remember engaging in this new favorite hobby in our living room when my parents, my godfather, Uncle Bob, and his wife, Aunt Nancy, walked into the house following the burial of Aunt Nancy's mother in the fall of 1989.

I hadn't seen as much of Uncle Bob as I did when I was younger. He married in 1981—I was barely old enough to remember my parents preparing for the wedding while an infant Sean and I stayed overnight at Nana and Grandpa's house. They promptly had their first son together, Robert Jr.—or "Robbie" (Aunt Nancy had a son from a previous marriage, Anthony, two years my senior, and it was pretty cool to have an instant older guy cousin). But not long after, Sean and I had new cousins within two years of each other. Uncle Bob's family followed so many out of the direct New York City area and towards the blossoming Central Jersey gateway to the shore, where they would welcome my youngest cousin, Daniel (Danny) Arthur, a few months after Elizabeth was born.

The area, made famous by Bruce Springsteen in his youth in Freehold, New Jersey, offered twice the house for a fraction of the price. Nobody had complained about gas prices since the late 1970s, so this new "super commuting" became increasingly prevalent in our neighborhoods and, more noticeably, on our highways.

I had missed Uncle Bob. My dad's hulking, twin-brother police officer was a sharp contrast to my father's smaller stature and relatively innocuous shirt-and-tie office career. But this solemn occasion wasn't the time to catch up. I was fortunate that there were more pressing emotional issues to deal with, like the loss of a loved one, because I had just brought home the worst report card of my life.

It wasn't surprising. Seventh grade was a circus as we broke in a first-time teacher who could not corral twelve- and thirteen-year-old children who were discovering their hormones. Report card day should have been the kick-in-the-ass needed to reverse course. Just last spring I made the state finals of the National Geographic Geography Bee—I didn't suddenly forget how to learn. I just wasn't as interested in learning about academics as I was in music, sports, and, suddenly, girls.

My parents wouldn't have much time or ability to straighten me out—and my developing rebellious attitude sent signals it wasn't worth the effort. They'd soon receive and pass along the news to me that would alter the trajectory of my family life forever: doctors diagnosed Uncle Bob with late-stage abdominal cancer. Optimistically, doctors gave him ninety days to live.

The news hit my father like a ton of bricks, but it transformed him into a borderline superhero. He spent every Saturday at Uncle Bob's while his twin rapidly deteriorated. He insisted I came as well, as we would handle "man of the house" tasks like putting up the Christmas tree and hanging the outside lights.

I couldn't tell the pain my father was most certainly in. I would pepper him with questions about his upbringing with Uncle Bob. Stupid questions, too, like "Why doesn't he like the Yankees as much as you do?" (Before I learned the truth, few people loved the Yankees as Dad did). But Dad showed neither emotion nor frustration. He answered every question earnestly and to the best of his ability.

That emotional front changed on the morning of February 19, 1990. Mom and I were walking in from 7:00 mass, which I had just served. It was an especially frigid, dark morning. We returned to see Dad on the kitchen telephone, tears welling up in his eyes.

We lost Uncle Bob.

Breaking it to Robbie and Danny (along with Sean, Elizabeth, and a toddler Erin with no memory of the man who was her godfather) fell to Dad. The cousins were sleeping with us for the weekend; the adults expected it would be their father's last as he was visibly near the conclusion of his courageous battle. He woke up the house and summoned all the children into my parents' bedroom.

Dad asked Robbie and Danny to sit on either side of him. He put an arm around each of them and took a deep breath.

"Boys, you know your dad was very sick", he paused, reaching for the strength to fight back his own tears, before finishing, "He's in heaven now."

And that was the precise moment when the Dad I knew ceased to exist, and the broken old man began his incubation.

...

Sensing my emotional vulnerability, Father Gerry made himself extremely available to me. He would call me out of class to ask how my family was coping—how I was coping. He would repeat the same following masses I served. During those masses, he would include "Robert Hanratty" during the prayers of intentions. This was what being a priest was all about, right? My parents couldn't have been happier that their thirteen-year-old son sought solace and advice from the parish priest.

Who could blame them? St. Francis had just enrolled in the "Drug Abuse and Resistance Education (D.A.R.E.)". Their slogan, "D.A.R.E. To Keep Kids off Drugs adorned t-shirts, hats, and bumper stickers so heavily that it was odd to go a day without seeing the logo at least once. After First Lady Nancy Reagan adopted combatting teen drug use as her signature issue, the airwaves were flooded with Public Service Announcements to boomers about the risks of marijuana and cocaine, devoid of any irony. (Save for one infamous commercial where a burned-out teenage son tells his Wall Street-type dad he did drugs because he "learned it from watching you!")

The War on Drugs was in full effect.

Thank God kids in distress had a trusted adult like Father Gerry (and his Youth Group!) instead of turning to the scourge of drugs. Because parents in the 80s weren't as concerned with *WHY* their kids were doing drugs as much as *THAT* they were doing them, there was a pervasive misguided belief that it was merely teen curiosity or peer pressure that inspired children to turn to drugs. I don't believe that's entirely false, but in my experience, both teens and adults who want to alter their minds aren't always doing so because their friends are doing it, too.

Ridgefield Park Police Officer Nicole Verrazano, referred to as "Officer Nicole" even during future teenage traffic stops, had good intentions when she taught us what drugs looked like, what they did to you, how much they cost, and where in town to avoid them in her capacity as the D.A.R.E. Officer in town. I'm sure she was following the D.A.R.E. procedural manner/script. But being continually told "No" is a surefire road to "Maybe" at the very least.

One thing Officer Nicole picked up on, an ode to her policing skills, was just how badly we were bullying Matthew Baker. One morning, she pulled me aside in the hallway to ask why we were so obviously mean to the kid. I feigned ignorance; she told me she knew I was better than that. I tried to flip it as "he doesn't like us either," but I again got a stern look and a reminder that I should be better than that.

Even with the benefit of hindsight highlighting the program's clear flaws, it doesn't negate that it had the desired impact at specific points in our youth. In seventh grade and in emotional distress, my mind wasn't wandering toward the abandoned gas station on Main Street to score angel dust. Instead, I sincerely appreciated the compassion and attention Father Gerry extended my way. On one occasion, I mustered the courage to request permission to leave class and converse with him, as he consistently encouraged me to do whenever needed. After all, it was in his post-mass blessing. *"Any needs that might make you worried, anxious, or afraid."* I was all three of them.

Every meeting would be sealed with a kiss—kisses that were getting progressively longer at this point. These one-on-one settings were more intimate than the already-too-touchy altar boy blessings. The hugs were tighter, sometimes lifting me as I approached 6 feet tall. It was around this time that I became conscious of the fact that this made me uncomfortable.

However, so did the dentist. So did the barber. So did the pediatrician. So did math. Father Gerry's forced, slobbering kisses were an annoying part of the mass, like the sign of peace or the uncomfortable silence after communion but before the prayer of dismissal. What is mass to a thirteen-year-old if not an obligation? Obligations are annoying and uncomfortable.

Apparently, I divorced the man from the behavior because I continued seeking his counsel and attention. Grieving at home was not an option.

From my inaugural day at St. James in 1981 until Erin's high school graduation in 2005, there was always at least one Hanratty child navigating the halls of education. Mom's stress levels increased with each child that entered the American education mechanism. She had the added stress of being a regular volunteer at the school—class mother, milk program administrator, and a few other hats as needed. By the end of the 80s, her anxieties were palpable.

The passing of Uncle Bob only exacerbated matters as Elizabeth was navigating kindergarten, Sean was entrenched in 4th grade, and Erin was emerging from diapers. Her emotional bandwidth was fully stretched.

Dad was falling apart into himself. Always a weekend warrior with drinking, he began stopping to pick up a twelve-pack of Budweiser multiple days a week. The more he drank, the more his face dropped, the more anger consumed him. Losing his twin sixth months before what would have been their fortieth birthday was a blow too devastating to bounce back up from.

It's not the most sanitary way to honor the deceased, but Dad inherited Uncle Bob's bathrobe. It was poop-brown and many years old. He'd come home from work, get into that godforsaken robe, and drink until his face looked like a boardwalk water balloon race clown. He was the antithesis of approachable during this period of family trauma.

…

To Dad's credit, he did his best to find healthier, more lasting ways to honor his brother. He made a capital donation to the town's Little League to have a plaque placed in honor of Uncle Bob in the Little League clubhouse. He took the family and invited Aunt Nancy, Robbie, and Danny—to Disney World in June of '90 to purge the toxicity of what we had all endured. It was a glorious trip, and it had the intended consequences. There was joy within the Hanratty family again.

When we returned, I had a new role waiting for me. After several votes, I narrowly defeated Matthew Baker to be elected president of the St. Francis of Assisi Altar Boys' organization.

They gave me a gavel and the job of finding altar boys to serve funerals. I used that power like any good New Jersey Democrat would: corruptly. The going rate was $3 a funeral; there could be five funerals in a week. All with the bonus, after September, of an excused 90 minutes from school, where you'd return just in time for lunch. It was the sweetest gig on Mount Vernon Street. Making money to buy cassettes when you're supposed to be learning about the Ascension? Jackpot.

I would take as many of those gigs as I wanted and then would leave it to the other altar boys in my class to work out a schedule. If I got friendly with an underclassman during recess, at the park, or during organized town sports, I might offer him a midweek spot alongside a friend and me.

But I wasn't the only one with a passion for my newfound authority. This was the summer when the kissing intensified to the next level. The bear claw grip on the cheeks got firmer. The lip contact even longer. And now he was forcing his tongue into my mouth.

The vulnerability I felt after my godfather's untimely passing, combined with the newfound responsibility as president of the Altar Boys, positioned me regularly in the grip of this larger-than-life man.

My first "French Kiss" was with a 300 lb., thirty-something dude named Gerry.

VIII

I had my second "French Kiss" about halfway through an opening-weekend showing of "Home Alone" in late November 1990 with a nice girl from our class. Fueled with no knowledge from older brothers, I had only sitcoms like "Growing Pains" and "Family Ties" to teach me how to "date." My only other first-hand knowledge of intimacy told me I could have trapped her with bear claws on the sides of her head and forced my tongue down her throat against her will, but what I knew as an "altar boy blessing" is defined by law as "sexual assault," so I guess I was fortunate in a way to have Alex P. Keaton and Mike Seaver.

By eighth grade, our hormones were fully raging. In the tiny pond of St. Francis, half of the boys and girls started pairing up to, depending on your generation, "hook up" (X), "make out" (boomer), or "neck" (so-called-greatest).

For most people, discovering the joys and heartbreaks of early-teenage romance would be what they would likely remember most about their eighth-grade year. If "Home Alone" didn't become an annual Christmas staple for kids of all generations, I don't know if it would survive in my memory bank.

...

Sunday family dinners were a staple growing up—and beyond. With Nana, Grandpa, and Aunt Breda living a mere 3.5 miles away, it was always a thing. I never thought much of the rhyme or reason when they would be at our home or theirs, but in retrospect, we spent more Sundays at our place during the summer months with the pool. Colder months would see us spend more time in Teaneck, with Nana's savory cooking filling the air, the gas fireplace burning, and the general feelings of warmth and coziness you crave in the winter.

They weren't at our house one Sunday in the Summer of '90, though. I'm now confident it was because my grandfather was uncomfortable with another dinner guest that afternoon: Father Gerry.

I wasn't the only family member with whom he checked in following Uncle Bob's passing. Outside the church most Sundays, he'd hold up his blossoming "receiving line" to hug my parents and ensure they were holding up as well as they could. His concern carried throughout the school year, beyond our Disney trip. My parents reciprocated by inviting him over for a Sunday barbecue.

After a usual Hanratty cookout of burned chicken legs, delicious Sabrett's hot dogs, and well-done burgers, I found myself alone with him in the pool. The details of how escapes me. I couldn't tell if my parents or siblings had been there and left, or if he had been alone and I joined, or vice versa. Regardless, we were there.

He began talking about the soothing nature of water, drawing a comparison to John the Baptist. Then, he asked me to float on my back and close my eyes, and instinctively, I complied. I don't recall putting up resistance initially. I still held onto the belief in "the role of the Priest" and thought I was "chosen" and destined for heaven—all that other misinformation. He positioned one arm beneath my shoulder and the other under my upper thigh, mirroring the pose often depicted of the Blessed Mother cradling her son's lifeless body after being taken down from the cross.

At that moment, I genuinely thought it was the beginning of some ritual. The conversation shifted toward my changing body as he continued talking about John the Baptist. He asked a series of uncomfortable questions that had nothing to do with faith or spirituality:

- *Have you noticed an increased need to shower?*

- *When you shower, do you find yourself paying more attention to different areas and crevices?*

- *Are you observing hair in places you didn't before? Perhaps on your legs or armpits...*

As if that wasn't discomforting enough:

- *Maybe on your testicles? Maybe above your penis?*

As I was floating, I noticed Gerry moving in a slightly different direction from the natural flow of the water. I felt a pressure point in my lower back. It was clicking. He was rubbing his erect penis up against my lower back. His grip on me got tighter. He was a big fellow with an enormous belly, and the bear claw gripped my left rib and thigh and trapped them on the right side of my body.

I could do nothing but stare into the sky above 208 Teaneck Road. The muggy haze of mid-summer heat. The massive maple tree that would inevitably shed her leaves before Dad closed the pool each year, always hoping for "Indian Summa," as he called late September heat waves in his Bronx accent. There was the sound of the water waving above and below my ear drum. I could do nothing but pretend it wasn't happening.

I'm not sure what excuse I used to get out of the pool, but I remember getting my towel and high-tailing it inside, where mom was doing the dishes, my siblings were watching television, and dad was in the basement drinking beer. He came up to offer Gerry "another one?" and the man of the cloth obliged.

He should have offered him a cigarette.

•••

For as much torment as being an altar boy would cause me, there's great irony in the solace that the St. Francis Altar Boy's Organization concurrently brought to me. Mrs. Kennedy was a staid, solid rock whose personality became even more disarming as the internal turmoil continued. I had the Altar Boys, of which I was now the fearless leader, and I had my new room after my grandfather spent the first year of his retirement converting the attic at 208 Teaneck into a fourth bedroom—finally my own space.

It was a space I would personalize at a frenetic pace—posters of Lawrence Taylor, Cindy Crawford, the cast of Young Guns II, Don Mattingly, and an American flag that said "These Colors Don't Run" (I fancied myself quite the "patriot"). And I would retreat there. I would spend almost all of my time at home in the attic. I'd have the cordless phone to speak with friends for maybe a half hour a night. I didn't have cable. I had the radio and myself.

I gravitated towards slower power ballads and R&B breakup songs. The more depressing, the better. Give me a tune about death or suicide like LA Guns' "The Ballad of Jayne" or Kix's "Don't Close Your Eyes," and I was in my comfort zone.

It was a sanctuary I would soon need more than ever.

Early into the academic year, Mrs. Kennedy summoned the 8th-grade altar boys to an emergency meeting. She made a very brief statement that she was resigning immediately; Father Gerry was now in charge of the Altar Boys Organization. Mr. Paddock was following her out the door.

She read off a detailed list of "assets" that the altar boys possessed—from the significant (roughly $200 cash on hand) to the minor (28 individual packets of Sanka coffee). But all I could think about was what this meant for the following year. My safety was being ripped away. The Altar Boys Organization was always the framework within the church that brought solace and quiet. Father Gerry hit the rest of the parish like a flash grenade — from the mass to the school to the youth group. He was pervasive in every other parish corner except for the Organization.

Now, that would all change.

I wasn't aware of how afraid I had become of Gerry, but I remember great fear and trepidation when Mrs. Kennedy broke this news to us. losing our guiding light for my "presidential administration" left me heartbroken.

It left Gerry with the opportunity to fulfill the vision he had been pushing since he arrived on Mt. Vernon Street four years prior: opening the Altar Boys to public school students. But that wasn't enough of a move. He also opened it up to high school students—"to keep them involved in the church."

I knew immediately what that would mean: my presidency would expire upon graduation, but my Altar Boy involvement would continue beyond 8th grade. I had no choice, just as I felt I had no choice but to become an altar boy.

Only this time, it wasn't because I was an impressionable nine-year-old captivated by the experience and expectations. It was because there was no way I'd be able to tell Father Gerry "No." I was thirteen and had a girlfriend, but unwittingly beholden to a man who made me feel all sorts of uncomfortable.

Before I knew it, Dad had considered another way to honor Uncle Bob's soul. I found myself in the Astrovan with Gerry, Dad, and a few other altar boys en route to Western Jersey, where we would purchase new cassocks and vestments for the "Senior Altar Boys," as we would be called.

•••

Radical change wasn't limited to my tongue or the altar boys. From the end of seventh grade to the start of eighth grade, St. Francis underwent more turnover than any year since Sudol and Sister Patricia arrived. We had a new nun, Sister Dianne, and her god-awful luck would have her assigned to our class.

Our class was brutal throughout all of the seventh grade. Even had regular interventions from the principal, other teachers, and clergy, but that civilian teacher never got a handle on us. And if they thought a new nun, who replaced the retiring Sister Marianne (who commanded respect), would fare any better, the school administration was foolish. Before October, we had already christened her "Sister Buffalo" (she was on the heavier side) and doodled cartoons of her, focusing on the greenish hue of her graying blonde hair. We were brutal.

Across the parking lot, the rectory welcomed its first new priest since Gerry Sudol came four years earlier. Father Vaccaro recently announced that he had sought permission to seek a life of solitude and prayer at a monastery. See no evil, speak no evil, hear no evil. Reverend Joe Doyle would fill the opening: a firm and fit, ginger-haired Jersey-born baby boomer who looked more Irish than Paddy's pig. With red hair, freckles, wire-rimmed glasses, and a generous smile and laugh, he perfectly suited a parish whose financial base comprised retired Irish and Italian-American Catholics and their baby boomer children.

Unlike Sudol, Francis, and Vaccaro, Doyle didn't come from ministering elsewhere. He was part of the Archdiocese Bureaucracy in Newark. A well-educated and intelligent conversationalist, he was more well-rounded than the average priest. Even us students saw the writing on the wall—this would be the next pastor.

The Boomers were asserting themselves in positions of power nationwide. The governor of Arkansas, Bill Clinton, was preparing to shock the world two years later and defeat the greatest generation's War Hero, President George Bush. At St. Francis, our pastor was long past the point where he should buy green bananas. Father Francis was deteriorating in front of our eyes. He had tremors that were no longer concealable. The priest struggled to turn the pages of the prayer book we had to hold in front of him. He shook while dispersing communion. His sermons were brief and often inaudible.

Before Doyle, the conventional wisdom was that the pastoral role would be offered to Vaccaro—who would decline it, not being someone comfortable with attention—and then to Sudol, who would do backflips to have that type of attention and authority.

Now, the paradigm shifted.

IX

In retrospect, January 1991 was a watershed month on my journey on earth. I learned three things that would remain true and at the forefront of my thoughts and actions for decades:

1. The United States had an unhealthy obsession with Saddam Hussein and Iraq.

2. Nicotine calms.

3. Alcohol erases.

America wept on January 27th. New Jersey's own Whitney Houston performed arguably the most memorable version of The Star-Spangled Banner in history. The United States was at war! Gulf War fever gripped the US. It was no different in Ridgefield Park. Yellow ribbons dotted homes throughout the village. USO or Red Cross donation tins were on every countertop on Main Street. And because, you know, capitalism, you had your choice of "official" Operation: Desert Storm t-shirts, hats, trading cards, and teddy bears, among countless other knick-knacks.

Against this backdrop, an unusually odd number of St. Francis birthday parties were being celebrated that winter. It was strange how the sexes reintegrated. From Pre-K till 3rd, you invite the entire class to your birthday. 4th and 5th are just the members of your assigned sex. 6th and 7th are more toned-down versions, as you're cool or not by now—and those subgroups celebrated their special days separately. But by eighth grade, when you get tingles in the jeans, it's back to mingling with the opposite sex. Only by now, there are a few more friends to bring to the dance: alcohol and cigarettes.

Everybody in Ridgefield Park knew someone who had access to "a hall." And for a town a mile square, we had a lot of "halls." We had the Elks Club, the Knights of Columbus, four firehouses, a VFW, and an Episcopal Church. All were unique in their way, but they were basically the same—a central location in town with enough open space, collapsible tables, a bar, and folding chairs to host a gathering. All anyone ever cared about was the bar, though.

These halls and proceeding sleepovers became the rotation for the birthday parties. Many of them involved contraband. The booze was almost always stolen. A handful of us had access to abundant spirits merely by living at home. By a handful, it was everyone. Ridgefield Park was a hard-drinking town in the 90s.

Cigarettes were even more effortless. I had been buying them for my parents since we moved to 208 Teaneck Road by walking up the block and asking for "A pack of Marlboro lights for my father and a pack of Virginia Slims for my mother." Sometimes, the shopkeeper would remind me to "bring a note next time," almost as if it was a library card that needed to be renewed. But with no less than two dozen places within town limits to buy cigarettes, acquiring them was never a problem.

One puff of a cigarette, and you wondered why an adult would ever do such a stupid thing. Three puffs and you understand. A new smoker can physically feel the nicotine move through their bloodstream, bringing a sense of calm to every part of the body as it travels through their veins.

For the longest time, that was all the answer I needed to the question a therapist or three has asked me: Why did you start drinking and smoking? *Because it was there, I could, and it's what the grown-ups do.*

There's still plenty of truth in that; we were hardly the first cohorts to share a rebellious spirit. You must expect a yearning for expression when you stifle kids' creativity by putting them in uniforms. Even if that was the reason for the inaugural sip in what would become quite the partnership, there was no avoiding how good it made me feel.

My entire footing changed. I didn't realize what my base level was until it was altered. I was edgy and shaky, constantly looking over my shoulder, waiting for the other shoe to drop, and afraid to speak without being boisterous. Not after a drink, though.

It put a smile on my face, made me (too) comfortable speaking, made me laugh, and made me feel invincible.

It made me forget everything that made me *"worried, anxious, or afraid."*

•••

I didn't "have a guy" with a hall—at least not yet. My father was still a few years away from joining, becoming engulfed, and practically moving into the Knights of Columbus. My fourteenth birthday was a pizza party. I invited the entire class, even Baker. Sister Patricia recently appointed me to a student leadership conference at Paramus Catholic High School, making me feel inclusivity was the way to go.

After the party, I had thrown the invitation out to the basketball team, inviting them over "to watch wrestling videos and horror movies." As soon as the lights went out upstairs, we rendezvoused with my parents' liquor cabinet. Hence, I'm likely one of the rare souls who vividly recalls the date of their inaugural hangover: February 6, 1991.

The usual protocol was that parents would chaperone and provide rides to as many kids as they could in their car to away games, always within 5 miles. This is a true testament to the widespread influence of the Catholic Church on the immediate area. But when half of the team slept over at my house—and my parents' bandwidth for adolescents expired following a loud and sleepless night—there weren't enough rides to satisfy the team.

With five of us, including me, left ride-less, Father Gerry—who was walking through the church parking lot—intervened. He volunteered the Astrovan for our transportation, averting the crisis until Harry Graves overheard.

Every town boasts a Harry Graves—a lifelong fixture, recognizable by all, who wear many hats throughout the community. In my youth, Harry wore the hats of soccer coach, Fire Chief, salesman, head of maintenance at St. Francis, and scout leader. Harry, perhaps dropping off his daughter Sara for cheerleading at the same event (though with the many hats over his trademark bald head and bushy mustache, one could never be sure), stepped in and said, "You don't have to do that, Father. I can fit them in the van."

He hadn't planned on attending the game, certainly not expecting to chauffeur a group of hungover teens in his utility-packed van. Yet, sitting on buckets of spackle seemed far more appealing than the spacious Astrovan.

My body and mind were in sync, cautioning against mixing Father Gerry with the guilt-ridden aftermath of pilfered Jack Daniels and Bushmills. Even if I couldn't fully fathom why, riding with him to the Holy Trinity gym on any other Saturday would have been welcome. Just not this Saturday. Thank the heavens for Harry Graves.

•••

The start of spring was the last time we would mingle with the public school Catholics during our time at St. Francis. As we prepared to leave the protection of elementary schools, we were expected to *confirm* our commitment to our faith and the Church via the sacrament of Confirmation. As taught, confirmation was our opportunity to make the vow as an adult that our godparents made for us at our baptism. They didn't teach us it had its foundations in Judaism, as it's a pretty cheap knock-off of a Bar/Bat-Mitzvah.

You choose only one "Sponsor" for this sacrament—someone already confirmed and in good standing with the church. It didn't need to be a relative—though almost everyone with an older sibling chose them. I also kept it in the family, choosing Aunt Breda to reprise her role as godmother.

Candidates, as we were called, were also required to select a Confirmation "Name"—the name of a saint separate from your first and middle names. In honor of my godfather, who was no longer with us, I chose "Robert." I had no idea if a Saint Robert existed, though I'm sure there's an easy trace of the name via Latin.

What's not to be excited about when you could reasonably expect to bank at least $300 in gifts, like more?

And what's not to love about another round of parties with bootleg hooch and Marlboro? Our confirmation parties, like our birthday parties, became sneaky and full of vice and experimentation.

...

I continued to spend most of my time at home in my attic bedroom. It was moderately spacious, 2.5 times longer than its width, and featured dark brown carpets and walls adorned with pale oak paneling. The east-facing window provided a clear view of the Empire State Building on select nights. The room offered peaceful isolation, muffling the anxious sounds from the rest of the busy household.

Music remained *my special friend.* I was still a sucker for the slow power ballad stuff, but I was discovering the angst of rap. Unfortunately, that rap was Vanilla Ice and contained absolutely no legitimate angst, as Robert Van Winkle would become a punchline/trivia answer/reality television participant. But that choice to "stop, collaborate, and listen" would lead to avenues that had me in a prime position to enjoy the Golden Age of rap, which would begin soon.

The one type of music I hadn't considered listening to yet was "The oldies"—anything recorded before Michael Jackson's "Thriller" in my mind. If someone recorded it all the way back, twenty years ago, while my parents were in high school, there wouldn't have been a snowball's chance in hell that I would have enjoyed it.

Then I saw Oliver Stone's "The Doors".

Being exposed to the dark poetry of Jim Morrison, hiding behind the music that took a listener on a journey rather than following along with a beat, changed my consciousness forever. Music could be about so much more than cars or fucking or friends. Music could be about pain. Music could be about sorrow. Music could be about confusion. Weeks later, Sister Dianne scolded me for doing an art project centered on Morrison performing at the Hollywood Bowl.

Growing up, my parents had some solid rock and roll tapes, and it opened up pathways to catalogs of some of the greats. However, I was listening to Morrison dryly croon "When the Music's Over" when I was by myself, stewing over Gerry's decision to give the starring role of The Big Kahuna in St. Francis' "Living Stations of the Cross"—rebranded by Catholics from "Passion Play" when the obvious antisemitic overtones of the latter became too big to ignore—to Matthew Baker.

The Altar Boys had traditionally been responsible for the production—upperclassmen only —which took place in the aisle and altar of the church every Good Friday near sundown. The President of the Altar Boys was traditionally Jesus, and then the officers took their roles—Roman Soldiers, St Peter, Pontius Pilate, Barabbas, etc. There was a reader—an 8th-grade girl (these weren't speaking roles. You just had to pose in your role as the narrator read the "station").

Mrs. Kennedy did nothing more than direct us to our positions once during a single rehearsal, and we retained it. She never threw herself into it. On the other hand, Gerry thought he was directing on the corner of 42nd St. and Broadway. He decided the production would be in the gym in lieu of the center aisle of the church. He asked parents to create biblical robes from blankets and sheets, as it would now be open to the entire school.

He decided he was the Producer, and I, having lost out on my assumed divine right to play Jesus and not taking it well, would be the Director. It was all a load of shit. Such a load of shit that the night before the play, during some roughhousing at home, I shredded Sean's makeshift "Man in the Crowd" robe into two pieces.

My folks were furious, and for the first time I could remember, I felt no guilt. I didn't know why. I almost instantly felt terrible when I realized I made someone else feel bad, or at least thought I did. Not this time.

But when the ending scene opened with the Risen Jesus posing on a cross in his underwear in front of the parish, I suddenly felt better.

•••

The day after the play, Easter was ruined forever. It would just take a couple of decades for me to realize it. While the simple Stations of the Cross had to become an off-Broadway production, transforming the inside of the church from its Lenten décor, reflecting on Christ's suffering, to Easter, which celebrates his alleged Resurrection, was a job for solely Father Gerry and the President of the Altar Boys.

No one else received the same demand, just me. The responsibility for something I didn't understand settled on my shoulders. The day was uncomfortable from the jump when Father Gerry insisted on multiple hugs. Each embrace felt like an invasion, leaving a palpable discomfort lingering.

As the day unfolded, Father Gerry's actions escalated. He sought hugs and planted what we called "Gerry kisses" (long, direct mouth-to-mouth contact) on me. Each moment with Father

Gerry became increasingly distressing, and I counted the minutes until I could escape the church grounds.

Walking home alone in the rain, the somber notes of the Doors in my ears became a soundtrack to my uneasy thoughts. The lyrics of "Riders on the Storm" seemed to echo the disquiet in my mind, and I couldn't shake off the unease.

•••

The worst-kept secret came to light around this time: Joe Doyle would replace Father Francis as pastor; the latter finally being sent out to pasture at a retirement home for priests. I wasn't in the room where it happened, and neither were my parents, but the rumors around the parish were that Gerry didn't take the snub all that well.

But it wouldn't be our problem much longer because graduation day was rapidly approaching. After ten long, consequential years, our sentence was approaching its expiration date. St. Francis tried each year to make graduation a spectacle. They created a photocopied yearbook with overexposed reproductions of our graduation pictures—boys in royal blue and girls in baby blue—not that you could tell from a photocopy.

There was a graduation mass on the morning of our last day of school. It was followed by the misogynistically labeled "Mother's Breakfast" for the moms of all the graduates. Dads were welcome, too, as was the faculty. But moms were the only ones to get a rose and a kiss on the cheek. The day ended with a Graduation "Convocation" that evening at the church, which was nothing but a fancy way of saying "one more blessing" and a chance for the parents who missed the mass that morning to see you in your gown.

Gerry said our graduation mass. His sermon was about our unlimited potential. He was reading fictional headlines from the year 2021 (Hah! If he only knew). The best athlete in the class was retiring as the NBA's all-time leading scorer. The most intelligent person in the class had just cured cancer. I was President of the United States. His departing love letter to me.

Once the official duties were over, it was Graduation Party season. Everyone in the class who wanted to have a party had one. I never ate as much catered pasta and party-sized Italian heroes as I did that fortnight. There was no way we could pull off day drinking in front of our folks, so there was plenty of stomach room for food. Families went all out to celebrate the Class of '91.

Not to be outdone, however, and to ensure he got the attention he craved from the people he sought it from, Gerry threw a graduation sleepover for the graduating altar boys at his Pennsylvania cabin. Some parents chaperoned it, but I have minimal memories of it. All I can recall was that he remained topless for all or most of the overnight visit, which was odd because the nearest place to swim was about a twenty-minute walk away. There was a cookout. The morning smelled like campfire smoke.

It wouldn't be my last visit to his Poconos retreat, but the fact that I can't recall anything from that stay still bothers me. I'm confident nothing unsavory occurred, especially with chaperones and many kids. Nevertheless, the graduation party at his home in Hawley, Pennsylvania, is a memory gap that I can't seem to fill.

The family hosted my graduation party the following Friday night.

Gerry showed up in his bathing suit.

X

I never wanted the summer of 1991 to end. No child ever wants any summer to finish, but once Labor Day rolled by, I was going to be something I never thought possible: a public school student.

It wasn't supposed to be this way. I took the aptitude tests for all Catholic high schools in Newark's Archdiocese: Bergen Catholic in Oradell—Don Bosco in Ramsey, Saint Joseph's in Montvale, and Paramus Catholic in Paramus. I also visited them and attended their open houses for prospective students.

Applicants were required to list schools in order of choice. While it wasn't formal policy, Bergen and Bosco made it known they would only take you if you listed them as your first choice, Paramus would only take you if you listed them as your top two choices, and I have no recollection of the ranking requirements for Joe's. It didn't matter; I was dead-set on attending Bergen Catholic High School.

That changed suddenly and abruptly in ways I still don't fully comprehend. I intended to choose Bergen; pleasing my folks that I voluntarily wanted to pursue a Catholic High School Education, and there was very little to discuss. Until my mother came up to my room one night early in the school year to tell me they'd like me to reconsider going to Bergen and attending Ridgefield Park High School instead. She said that Dad was worried about losing his job, and Bergen was expensive. Selfishly, I thought about it and decided I still wanted to go to Bergen. That's when she broke it to me; I had no choice. They couldn't afford it. It devastated me.

I would have company. A supermajority of students from the St. Francis Class of '91 went from 8th grade to public high school—the only class in my time there to have numbers like that. I would estimate that at least half of each class attended Catholic high school before our class, likely more.

Despite my excitement about leaving St. Francis, I couldn't shake off the feeling of intimidation that loomed over me in the presence of public school students. Their confidence and casual demeanor contrasted with the sheltered environment I was accustomed to, making me feel like an outsider navigating unfamiliar territory. The "St. Francis Sissies" nickname still scarred me, and my anxiety was more palpable than it had ever been. They were intimidating, as was the building itself compared to St. Francis in its tree-lined center of town location.

Ridgefield Park High School is nestled next to the New Jersey Turnpike, surrounded by the swamps of Ridgefield Park. The proximity to the Turnpike meant a constant hum of noise beating through the atmosphere as we tried to concentrate. The school had a unique courtyard-style layout featuring a central main hall housing administrative offices, the library, and the cafeteria. The large gym, painted primarily in scarlet red, paid homage to its nickname, "The Scarlets." Baby blue-painted cylinders dotted the hallways, each containing gray metal lockers.

It was a far cry from St. Francis, where I was among the biggest fish in a miniscule pond.

• • •

In the 1991 baseball season, the Ridgefield Park Baseball Association introduced an extra dimension by creating a traveling team for players who didn't make the cut for the advanced Babe Ruth League. Players like me and half my friends. The decision was made at the Knights of Columbus hall, and, somewhat unexpectedly, my dad volunteered to coach while under the influence of alcohol. This left me mortified, considering his only coaching experience was 7-year-old tee ball, and now he was taking charge of me and my friends. One evening, he stumbled home, leaning heavily on a cane at 40 because of an arthritic hip, and in a somewhat slurred manner, he conveyed the news that he would be my coach. He enlisted the help of 22-year-old Dave Ronan, a St. Francis alum known for his friendly and approachable nature.

Our inaugural game pitted us against Little Ferry, a formidable baseball powerhouse littered with future classmates. In his coaching wisdom, Dad designated me as the starting pitcher. However, he overlooked that it wasn't Little League anymore, we played by MLB baserunning rules, a crucial detail left unexplained. As the first batter walked and promptly stole second when I failed to pitch from the stretch, it became apparent that I needed to familiarize myself with this fundamental aspect of the game.

In baseball, "pitching from the stretch" is when the pitcher throws the ball to the batter with runners on base. Instead of using a full windup, the pitcher adopts a simplified stance. With one foot on the rubber and the other stretched toward the base, the pitcher aims to control the runner's lead while delivering an effective pitch.

Dad dispatched Dave to clarify the situation. Confused and unaware, I sought an explanation for pitching from the stretch. Dave explained the concept simply, but the information failed to register. Amidst the unfolding confusion, I felt as if I had heard nothing. I drew blanks. I was sweating profusely, my face reddening, and my heart racing.

Dave returned to the dugout, and I ignored his advice, opting for the traditional windup. He came out again, and this time I heard less. The noises of nothing gave way to the sound of what I assumed was blood rushing through my brain, like violent waves crashing against my cranium walls.

I was having my first known anxiety attack.

• • •

Jaime Reap was another reason I didn't want the summer to end. She had been an enduring crush of my life—on and off - a thread woven into the fabric of my experiences since kindergarten. When girls were cool, she was all I wanted to hang out with. When girls were "yucky," she was the "yuckiest." And when girls became interesting again, she was who I wanted to be around. Girls were fascinating in the weeks following graduation, and boys were finally attractive to them, as I found out when a lazy afternoon at a classmate's house gave way to "Seven Minutes in Heaven."

Locked inside the closet with Jaime for seven timed minutes, the air thick with anticipation, the crush that had endured for years suddenly manifested into something tangible. Our lips met in a brief but impactful kiss, culminating in feelings that had simmered beneath the surface for far too long. Although nothing formal materialized from that encounter, it began a shift in our dynamic.

After that clandestine moment, Jaime and I spent more time together. There was an unspoken connection, a shared understanding beyond the confines of formal labels. We were two scared kids being thrown from the frying pan into the fire as she was likewise heading to RPHS. And in her kiss, she told me I was okay, and that I was good enough.

We wouldn't form a romantic relationship that summer. Before the doors of RPHS opened, we hung out only in groups, where we attempted to forge our own paths. But in Jaime's company, I felt something I never knew I was missing: security.

•••

My first class on the first day of my first year of public high school was Introduction to Physical Science (IPS), taught by the hyper-memorable Gil Duff. Known equally for his short temper and armpit-stained button-down shirts, Mr. Duff had a three-decade tradition of wearing Hawaiian shirts the entire first week of school and never again until the following September.

A short, stubby man whose face bore the scars of the drink, his first demand of us was to pair off into lab partners. He made clear in no uncertain terms that our decisions were final and wouldn't tolerate requests to change partners after today. As luck had it, IPS was the only class I had that year with no fellow St. Francis Class of '91 folk. I knew a relatively small few people in the class in town, but they naturally paired up. Didn't know a single girl in the class. The two nerd-facing kids paired up. I was standing in front of my desk, mortified that all my nightmares were coming true. That I was being rejected. I was being mocked and laughed at. Everybody was noticing everything was wrong with me.

"Wanna pair up?" a voice said, breaking the panic. I looked down to see a face I had never noticed before. *It must be a Little Ferry kid.* I spoke to myself, referring to the other municipality that shared RPHS. But he didn't pair up with the other Little Ferry pupils. The more I thought about it, the more he looked as lost in that first-period class as I did.

"Sure," I said, thinking that neither of us had a choice. "I'm Ed," I said, extending my hand for a shake because that's what grown-ups do.

"Ryan", he responded.

Ryan Henderson was not only new to the school but also to Ridgefield Park and my direct neighborhood. 208 Teaneck Road, a county thoroughfare, sits between cross streets Vorhees to the south and Brinkerhoff Street to the north. Ryan lived at the northeast end of Brinkerhoff, a short walk to the Ridgefield Park town pool but an even shorter walk to my house.

That accidental lab pairing, the last two remaining students picking each other by default, would be the origin of a life-lasting friendship, as I found a blank canvas on the boy who would be nicknamed "Doc" later in life. Someone with no knowledge, memory, or understanding of St. Francis. It was impossible to know this at fourteen, but Doc offered me a fresh way to explore myself as someone other than Eddie the Altar Boy.

He would be the first person I told when I lost my virginity in the summer of '92. He got the directions for our first trip to Taco Bell the day I got my driver's license. He'd ride shotgun with me to the first Yankee Game I'd drive to without parental supervision. We smoked pot for the first time together. He would come to Wildwood on Hanratty family vacations. Later in life, we would be ushers in each other's weddings and attend the funerals of each other's loved ones.

RPHS isn't a large high school compared to other behemoths in North Jersey. Our paths would have crossed, eventually. But the genesis of our friendship emerged out of survival instincts, and the fear of rejection forged a brotherhood.

•••

IPS revealed another disturbing trend that began manifesting in the sixth grade: if I wasn't interested in it, I couldn't comprehend it. The honor roll student had been replaced with someone with a ferocious appetite for learning more of what he already knew rather than wanting to discover new things.

New things weren't just intimidating; they were scary.

Before the end of the first quarterly marking period, I was carrying A's in History, English, Art, and Gym while struggling to maintain a D average in Spanish, Algebra, and IPS. This fear of the unknown and a scrawny 6'1", 155 lbs. frame kept me from trying out for football.

In the next few years, I would make many adjustments and put in extra effort to make my overall grades and comprehensive student profile desirable to college admissions officers. Still, this remained a constant theme for my academic travels.

XI

You can take the boy out of St. Francis, but you can't take St. Francis out of the boy. Even with the migration to wearing civilian clothes to school, the burgeoning lifelong friendship with Doc, commitments to the RPHS freshman basketball team, and an increase in chances and people to party with, I remained stubbornly allegiant to that gothic monstrosity on the corner of Euclid and Mount Vernon Streets as I found my footing in high school.

Gerry's grand vision—and Dad's generous purchase of Senior vestments—kept me shackled to the ritual of serving mass into my RPHS years. For most of freshman year, I would serve a Sunday mass—celebrated by Doyle or Sudol. Because of a decline in attendance, there was no need to replace Father Francis, as a third live-in parish priest was no longer necessary.

I no longer had a sense of pride in the parish—or any of the positive, affirming emotions that adjoined being an altar boy while Mrs. Kennedy was in charge. Instead, it fell somewhere between an obligation and a sentence. I could rationalize it, however, by using one of the most irrational tools ever created by man: religion.

Thanks to the St. Francis indoctrination, I was still a fire and brimstone believer; I would attend Sunday mass regardless, lest my soul burn for all of damnation. So, I may as well serve mass for extra credit with the man upstairs. It didn't hurt that clergy, guidance counselors, parents, and mentors told us that taking part in a church organization through high school would look great on college applications.

The longer it lasted, however, the more awkward I felt. My face was breaking out like the cheesy, saucy pizzas you could get at one of the six pizzerias in our little village. There were hot girls that I was thinking about when I discovered self-pleasure attending these masses. It was increasingly mortifying with every mass served.

I could never immediately tell my parents I didn't want to do something. I had long thought that it was a simple fear of disappointing, as I've displayed with many other close ones over the years, but like everything else upstairs, it's deeper than that. I would make passive-aggressive comments and mope around the house until they figured out what I was trying to convey.

So when I began dropping hints that serving mass wasn't all that it was cracked up to be anymore, they received the message, but the response was not what I intended. "Why don't you cut down to once a month?" my mother suggested.

That didn't solve my problem. It locked me into an unwelcome solution. But I did it anyway. I dropped a note in the scheduling box inside the sacristy, kindly asking to reduce my availability to once a month.

•••

The last substantial time I spent with Father Gerry Sudol was the first Thursday and Friday of November '91. Like clockwork, the New Jersey Education Association holds its annual Teachers' Convention in Atlantic City, NJ, on the first weekend of November each year. St. Francis teachers are not unionized or part of the NJEA and never partook. But for public school kids, this meant two days off and a four-day weekend just as you hit the school year's two-month mark. Perfectly timed for the teachers, but not too shabby for the students, either.

Gerry invited a few senior altar boys to his cabin in Hawley, Pennsylvania, the same place he had held a graduation party months earlier.

My memories from that trip—like the graduation party—are relatively minimal, encapsulated in mundane details. One notable aspect was his request for a financial contribution to cover food expenses. On the way out, we ate McDonald's breakfast, and in the evening, we drove to a local pub to chow down on burgers while Gerry drank beer.

A prevailing theme throughout the trip was a subtle yet deliberate effort to distance ourselves from his company. This avoidance reached a point where he had to ask about joining us on a hike.

From what's survived in my memory, these snapshots stand out as the defining features of that 48-hour getaway, a minimal recollection compared to every other vacation/getaway/sleepover I've ever been to—even the ones where I got blind, blackout drunk. Feelings indented themselves into my mind more than visual remembrances. I was uncomfortable; I did not want to be there, but I still had no idea why.

I chalked it up to puberty or all of life's changes over the last year plus, really beginning with the loss of Uncle Bob. But when we came home from that trip, I spent the rest of the long weekend buried in the attic. Decades of experience now lead me to assume that this was my first extended bout of depression.

•••

I would have my last real interaction with Gerry a few weeks later. Before the fall of 1991, every time I partook in the Sacrament of Confession, it was at the mandatory direction of either St. Francis School or their Ministry that oversaw other sacraments like Confirmation or Communion.

Before Advent kicked off in early December, St. Francis publicized special hours for pre-holiday confession. I remember feeling like it was my duty to go. My parents didn't pressure me to go. Both of them—like millions of adult Catholics—decided confession "wasn't for them." I had to ask for a ride to the church.

I had every intention of having Joe Doyle hear my confession, but once Gerry made eye contact, he motioned to me as if to say, "I have a shorter line." I took the bait.

The confessionals were built into the outer walls of St. Francis. They were three-chamber vestibules with the priest's location in the middle. The sinner could choose the traditional route by entering on the right, where they would be screened off from the priest. Or they could go left, and the priest would hear their confession face-to-face.

I entered the confessional. Gerry would often shame young people into face-to-face confession as opposed to the more traditional "behind the screen" confession popularized in television and movies. If a child entered the screened-in chamber, he'd tell them to walk around and use the other door.

I intended to give him a soft confession. I would not say I experimented with alcohol with increasing regularity; I was going to say, "I've lied to my parents multiple times." Certainly would not say I got a premarital blow job (technically, I don't even know if that's considered a by-the-book-sin); instead, I would say, "I had impure thoughts."

Gerry would have none of it. He asked the questions, running through the commandments, asking if I'd lied or how I'd treated my loved ones. Then he asked if I had impure thoughts, and I said sometimes. He wondered what type of thoughts I had about girls. He asked how, to which I said awkwardly, "I dunno, isn't it obvious?" He pushed until I admitted they were sexual. He asked if I masturbated. What high school freshman didn't? I answered in the affirmative.

I don't remember what my penance was that night. But as of 2024, it's been thirty-three years since my last confession.

•••

The end of my eight-year run as an altar boy ended unceremoniously, with none of the pomp and circumstance or familial attendance that my first mass in 1986 had. After 1992's feelings of awkwardness, even after cutting back to once per month, I decided I had had enough. To my delight, I informed my parents, and there was no pushback. Effective immediately, I was no longer an active member of the St. Francis of Assisi Altar Boys.

I would still attend Sunday mass. But after a decade of serving mass, it was time to hang up the vestments.

Father Gerry's Youth Group flourished during my time as a Senior Altar Boy. Many engaging activities for young people were far from the stereotypical version of what Frank Zappa called "church-oriented activities." This wasn't Christmas Caroling with Mrs. Kennedy; it was overnight lock-in pizza parties in the gym, ski weekends, or a rebooted CYO

Basketball league for high school students who didn't play at their schools for whatever reason. The Youth group drew significantly more young people from the public school system than it did St. Francis alumni.

I'm not saying the coolest of the cool were part of the Youth Group, but it didn't have the stigma of a nerdy, bible-based gaggle of goody-two-shoes that "Church Youth Group" may conjure up in the mind. Still, I wanted nothing to do with it.

It didn't start like that. I did a few activities—including the lock-in pizza party right after I had graduated from the school. I didn't stick with it. I gave no reason or explanation. And it's not like I wasn't involved in other things. I wasn't withdrawing. But my body and mind would not allow me to get involved in Gerry's Youth Group as I always assumed I would in my post-altar boy life.

...

I maintained my Sunday mass attendance schedule, though. I was walking up to St. Francis by myself and hanging out in the back of the church for the entire mass. I left right after receiving communion—what we called "Beating the traffic."

Following communion, all that remained of the mass were special announcements ("The Rosary Committee will meet Tuesday night in the lower church at 7:30") and the final blessing. It's not as if I was skirting the entire liturgy. I was meeting my minimum requirements to keep my soul in a state of grace in case I got hit by a truck.

Around this time, circa 1993, I furnished an identity independent from whom I always considered myself, Eddie the Altar Boy. Nirvana exploded onto the music scene in late 1991, and the game of Rock'n Roll changed forever. While their instruments sounded like a stripped-down version of the glam bands that dominated my cassette collection, their words and the meaning behind them were vastly different, almost like The Doors. Darker, bolder, more emotionally honest.

Pearl Jam broke through around the same time, and in them, I found the voice I had been yearning to hear since I gained adolescent consciousness. They sang of abandonment and pain, love and ecstasy, loss and grief. There are only so many songs about making out in the back of a car that you can get excited about, and that was the more significant part of my collection until the Seattle garage sound went nationwide.

With that, I took my appearance more seriously. I was still breaking out like hell, which did wonders for my already damaged self-esteem, but I could still work on the rest of me. Gone were the generic Yankees and Giants t-shirts with big bubbly letters popularized then; in were open flannels and band t-shirts. I mothballed the basketball sneakers in favor of black Converse Chuck Taylor-All Stars or a pair of Vans. The neat flat-top haircut I was sporting would grow out. I never again allowed myself to be confused with some dude in basic training. I even got my ear pierced.

The basketball shoes may as well have gone into the trash at that point, come to think of it. While I remained a die-hard fan of college and professional sports, I stopped trying to convince myself I was an athlete. On Martin Luther King Day, 1992, I was at a varsity basketball practice shooting around. I ended up landing on a ball already on the ground, twisting my ankle to where I was on crutches for three weeks. It was the end of my season, and I decided I would never partake in organized sports again.

...

I was getting comfortable in my new skin by the fall of 1994. We were seniors now. I'd pick up Doc on the way to school each morning, sometimes stopping to get this magical elixir that helped you stay awake through first-period physics called coffee. We'd listen to Green Day's album "Dookie" because that's all anyone listened to. I was looking at colleges and thinking about life after Ridgefield Park.

I was still attending mass each Sunday, though by now, I was driving up alone and lurking in the back before beating the traffic. That's how something peculiar became noticeable: Father Gerry wasn't there anymore.

His name remained on the masthead of the weekly newsletter, "The Bulletin," provided at mass each Sunday. There was no formal announcement about a leave, vacation, or anything else that would explain a priest's noticeable multi-week absence.

I asked my mom if she knew anything—she was always up on the latest gossip around the parish—and she said she didn't, but people were wondering. A few days after I came home from school, my mom had some answers.

It turns out that Father Gerry Sudol was leaving St. Francis for good. He had a series of nosebleeds that required medical attention, and the Church doctors diagnosed him with "Nervous Exhaustion." The parish would receive no more official information.

Ever.

The era of Father Gerry Sudol at St. Francis began like a hurricane. It ended with barely a whimper.

At least, as far as any of us knew. What we would eventually learn about his departure would implicate not only St. Francis but the Archdiocese of Newark in its entirety.

XII

Ridgefield Park's mid-90s social fabric featured a drinking culture that permeated all facets of community life. Civic and family gatherings found their home in local halls, fostering an environment conducive to socializing over drinks. Membership in organizations like the Knights of Columbus, Elk's Club, and VFW (at least back then, when there was still a noticeable collection of WWII and Korean veterans among us) reflected a strong presence of social clubs where alcohol consumption remained normalized, encouraged, or expected. The heart of Main Street boasted four establishments dedicated to selling alcoholic beverages.

The annual Independence Day Parade—the village's pride and joy- was a long, fourteen-hour open bar from house to house. It would start with a bomb blast at 7:45 AM and rage on until the grand finale of the fireworks down by RPHS an hour after sundown. Poorly hidden kegs would dot the residential areas of the nation's longest continuous 4th of July Parade. It wasn't unusual to see the Governor of New Jersey or New Jersey's senators and Congresspeople show up to march in it. Likewise, it wasn't uncommon for some overly-imbibed-by-11 AM residents to let the politicians know what they thought of them in not-so-kind language.

The prevalence of alcohol extended beyond social settings to more personal realms, with a notable presence in the lives of many residents. AA meetings drew a significant crowd. They kept the lights on the lower church for all those years before Gerry's youth group. It was a trend that extended significantly among our boomer parents. Heavy drinking among fathers was commonplace. Within the circles of the St. Francis community, alcoholism was an undeniable reality, with every significant church event either sporting a cash bar or the option to bring your own booze, depending on the venue. People didn't gather without booze.

Public safety institutions like volunteer firehouses and the police firing range were not exempt from this culture, with refrigerators stocked with beer as a casual accompaniment to their respective activities. What goes better with your service revolver than cold (free) iced bottles of Budweiser?

As luck would have it, one of those volunteer fire departments provided the beer for the party that set the tone for what the next four years of my social life would look like, only three weeks into my freshman year. The situation was cut directly from our youth's raunchy and silly teen comedies.

A classmate who lived just blocks away found himself home alone for the weekend and invited freshman boys over during lunch on Friday. What started with a few attendees sprouted into about two dozen freshmen. With access to one of the fire departments through his father, he snuck in and stole three cases of Budweiser nips—smaller, 6 oz cans of beer. As the gathering progressed, someone jokingly suggested ordering a stripper, prompting us to check the Yellow Pages, where we surprisingly found listings for both strippers and strip clubs.

We called under the guise of hosting an 18th birthday party, and a neighbor and former altar boy, two years our senior, volunteered to impersonate the birthday boy. To our amazement, the dancer showed up with a rock-solid-built security escort who didn't bother checking IDs, taking our story at face value. As the dancer began her performance, giving personal dances to the birthday boy and anyone willing to pay $5, she quickly cleared $100. Meanwhile, I attempted to sneak home quietly, only to find both my parents still awake.

My dad, inebriated himself and stationed in the basement, remained silent. However, my mom insisted on talking to me. Exhausted, I claimed I was tired and needed to be up early to watch the freshman football game. Rushing to the attic, I couldn't contain the alcohol's effects and ended up vomiting in the closet.

It wasn't a fun morning the next day, but it's not like I learned my lesson.

...

Getting my driver's license marked a significant shift in my teenage life. I was liberated from the confined walking distances within Ridgefield Park. This newfound freedom meant I could spend less time at home, where I was constantly sequestering myself in the attic. The more I distanced myself from home, the less time I spent trapped in my thoughts. Hours after the state licensed me to drive, I eagerly picked up Doc and some other friends to celebrate my newfound mobility in my mom's Dodge minivan.

I don't know why it seemed to fit hand in hand, but having the responsibility of being behind the wheel made another adult behavior seem like the next natural progression: pulling into the Mobil gas station and buying a pack of cigarettes. I opted for a pack of Marlboro Mediums and soon had a few cigarettes every day. Little did I know this habit would persist for decades. The experimentation with alcohol and cigarettes naturally led to a curiosity about marijuana. A desire to try this new substance prompted me, Doc, and a couple of friends to approach a member of the football team whom we assumed would have access to weed.

Seizing an opportune moment when my parents were attending a formal function at the Knights of Columbus and my sisters were sleeping at Aunt Breda's; our friend came over. He brought a small metal pipe and a tiny Ziploc of weed, which we later learned was called a "dime bag" because of its $10 price tag. I set the atmosphere in my room with The Doors playing in the background, lights dimmed, and incense burning because I was dramatic like that.

As we indulged in the first rush of cannabis, uncontrollable fits of laughter and euphoria overcame us. The experience was exhilarating, and an hour later, we found ourselves on the phone with Domino's, ordering pizza. When my parents returned home, they were none the wiser, believing that I and my three friends had enjoyed a night of pizza and watched the NBA Slam Dunk Contest.

Or, more likely, Dad got himself trashed, and Mom exhausted herself dealing with the Knights of Columbus folk; she knew but figured, "Fuck it, they're home."

Whatever was going through her mind, I tuned into another avenue of escape.

•••

Little Ferry, with whom we shared RPHS, was a town of economic diversity featuring an eastern edge characterized by industrial areas and low-income housing, the main access road, Rt 46, littered with used car lots, hourly rate hotels, and fast-food joints. But amidst this gritty landscape, Mariani Drive stood out as the crown jewel of Little Ferry addresses. Business owners, Wall Street types, and other legitimate businessmen populated this street, showcasing McMansions before the term gained popularity. At the northeast end of Mariani Drive, behind a row of these impressive homes, lay a clearing of woods spanning approximately three acres, accessible from three different roads, although thorn bushes hindered one route. In the summer of 1994, this tree-canopied clearing became the official weekend hangout for the Class of 1995.

Regardless of the unpredictable North Jersey weather, our weekends in the wooded sanctuary were a consistent ritual. Friday mornings would be full of greetings like "Woods tonight?" or "Will I see ya in the Woods later?" The acquisition of cases of beer, often facilitated by a cooperative legal adult relative, became an integral part of our routine, with Coors Light and Zima emerging as the beverages of choice, as pathetic as that sounds. Although Goldschlager—a famous German liqueur at the time — achieved legendary status among us nubile drinkers because "you shit out the gold flakes tomorrow."

When in the woods, our parties unfolded into the same tapestry of activities: heavy, heavy drinking, sharing the camaraderie of cheap marijuana smoke, and contemporary songs sung in drunken baritones. Teenage romances would blossom and wither in the natural surroundings, often on the same night.

As the night matured, we would migrate towards the Plaza 46 diner. This late-night highway pilgrimage for munchies became a tradition, much to the dismay of the wait staff, who had no interest in catering to three tables of low-tipping teenagers. The juxtaposition of nature's embrace and the diner's neon glow was as dichotomous as Little Ferry itself.

As was the juxtaposition of being a vigorous seventeen-year-old who consumed beer like a seasoned vet on a dive-bar stool.

This was the only way of life, and I fit the lifestyle brilliantly. An identity was forming, and not a healthy one.

•••

Veterans Park was the recreational epicenter of RP. The tract of land unfolds from the southern vicinity near the Town Pool to the northern bounds adjoining Ridgefield Park High School. The park is next to the New Jersey Turnpike and has a diverse array of amenities. Among them are three ball fields, including a little league stadium, a dedicated soccer field, and a hockey rink. A playground graces the park, featuring a slide that, with its distinctive bump, evolved into an eccentric town icon.

While not entirely secluded like The Woods, the park takes on an enigmatic quality after sundown, with its ample dark spaces providing a gathering ground for teens seeking to blow off steam and party. Seeing the swampy creek that abuts the turnpike littered with the remnants of many unsanctioned parties wasn't unusual. Half of the refuse could have easily belonged to the beer league softball teams among the dozens of organizations that used the park.

And on December 27, 1994, it was where I shared the most consequential kiss of my life with Jaime Reap.

As we started high school, she remained active in the St. Francis Youth Group. I was finding my way, attempting to separate myself from Eddie the Altar Boy, heading in a different direction. As senior year began, water found its level, and the cliques that formed were more of a choice than by upbringing, everyday activity, or neighborhood. It was more organic.

We hung out often as part of a bigger crowd interested in doing the same things—primarily partying, which is precisely what we did that night when I ended up looking thoroughly like a clown with an empty 12-pack of Coors Light on my head, along with her on a bench along the third base side of Softball Field 1.

I had kissed a lot of girls at this point. But I refused to commit to almost all of them. I was so intent on proving my masculinity to myself. Internally I thought that my feelings of being less-than emanated from being a horrible athlete, a bit of a spaz, and awkward. Hooking up with girls was something I could do to prove that wasn't the case. I had no varsity letters, and my refusal to open up to new things prohibited my grades from being elite-university-worthy. Still, I could find a date most Friday nights with minimal effort. It wasn't because I had an instant attraction to a girl as much as I had to prove to myself I could—that I was an ordinary man.

Despite the relative ease at which I could find female companionship, every single time, I would say to myself, *damn, I cannot fathom why she would want to spend time with me.* It would inevitably lead me towards being inauthentic to myself, feigning interests and trying to portray myself as the knight in shining armor to every damsel in distress I would go out with. No wonder there was no commitment.

That wasn't the case with Jay, as I would now call her.

It was unlike any kiss I had ever shared. And I couldn't help but note the irony that in my final year of public high school, I was settling down with a St. Francis girl.

•••

By now, Father Gerry was a punchline. Following his abrupt departure, rumors quickly circulated that he was seeking help at a "hospital for priests" in Philadelphia to treat his nervous exhaustion. To an entire generation of kids, however, we knew something was fishy. We just did not understand pedophilia.

To a man, every one of us who cracked a joke about Father Gerry's "proclivities" did so under the guise that Sudol was a homosexual male. The mid-90s awakened many overlooked parts of the American fabric, but in Ridgefield Park, New Jersey, in 1995, nobody was looking at the exiled priest for his attention to boys. They were looking at his attention towards males. Like many other dads at St. Francis, my father was as close or closer to him as my mother was. This was the case in similar households.

Even some wiser parents or grandparents would make a flippant remark or sarcastic joke about Gerry being "light in the loafers" or "queerer than a three-dollar bill." This misconception wasn't just wrong; it was dangerous.

I still viewed the entire Sudol saga as I did when I first became uncomfortable with his kisses. It sucks, and it's annoying, but it comes with the territory. He did nothing wrong; he just maybe liked men the way I liked women. The dramatic age difference never factored into my continually evolving thinking.

We would joke about him with regularity. During a pickup basketball game, one former altar boy started reciting the "For all that you are" blessing while reaching around to steal the ball from me. There were yearbook signings of the same blessing. "Going to Pennsylvania with Father Gerry" became a line you'd rag on someone with. Nothing was funnier than Father Gerry jokes in the classroom or The Woods.

Tears of a clown.

•••

In the latter part of senior year, festivities swirled around Jay and me, the celebratory mood infusing our relationship with vitality. Our Memorial Day weekend unfolded in the familiar setting of Wildwood Crest at the Admiral West Motel, a long-standing RPHS tradition. Brimming with excitement and well-stocked, we embarked on the journey, slyly hiding nine thirty packs of Coors Light in my Dad's station wagon, cleverly concealed beneath the collapsible back seat, the weekend seamlessly blended into a continuous stream of revelry, from dawn till dusk, with the Admiral West morphing into a bustling hub of celebration, inundated by the lively presence of RPHS students and both recent and not-so-recent (balding) alumni reliving their glory days.

Amid the lingering euphoria, the excitement for our senior prom reached its zenith in the following week. The prom weekend unfolded at a run-down hotel in Seaside, New Jersey, where Jay's fair Irish complexion succumbed to a painful sunburn, confining us to the room while our friends reveled on the beach at night with all the party favors. It marked the first instance my inability to partake in the drinking visibly bothered me.

The next time I found myself all dressed up in a suit with Jay, I would have no problem finding alcohol despite still being only eighteen years old. She asked me to be her guest at her Uncle John's wedding. She informed me that her family had booked a hotel suite, and we were welcome to stay. Translation: You can get as drunk as you'd like.

The dynamics of a wedding fascinated me. People got dressed up for a never-ending stream of food and drink. When we arrived at the venue, attendants guided us to "The Ice Sculpture"—a giant swan under which, encased in ice, was ten different beers to choose from. I looked at Jay and her oldest brother and said, "We can really just help ourselves?"

Fast-forward a few hours, and I'm singing "Paradise by the Dashboard Light" with a lesbian barbershop quartet in the hotel lobby. The party continued into the bridal suite, where John and his new wife, Dianne, were immensely patient with a wandering group of friends, relatives, and their dates as we moved in and out of their room.

Jay's greater family immediately embraced me—and they were great in numbers, with Jay's mom being one of thirteen children and John being the youngest. I felt a sense of comfort with the adult they treated me as. It was a far cry from the restrictive "Just Say No" household that I was living in.

It felt like I was more authentic when I was further removed from home, St. Francis, and RP. But I also felt more genuine when I could unwind with alcohol.

...

On the Sunday of Labor Day weekend, I attended the 9:15 mass with some former altar boys. We were all set to depart for college later that day. After mass concluded, we went our separate ways for good. I left Eddie the Altar Boy sitting in the pews of St. Francis that day and never looked back.

XIII

Of all the things I miss about life before antidepressants, the ability to cry is at or near the top of the list.

Dad was a crier. He had a particular Budweiser-to-tear ratio—and for a while; I related to that better than any other emotion I ever shared with him. And when he caught my eye after the third and final trip to unload my belongings to Pine Hall 203 B, shit got real. He broke down crying while telling me how proud he was of me. I could barely keep myself together.

The ride to Ramapo College of New Jersey from St. Francis on a Sunday of a holiday weekend was a breeze that wasn't fast enough. I didn't know it then, but I yearned to shed everything I ever convinced myself was my core.

I was looking to recast my life, plant a new flag in this bucolic surrounding as "Ed." Not Eddie, altar boy or not. I realized one of the few—and underrated benefits—of being a "legal adult" is that people will call you what you tell them to call you. Professors even gave you the courtesy of asking how they should refer to you.

That last mass with the altar boys might have only been six or seven hours away, but it might as well have already been a lifetime before sunset. I had emotional goodbyes, hugs, and kisses with Mom and Elizabeth. I knelt to hug Erin goodbye and reassure her I'd be home every weekend. And Big Ed and I shared that emotional embrace.

I was stronger than him. Significantly.

This wasn't me outlasting him for seven extra points when we played "21" at the Fairleigh Dickinson black tops down the block from my grandparents' house four years ago. I felt it in his bones that it took every drop of hope and aspiration to get a child into college. And I knew he wasn't full of shit. He was done. And I knew at that point—when I was misty-eyed and hugging my dad, my namesake—that my siblings would NOT have the same father I did.

None of that was near the forefront of my thinking when my family *finally* left. Before I dove into my luggage, crates, and Bed, Bath, and Beyond dorm room essentials, I reached for the shoebox within a tote bag that had "my sins"—my ashtray with a Grateful Dead logo in the middle of it, a carton of Marlboro Lights, Toby my pot bowl, and a fifth of Blackberry Brandy I found in the back of the liquor cabinet at home.

This was it. This was my opportunity to break free from everything I had been carrying with me for most of the last decade. The tension, the awkwardness in solitude, shit—even the acne—was gone. I was a new fucking person.

A few hours later, though, I was back in front of Jay's house across the street from St. Francis, picking her up for coffee. I wasn't anywhere close to shedding my St. Francis skin, but it was okay. Old habits die hard. It was going to be a process.

•••

In the fall of 1995, my new schoolmates and my old RP friends were given access to a futuristic platform that until then seemed like something out of *The Jetsons*—an electronic mail address.

EHANRATT@RAMAPO.ORION.EDU would be the first sign-on for my inaugural venture into electronic communications and the information superhighway. We had plenty of cursory lectures by teachers and other adults about how "The Internet" would change everything. It was usually something blunter like "Computers are the wave of the future"- generic platitudes my old man probably heard when he was eighteen. Still, to this day, I don't think many younger folks realize exactly how life-altering email was.

I sure as hell never assumed that one day, it would be the medium in which I would change the entire trajectory of my life, for better or worse.

Doc was one of those high school friends with whom I would keep in touch via this new emerging technology, but he was also the only friend I would somewhat regularly speak on the telephone. He may be the only friend to whom I never sent "a letter" since neither of us had to work too hard to get in touch with the other. Given Ramapo's relative proximity to RP, he'd usually come up and crash for a night when he was home from school on the weekends.

On the familial front, I did my darndest to control communications and, to a degree, narratives. I was brick by brick, building walls around my pre-existing relationships once I settled into school. I kept in regular touch with Sean - his football career was blossoming as he made varsity in his sophomore season. And I could follow it with relative ease given the extensive high school football coverage in "The Record," a newspaper abundantly available on every corner of campus: student center, library, cafeteria, and bookstore.

Elizabeth was approaching her teenage years and quickly assumed my private landline. It was nice to have a direct line to her to bypass whoever else answered the phone when I was looking solely to speak with her. However, she was primarily concerned with her junior high and high school years as I was with college.

Erin caught me completely by surprise. She was ten years younger than me. By the time she developed a personality and identity of her own, I was navigating the oddities and insecurities of adolescence, with, unbeknownst to me at this time, added awkwardness and confusion from trauma.

Beyond that, Erin often felt "different" from Sean and Elizabeth. She had no recollection of the family's apartment, the only one of us to have known one home for their entire childhood. Ironically, while she shared the same godparents as me, she had little to no memory of Uncle Bob, who passed away two weeks after her third birthday. The family life she was experiencing was immensely different from mine, not just because of the day-to-day changes in life and technology over a decade.

No, the gulf between our upbringings was familial, financial, and emotional. To that point, I assumed I would always be her big brother and she my baby sister. And while that still holds to a degree today, moving out of Teaneck Road and onto campus at Ramapo College changed the entire dynamic of our relationship.

Not long after I settled in, I got regular telephone calls from her around 2:45 most days when she got home from St. Francis. I don't know if, in her previous eight years, I had ever spoken on the phone with her—I don't know why I would have—but now we were recapping her day at least three times a week.

Sometimes, she would catch me while friends and I were taking bong hits in our dorm room, which not only made for interesting conversation but endeared her to all my stoned-out-of-their-minds friends. None of them had sisters that young, and for a bunch of testosterone-fueled-young-adults that wouldn't hesitate to go nose-to-nose with each other over whose football team was better, they would melt with regularity when the phone rang and patiently waited for me to finish the conversation before passing our contraption back around the room.

Those phone calls connected me to the innocence of youth. It's hard to imagine an 18-year-old thinking that he has it insurmountably tough, given the benefit of hindsight, but I did. Even then, I had a longstanding feeling that the walls were closing in on me, that something was suffocating. But those stoned calls with my baby sister reminded me someone was in my corner as I tried to forge a path in what felt like a confusing, frantic, directionless life—despite my efforts to reimagine myself.

•••

In September 1995, the New York Yankees were preparing for their first postseason appearance within my memory. Their march to October was palpable, with the navy blue Yankees cap, the most famous headwear on campus. During the first two weeks of the semester, the Greek Organizations (Fraternities, Sororities) hold "Open Houses" for freshman—parties with copious amounts of alcohol where they attempt to recruit you into their don't-call-it-a-cult. These two events collided at a generic frat open house the second week of school when I made the acquaintance of Ben Merrill.

I noticed Ben and a few other gentlemen at earlier parties. Like me, they seemed to gravitate towards where the alcohol was being served and had little to no interest in hearing pitches about membership from our gracious hosts. The fraternities were timeshares; we were only interested in the free ride accompanying the hard sell. On this night, he and I were the only ones hovering around an innocuous game between the Yanks and the Baltimore Orioles in the corner of the fraternity apartment.

The more we talked, the more we realized we had an equal passion for sports, drinking, music, and, most importantly, life. From first impression, Ben was a bright and astute dude. He didn't appear a pompous know-it-all like so many first-year college students looking to impress; quite the contrary. Despite a reserved personality, he confidently expressed his opinions and perspectives without hesitation.

We realized we had a Remedial Math class together, and following our next session, he invited me back to his dorm to pull bong hits. While listening to the Grateful Dead's "Terrapin Station," we talked about his favorite band, Nirvana. We rattled off the names of obscure Yankees from the team's less-than-stellar run in the late 1980s. But most impressive, we discussed our classes. He wanted to know as much about history as he could, and I peppered him on literature—his major—and we would discuss how they often intersected with works like "The Prince" or "Uncle Tom's Cabin."

The first Sunday of October found me rolling back into Pine Hall with time to spare before the deciding game of the Yankees' first playoff series I would ever witness. Watching the deciding game with Ben and other newfound friends who shared our interests in sports, beer, weed, music, and conversation added to the excitement. However, as the game went into extra innings, Ben asked me, "Are you Catholic?" Despite our shared experiences, he had no idea about my religious background. In response, I affirmed my Catholicism, and Ben proposed, "Want to go pray?"

Without questioning the absurdity, we knelt in the bathroom of 203, reciting Hail Marys with rosary beads until we heard the game return from the commercial. However, as the young Panamanian rookie Mariano Rivera looked on from the bullpen, the Yankees' pitching imploded, and the Mariners celebrated their victory, ending the World Series dream.

"Well, that's the last time I'll ever fucking pray. Thanks for nothing, God," Ben remarked with a twinge of blasphemous guilt.

I replied—not wholly in jest, "Same."

•••

In the first fall semester, while unconsciously distancing myself from prayer, I remained firmly rooted in Catholicism's faith and traditions, and weekends meant returning home for some Pizza Hut delivery cash and attending Sunday Mass at St. Francis, always flying solo. Discussing religion during the early college days mirrored conversations about our ethnic heritage—a statement of birth circumstances rather than a circle of "Born Again" or "Saved" individuals, fitting for a North Jersey Liberal Arts College.

My initial impression of a guy named "Sprengel" reflected ingrained prejudices. Assuming he escaped the methy parts of Appalachia, I soon discovered he was the son of two devout urban Irish Catholics. He enjoyed "Hootie and the Blowfish" and chewing tobacco. Basketball rivals since sixth grade and occasional opponents in baseball, Mark and I also realized that we attended the same Jubilee for Altar Boys officiated by Archbishop McCarrick.

Mark was the only friend I made after St. Francis, who was a practicing, church-attending Catholic, and those weekend rituals continued into college. Holy Days of Obligation, like All Saints' Day on November 1, added to the religious calendar. At a party where Mark (Leatherman) and I (construction worker) dressed up like the Village People, I told him I planned to attend the evening All Saints' Day Mass at St. Paul's Catholic Church. He said he'd meet me in my room 10 minutes before.

As 6:30 approached on November 1, I found myself unintentionally high, forgetting our plans, forgetting that it was even All Saints' Day; I followed my usual routine of meeting Ben in his room for bong hits after our 3:30 class ended and before we hit meal plan for dinner.

Mark showed up in my room, and I immediately thought, "Oh fuck, yeah, All Saints' Day."

I would set a then-record for uncontrollable church giggles. Seated in the last row of a tiny vestibule during All Saints' Day Mass, uncontrollable laughter disrupted the entire service. Every word the priest uttered prompted me to chuckle. Mark was powerless to resist, and church giggles were more contagious than the common cold, so we left promptly after communion.

Reflecting on these experiences, I shudder at the unfounded fears and judgments I once harbored about being Catholic. I questioned why I was still attending mass. Jay had already ceased attending, but I held on.

It was fun attending with Mark, but not fun in any way that provided spiritual fulfillment or contentment. It was more ironic fun than anything else.

Sunday Mass at home was a personal escape, free from accountability to others. But away at school, there is no need to bail on activities like video game tournaments or Yankees games. While my Catholic identity was clear, the lingering shame surrounding my faith reflected imagined ridicule from friends like Ben, chanting "St. Francis Sissy"—something Ben or any of my new friends would never entertain.

But walking back into the dorm room after All Saints' Day brought back memories of comingling with public school kids—and the insecurities that accompanied them.

Mark's comment on the way out of the church, "Well, that was pointless," resonated with my sentiment. Except for Christmas, it marked the last time I attended Mass for a Holy Day of Obligation. Little did I know, this subtle shift signaled a changing relationship with Catholicism.

In the aftermath of an unintended high on November 1, I continued my routine, attending Sunday Mass at home and reflecting on the unfounded fears and judgments I had once harbored about being Catholic.

•••

After the initial chaotic month of college, routines and a sense of normalcy emerged, akin to forging order out of the liberating chaos of newfound freedom. As friendships developed, specific individuals became constants in the evolving college experience. One such constant was David G. Hayes, known simply to all as "Hayes" or "G-Hayes," who seamlessly integrated into various aspects of campus life, from big parties to smaller gatherings and shared classes.

I spent leisure time in familiar circles as this routine solidified friendships. On a random weekday afternoon, a search for Mark led to a spontaneous encounter with Hayes. The familiarity had reached a point where a casual knock-and-nudge allowed entry into each other's living spaces.

During this unplanned visit, Hayes invited me into the suite's common area with his distinctive South Jersey accent. Our preliminary group had condensed their social lives into three rooms: my 203, Ben's 305, and Mark's 405. Hayes lived with Mark in 405.

Hayes quickly became integral to my college experience, extending beyond campus life to various aspects of my daily routine. In Pine Hall, where Ben, Mark, and I lived, his presence added a unique dynamic shaped by our diverse regional accents.

Our friendship blossomed over shared interests in partying, sports, and academic pursuits. Despite not formally introducing ourselves, mutual recognition grew steadily over a month.

The turning point came when Hayes suggested playing NBA Live '96 on Sega Genesis. This casual invitation sparked a more profound connection beyond surface-level similarities. As we played, Hayes offered a homemade vodka and Mountain Dew concoction and, through slightly buzzed conversation, offered me glimpses into his life outside Ramapo.

Our routine of setting up video games while sharing stories allowed us to establish a profound connection beyond the college setting. During these interactions, I discovered Hayes's serious passion for sports, particularly basketball, which we both shared.

We uncovered commonalities as we delved into our backgrounds, including our upbringing in Irish Catholic households, fathers with urban backgrounds, and family moves to New Jersey. These shared experiences formed a firm foundation for our burgeoning friendship despite some major New York v Philadelphia differences. My encounter with David G. began a meaningful connection that transcended the typical surface-level friendships of college life, laying the groundwork for a lasting bond.

...

The last night of our first semester was memorable for many reasons. About a third of the campus had vacated, having finished their finals. Our finals were likewise done, but we wanted to milk every second of college independence before returning to life under our parents' roofs.

A mid-May thunderstorm had rolled through campus, breaking the humidity and saturating the grassy areas of the college. Our last thirty packs of the year were being crushed. Naturally, heading out to throw the football around was the obvious next step in the evening's activities. Our friend Duce—a gentleman whose presence guarantees a fun and exciting adventure joined Ben, Hayes, and me. Likewise, there was another freshman beginning to spend more time with us through mutual pot-purchasing friends.

Walter Walker was one of those distinguishable faces in the crowd. I remember noticing him the prior summer during freshman proficiency testing (the reason guys like Ben and I ended up in Remedial Math). A mixed-race kid from South Jersey, he stood tall with a frame similar to mine at the time - standing over 6 feet, with a slim waist and broad shoulders. His curly black shoulder-length hair hinted at the same rebellious spirit as Ben's fuchsia dye jobs or my burgeoning ponytail that grew from making it the entire first year of college without a haircut. Walter had that spirit by the bucket and wore it on his sleeve.

Slipping and sliding in a grassy area by the campus academic buildings sounded the best way to cap off the first year of college. Campus Security, soon to be our well-known nemesis, felt otherwise.

Ramapo Campus security was a hired security force, distinct from most other New Jersey colleges and universities equipped with dedicated police forces. This distinction meant we lacked the threat of genuine criminal consequences or the possibility of driver's license suspensions for illegal parking.

In theory, if security involved the Mahwah Township Police, we could face arrest. However, the practicality of contacting actual law enforcement for tasks they were prohibited from performing by a group of middle-aged individuals ineligible to be real cops made such occurrences exceptionally rare.

So when their SUV pulled up next to the lawn where we were throwing the football around, they demanded we cease immediately. Duce and Walter had a straightforward question in response: "Why?"

Their reasoning bordered on the absurd and a dash of laziness: Ramapo was an empty campus, and everyone had to vacate by noon the next day. Duce assured them we were already packed, and that it posed no issue. Now the guards had stepped out of their vehicle. The senior guard snatched the ball from Duce's hands, stating that he could retrieve it at 9:00 from the security office the following day.

Ben, Hayes, and I avoided conflicts. Still, there was a noticeable shift in Hayes when one of the security guards confiscated the football from Duce and refused to return it. Hayes, uncharacteristically, marched up to the guard and demanded the ball back. The other guard deemed it contraband. Here's where I wish my memory served me better because, in the blink of an eye, security escorted Duce and Hayes off campus for the evening (the guards drove you to the northern end of the school property and told you to get out).

Back in Pine Hall, Walter's enthusiasm showed no signs of waning. Removed from the potential conflict and tension with the men in not-quite-blue, my indignation had reached a boiling point. Ben, quietly agreeing with both of us, witnessed Walter passionately asserting that atrocities like this would persist until the United States underwent a "bloody revolution." I, equally passionately, argued that the tools were already within the country's framework, and we could affect change from within if only we could mobilize people to the polls.

In a paraphrase of Walter's astute response, he remarked, "The Boomers will never let that happen."

...

I spoke almost weekly with Walter over the summer following our first year in Ramapo. He wasn't quite as revolutionary for dealing with historical injustices like the confiscation of a Nerf football or the fuel of final-night-on-campus-binge drinking. Still, he remained steadfast in his resolve on every topic, from Gayle Sayers being a better running back than Jim Brown to the US presence in the Balkans being nothing more than a military-industrial money grab.

I spoke even more frequently with Ben, and we planned multiple visits to each other's houses, Yankee Stadium, and even a couple of concerts to see this hot-shit college band called Phish in Pennsylvania and on the Canadian border. Our twin-brotherly conversations carried through the summer. We'd reflect on the surges and slumps of the 1996 Yankees season. We'd meticulously plan the landscape and soundscape of the dorm room we would share our sophomore year.

Mark and I often hung out during college's "off-season." He lived closest among my college friends, so meeting up didn't involve the logistical hurdles of seeing the others. Our get-togethers usually revolved around inviting each other over for drinks when we had the house to ourselves, although I had no qualms about having Mark stop by when my parents were home. I recall joking about how Mark was the ideal guy for a girl to introduce to her family, and he also proved to be the perfect friend. My parents took to him immediately, and he effortlessly put my sisters at ease, which wasn't always the case when I brought new people around.

Hayes and I opted for a different mode of communication: writing letters. It suited our conversational pace better. Our discussions veered more towards the big-picture aspects of sports rather than the day-to-day minutiae that Ben favored, with his Philadelphia allegiance antithetical to all that I love and root for in the realm of fandom. We'd exchange updates on sightings of other Ramapo acquaintances, creating a sort of friend circle newsletter. We'd also spend a lot of time talking shit about our respective lousy summer jobs - his at a warehouse, mine at a supermarket deli.

I saw a better version of myself in each of these four men.

All four were sharp minds, each profoundly attuned to my passions for music, sports, and a delightful party. Ben, the consummate intellectual, possessed the knack for engaging in conversations on various subjects with anyone willing. A fiery yet principled individual, Walter unwaveringly stood by every word he uttered, devoid of empty rhetoric. Hayes, the amiable, easygoing companion, was someone you couldn't find fault in for anything. He enjoyed having a good time, drinking a good beer, and enjoying life. And Mark, a practicing Catholic, carried the discipline, respect, and appreciation of an altar boy well into his young adult years.

Around the time I made my First Holy Communion in 1985, the most popular toy and after-school cartoon was a Japanese-based series called "Voltron" - where a team of space explorers piloted robotic lions that combined to form the mighty Voltron, a colossal humanoid robot.

They were a "Voltron" of my ideal sense of self, each pillar of what I wished I could be: brilliant, genuine, relaxed, respected. Only now was I developing an inner monologue, pointing out the stark differences between who they were and how I perceived myself.

They're better than you. They hold their liquor better than you. They get better grades than you. They go to class more often than you do. Don't let them see the real you.

XIV

Society often promotes college as a time of profound intellectual and personal growth. Yet, amidst academic pursuits and social adventures, the topic of spiritual growth frequently remains in the shadows. While some may find enlightenment at religious institutions like Brigham Young or Liberty University, my journey at Ramapo took me on a divergent path.

Leaving Ridgefield Park as a devout Catholic, I entered Ramapo with unwavering faith in the mysteries of Catholicism. However, as the years unfolded, my beliefs underwent a radical transformation. By the time I left, I had shed my religious identity. I embraced atheism with fervor, questioning not only Catholicism but organized religion in the modern era.

My journey away from faith had nothing conscious to do with Sudol. I barely, if ever, thought of him and remained in psychological denial that anything untoward or improper happened during my time serving as an altar boy. Instead, the openness with which professors spoke about the Catholic Church, religion, and spirituality captivated me.

In St. Francis, nuns taught faith as fact. In 1986, there was a devastating earthquake in the (primarily Catholic) nation of Argentina. Sister Therese sorrowfully taught us that these things can happen when people turn away from God — and nothing about tectonic plates.

At RPHS, the teaching was more agnostic. There were no lessons on dogma; we would pragmatically learn about the Church's historical impact: the spread of Christianity, the Holy Roman Empire, the Inquisition, the Schism, Martin Luther, Henry VIII, and so on. Regarding Luther's split from Rome, we were taught about his disputes with Vatican leadership and corruption, not the adoration of the Blessed Mother or any other theological disagreements.

Religion in the classrooms of Ramapo College was a different animal.

Before registering for a class, I majored in History. I adored my high school teacher, Dr. Ed Michels, a brilliant and stern historian who taught the subject as a cold, hard fact—no ambiguity or agenda. This happened on this date—end of the story. That was the path I wanted to emulate: become an expert in a field you love, educate the shit out of yourself in it, and then pass that knowledge along to the next generation–as historians have been doing since humankind developed language.

In history, you couldn't avoid Catholicism or the Catholic Church. With no pride or prejudice, Ramapo professors educated me on the atrocities and genocide of indigenous people in the Western Hemisphere in search of gold and evangelism (Western Civ), the role of Pope Pius XII in appeasing Hitler's Final Solution (Jews in the 20th Century Europe); and their financing and support of the Trans-Atlantic Slave trade (African-American History 101, The American Civil War), even the demagoguery and antisemitism of radio priest Father Charles Coughlin in the 1930s during the nascent "America First" movement (America

Between the Wars). And how my Ancient Rome professor would flip his lid if you referred to a year as "Before Christ" and not "Before the Common Era."

Hannibal crossed the Alps in the year 218 Before the Common Era unless you wanted a failing grade.

Many of these professors were admitted and avowed atheists, often letting us know from the start that they were not religious people. One professor was different. Dr. Alex Urbiel was a first-year associate professor in the Fall of 1996. A Michigander from a twelve-child Polish Catholic household, Dr. Urbiel took a more personable approach to teaching and attempted to reach students.

Discussions rarely focused on matters of faith. History was about the people making history—the soldiers fighting the wars, the communities electing the leaders, and the books, art, film, and music telling tales of the generations of Americans who came before us. We learned about Charles Coughlin as a demagogue tapping into the antisemitic zeitgeist that captured too significant a portion of the West's imagination—NOT as a priest.

Religion wasn't matter-of-fact as taught in high school, but Dr. Urbiel's faith or opinions on faith never spilled into discussion. Religion existed as part of a multifaceted sense of the American self, just as "The Twist," "Easy Rider," or The Know Nothing Movement did.

That was the first time I considered the concept of identity without religion. I was Catholic. I knew the faith of every single person in my life and looked at them through that prism. Dr. Urbiel's teaching of social history showed me that did not have to be the case.

Once the crack in the window appeared, I threw a bowling ball through it.

...

I was attending mass weekly well into the Spring of '96 semester. I maintained delivery jobs at home; that was my beer and cigarette money, and Jay was home most weekends. Not that it mattered if she wasn't; we saw plenty of each other, with William Patterson being a fifteen-minute ride to Ramapo. Most weekends would end with me swinging by St. Francis on the way back to campus—9:15 if I worked and did nothing the night before, 12:30 PM in the rare event that something was going on in RP that I wanted to attend.

Every weekend that I left, my mother would remind me I was more than welcome to have some friends come over for Sunday dinner. I must have mentioned it in passing in a Pine Hall bong session because the fellas became instantly excited about a home-cooked meal, with the bonus of getting off campus for Walter and Hayes—who rarely ventured home to the Philadelphia metro area but had no friends or kin outside of the school in the northern part of the state, on what was Palm Sunday—the Sunday before Easter, my family plans aligned with my college plans. The Ramapo Crew was heading to RP for a Sunday dinner.

We made it a point to smoke some weed right before we embarked on the thirty-minute sojourn. We wanted optimal munchie hunger for unlimited Prime Rib and mashed potatoes, head and shoulders over the campus cafeteria on its most impressive night. Mom wasn't as oblivious as I thought, asking if allergies were terrible on campus with our red eyes.

Crossing realities was a great feeling. Bringing new friends into my familial home was a flag-planting of sorts. I brought them up to the attic to give them an idea of where I came from. The view of the Empire State Building enamored Ben. They spent some more time with Sean, who had made a visit or three to partake in college fun.

After we left, I had to confess something to the boys in my station wagon. I had to make an appearance at Palm Sunday Mass, at least. They thought I was joking until I pulled into the lot of St. Anastasia's in Teaneck. A right turn where I would have remained straight to catch Route 4 back to campus.

Hayes was beside himself. Walter and Ben were confused. I walked in and grabbed a palm in the church's vestibule. Then I cracked. I had no idea why I was even there. It was some honing beam that told me I had to be at a place of worship to honor the start of the Easter season when you don't even have faith in this crap anymore if you're being honest with yourself.

"Hayes is right. Let's head home," I said before ever crossing the threshold into the church.

Weeks later, after the semester ended, and I was home and back in my routine, I would call Doc at 6:45 on Sunday nights. I'd ask if he minded driving around for an hour because I couldn't do mass anymore, but didn't feel like letting my parents know church wasn't my thing anymore. He never laughed about it or questioned it. He'd say he'd be outside in five.

By August, I couldn't bother keeping up the charade anymore. The Sunday finally came when I wasn't even going to pretend. Around 7:00 PM, my dad—surprisingly sober—called me downstairs from my room.

"You have to go to mass," he said uncomfortably. Mom was sitting in the kitchen—out of my view from halfway down the living room stairs, not fully committing to a face-to-face conversation.

"I'm not going to; I don't see the need to anymore."

With that, Mom stormed out of the kitchen and tried to give me a much sterner demand to head up to St. Anastasia's for the last local mass of the day.

And that's where my rage rose and met hers.

I don't remember my response to her; I know I got animated and making myself appear larger—arms flailing, the veins in my neck strained by the tension in every facial muscle being pulled in different directions. No recollection exists of what I said or for how long I was going until my father finally yelled "HAY!" (his one and only "I've had enough" holler).

When I came to my senses, I was cruising around Lower Bergen County with Doc and Jay, like so many other summer nights when the stash was dry and the cooler empty for a trio of nineteen-year-olds.

I would never go to Sunday mass regularly again in my life.

•••

My explosive outburst directed at my mother over her demand I attend mass at 19 years of age would fit into a much neater box if it were a one-off, an isolated incident that can be pretty easily explained. The church harmed me as a child; I don't want to patronize it as an adult; respect that and move on.

But my behaviors were muddying those waters, as I would be prone to flip my lid around my family, over any topic. And I'd inevitably bring it back to Catholicism. I could walk through the kitchen and overhear Erin or Elizabeth talking about school, and I'd interject with something like, "You know how stupid the idea of Catholic School is? Are they still teaching bullshit like Adam and Eve?"

All the while, I would think that I had moral clarity and certainty. *Look at these sheep. I am more concerned with the afterlife than what's happening here. They spend every Sunday with the rest of the hypocrites, giving them money hand over fist.*

I had a hairpin trigger.

My political leanings formed around this time, adding a unique color to my commentary. Our household was a typical Republican home for the entire 1980s and 1990s. In RPHS, I fancied myself a Republican even though I couldn't vote until college.

Democrats were communists. Democrats were welfare queens. If you loved America and you loved freedom, you were a Republican. All of which glosses over the fundamental distinction that became clearer with each passing election cycle of my life: If you agreed with the Civil and Voting Rights Acts, you were most likely a Democrat. If you preferred what America looked like before the landmark legislation, you were definitely a Republican. One need only to look at electoral maps before and after.

College in the 1990s wasn't necessarily a bastion of liberalism. Still, there was no intellectual defense or appreciation for the wealth-robbing Reaganomics or the racist dog whistles buried within Newt Gingrich's "Contract with America" to be heard in the classroom.

I carried this, along with a sudden sharp disdain for cops and law enforcement, which didn't sit well with Dad given that his father and Uncle Bob were both "on the job," as they said in the Bronx. But I couldn't help it. The realities of Driving While Black were regularly on the front page circa this era, as "The Record" did a deep dive into State Police records.

In New York City, a Haitian immigrant named Abner Louima was sodomized with a plunger by some sick fuck in the precinct while being questioned about a noise violation. We were only one election cycle removed from Rodney King, and the OJ Simpson trial was still at the tip of national consciousness. The headlines gave me all the ammunition I needed, as did personal experience.

I fostered a look of what I could only describe as "hippiejock" throughout the first year of school. It wasn't the best of looks. (I still adhere to it, and it's still not the best of looks.) There were a lot of tie-die shirts, topped off with a Yankees cap—Corduroy pants, and vans below a satin Giants Starter jacket.

My hair was well past my shoulders now, often worn in a pulled-back, lazy ponytail—my Dad called it "embarrassing" once—and my station wagon's back used bumper stickers to express my developing frenetic personality: Sports, Bands, "Question Authority," "Hootie Blows," etc. I became quite the target for traffic stops myself.

Between 1995 and 2000, police stopped me at least a dozen times and never issued a ticket. Cops are fishing for weed because I fit a profile; it was nothing more than that because then, as now, I drove like a seventy-five-year-old grandparent.

And every time I came home hotter than a blister in the sun about being stopped, Dad would calmly point out I should get a haircut and get rid of my bumper stickers. My favorite retort to that was always, "So Freedom of Expression? That was bullshit?" I developed a propensity for taking much bigger ticket items and personalizing them.

•••

The most noteworthy traffic stop occurred in the summer heat of August 1998. I worked at the Grand Union supermarket in Ramsey, New Jersey, one town south of campus and about 22 minutes from RP, with no traffic from RP during the summer. This particular Friday was slightly congested, like most in the summer, as rush hour saw North Jerseyans head for the Garden State Parkway: Shore Points and All Points South. I remember the traffic conditions because the bullshit excuse they gave me for the stop was, "I was tailgating."

The officer who made the stop immediately called for backup. Turns out he was the township's D.A.R.E. Officer. Fucking great, I knew what that meant.

"Tell you what, if you consent to a search of the car, I'll let you go with a warning."

I hyperventilated. I had no idea why. There was not a single stem or seed of marijuana in the car. No open containers. Nothing on my person. I had nothing to hide. That didn't change the fact that I was sweating profusely and probably looked to that cop like I was concealing 50 grams of blow in my glove compartment.

"Uh, sure," I said.

"Step out of the car, please," he said, and as I exited onto the shoulder of Route 17, he immediately laid his hands on me to turn me around to search my person. Whoa. I consented to a vehicle search, or at least that's what I thought I was consenting. I'm sure there was some legalese or cop-speak at the time that gave him the right to lay a finger on me.

He began patting me down intensely, anywhere I could conceal anything. Pockets, socks, waistline. He verbally pointed out that I was tensing up.

Of course, I'm tensing up, you perverted swine! I'm being touched against my will. I'm being touched around my waist against my fucking will by some goon who thinks he has authority over me. Do most of the young men you do this to enjoy it!?

I don't know how I had the composure to drive home the additional 18 minutes. I was probably *tailgating* again. But I had fits of heavy breathing and a cold, damp sweat on the back of my neck that was not the type of perspiration you'd expect on a humid August drive-time on a slow-moving highway in a gas guzzler with no air conditioning.

When I got home, Dad and I had the fight of our lives. I stormed into 208's kitchen with vigor, flailing my arms again. "I WAS MOLESTED BY RAMSEY PD!" I screamed through tears. I didn't know where they came from. I had this massive ball of anger I was ready to unload, and it came out as the cry of a child.

My parents, who were in the kitchen then, let me finish. Dad, who had been drinking, said calmly if that's the case, I should get on the phone and file a report with Ramsey PD.

I was aghast. That's your instant solution, I thought to myself. Jesus, it's a good thing I never thought there was anything wrong with the Gerry kisses. What would you have said, "Get on the horn and call the Vatican"?

"FUCK YOU, YOU FUCKING PIG LOVER" I screamed back. Mom got in between us. She knew that if I laid a hand on him with this rage, I could never walk it back. I spent the rest of that summer Friday night in the attic. I was wholly uninterested in taking Jay out, seeing what Doc was up to, or both.

There was no longer a hint of the Catholic faith in my blood. Anger was my new religion. Rage, my new God.

XV

Because Ridgefield Park is the type of town it is, I wasn't the only one who caught a case of alcoholism in the first semester. Shortly after Christmas, friends from the Class of '95 invited us to a small gathering. After many beers, we all talked ourselves into reuniting to go to the Admiral West in Wildwood Crest for Memorial Day the following spring. We would now be the alumni reliving glory days. Jay, Doc, and I discussed it soberly the next day and decided it was something we should do. We had a great time the prior year, and even if we weren't as close to the RP crew as we were nine months ago, we'd still have each other.

We were square pegs in round holes. There was no longer any connection to this crowd of fine people, some of whom I considered "ride or die" friends a year prior. Hayes was also in Wildwood on that holiday weekend. There were no cell phones at all, so I have no idea how we met him, but we spent the entire second of three days a mile north hanging out with our relatively new college friend as opposed to the two dozen friends from a former life that we were staying with.

There was one thing that our old pals had on offer that could lure us back to the Admiral, however—the promise of LSD. Rumors had it that there would be acid available for sale on Saturday. In retrospect, it was pretty funny how Jay, Doc, and I jumped at the opportunity while everyone else from the Class of '95—most of them with a year away at college–shuddered at the thought of it. It would be the three of us alone having a trip within a trip.

I was no stranger to LSD at this point. Unlike my first experience a few weeks into the fall semester, I knew to block off 7-8 hours for the experience. We paid $10 each for the little "tab"—a small piece of paper covered in the compound you let dissolve on your tongue. Within 30 minutes, the effects become noticeable. After that, you find out where you're going.

So much of how an acid trip plays out depends on what's already occupying your mind. I wouldn't recommend it if you're in an anxious or depressive state because the odds of a "bad trip" (a miserable experience if ever there was one) increase exponentially when that's the case. So when I found myself with Jay and Doc and nobody else, long after sundown, with our toes in the water of the Atlantic Ocean, a theme of familyhood was forming.

My altered mind acted as if it was and always would be the three of us against the world; every fiber of my being told me I was safe with these people, a clear juxtaposition against what was likely going on at the Admiral at the same time: binge-drinking, orgies, and general debauchery (not that I object to any of that).

That visit marked our informal end as members of the Ridgefield Park crowd; we were no longer actively "Scarlets." I can't speak to Jay or Doc's motivations, but I knew from that point forward that it was no longer a realm in which I felt secure.

•••

"Do you remember Willie Foster?" Mom asked me one afternoon in June of '96.

How could I forget Willie, the kind and interesting altar boy who disarmed me a decade earlier when we met His Eminence, Archbishop Theodore McCarrick? I was only somewhat friendly with Willie after he graduated from St. Francis two years before me. I would see him from time to time on Main Street, hanging out with a pretty intimidating crew, smoking cigarettes, and giving off a discerning vibe. Still, he never failed to look me in the eye when I would pass him by en route to any of the odd delivery jobs I held in the center of town when I was home, nod and say, "Hey, Eddie."

It was disarming. And timesaving. I would cross the street when Willie wasn't with that crew to avoid eye contact.

"He passed away," she said, barely able to keep it together herself.

My heart dropped to the floor. Instantly, I knew the root cause of his passing, if not the official reason. I knew he was close to Sudol. Like me, he was the oldest son. He was introspective and known for his talent, as I was with my grades when I was younger. His poor mother worked as a receptionist at the Rectory, taking phone calls for Gerry, Father Francis, Vaccaro, and other priests who called St. Francis home.

I couldn't shake the feeling that Father Gerry Sudol was responsible for this death. Unable to see that I was self-medicating dramatically due to the same figure and similar trauma, I instinctively knew that interactions between Sudol and Willie were at the heart of why this young man of barely twenty-one was no longer among us.

•••

It was merely availability that differentiated the avenues of escape that Willie and I chose. I would never be one to follow Nancy Reagan's wishes and "just say 'No.'" I don't know what substances Willie used; I don't even know what type of event caused the extinguishing of his flame at too young an age. But I understand I had never experimented with heroin, as an example, not because I was deathly afraid of addiction, overdose, and death, but because I didn't hang around with people who used heroin. Believe me, if Doc had picked it up one day, I would have been filing the syringe for him and waiting my turn.

The escapism of drugs was too hard to ignore. I was only fortunate that nobody I enjoyed had a fancy for the hazardous and destructive substances. For better or worse, I geared my drug use more toward avoidance than soothing. Booze was for soothing. Pot, LSD, and psilocybin (the ingredient in magic mushrooms) didn't numb; they cut off access. The heady stuff I didn't want to think about—the heavy shit I didn't even know I was carrying—would be cut off, and my mind would focus on something entirely different. Maybe an episode of "The Simpsons" was on in the background; perhaps it was the bass line in a Pink Floyd album or even a trippy circular pattern on Ben's button-down shirt that day. But it would be something harmless. Something safe.

It wasn't foolproof, especially with marijuana, where you can get stuck in the wrong neighborhood of your head, and you're too stoned to ask for directions out. There were aforementioned "bad trips" on LSD, but I only had one experience that bordered on "bad," where I got hung up on a couple of poor grades.

Most of the time, though, tripping would open up some pathway in my mind that wasn't accessible the day before. I'm convinced I hold Tupac Shakur as one of America's five most legendary poets because I was tripping my face off on mushrooms when I found out he died that September Friday night in 1996. If I was merely drinking, perhaps I only put him on the still-lofty level of Dr. Dre or Billy Joel.

In 1996, the ultimate destination for a psychedelic journey via mushrooms was undoubtedly the Clifford Ball. This three-day extravaganza unfolded as a Phish festival, featuring the band's dynamic performances with two sets each day. Nestled within the confines of the decommissioned Plattsburgh Air Force Base in Plattsburgh, NJ, it became the focal point for Phish fans during August '96. The festival held a magnetic appeal for the predominantly college-aged Phish heads, drawing in enthusiasts like Ben, Hayes, and Duce, each accompanied by their hometown crews. Meanwhile, Doc, Jay, and I opted for a road trip, kicking off our Phish adventure in Hershey, Pennsylvania, before embarking on a full-day ride to the festival site near the Canadian border.

As we arrived, anticipation hung in the air, and our excitement wasn't just limited to the music. Before unloading the tents from our cart, we secured an ounce of grass for an extra dose of "freedom." While the event discouraged the bringing of alcohol, getting multiple beers on demand was surprisingly effortless.

During the second day, a member of Ben's crew struck gold with a mushroom connection, and the effects were instantaneous. Amidst the festival's vibrant atmosphere, a man adorned as Uncle Sam towered on stilts, eliciting a mixture of awe and trepidation from the crowd. Seeking respite from the scorching sun, we stumbled upon a mist tent, a sanctuary from the heat that Jay, already showing signs of sunburn, eagerly embraced. Entering the misty haven while reaching the peak of my mushroom experience, a surreal sensation enveloped me as the mist danced upon my face like a cascade of a million tiny leprechauns.

In this altered state, my thoughts turned poignant, shifting to memories of my baby sister Erin and her special place in my heart. Recollections flooded my mind of her endearing habit of sending me $5 bills whenever our Nana or Grandpa gave her money, despite her age of nine. Contemplating the turbulent dynamics within my family, particularly my father's struggles with alcohol, I realized the weighty responsibility I carried as Erin's older brother. As emotions surged, I vowed silently to myself to always protect and care for her, determined to shield her from the challenges I had faced, even as I momentarily overlooked my own unresolved trauma.

I was putting together a life plan by the seam of my pants while tripping balls at a Phish show with 70,000 other people. And I thought to myself, "I think this is who I want to be."

•••

As my twentieth birthday approached, I eagerly embarked on a countdown to my twenty-first. To mark each passing day, I crafted a tear-away calendar, its numbered sheets a tangible reminder of the impending celebration. The ritual began in the confines of my dorm room in January, but as the months unfolded, the countdown moved to the basement at 208, where I now lived after Sean had claimed the attic as his domain in my extended absence.

When January 27, 1998, finally rolled around, Dad orchestrated a peculiar yet memorable rite of passage for my first legal drink. Insisting that I rendezvous with him at the Knights of Columbus, conveniently located diagonally across the street from St. Francis, he planned for the momentous occasion to coincide with the stroke of midnight, marking the transition to the 28th. As the expected hour approached, Dad, in a generous and festive spirit, engaged in the tradition of "buying the bar," covering the next round for everyone present.

There was a council meeting earlier that evening, compelling Dad and his circle of friends to linger at the bar, patiently awaiting my entrance into legal imbibing. A majority of the bar was well into their forties, if not older, and showing the long faces of middle age mixed with a few hours of feeding their alcoholism. When the clock finally struck midnight, I confidently ordered a Budweiser and a shot of Southern Comfort, only to discover they were out of SoCo. Undeterred, I embraced the substitution of Wild Turkey, savoring the peculiar blend of excitement and nostalgia that marked the initiation of my countless future bar orders.

We drank until 2 AM when my father ignored the advice he'd yell at me many a night about not getting into the car with a driver who'd been drinking when he queried a fellow barfly to take us home—since Mom made two trips to drop each of us off that night.

The following day, I lurked around home until 11:00, when the local liquor store opened. I purchased two four-packs of Guinness Stout pub cans, my grandfather's favorite beer.

I returned to campus prepared for a night of Happy Hour with my legal friends and then an apartment party for all. I was twenty-one now. The law couldn't stop me from drinking; the only thing that could was myself.

And I had no interest in doing that.

XVI

Prince's anthem from 1982, "Tonight we're going to party like it's Nineteen Ninety-Nine," became my mantra as the first quarter of the year aligned with my last semester in Ramapo. I dove headfirst into a relentless cascade of drinks and festivities, relishing the waning moments of academia, the illusion of carefree living, and the impending turn of the millennium. It was my way of grappling with the tidal wave of change on the horizon.

Amidst the chaos, I found solace in a daily pilgrimage to "The Shack," a newly discovered liquor store conveniently located a few miles from campus. The owners, recognizing our regular presence, dubbed Ben and I the "Keystone twins" because of our frequent purchases of a $4.99 twelve-pack of Keystone beer (each).

Ben and I had seamlessly become nightly drinking companions, sharing our thoughts and navigating the uncertain terrain of our post-graduation futures. It wasn't just about the drinks; it was a ritual, a nightly rendezvous that went beyond the casual camaraderie of group gatherings. In the sea of faces sipping drinks each night, it was always Ben and me, forming a unique bond over shared aspirations and contemplations about what lay ahead.

As the evenings unfolded in a symphony of clinking glasses, crushed cans, and laughter, Ben projected an air of certainty about his future, starkly contrasting my uncertainty. While he charted a logical course for the coming year, I needed help with the basics, like submitting my graduation paperwork on time. Ben seemed to have a roadmap for what lay beyond the comfortable confines of college, a plan that eluded me entirely.

Our nightly sessions became a platform for more than just revelry; they were a space for sharing dreams, fears, and the tangled threads of our post-graduation ambitions. Ben's decisiveness and foresight constantly reminded me of my need for direction. The future loomed large, and I was grappling with the overwhelming question of what the rest of my life held. It wasn't just about finding a job or settling into a routine; it was about navigating the vast expanse of adulthood without a compass.

I didn't decide to abandon the pursuit of a teacher's certification lightly, and it intensified the anxiety that already coursed through me. It wasn't because of a lack of desire to teach; quite the contrary, I held the teaching profession in the highest regard, considering it among the noblest of callings. I didn't base my decision on a misguided pressure to step into the "real world right away."

In my eyes, those who inspired my initial interest in teaching were ideals of knowledge and charisma beyond my reach. Dr. Michels, a living encyclopedia in the era when Wikipedia was just five random syllables, possessed a reservoir of unattainable expertise, like a distant peak I couldn't fathom climbing. The idea of maintaining such a wealth of information seemed daunting, and I questioned my capacity to match his intellectual prowess.

Then there was Dr. Urbiel, whose infectious personality radiated the belief that history mattered. His remarkable ability to forge connections with each student and an unwavering commitment to ensuring no one felt left behind left an indelible impression on me. Possessing that level of confidence and likability, creating an environment where every student felt seen and valued felt like an elusive aspiration.

The fear of falling short of the standards set by these mentors, both in terms of knowledge and interpersonal skills, contributed to a sense of inadequacy that reverberated through my choice to alter my academic trajectory.

You can't teach, the internal voice in my head said; *you'll never be as bright as Michels. You'll never be as liked as Urbiel. You'll be another Mr. Duff—a sad laughingstock counting the days to retirement and the first drink after work each day. Go withdraw from the program. It's not who you are.*

…

By graduation day, I was a bloated, puffy, red-faced mess. I entered Ramapo weighing approximately 185 lbs. I'd leave 35 lbs. heavier. It made little difference that Ben and I would occasionally get Keystone Light. Getting myself in shape would take a legitimate effort, but I had no idea how to do that independently.

Physical fitness wasn't an interest in the way history or sport was. The slender shape I kept myself in for the entirety of my youth had nothing to do with me and everything to do with circumstance: my mother provided my meals, my organized activities provided structured exercise, and everything was within walking distance in Ridgefield Park.

Food, recreation, and transportation all converged to keep me fit, svelte, and active. Late-night pizza, cheap beer, and cigarettes conspired to undo that in four short years. The morning I would depart Ramapo College of New Jersey, their impacts were on full display.

Lucasfilm released "Star Wars: Episode I: The Phantom Menace" the day before. Doc and Sean drove up to catch an early morning show with Ben, Walter, Duce, and me. It may have been universally panned, and its reputation further sullied as movies evolved, but it was still Star Wars. Few cultural tent-poles are as firmly entrenched in Generation X as The Force is. We were head over heels, leaving the theater. And in 1999, if we were enthusiastic about anything, it called for drinks. When we returned to campus, Duce presented me with a handle bottle of Seagram's 7 because, as he put it, "Every Irishman deserves a handle of whiskey upon his graduation." Who was I to argue?

We killed that bottle before a larger group of friends gathered in our apartment for the 7:00 showing of "The Phantom Menace." Seeing it a second time, thoroughly intoxicated, made me love it even more. Loving it like that called for many more drinks after the show!

Graduation morning was one of the worst hangovers I had experienced at that point. Adrenaline was the only thing that could spark me out of bed and into the kitchen to use the only other appliance besides the stereo still plugged in — the coffee maker.

It was boiling with a high sun, even by today's pre-climate change expectations. I was sitting in a black robe and gown in a seating area on the sunniest patch of land on the entire campus. Sitting through the commencement address delivered by the descendant of one of Thomas Jefferson's rape victims, all I could think about was going back to bed.

Six weeks later, my parents hosted a celebration for my friends at our house. The festivities began early, with me drinking when Walter arrived, a good two hours before the party's scheduled start time. With a keg on tap and guests bringing their liquor stash, the party quickly gained momentum, attracting over 30 people at its peak. As the sun dipped below the horizon, I horsed around with friends in the pool, only to feel the urge to exit the water abruptly. Ignoring the conventional ladder, I attempted a less orthodox approach by scaling the pool's outer wall. Unfortunately, my unconventional exit strategy ended in a tumble onto the pavement, where I found myself sprawled on the lawn with my bathing suit partially dislodged, leaving my backside exposed to the entire party.

After my less-than-graceful descent, the atmosphere shifted dramatically when my mother stormed out of the house. Her voice cut through the evening air with a sharp command to cease the revelry. With her decisive intervention, the party came to an abrupt halt.

I suffered another humiliation in the pool at 208 Teaneck Road while Jay was inside, confessing to my parents that she couldn't be with me anymore because I had been self-destructing. They knew. They had to. But heating it from someone else, someone so intimate, was jarring to them.

And to me, because for the first time since high school, I was single.

...

I secured a summer job at a Day Camp for children of affluent parents across the state line in Rockland County, NY. They trusted me to drive a school bus daily and safely and to not smoke in it. Managed to do so safely. The role was "gym teacher," which meant most of my day was outdoors doing physical activities with kids between the ages of 3 and 9. It wasn't cross-fit, but it kept me moving. I shed some of the poundage I added to my body in college.

There was a fun group of counselors—most living much closer to the camp. We varied in age from 18 to 25, with that twenty-five-year-old being referred to as "Old Karen" unironically to differentiate her in conversation from the 22-year-old "Young Karen." Man, young people can be dicks.

In the middle of that group was New Girl, the last counselor to join the crew before the summer of '99. She embodied a striking blend of contemporary style and physical allure. Her shoulder-length trendy blonde hair framed a face dominated by deep blue eyes that hinted at the promise of a good time. Her firm figure stood out regularly thanks to the required daily donning of bathing suits. Behind the reserved exterior lurked a bit of a party animal, a dynamic contrast to her initial impression. We had much in common after graduating and concluding a year-long relationship.

That commonality lit a spark on the evening of July 23. The camp owners did an outstanding job keeping the counselors feeling appreciated for their tireless work corralling toddlers and preschoolers. On this particular Friday, they showed their gratitude with group tickets to a Yankees game. Yanks' ace David Cone was making his first start since throwing a Perfect Game the previous Sunday against the Montreal Expos.

Friday nights in the late 90s at Yankee Stadium were an incredible experience. The team was in the middle of a run that would see them win four World Series championships in the five seasons between 1996 and 2000. America's economy was pretty good, or so the Boomers said. Our world was calm a decade after the Berlin Wall fell. Catching this burgeoning dynasty on a hot summer night was the thing to do in the NYC metro area. Cone's historic performance only added to the adrenaline in the stadium.

However, I didn't need a legendary pitcher's return to the mound to spark my juices. The counselors assembled back at the camp to depart in one of their minivans about 90 minutes after the workday. I confessed I wasn't heading back to Jersey, battling bridge traffic, only to return to battle the same traffic we'll face again when we cross the bridge. Instead, I'd "swim it off" and take a "whore's bath," as we called it back then—wash your face, hands, and pits, throw on a fresh coat of deodorant, and maybe brush your teeth. Then I would find a local watering hole and wait for everyone to return.

New Girl announced her intentions to do the same thing. Odd, I thought, considering how her home was so close; it was a long one of our bus routes. Without hesitation, I asked her if she knew of an excellent place to hit up, as I only knew of Company B's—a quasi-chain that I popped into for two Becks and three cigarettes at the end of a few shifts per week. She assured me she did.

I guess it was a date.

I feared nothing more than getting pinched for drinking and driving. I could handle the 2 or 3 Becks and ride home—blending easily into that same bridge traffic, but anything more than that, I would do my darndest to trick someone else into driving. Luckily, the 1985 Chevy Caprice Classic station wagon I was still driving made the attempts to defraud eminently believable. New Girl had a brand new Volkswagen Jetta, and my air conditioner wasn't working. She drove.

It didn't make a difference in terms of legal blood alcohol levels. She had two Labatt Blues to my three Bass Ales. The bartender drew a few bucks from the $10 I threw down on the bar for each drink. When we left, I replenished it and threw a few more dollars on top for the tip.

Fuck, it really was a date.

Baseball-Reference Dot Com tells me that the Yanks beat the Cleveland Indians 9-8 in 10 innings that night. Sounds like it was an exhilarating game. Paul O'Neill homered, and Derek Jeter drove in the winning runs in extra innings. I remember nothing about it other than flirting with New Girl. The pre-game started in the parking lot, and there was a nonstop train of everyone but our designated driver making beer runs. New Girl was even coming on smoke breaks, claiming to be a "smoker when she drinks"—which wasn't that unusual back in the 90s, as foreign as it may sound for young people today.

We were the impetus for the party to continue back in Company B's—to the chagrin of the underage folks on the trip. To hell with them. This was a date.

After one round of drinks, I asked her if she wanted to step out for a smoke. She happily agreed, and we walked out back—even though smoking in bars was still 100% legal. We got down to business and made out furiously and, I'm sure, sloppily. We had missed our ride back to the camp. Neither of us could drive or was in any rush to leave. I was a good 25 minutes from home and called Sean, who, as luck had it for me, was home and not partying with friends himself. Life before Uber was rough.

...

Now, I had to navigate something wholly foreign to my life: a relationship with someone who didn't know me from RP and more and didn't know the way I derailed as my college years went on.

Haunted by the memory of my ignominious poolside tumble, I distanced myself from my college friends during the aftermath of the graduation party. The hungover feelings of guilt lasted weeks. To erase the stain of that evening, I redirected my focus toward New Girl, molding myself into what I perceived as her ideal.

The tie-dye shirts got tossed in favor of sleek Calvin Klein polos, and I transformed my unkempt appearance with regular haircuts—quite a departure from the laissez-faire approach since junior year at Ridgefield Park High School. The change also extended to olfactory aesthetics, with the introduction of cologne ("Cool Water") to my daily routine. Musical preferences underwent a drastic shift; my classic rock staples, Dylan and the Grateful Dead took a hiatus as I immersed myself in the Dave Matthews Band. Simultaneously, I bid farewell to the once-cherished pastime of smoking pot, figuring simply, "That's not who I am anymore."

And was this going to be a permanent story in my life? Quadrennial metamorphoses into someone new? I had barely established myself as someone other than Eddie the Altar Boy. Was College Ed going to be relegated to the attic alongside him?

New Girl and I quickly became a grossly typical young American couple. Our usual Friday nights were dinner at a mall-chain restaurant like Friday's or Chili's before seeing a movie in the same mall. 1999 was a killer year for film. You had the Americans: "Pie" and "Beauty." "The Insider". "The Sixth Sense". We saw them all.

We even went fucking apple picking.

Drinking wasn't a priority because it wasn't much of a possibility. We both lived at home, and neither of us had a set of permissive parents who'd let a significant other spend the night, and we were too far from each other to depend on taxis reliably—not to mention the cost. Once or twice a month, however, we would book a room at the Inn at Ramsey.

On Route 17, just two exits south of Ramapo College, it adjoined another Company B's location. With hot tubs and thematic rooms like "Jungle" and "Romantic," it was the perfect getaway for two 22-year-olds with raging feelings for each other and no domestic privacy. But it also had another Company B's.

The friends I moved through high school with and the friends I honed in on to form a familial bond with at Ramapo shared one common thread: a desire to party. We were never mall walkers, moviegoers, or apple pickers. I went into the world assuming that was the norm. I discovered it wasn't when asked, "Why would you order a bucket of beers just for yourself?"

Not everyone thinks that's a rhetorical question, it turns out.

...

On Labor Day weekend, another sign emerged that I was projecting my drinking habits onto others when, in reality, they differed significantly from the norm. New Girl and I stole one more summer weekend before the fall began. We ended up at the same hotel where I spent that dry prom weekend four years earlier, only this time, I was anything but booze-deprived.

After a morning at the beach, I suggested watching the Notre Dame-Michigan game, asking if New Girl preferred a bar or the room. Learning it was at 1:00 during peak sun, she questioned why it had to be either or. I got my way. Game in the motel. Throughout the game, she repeatedly asked if it was almost over, forgetting the typical duration of football games.

Meanwhile, I consumed roughly a twelve-pack of Corona. Once the game concluded, we showered and headed to the boardwalk for the tiki bars I couldn't access at 18. We spent the evening indulging in tropically colored cocktails and whatever light beer was on special. Upon returning to the room, she expressed an interest in intimacy, but I experienced the worst performance anxiety of my life up to that point.

Two days later, it was time to choose a fantasy football team name. Because I know nothing if I don't know self-depreciation, I christened my team "The Whiskey Dicks". It fits into a neat little box. I had too much fun at the bar and couldn't satisfy my girlfriend–make light of it and move on. Nobody else had to know unless I brought it up, but that didn't matter. I had to convince myself it was normal.

Because I knew it was anything but. Sure, "whiskey dick"—the inability to achieve or maintain an erection after drinking alcohol has impacted anyone who's ever been around a dick and booze since humans discovered how much fun both can be. It happened with New Girl, likewise when alcohol wasn't involved. Not always, not even frequently, but too often for a relatively fit 22-year-old (I had dipped under 200 lbs.) fiercely attracted to a girl he convinced himself he was madly in love with. The minute my inner monologue grew louder than the million little eddies gathering below, it was all over. *You're not good enough for this. Who do you think you are? You don't know how to have sex.*

That never happened with Jay.

...

Nowhere was the delineation between who I was and who I was pretending to be more straightforward than on September the Eleventh (of 1999, of course). The Dave Matthews Band was performing at the Continental Airlines Arena, five miles from home in the middle of the Jersey Meadowlands. New Girl and I had tickets to attend, along with four other counselors. Doc and Hayes also had tickets. I gave them a heads-up so they could meet us for a tailgate.

The tailgate turned into a rager. I had just purchased my first new car—a 2000 Hyundai Elantra for $11,000. Was totally clueless and had no idea how this worked, but I knew I was sending Fleet Auto Finance $300 monthly for the foreseeable future. I was excited to drive it and figured I'd drink responsibly through the tailgate and drive home. Thirty minutes into the tailgate, I asked another counselor if she wanted to drive the new car home, and she agreed.

As luck wouldn't have it, Arena Security halted alcohol sales before the show even started. All of that heavy parking lot drinking had to ease into an equally intense crash. Two hours into the show, I was starving and exhausted, sitting down during a rousing version of "Crash Into Me" and eating concession stand popcorn. I was already hungover and wanted to go home. And that's when Doc and Hayes showed up in our section.

Rarely has a year gone by since where one or both of them hasn't made some joke about "that time we saw Ed at the Dave show, sitting down and eating popcorn during Crash."

That's who I thought I was supposed to be. However, my slovenly posture and popcorn feast had a lot more to do with the crash of a hastily chugged twelve-pack with no further alcohol available to soothe the need than it did Cool Water or whatever name-brand articles of clothing I wore that day.

...

The Grateful Dead once sang about a "summer love in the spring, fall, and winter," a noble wish not written for me and New Girl. We crashed as rapidly as we soared. We were discussing looking for a place to live for a hot minute.

I just got my first career-oriented position as an archivist at a small firm called KLJ Review. The company, privately owned by a man we called The Boss, had the responsibility of archiving broadcasts of NBC News and MSNBC Cable. I found it in the Bergen Record classifieds. I faxed a resume from my parents' basement, aced an interview, and received a job offer on the spot.

It didn't pay exceptionally well—the starting salary was around $26,000 per year in 1999—but it paid enough to consider moving out of 208 Teaneck Road and shacking up with a woman I didn't know five months earlier.

But reality settled in when we took a trip to a casino run by the Oneonta Tribe about three hours north of us in New York State. Nothing says "Sorry for the genocide" like favorable gaming licenses. We found the casino itself to be dry—I don't know how we kept finding things like concerts and casinos that prohibited alcohol—but this time, New Girl came prepared with shot bottles aplenty in her purse.

We were with another couple—college friends of hers—and had tickets to see a stand-up special with the TV stars of yesterday: The Guy who played Skippy on "Family Ties," the guy who played George Jefferson on "The Jeffersons" (Sherman Hemsley), and the guy who played JJ Evans on "Good Times" (Jimmie Walker). Our seats were front and center; never the place to be at a stand-up, it seems, and we became Jimmie Walker's fodder. The more he spoke to us, the more I belligerently laughed at my reply to him. Before I knew it, Kid Dy-no-MITE was mocking my alma mater and my sex life.

I was more interested in loading up on gas-station beer from the Mobil next door than retiring to bed.

And that was the end of us. It turns out 22-year-old ladies fresh out of college want something more in a man than the ability to laugh it up JJ Evans and ongoing cases of whiskey dick.

...

I felt chewed up and spit out by the real world, and there was only one place for me to retreat to: Ramapo College. Walter, Hayes, and Duce were still studying in the 99-00 academic year, the latter two living on campus—the refuge remained. I tried their haircuts, cologne, razors and picked apples. If that was the real world, I wanted no part of it. It was time to get back to my comfort zone.

I apologized one Friday night in early December as the countdown to the end of the millennium intensified. My friends were more than understanding, assuring me they had my back through thick and thin and that all they cared about was my happiness. After four years and counting, they knew how to handle me better than anyone I had ever met.

I didn't know what I did to deserve them.

You did nothing to deserve them; you're such a burden to them. Look at you, whining on a Friday night about a breakup. Boo-fucking-hoo.

XVII

I can live a thousand lifetimes, and I don't think I'll ever experience something as fucking stupid as Y2K panic—and I place it squarely on the Boomers. The "greatest" generation that liberated Europe was picking up the pace on their expiration; Gen X didn't get near decision-making prowess in any sector of society. At the end of the nineties, the oldest Boomers were in their early fifties and squarely in the seat of influence.

And they thought that all of humanity would come to a crashing, fiery demise because, for years, electronics only asked you to program the last two digits of the year. Every piece of home entertainment in the retail stores was now labeled "Y2K Compliant". There were actual, legitimate fears that our banking system—which seamlessly handles the debits and credits of some half a billion individuals and businesses to the fucking penny daily—was just going to come to an abrupt halt, and all our wealth would disappear.

It sounds as ridiculous in retrospect as it was in real-time. The entire craze was an exercise in just letting the Boomers tire themselves out because I didn't know a solitary person under thirty who was buying into the apocalyptic worry-fest.

Walter and I solidified plans to ring in the New Year, New Decade, New Century, and New Millennium at a bar close to his home, which he was renting off campus in Suffern, NY. Ireland's 32 was the bar's name, a reference to the united total of Irish counties when you add the 26 in the Republic to the 6 in Northern Ireland, still under British rule in 1999.

It would be a double date. He was living with his college-long girlfriend Tiff in Suffern, and I had been spending a lot of time with Jay lately. We weren't formally back together, but it headed that way. She and Tiff were set to depart for Prague a few days into January for a study-abroad trip. There was an understanding that upon her return, we would decide if we would give "Ed and Jay" one more shot or remain perfect, soulmate-level friends with obvious occasional benefits because that's how we rolled.

The clock struck midnight, and wouldn't you know it, nothing happened at all. Computers kept running. VCRs kept recording. Our collective wealth shockingly didn't evaporate. Nary a satellite fell from the sky.

The first day of the millennium found us bonding over thirteen hours of a "Law and Order" marathon on the USA Network. We ordered from the same pizza parlor five times, primarily to restock bottles of soda that we were craving and couldn't get enough of. It was a five-star hangover nursed with copious amounts of sugary drinks, great friends, Lenny Briscoe, and the woman I knew I would be falling back into the arms of once she returned from behind the former Iron Curtain.

This new century wasn't looking too bad.

I lived with Walter in his house for the month Jay and Tiff were in the Czech Republic. It was my only authentic taste of bachelor living. He was finishing his degree with evening classes; I worked a 12-8 shift at KLJ, about 25 minutes south of his home. It couldn't have worked out any better.

Walter and I had a perfect roommate synergy. There was always cold beer in the fridge. We'd spend many nights walking across the New Jersey Transit commuter train tracks to the tight collection of bars in Downton Suffern. Even saw the same faces at the same establishments. We became honorary townies for a month.

We also devoured the 1998 Mitch Albom novel "Tuesdays with Morrie," a book about the author's journey and reflections on his professor—Morrie—at the end of his mentor's life. Albom was a national sportswriter based in Detroit, and I knew him well. I heard him describe Morrie in an interview, and he reminded me of the Yoda-like figure that Dr. Urbiel was: the quiet, happy warrior with an ability to lead you somewhere and make you feel you got there yourself. The type of educator I never believed I could be.

There was a new website where you can purchase books: Amazon.com. I had a desk job with an internet connection, a steady paycheck, and limited financial obligations. My friends were all getting a copy of "Morrie." Walter and Ben enjoyed it so much that I couldn't engage them in a blowout NFL playoff game—Dan Marino's last ever — because they were knee-deep into "Tuesdays with Morrie."

I didn't want January to end, and not because we didn't miss the ladies—of course, we did and kept each other abreast when we got an email from them. But I knew what lurked after this taste of freedom. It was back to RP, back to my reclaimed attic.

...

The 208 that I returned to was a far, far cry from the home from which I departed for Ramapo. Dad had been going on two years without steady work, and his computer leasing company had become unnecessary with the steady decrease in office computing hardware prices. Computers were abundant and disposable, so there was no longer any need for specialty financing. They were office supplies akin to telephones or staplers.

Mom was still in a grief spiral over losing Nana and Grandpa, who passed in consecutive years in '98 and '99. She moved through the day with a depressed demeanor, and every conversation circled back to how hard it was.

Sean had recently found full-time work for the state government, a job requiring him to wear a shirt and tie daily. Still just 20 years old, he ran all the (increasingly necessary) electronics in the house that Mom and Dad had no time for. He was the only adult showering and putting on clothes to earn a paycheck every day. By all but biological metrics, he was the man of the house.

Elizabeth was in her second year at the Academy of the Holy Angels' High School. During the Bush recession, I had no money to attend Bergen Catholic. After almost eight full years of Bill Clinton, Elizabeth was going to the most exclusive (read: expensive) Catholic high school in North Jersey while the old man wasn't working. I was sure to make a note of it.

She was everything an ordinary sixteen-year-old girl in North Jersey was supposed to be. She developed a personality independent of the family structure and showed interest in the liberal arts and, ironically, the Dave Matthews Band.

And poor Erin remained trapped in St. Francis, which was now a shell of what it was even in my day. Only Sisters Patricia and Therese remained; both had tacked on a decade-plus since they handled my education. The rest of the faculty became a revolving door of desperate teachers taking a barely minimum-wage job for a year until they found something better, like working at Blockbuster Video. At twelve years old, she was the one member of the household excited about my return home.

The lack of structure did me no favors at all. I spent the first year partying at home as if it was still college. My later shifts allowed me to enjoy midweek nightlife and still get plenty of sleep before work. Hangovers aren't crippling at twenty-three as long as they don't require a "Law & Order" marathon. It wasn't uncommon for me to leave work and head directly south for 45 minutes and hit Ben's place—or wait for him to come up to 208—to only begin a five-hour drinking shift at 10:00 PM.

Mark, still the closest geographic friend, was single and always interested in spending a weeknight at any of the various pre-internet-dating hotspots in North Jersey that lured revelers in with live music and drink specials. There was many a Thursday night when he'd pick Jay and me up from our respective homes a half-mile apart, take us to some ironically named venue like "The Junkyard," and then bring us to refuel on greasy breakfast foods at the Heritage diner before safely returning us home.

With the Yankees dynastic run showing no signs of slowing down, many Friday nights saw Walter shoot down Route 17 to meet me, Doc, and whomever the poor sucker was that we hoodwinked into driving us to Yankee Stadium. More than once, those nights ended in one of a handful of RP dive bars—the only local socialization I ever did.

In January 2001, Sean celebrated his twenty-first birthday, which was booze-soaked and involved Ben and I, who began the day pregaming a Rangers-Devils hockey game at a Port Authority bar at 11 AM. The state that we returned home in made it clear to my parents that it was time for me to go.

...

My folks cycled through friends for most of the first twenty-five years of my life. I never knew if it was the normal evolution of adult relationships or if it was something more. Their circle of friends aligned with the four of us children growing up; as each one of us entered St. Francis, it was an opportunity to meet new families that may not have previously had kids in the school. Occasionally, shared interests or culture led my mom to find a new best friend.

My Dad's friends came from one of two places—the heavy-drinking husbands of my mom's friends or the barstools at the Knights of Columbus lodge. In February 2001, he was leaning heavily into the latter crowd, and the impact of those relationships would strip me of any choice or agency, just like becoming an altar boy did.

A drinking buddy du jour was the new superintendent at 55 Teaneck Road, the same apartment Sean and I grew up in before moving to 208. He told my father that the rental market was hyper-competitive, but he could get an apartment for Jay and me for a $500 finder's fee. A typical "leave the money on the nightstand" situation. The only problem was that Jay and I weren't seriously considering moving in together yet; we never asked for help.

And when we eventually cohabitated, staying in RP wasn't at the top of our wish list. Neither was a basement apartment. It didn't matter.

I let myself get talked into it. The more hesitation I showed, the more Dad pushed. The final straw was when he came up unannounced to the attic, where Jay and I were under the covers and watching "The West Wing"—a sacrosanct moment of our 2001 weekly schedule. Reeking of beer in his barely closed bathrobe, he sat on the corner of the bed and stuttered through why we should be grateful for this opportunity.

Similar to the altar boy decision, there *were* alluring reasons to proceed. Privacy was the first among them—it would be nice to watch President Jed Bartlett on the TV without an old man in his bathrobe. A place to party was second, at least for me, definitely not for Jay. It remained equidistant to both of our jobs under ten minutes, door to door. And we were heading in this direction, anyway.

Dad paid the super, and we signed our lease to move in on March 1, 2001.

The first month of cohabitation was ripe with growing pains, but we quickly settled into a routine. Being in RP, we would have one or both sets of parents over each weekend—which was probably the point from the jump. But living with Jay felt natural and secure.

On June 12 of that year, I asked her to be my wife. Life was moving on, whether or not I was ready for it.

XVIII

The quickest way to bond with someone is to plan a wedding that marries two Irish Catholic families. It would be best if you had a bunker mentality to deal with the incoming, and when all is said and done, you accomplish the unthinkable together.

Both sets of parents were adamant that we get married in St. Francis. That was unaligned with how Jay had dreamed about her wedding day since childhood. She hoped to be wed at or near her grandparents' Highland Lakes, NJ, lake house. It would have been a dream venue, weather permitting. She had visions of a moon gate over the dock and taking vows above the water on the rural parcel of land where she spent so much of the first quarter of her life.

Her parents were polite but stern in that they would only pay for the wedding if it took place in St. Francis. And it had to be a full mass as well, rebuffing Jay's suggestion that if we married there, it would only be a brief ceremony. But Jay had severe issues with the greater Catholic Church. She found them to be a misogynistic junta with a history of suppressing women's rights, pillaging the globe, and exploiting the poor. She also made more than one allusion to the "creeps" in the priestly profession. (She wasn't wrong—on any count).

My parents had no such leverage, but they expressed their demands just as sternly. Not only should it be in St. Francis, and it must be a full mass, but Joe Doyle must officiate it.

They should teach you about people-pleasing in High School so you can quickly identify the tendency earlier in life than most. I went into a full-on people-pleasing mode with the wedding debate. I sold Jay out, convincing her she deserved the best wedding possible. If it's a choice between a backyard wedding at her parent's house across the street from St. Francis or a wedding in the church and a venue of our choosing, we were better off with the latter.

We would be married where we first met. How many couples can say that?

I would be married where I was abused. How many people can say that?

•••

Fantasy Football was on the verge of exploding in 2001. It was the fourth season of the Ramapo Fantasy Football League (RFFL), and my friends and I were as rabid about our teams as we've been with anything. We had our unique nicknames that quickly became our personalities and the center of the social universe. Whiskey Dick Football was alive and well. I would host a draft for ten people crammed into our one-bedroom basement apartment. The appetite for all things football was insatiable.

By the time the season finally kicked off, the yearning for football games reached its peak. For the past two seasons, we had made it a point to meet at a "football bar"—any pub or restaurant that carried the satellite Sunday Ticket package—for the first week. In 2001, however, the plans centered on Monday Night Football.

Fresh off a Super Bowl appearance, the Giants traveled to Denver to face the Broncos on the season's first Monday. Ben made plans to spend the night at our apartment, where we would finish all but two beers from a 30-pack of Genesee Cream Ale, watching the Broncos piss on the Giants. We drank beer out of the RFFL trophy. I thought I'd remember that game, on September 10, 2001, primarily for my fantasy year going down the drain when Denver receiver Ed McCaffrey tore his ACL and his season was over.

A few hours later, a phone call woke us up with the message millions of Americans were receiving around the same time: "Turn on the TV."

Jay answered the call, and the bedroom television flickered to life. I awoke to the jarring images of the World Trade Center engulfed in billowing black smoke. Reacting swiftly, we rushed out of the bedroom to awaken Ben, sleeping on the couch. As he shook off his slumber, we grasped the gravity of the situation just in time to witness the horrifying impact of another plane striking the Second World Trade Center tower. The reality sank in — America was under attack.

In the ensuing chaos, amid reports of potential threats beyond the four identified planes, there were alarming accounts of bombs in Washington, DC. The tension escalated as fighter jets roared overhead, prompting us to dash to the apartment's parking lot for a clearer view. In the southeast sky, smoke rose ominously just eleven miles away, marking the epicenter of what would soon gain global recognition as "Ground Zero." The surreal events of that fateful day left an indelible mark, forever altering the course of our lives and the trajectory of the nation, and it would become the first time that my damaged trauma responses allowed me to craft a personal narrative from a global event.

A shameful period of Islamophobia swept through America, targeting Muslim businesses and individuals in response to the attacks. I turned my angst and confusion elsewhere—ALL religion.

My atheism hardened since leaving Ramapo. I started commenting on how St. Francis was an awful place without context. I would tell anyone who would listen that Pope John Paul II was a tyrant and an enabler of horrendous behavior. And I would occasionally sprinkle in criticism of Judaism, Islam, hell, and even Buddhism just to be an equal-opportunity offender. Still, it was becoming less of a secret to everyone but myself that what I experienced as an altar boy wasn't right.

While the darkest parts of the American soul targeted our Muslim brothers and sisters, I turned my anger and confusion toward the only faith I had ever known. Family dinners, gatherings with friends, football Sundays with my in-laws — the setting mattered not. The minute anyone said anything about the attack—and it was all that anyone was speaking about—I saw the opening to denigrate religion. As far as I could tell, the prospects of heaven were the motivation for suicide bombers but never for the terrorist plotters. Osama bin Laden didn't give a fuck about the Quran; he just used it as a tool to motivate the devoted. If we stopped these foolish devotions, we'd be cutting off the most useful terrorist recruitment tool out there.

Frankly, it confounded me why few others could see what I thought to be so obvious. If I, with my Catholic upbringing, can modernize myself and move away from ancient answers to everyday questions science and technology long ago answered, anyone should be able to.

•••

Bachelor Parties would become some of the more noteworthy experiences of our collective friendship. Ben, Walter, and Doc were all giving farewell-to-freedom celebrations in Atlantic City. We drank, smoked, and gambled from lunch to breakfast the following day. Hayes' was in Hoboken, NJ, because of a last-minute cancellation of a party bus intended to bring us into Manhattan. I got so drunk I was kicked out of one bar and then pre-banned from entering the bar down the block. Good times.

Mark's would be a long weekend of golf, drinking, and fine meats at a massive McMansion in the Pocono region of Pennsylvania. We were a little older, and our bodies couldn't hang like they did for the Atlantic City ones, but near-record amounts of craft beer were routinely crushed from sunrise to pass out.

They hosted mine at the Knights of Columbus, with a nightcap in the 208 Pool.

Organized by my best man and brother Sean, the bash was a straightforward yet enjoyable affair. To keep it affordable for everyone, Sean chose the basement of the K of C, which had two halls, one upstairs and the other next to the bar. I've long suspected that my father was the real mastermind behind the decision to hold it there—he was all about his comfort zones, and by this point, they were 208 and the Knights of Columbus and nothing else.

The gathering included about thirty people: friends, my dad, future father-in-law, brothers-in-law, and other relatives. The Knights hosted a traditional beefsteak dinner with unlimited platters of sliced sirloin and French fries. Sean's attention to detail was clear in the setup of beer pong tables, starting a beer pong tournament reminiscent of the finest tournaments we ran at Ramapo.

The atmosphere was casual yet vibrant during the event, with the Yankees playing on every TV in the house and the Jukebox filling the air with the Dave Matthews Band. The gift I received—a PlayStation 2 from my groomsmen exemplified Sean's commitment to capturing everything I love about basic partying. It was Madden Time!

Sean and my groomsmen went all out. There was only one problem that was well beyond their control: the parade banner.

Earlier in 2002, a Massachusetts jury convicted Father John Geoghan of sexual assault and battery for grabbing the ass of a ten-year-old boy in a swimming pool. (Maybe let's keep the priests out of pools?) Following his sentencing, drips and drabs of information about Geoghan's trajectory continued to be made public: allegations against him date back to 1967; He admitted to molesting seven boys in 1974; he had seven other families demand his removal over molesting their sons in the parish in 1981; they put him in charge of a youth group at his next parish because the church believed he was "fully recovered"; church doctors eventually diagnosed him with "atypical pedophilia in remission."

The public scrutiny of the Church was unlike anything I had ever seen in my 25 years. News programs featured guests who openly called not only for the Archbishop of Boston, Cardinal Bernard Law, to resign but for Pope John Paul II to do the same. Geoghan's tale exposed the meticulous and intentional details the Church would go to not only to shield abusers from prosecution but to keep them active around children.

They threw my bachelor party on Saturday, July 6, 48 hours after the nationally renowned Ridgefield Park 4th of July Parade. The K of C, like every other organization in the village, marched in the parade. Each group would typically carry a banner about 8 feet wide and 4 feet tall, introducing their group to the parade watchers.

In response to the public outcry, the K of C banner for 2002 read: "KNIGHTS OF COLUMBUS COUNCIL #229—STANDING IN SOLIDARITY WITH OUR PRIESTS."

I eyed that banner up all night long. I have no idea where the Sharpie came from—probably the beer pong sign-up sheet. But after the right amount of liquid courage to draw a massive "X" through priests and scribble what my drunk ass believed to be the more appropriate description of the recipients of their solidarity:

"PEDOPHILES,"

Sean gave me a look of "Oh, what the fuck, man?" There were uncomfortable chuckles and laughter. My future brothers-in-law grew up in RP; they knew who I was referring to. Everybody with a St. Francis connection did by now. "Father Gerry" had become a punchline among anyone who remembered him by this time. Willie Foster's death brought the suspicions, if not to conversational volume, then at least to a whisper.

And the more folks would talk—I limited my chatter primarily to Jay, my family, and hers, as despite living and marrying in RP, I still opposed to reconnecting with my past, pre-Ramapo life—the more they'd eventually get back to their older suspicions of Father David Ernst, who was a Sudol-like figure in the parish between 1969 and 1975.

It was just understood and accepted by the time of Geoghan that Ernst and Sudol were both "one of those priests"—the vocabulary I—and others often used to describe abusive clergy.

The following day, I got a phone call from my mother saying the K of C expected an apology. I politely told her they could go fuck themselves; I no longer had any business with them.

•••

July 27, 2002, began with an unusual atmosphere characterized by a dreary, overcast sky and oppressive humidity. Eager to pass the time before the impending nuptials, I spent the initial three hours engaged in a spirited game of "Madden" with Sean on the newly gained PlayStation 2.

However, amid the excitement, a strange and nervous energy gripped me. All I wanted in those moments was for Jay to become my wife, and I envisioned our wedding day as a culmination of dreams, surrounded by our closest friends and relatives. Despite these positive aspirations, an underlying tension manifested as a cold sweat behind my neck, making it challenging to maintain focus.

Around ten, seeking a reprieve from anxiety, I cracked open a beer for my shower. The cold can of Budweiser seemed to do wonders, providing respite and settling my nerves. The beer became a simple remedy, a brief calm interlude before the impending ceremony's whirlwind. So I had another.

We caught a ride up to the Church. Father Joe asked us to wait in the sacristy. Hadn't really considered that in the days leading up to the ceremony. I told Sean we should wait outside by the rectory entrance so we could smoke—I went through a quarter of a pack before the wedding began. I wasn't waiting for a second longer than I had to stay in that damned sacristy.

The ceremony itself began with Jay's father escorting her down the aisle. At that moment, Jay looked more beautiful than ever. Her blue Irish eyes sparkled like precious gems, and her radiant smile could have outshone a thousand suns. With professionally done hair and makeup, she possessed a magazine-cover gorgeousness that captivated everyone present.

The following reception occurred at a beautiful rustic preserve in the heart of the Meadowlands, far removed from the urban hustle and bustle of the turnpike (But with the newly altered New York City skyline in the distance). As fate would have it, the sun made a welcome return.

Our first dance, set to the heartfelt lyrics of "To Make You Feel My Love" by Bob Dylan, was a moment of connection and intimacy amidst the grandeur of the celebration. The dance floor witnessed the beginning of the party of our lives.

The evening was a nonstop highlight reel of memories. There was an unexpected depletion of vodka before a cocktail hour had concluded. Jay's Uncle Fred, a short, ginger-haired figure, injected humor into the festivities by dressing up as a leprechaun and joining Jay in a spirited Irish jig. The musical repertoire took me back almost a decade, as I passionately sang "Paradise by the Dashboard Light" with the same enthusiasm as a performance as I did with that lesbian barbershop quartet in that hotel lobby at Jay's uncle's 1995 wedding.

As the night unfolded, there was a palpable reluctance to conclude, and it almost didn't. Within an hour of our return from the ceremony, our wedding party drank the hotel bar out of beer. My friends, each bringing their own cooler with more than enough beer, graciously brought the coolers into the bar. Drivers delivered multiple large orders of pizza to the lobby.

This happens when you marry two Irish Catholic families and have them start their day in a church. They inevitably liquor themselves up into party machines as if they're collectively trying to suppress something. Ironically, it usually leads to a phenomenal time, and the wedding of Jaime and Ed Hanratty was just that.

I believed I had a future—for the first time that I could remember.

XIX

Father John Geoghan continued to make news beyond 2002. The following year, inspired by the Geoghan trial and Cardinal Law's blatantly bold negligence, the *Boston Globe* rocked the world with its groundbreaking investigative journalism, uncovering a scandal of monumental proportions. The Globe's renowned Spotlight team delved deep into the dark underbelly of the Catholic Church, exposing widespread sexual abuse perpetrated by priests and the systemic cover-up orchestrated by the Church hierarchy. Their meticulous reporting shed light on the harrowing experiences of victims who had long been silenced and ignored.

The scandal sent shockwaves through the Catholic community and beyond, prompting widespread outrage and demands for accountability. The Globe's relentless pursuit of the truth forced the Church to confront its complicity in protecting predatory priests at the expense of vulnerable children. This groundbreaking exposé sparked a global reckoning with clergy abuse and sparked a wave of similar investigations in other cities and countries.

And barely over a year into it, it would cast a pall over our marriage.

The fall of 2003 descended into Animal House at my parents' house. Sean was 23, living at home, and settling more and more into the role of "Man of the House". He began paying the cable bill, made sure the house was up to date on modern electronics, and wasn't shy about throwing a party.

The girls were 19 and 16, the prime age for teenage partying. Dad still wasn't working and was drinking every day. Mom remained preoccupied with the grief over losing her parents. Elizabeth and Erin had much more permissive teenage years than I did; that was clear.

The Yankees returned to the World Series after missing out in 2002. The longer they advanced in the playoffs, the more opportunities there were to have a watch party. For three consecutive Saturdays, Sean and I purchased kegs for the game. We'd buy them before even having a guest list. And if enough people didn't show up to kill it, there were football games the next day, and I only lived a third of a mile down the block.

On the third Saturday of our October bender, I was outside on the deck having a cigarette with my folks, Jay and Sean. Yes, we were the five oldest members of the family, but the sixth (Elizabeth) made it aggressively clear years earlier that smoking inside was unacceptable (and time has proven that it, indeed, was an unacceptable practice.)

The *Boston Globe* expose inevitably came up. I inevitably brought it up. Repeatedly. I did it so often that my mother snapped, "Did Father Gerry do something to you? You're always making these comments," with a hint of frustration over my incessant needling about St. Francis since I left for college.

"Yes, he did something, alright?" I replied, a faint hint of emotion in my voice.

The faces of all four on the deck froze.

"It's not what you think," I replied, knowing that the Globe's reporting brought horrible details of rape and sodomy to the forefront. "I didn't have it as bad as others probably did. But he crossed plenty of boundaries. There was a lot of inappropriate romantic-style kissing", internally gagging at the thought of using the term "French Kiss" to my family (or, given the 2003 parlance, "Freedom Kiss" because Americans have such a thick skin.)

That's all I could admit to them. That's all I could admit to myself. *I didn't have it as bad as others.* Sure, what happened to me was fucked up, but did you hear about those poor altar boys in Massachusetts? Or the others Gerry probably abused "worse" than me. That's what I had settled on in 2003. That was my justification why I wasn't a victim of childhood sexual abuse.

My words shocked my family. One by one, they approached me to hug me, reaffirm that they loved me, and let me know they had my back.

I told them I appreciated it and that I loved them, too. While I didn't think it needed to be said, I didn't expect that conversation to go beyond the deck that night. All I wanted to do was get back inside and watch the Yankees and Marlins battle it out in the World Series.

...

I remember vividly the emotions I woke up with the following day. I was becoming an expert in early recognition of that blend of shame and guilt from the feeling that you did something mortifying the night before. Often, the case would be that I did nothing particularly egregious; it was merely the level of intoxication I reached around other people.

But the morning after I made the admission, I knew exactly what I did last night. I overshared something I was not emotionally prepared to do. My internal voice was shaming the shit out of me.

Look what you did now. Everyone's pissed at you for ruining a good time. Why do you keep getting that drunk? It would be best if you didn't show your face around them for some time. Jay is going to eviscerate you when you wake up.

I rolled over to find Jay resting her head on the corner of my pillow. My movement jarred her awake, and she said with eyes still closed, "I'm so proud of you," as she reached over to my shoulder to pull me closer.

She wasn't pissed! Quite the opposite. She was sympathetic.

As we settled into our Saturday Morning coffee and cigarettes routine, she explained she had long felt there was a reason for my occasional fits of anger. There must have been a reason I would drink harder than everyone else. She hoped with all of her might that this would change both.

I felt a relief unlike any before. My partner did not think less of me about my truth. She wasn't upset with me for over-drinking; I had her full support. I told her I couldn't muster up the emotional bandwidth to repeat the situation, but she was free to tell her parents. They were family. They lived across the street from St. Francis since the very early 80s. They knew who Father Gerry was.

When the phone rang later that morning, I knew it was my mother before even checking the caller ID.

"Hi honey, how are you doing today?" she asked before getting to her point. "I just spoke to Father Doyle. He was sick to his stomach; he said the Church wanted to root these priests out, but they needed people to testify about them. I have the number for you to call; an entire department at the Archdiocese of Newark exists to handle these issues."

What the actual fuck?!? What part of "this doesn't leave the deck" did she not understand? This was far and above what I was willing to do. It was bordering on my worst fears exposed—sharing my vulnerabilities not only with a stranger but also with a stranger within the infrastructure of the Catholic Church.

The entire situation was unbearable because I hadn't confronted myself with what had happened. I didn't talk about the pool. I didn't mention the Holy Saturday incident. Said nothing about his flaunting around half-naked at his Pocono house. I told them about the "Gerry kisses", and that was it. I was in no way, shape, or form prepared to make any formal statement.

I told her I would think about it; that was the most my People Pleasing would allow me to concede. I wanted to say, "Not a chance in hell." I wanted to say, "Of all the fucking organizations on earth, why would I trust the Catholic Church?"

That's the depth of the power of the Roman Catholic Church. My parents' first instinct was to report a fire to the arsonist, defying all logic, perfectly captured how they continued to hold over the faithful.

I don't know if it's a product of their parents' lifestyle or whether they engaged it themselves in the workplace. Still, in my limited experience, the Boomers had no hesitation about calling you at work. Sometimes, it was to talk about the mundane, perhaps invite you over to dinner. Others, it was to pressure you into speaking to the church.

Joe Doyle jumped the gun and informed the Archdiocese of an informal complaint about Gerry Sudol. He called my parents to say speaking to them as soon as possible was imperative.

Imperative? IMPERATIVE? The Roman Catholic Church possessed not a shred of legal, ethical, or moral authority over me. They were an organization devoid of ethics and morals as far as I was concerned. How dare someone try to compel me to give those creeps a millisecond of the rest of my life? They took enough.

My dad called me at work to tell me this. He volunteered to come with me to Newark–because that was also "required" as part of their "protocol." You had to almost literally "kiss the ring" in the Archbishop's administrative offices in downtown Newark, NJ—about 25 minutes from my home in RP. Still the People Pleaser, I politely told him I'd let them know when I decided.

I didn't give it a second thought. What I would know as "avoidance" went into full effect. I spent the rest of that night decompressing with Jay, watching whatever we would watch on Monday nights in an era still dictated by network prime-time schedules.

Tuesday morning, not long after I logged into my workstation in that warehouse in the swamps of the Meadowlands (the swampy turnpike part, not the picturesque natural setting where we celebrated our wedding), a co-worker yelled out, "Ed, 2160"—the verbal code for a phone call on the line ending as such. And my suspicion that this wasn't work-related proved correct.

This time it was my mother. Her message was the same as Dad's the day before. The church wants to talk to me; they want to rid the church of these bad guys, but they can't do it without me.

The concept was utterly ridiculous to me. He was named in a suit with other priests that the Archdiocese settled for his role in Willie Foster's death. The church doesn't need me to know he's a menace.

I gave my mother the same stock answer I gave my father the day before. This is a lot to process. I'm working on it.

After lunch, I had another call on line 2610. When I answered, my heart sank to the floor.

"Hi Eddie, it's Father Joe Doyle…"

My parents gave him my fucking work number. I grabbed the phone receiver, clenching it with my teeth to resist smashing it through my computer monitor. How fucking dare they?

Given the jarring nature of the phone call, I remember little of the conversation. Though I know I told him a similar version of what I told my parents; I don't recall him offering pushback, but I'll never forget how he signed off on the conversation:

"I'm very sorry this happened to you."

He said it in the way you might say it to someone with a Nike full of dog shit after they walked through your yard when you haven't cleaned up after the puppy in weeks.

However, the fourth and final phone call to my workplace was the most horrific. The very next day, I was called by someone who introduced herself as a member of some task force within the Archdiocese responsible for complaints of this nature. She said, which is mandatory by church policy upon learning of an allegation, and would like me to make a formal statement.

When I told her I was examining my options, she warned me to look for "predators" looking to take advantage of my situation. She said that with no hint of irony or self-awareness. Again, I reiterated I couldn't commit, as I was still processing everything. For crying out loud, I got trashed and told my family members not five days ago, and now I'm being bullied by the Church clergy and staff alike? At my office?

I thanked her for her time, and then she told me she expected my decision soon if I expected the church to take me seriously and offer me their approved counseling "at no cost to me." As if any victim of the church would pay a penny out of pocket for Church-sanctioned help.

I couldn't believe the hubris of all parties involved. This was the solemn secret that I struggled to confront for so long. I couldn't even bring myself to get into the actual details of the abuse. By the end of the work week, I was being harassed and cajoled by the Church to let them handle it.

I lied to everyone, including myself, that I was considering speaking to the church. After the telecommunication abuse, however, there wasn't a chance in hell I was going to play ball with them.

•••

The whirlwind week concluded with Jay's parents coming down to our apartment for drinks after dinner on Friday night. Jay had briefed them on my "big reveal" the day after I made it. They both reached out to me to offer immediate support.

I don't believe it was a surprise to my Mother-in-law at all. She remembered Gerry asking her which of her three sons she planned to offer to the priesthood. But she remembered more than just Gerry. She spent all but the early years of her marriage living within two blocks of St. Francis—first at her parents' stately center-hall colonial, barely big enough for an Irish Catholic family of thirteen one block north, and then since 1983 directly across from the Euclid entrance. She remembered David Ernst.

Her friends told stories about overnight vacations with Ernst, camping trips, or uncomfortable conversations that sounded all too familiar to me. When Ernst was first shuffled to St. Francis, she was about five years older than Jay and I were for Sudol's arrival.

My Father-in-Law was likewise the product of a Catholic upbringing. Growing up in the Parish of the Holy Rosary on the banks of the Hudson River, he enrolled at Saint Cecelia's in Englewood, NJ, a school made famous by its one-time football coach, a Brooklyn kid named Vince Lombardi. It's where he met his wife.

After honorable service in the United States Marine Corps in the waning days of the Vietnam Draft, he returned to marry his high school sweetheart in her home parish of St. Francis. He was also familiar with Ernst, but from a married and responsible adult perspective, not that of a parishioner.

He worked multiple jobs throughout the 80s and early 90s so my mother-in-law could raise Jay and her three brothers. It paid off as they achieved the rare feat of putting four children through college. But it meant he wasn't around for the parish functions as much as some other dads were, and he may not have been a Sunday mass staple. But he was neither blind nor deaf. He heard the jokes and sarcastic comments that Jay, her oldest brothers, and I would crack around the dinner table about Father Gerry.

I was a year older than Jay's first brother and three older than her middle one, who was in Sean's class. They, along with the youngest, who was Elizabeth's age, withdrew from St. Francis one week into our high school journey when Jay complained to her parents about how far behind she felt in math and science coming from parochial school. "Because they don't pray the rosary" was not an acceptable answer to "Why did an earthquake strike Argentina in 1986?" when you get a proper education.

Jay and I told them we're not closing the door on pursuing anything with the Church, but they're aware of it, so we're keeping our options open.

They assured us we had their full backing regardless of our direction, but they recommended we first speak with a close family friend and attorney, Bruce Halligan.

•••

Bruce knew my mother-in-law for as long as she could remember. Throughout Jay's childhood, he was a prominent figure around the family until he fell out of favor for a hot minute. He could be stubborn and rubbed more than a fair share of people the wrong way, but everyone agreed that those qualities that could often cause so much consternation made him one hell of an attorney.

A short and stout man, he had a long face missing a half-chewed cigar and fedora to complete the "backroom power broker" look. He extended his hand from the hip—do they teach you to do that in law school?—and welcomed us into his office, directly next to the Bergen County Superior Courthouse.

He asked me if I was comfortable with Jay being present; he approached this as if I were his client to protect confidentiality. I appreciated it but affirmed that I was comfortable with her presence and preferred it.

Bruce asked me to take as much time as needed and let him know the details. And I did. I went into more detail than I did with my parents. I told him about the frequency of the Gerry kisses and how his grip would effectively trap me—I told him about prancing around topless at overnight getaways.

"Did he touch your penis?" Bruce asked.

"No".

"Did he make you touch his?"

I dropped an automatic "No". I gave no thought to his pool erection. When I heard "touch his," I thought about the lurid details from the *Boston Globe's* reporting. I thought about penetration and forcible sodomy. I thought of altar boys being instructed to masturbate priests. These are the parameters I was using. Everything could have been worse. I'm not a victim like THOSE kids were.

"Look, what happened to you was wrong," Bruce said, "but a court can be convinced that kissing is a cultural thing. Many European men will kiss other men as a casual greeting—even on the lips.

My recommendation would be to find a therapist. You need to work this out for you first, before you worry about the church."

He was entirely right in principle. The correct order of operations was to heal myself first, if possible. Then, seek acknowledgment and accountability. But that's not what the voice inside me heard.

See, nobody thinks it's a big deal. He was just "one of those priests." You're not the kids from Boston; you didn't have it bad at all. "Gerry kisses?" You're still upset about "Gerry kisses?" Give it up. Put this shit to bed and move on. You already had a lawyer tell you what happened was no big deal. You think a therapist will tell you any different?

Before we left, I had one last question for Bruce: "So, should I cooperate with the church?"

He extended his hand from his hip again and said, "Now, you're a very smart man. Why would you cooperate with the Church?"

He had a point. And while he, like everyone else, encouraged me to seek counseling, I was already subconsciously determined to re-bury my truth. The doubts I had about my abuse "not being horrific enough" even to warrant being called abuse had returned. The pressure from the church and the hinting by Bruce that this didn't rise to a significant enough allegation formed a lethal combination for my damaged psyche.

PART 2

XX

It would be fifteen years before my altar boy experience would be the focal point of my life, but it lurked around every corner. As I shuffled through life's events and expectations, lingering effects of the childhood trauma would manifest in different, but always adverse, ways. I took Bruce's advice and ghosted the church. They stopped calling after a few days. I couldn't accept their nonsense that they needed my attestation to remove a priest who was part of a larger settlement for clergy sexual abuse.

In 2006, I lived permanently in a zip code beside RP's 07660 for the first time since I was in a crib. Mid-00s real estate prices were skyrocketing when we settled into our marriage and thought about home ownership. New Jersey, already one of the most expensive states in the country, became nearly out of reach. With its proximity to New York City, buying in RP was a pipe dream.

Both working within 5 miles of our hometown, we needed to remain within an hour of work. We had about $1,300 total to our name, which meant the most we could afford was a $325,000 home (and people wonder why there was a mortgage crisis two years later). Moving due west was too expensive because of Route 80 access. An hour south forced us into Jersey Shore summer traffic—the pits of driving hell.

That left us looking north, to an area we were familiar with because of years of travels to Jay's grandparents' Lake House—the same one we should have married at retrospectively. The area had been undergoing a boom since the 9/11 attacks as nervous families looked to raise their kids further away from Ground Zero, but it remained within our price range.

We settled on a two-bedroom rustic log cabin in West Milford, New Jersey, that needed significantly more work than we wanted to admit to ourselves—a town as conservative as the rest of Jersey was progressive. Almost everything else was perfect. It was within the radius that we accepted would be our new commute. The home was affordable; it had a fireplace, and the entire town was naturally beautiful. Nestled in the Appalachian foothills, it was a desirous weekend spot for hikers. With South Shore access to Greenwood Lake, it was a haven for recreational boaters. We weren't hikers or boaters, but this little wood cabin on 1/3 an acre with a babbling creek running through its backyard offered significantly more than any other house we looked at.

The only thing that wasn't perfect was the town's conservative Christian values. There were churches galore—including two Catholic ones—and the general discourse of residents was more Rush Limbaugh than Walter Cronkite. At a neighbor's dinner party the first year we lived there, a guest snarkily chided that the primarily Black and Latino city of Patterson, New Jersey, "needed a Katrina"—referring to the infamous 2005 hurricane that nearly removed New Orleans from the map.

But for me, who stayed up at night with anxiety over wondering if I'd ever own a home, start a family, and be what everyone else appeared to be—normal—it was everything. It would be a point of pride—in good years and bad — when I hosted the annual RFFL Draft on the deck above the creek with my friends.

•••

Our property was about 85% natural and 15% structure. Spring meant playing whack-a-mole with weeds in every corner of the yard and any flower bed. I couldn't tell the difference between a weed or a flower half of the time, and I was brutal at identifying poison ivy, which led to no less than a dozen rashes the first few springs and summers.

I was pulling double beautification duty in the spring of 2007, trying to fend off nature in West Milford while attempting to add curbside appeal to 208 Teaneck Road on the weekends. Mom and Dad determined it was time to sell. They had no choice. Dad's decade without work had taken its toll. He successfully beat a colon cancer diagnosis in 2005, but he never got mentally well after that. You could make the argument that he hadn't been well since losing his twin brother fifteen years earlier, and you wouldn't be wrong. Extended grieving was something my siblings and I experienced from both parents as Mom struggled to cope with losing her parents a decade ago.

I spent a Saturday blasting a coat of white paint over the oak-paneled walls of the attic, the room where I spent many a melancholy evening in solitude. I remembered the emotions of teenage love and heartbreak, great laughter on the phone with Jay, and lonely evenings making mixtapes with names like "Heartbreak" and "Massive Depression." Why be subtle?

My efforts to clean up the home, have my parents sell, and recoup some value to make retirement easier were all for naught. The real estate market crumbled that year. 208's value went underwater compared to what my parents owed thanks to a foolish equity cash out that a bank gave a couple in their late fifties with no income. Again, people wonder why we had a housing crisis.

That Easter was the first Easter I had celebrated with my family since we got married. I had a management position in KLJ from early in my tenure. The Boss took a liking to me, and I gained more and more responsibility and the promise of running daily operations soon when the Boss moved into semi-retirement. I used that responsibility to ensure that I would work every Easter Sunday, as occasional weekends were required. Of course, I would abuse that power to ensure I didn't work weekends when there were exciting plans (and I did the same for Hayes, who joined my staff when he moved north after graduation). I also abused it to see that I worked every Easter (and many other family holidays).

Budget cuts coincided with the downturn in the economy, however, and one of the cost-saving measures was to cease being a seven-day operation. So I got beyond shitfaced at what would be the Last Easter at 208 Teaneck Road.

I pillaged the attic closet for any remaining traces of my former life, squeezing into a New York Rangers hockey sweater that was, by design, oversized and loose in 1994. Then I took a loaf of bread and a bottle of wine out onto the deck where the family had assembled—the same deck I came forward on five years ago. I did a mock consecration of the Eucharist over the deck table.

With hands extended out over the bread, I said, *"On the night he was betrayed for death, a death he truly accepted, Jesus turned to his apostles and said, 'Take this, all of you, and eat it. This is My Body, which has been given up for you. Do this in memory of me.'"*

As I continued, there was nervous laughter from all, and Aunt Breda ran inside as quickly as possible. I held a glass of cabernet and said, "Take this, all of you, and drink it. This is my blood—the blood of a new and everlasting covenant. Do this in memory of me."

The latter half of 2008 saw one last round of happy times as Elizabeth married her high school sweetheart and shed the Hanratty name. Sean fell madly in love with a college friend of Ben's wife, whom he met at their wedding. They married three months after Elizabeth's wedding. It was a fucking expensive year amid a financial collapse. But we survived it and had a final round of joy and toasts, and for one last time, 208 was filled with laughter.

•••

On a muggy afternoon in August 2010, I pulled my black Nissan Sentra into the tattered, macadamed parking lot of the Yankee Motor Lodge at the foot of the George Washington Bridge in Fort Lee, New Jersey. I was picking up Dad, who had been bombed. When I showed up, he offered me a Bud Light.

By this point, he had undergone two separate stints in rehab to kick drinking. Mission Not Accomplished. He would sneak out and purchase small plastic pints of Vodka anytime he was home alone—both at 208 and now at the rental he shared with Mom, Aunt Breda, and Erin on the northern tip of RP, almost a mile up and over from our old family house. He'd drink his day away.

Earlier that morning, I received a phone call at work. Cellphones were pervasive, so personal calls went directly there, a much-welcome development. The "Ignore" button is one of the greatest inventions I have ever seen.

It was Mom calling to inform me they dropped Dad off at the Yankee—a $50 per night hotel for all sorts of people down on their luck or in the throes of addiction and/or sex work—while they looked for some boarding house to place him.

I shared their pain and knew what they were dealing with. I couldn't bear to tolerate ten minutes of him in a drunken state. I had no earthly idea how they could tolerate it on a 24/7 basis.

I still knew the type of place where he was dumped, though. Lower Bergen County was littered with them, and there were always enough patrons to keep the lights on in America's second most expensive county. In high school, we would party in these types of hotels next to The Woods. The thought of my father—my namesake—spending multiple nights in a crack den was too much for me to process.

I called Jay, and the minute she heard where he was, she insisted I pick him up and bring him to our home. We'd figure out logistics in our awkward one-bathroom cabin later.

There was a backlash from everyone for our decision to rescue him from the whorehouse. They likely assumed he was going to go right back to the bottle—that now I was the one being manipulated by the addict.

What they failed to realize is that I never got that boozing buddy relationship with Dad. Sure, there was my first legal drink at the K of C, but at 21 years of age, I would not be socializing with the midlife crisis and late-life crisis brigades. By the time I was going out to bars not to party but just to be, he was too far gone for public consumption. The few times Sean and I took him out, he'd stutter so badly after one drink that we'd have to order the rest for him. That's not a drinking buddy.

I went into overdrive and collected all the booze from our house — all of it. Gifted bottles of whiskey and Bailey's that we barely ever touched, the entire wine rack, every beer in the fridge. I asked my neighbors, Gary and Jan, if we could store it in their basement, joking to Gary that I knew exactly how many beers there were because, unlike Dad, Gary was a Boomer who could handle a drink or ten. I could forge a drinking buddy relationship with him.

Jay came home that afternoon and laid down the law. He could stay here, but it was his last stop before the Passaic County YMCA, and he had to observe three rules:

1. No Drinking, period.
2. Attend an AA Meeting every day.
3. No Cooking after midnight.

He never had another drink as long as he lived. He grew into a loving grandfather of my three nieces and nephew. He became my most reliable golfing partner. The man my mother married returned to her after decades of processing his demons.

I would, not long after he left, have enough alcohol for both of us. The split traumas of being rejected by family (for trying to save our father's life) and the reality of your father—not yet 65 years old—depending on you for nourishment and shelter were too much for my untreated mind to handle.

I began to regularly drink by myself.

•••

My drinking throughout my thirties escalated along what I'm sure were the same lines my father did at a similar point in his life. In my earliest memories of beer, I only remember him drinking them with Grandpa on Sundays or when Uncle Bob or his friends were over. In my preteen years, he would drink alone, but only on the weekends, and he would remain sociable, which is where I found myself.

Weddings were the prima facia social event of our calendars in what seemed like every year since ours took place in 2002. After two dozen, an obvious pattern developed—if the wedding took place in a Catholic Church, I would get beyond annihilated beyond recognition. If it weren't, I'd get as tossed as everyone else—we could still party at or near Ramapo levels for fifteen years post-grad.

I have little recollection of Ben's wedding–where Sean met his future wife. We tailgated the church, popping our trunks and sharing beers intended for the hotel party an hour before the vows. Jay had to deliver stomach jabs to Doc and me to curtail our church giggles. I tried duck sausage for the first time and ate a slice of prosciutto that fell on the floor because, well, prosciutto. That's the extent of my recollections from a best friend's wedding. Everything else comes from very unflattering pictures.

When Doc married his wife Beth—a civil ceremony outdoors at the same venue where the reception took place—I drank from 2 p.m. to 2 a.m., fully remembered every aspect of the day and the party, and made it safely back to bed unharmed, waking up without that feeling of guilt and shame.

And that was par for the course at almost every wedding we attended. Unfortunately for me, I married into a massive Irish Catholic family. Jay was the second-oldest of thirty cousins. There were a lot of church weddings during this period.

During Dad's stay with us, a rinky-dink liquor store within reasonable walking distance underwent a facelift and transformed into a high-end wine and craft beer bar. *Uncorked* became a perfect 2-hour joint for Jay and me to escape when living with Dad was too much. It was unlike any of the other townie bars in West Milford. The closest pub to us before *Uncorked* featured Pabst Blue Ribbon on tap, unironically. *Uncorked* had brews from 8 different states on 8 different taps, a polished marble bar, mahogany and black accents, and dim lighting. It was an oasis.

And it would be where I spent at least two nights every week until a virus got out of hand a decade later.

...

They don't prep you for middle age the way they do for puberty. There's no thirtysomething version of "Are you there, God? It's Me, Margaret". One day, you can do what you've always done; the next one sneeze can incapacitate your back for hours. Middle Age hit me like a ton of 12 oz cans.

In February 2007, my body's dreaded "Check Engine Light" illuminated for the first time. Engaged in the mundane task of shoveling snow after a two-day bender, I suddenly felt my heart racing, vision blurring, and the back of my neck drenched in sweat despite the freezing weather. In the back of an ambulance, I reassured Jay that I felt fine, but an hour had passed since I dialed 9-1-1, fearing a heart attack.

My heart rate skyrocketed to over 160 beats per minute, and my blood pressure reached a concerning 200/120. The paramedics swiftly administered nitroglycerine under my tongue, stabilizing both. Although my vitals returned to normal after twenty minutes, the EMT strongly recommended an ambulance ride to the Emergency Room, emphasizing the life-threatening nature of the levels I had reached.

Despite stabilization, admission for the night followed, and subsequent cardiologist follow-ups became inevitable. The prescription of 50mg daily of Metoprolol, a beta blocker, became my routine, a drug already familiar to friends and relatives, all of whom were at least fifty.

A revelation surfaced during my stay on the cardiology floor at Chilton Hospital—severe sleep apnea. A subsequent sleep study halted after an hour, revealing "Hall of Fame level" obstructive sleep apnea. Introducing a CPAP machine into my life, I formed a love-hate relationship with it. While it granted me full, restless sleep, it interfered with everything bed-related, from closeness to Jay to rolling over.

Contrary to the weight loss experienced by many starting CPAP therapy, my waistline continued its upward trajectory, reaching 290 lbs. two years later. Pre-diabetic, doctors prescribed 100mg of Metformin daily. High bad cholesterol prompted the addition of 25mg of Crestor to keep the arteries flowing. Despite years of Metoprolol use, my blood pressure rose alongside my expanding girth. So 20mg of Benicar HTC, which makes you piss like a racehorse, entered my regimen as an ACE inhibitor, to keep the blood pressure down.

With each medication impacting other bodily functions, a 5mg prescription of Cialis joined the lineup.

I was not yet thirty-eight years old.

...

The most significant societal development of my thirties impacted me as much as it impacted the rest of the world — the rise of social media. I put in time and effort to distance myself from my youth and my trauma. And in seconds, all the memories came gushing back as friend requests.

Almost fifteen years after graduating from RPHS, I opened a Myspace account. The early social media platform allowed you to peruse other users by many criteria, including school and graduation year. The messages came in one by one.

"Oh my god, Ed?"

"How have you been?"

"What have you been up to?"

Virtual small talk with cast members from a life I had been not-so-subconsciously trying to forget since I left it.

Myspace was little more than a photo dump and song-sharing platform compared to the behemoth that would crush it. Facebook took all the quirky customizable shit that made Myspace unique and shit-canned it. With Soviet-style uniformity, their blue, white, and gray platform became the go-to place on the internet for everyone, including the Baby Boomers.

It was a great place until they arrived. If there were a post you found objectionable, you would breeze past it. If there were a pop culture reference someone didn't get, they wouldn't post to inform you they don't get it. And if something was going sideways in your life, you weren't vulnerable to some fifty-or-sixty-something white guy telling you it's Obama's fault.

I lived on Facebook like an open book. While others fretted about job security, I was secure in knowing that as long as KLJ existed, I could bullshit my way to $75,0000 per year — a salary that remained stagnant for the entire decade.

Some people had concerns over being so open in front of family and close friends. Not me. I was reaching a point where I had no tolerance for being beholden to family for anything. I desired to chart my course. After everything that we endured with my family's demise and our successful efforts to glue it back together again, my bandwidth was non-existent. A decade of choosing four family weddings a year over personal vacations or a nest egg caused even more lingering bitterness.

So no, I wasn't the type of poster who took the sensibilities of older relatives into perspective when he would post about the disgusting nature in which unarmed young Black men and boys were being lynched by law enforcement, not when Facebook was spreading the names of Michael Brown, Freddie Gray, Sandra Bland, and Eric Garner routinely through my feed.

The election of the nation's first Black President, Barack Obama, aligning with the growing cross-demographic, social media explosion, was a major ingredient in the cocktail that led to this Cold Civil War we pretend we're not witnessing. There were rabid, frothing, yet irrelevant retorts to any mere mention of his minor triumphs, like saving the country from George W. Bush's failed economic policies and ending the foolish war in Iraq. Always unsolicited and rarely reciprocated.

However, through these interactions, unfriending, and discussions, something was forming. My genuine feelings were now simmering above the surface. People noticed I was not who they always thought I was.

That's not Eddie the Altar Boy.

That's Ed Hanratty.

And he's kind of a dick.

XXI

By the holidays of 2015, Jay's career was taking off. She was accruing more responsibility, more salary, and more perks. For the first time in our marriage, the first time since we purchased the Money Pit cabin, a financial cushion existed, and with that, breathing room. Not having money always left me feeling impending doom for the first decade of home ownership. The newfound security was almost only because of her hard work and effort because I was at a dead end professionally.

I was still making the same salary I was seven years ago, where it went from an excellent wage to an adequate one to a shitty, unmotivating one. It was akin to the classic movie "Groundhog Day"—every day was the same routine: Wake up at 4:45 AM. Dilly dally in bed, checking my phone for fifteen minutes. Have coffee and fuck around on social media for another half hour. Meander around the room looking for clothes, hop in the shower, leave fifteen minutes after I needed to, arrive thirty minutes later than I was supposed to, but 10 minutes on most days before The Boss.

I would manage the workday by doing about 90 minutes of work and then shooting the shit on a personal message board a friend created we had christened "The Tank," short for "Overflow Tank," taken from a Phish lyric. The 8:30 AM—2:30 with Doc, Hayes, and Sean—other desk jockeys among our crew; was the workday's salvation. We'd primarily talk shit about sports, share details about lunch and dinner, and chat about drinking.

I'd get home and putz around the house until Jay got home, cook dinner, and it wouldn't be long until bedtime when I'd prepared to repeat the cycle in a few hours. Unless it was Thursday, I was off to *Uncorked* because Thursdays were a party night at Ramapo, so they had to be for the rest of my life.

Jay stopped being subtle about my innate ability to piss time away. For my 39th birthday, she bought me a laptop and a writing desk. She said I was happiest when I had an outlet, and she wasn't wrong. The time I spent writing critically about the Iraq War was one of the most enjoyable times in our marriage. Engaging with other readers and fellow members of the 20% of America who didn't think we should punish Iraq for the actions of Saudi and Egyptian nationals gave me a sense of purpose that I didn't get from rewatching MSNBC's footage of Michael Jackson walking in and out of court for eight hours did.

I didn't know what to write; I just had to. Something had to give. The strain of the last ten years and professional stagnation had the negative voices working overtime in my head.

Just about 40. You know you're never having kids, right? And that's a good thing, given that dead-end job you've got yourself stuck in. Now, you think you're going to be a writer? LMA Fucking O! That ship has sailed, and your life is halfway over.

I silenced those demons long enough to continue a dialogue with James Reader, managing editor of *Reverb Press*—a progressive-tilted online publication. He liked the sample article I had submitted (Why Bernie and Hillary Dems Must Tread Cautiously), and within days, I was churning out content and making decent supplemental income.

Reverb allowed me to branch out beyond the daily musings on The Tank. It gave me the vision of a better, more limitless future than being just the stuck-in-the-mud General Manager of KLJ Review. Working with a talented team of writers in our virtual newsroom exposed me to new people and new ideas in ways I hadn't experienced since the early days of Ramapo. Engaging with readers gave me a sense of community, the likes of which I had never encountered before. Suddenly, my Facebook page was a destination that users would visit and not a source of gossip and conjecture behind my back, as had been the case with family since the Boomers logged on.

Reverb gave me an identity.

...

The content was easy to produce for *Reverb* because there was an insatiable appetite among the American left to read about the latest sexist remark or racist dog whistle made by a former game show host. Attach a picture of this disheveled seventy-something with noticeable tan lines or his ferret's nest of hair blowing in the wind and watch the readership grow exponentially.

I didn't understand the appeal of Donald J. Trump in the early days of 2016, even after he began winning primaries. Like, people realized that "The Apprentice" was a scripted show, right? And that this guy went bankrupt six times? And he was the only person you ever heard of who lost money owning casinos habitually? And the bigotry, misogyny, and general crudeness.

All of that was easily verifiable externally. These weren't outlandish claims like "Obama's not a United States citizen, and his tan suit proves it." I couldn't wrap my head around how the party that, not that long ago, impeached Bill Clinton because he got a blowjob in the Oval Office, was falling head over heels for a serial philanderer that had high-profile affairs with each of his three wives. And two of them were immigrants, no less. How–and more importantly, why—could he captivate that same audience?

It reminded me of the hypocrisy of the Roman Catholic Church. There was no logical answer provided—just blind faith. There was no critical examination, just a declaration that this is salvation, the only answer.

The sudden fascination with him among the devoted triggered memories of another tall, heavy-set wolf in sheep's clothing thirty years earlier. There were countless allegations against Trump related to his aggressiveness with women. Underage beauty pageant contestants spoke about how he would gawk at them, barely dressed, in the dressing room.. He admitted on tape to "Access Hollywood" that when you're famous, women let you "Grab them by the Pussy". And there was an awkwardly silent slice of his base that seemed oblivious to the many pictures of The Donald with Sex Trafficker and Pedophile Jeffrey Epstein.

How. Could. People. Not. See?

It unraveled me.

•••

Jay's professional achievements landed her and a guest at a four-night celebration of all of her company's top performers. We were guests of the company at the Loews Ventura Canyon resort in the Catalina Foothills of Tucson, Arizona. I experienced five-star service for the first time in my life.

Every meal was delicious and abundant. Almost every drink was taken care of, except for the ones I ordered from the room. Also included were 18 holes of golf on their manicured desert course—one of the most beautiful I've ever played (one thing I reluctantly share with Trump—golf is my only exercise).

Jay and I connected better than at any time in our marriage. We spent the entire trip together and didn't get on each other's nerves once. I had been carrying a bit of baggage throughout the spring—the more I wrote about Trump, the more lost and confused I became; it was pretty disorienting. But those days in the desert were a welcome escape.

That was until breakfast on the third day.

We had a free day before an awards gala that night, at which Jay was among the dozens to be recognized with a glass corporate trophy. We planned to visit a few artist colonies in downtown Tucson for the day. I didn't have the healthiest of breakfast options from the buffet that morning, but it wasn't anything unusual: some scrambled eggs, a cup of coffee, a few samplings of various cured meats, and maybe a cranberry juice.

We took the scenic walk back to our room after the meal—choosing to walk through a sunny desert-scape on the grounds rather than through a labyrinth of hallways. About 5 minutes into the walk, something felt off. Dizziness was creeping in to where I felt I needed to lie down. As I told Jay, my heart raced. I felt the heat of the Arizona morning sun beating down on me as I sweat buckets. I had to get back to the hotel room.

She calmly led me back to the room, where I tucked myself into the fetal position, hyperventilating. It was reminiscent of the snow-shoveling panic attack six years ago, but only more intense and magnified by the knowledge that I was 2,500 miles from home. I feared I would have to dial 9-1-1 from the room. I panicked even more over how long I would be in a Tucson hospital. Panic begets panic.

Jay tried everything to soothe me. Lights on, lights off. She tried talking me down; she tried remaining silent. She wanted to hold me; she tried to give me physical space. After 45 minutes of thinking I was going to die, I could collect myself. I remained dizzy and fully drained, as if I had run a marathon and fallen down a flight of stairs.

I didn't find my footing again until we found a bar in downtown Tucson.

I had a similar incident the Monday following our return, luckily in the confines of my house. It caused me to skip a day of work, but I had to be seen by my physicians while these symptoms were still manifesting and the memories were fresh.

The doctor prescribed me 0.5MG of Xanax to take if I ever felt panic building again.

•••

By the fall of 2016, I was so afraid of another severe panic attack that I would pop a Xanax at the first sign of discomfort. If I walked up the stairs doing laundry too many times and was breathing heavily, I grabbed the bottle of Xanax. If my 299 lb. frame was succumbing to 100% humidity on the golf course, I reached into the glove pocket of my golf bag, found the pack of Tic-Tacs, and shook out a Xanax. Every time I took one, my day would effectively end. I had plenty of energy to get myself through whatever the anxiety-inducing moment was, and that was it. I was cooked.

We took a vacation to visit family in Dublin that autumn. Aunt Rosie was my mother's youngest aunt—she played more of a sisterly role in her youth than an authoritative one. She and her husband, our Uncle Peter, provided the most welcoming home in all of Dublin. Every morning, we arose to the smell of a full Irish breakfast being prepared in the cast-iron skillet.

Aunt Rosie would share stories of my mother's youth or my grandfather's temper when they'd try to pull something over on him. Uncle Peter would entertain with his gift of gab and unique quips for everyday situations, such as "every cripple has his own way of walking" to describe surviving day-to-day challenges and frustrations. Mornings in Aunt Rosie's kitchen would be the highlight of any vacation, anywhere on earth, but they always led to the same place—a Xanax after breakfast so I could bring myself to explore unknown places.

Other things were dominating my mind, to be sure. Back at home, we were planning a joint fortieth birthday party. We rented the clubhouse at our local lake club. The guest list included every friend and family member, totaling over 75 people.

I wasn't able to write for *Reverb* while I was overseas—during the election season, you needed to be glued to the computer to write about breaking developments as quickly as possible. And the election itself was inducing enough anxiety because Hillary Clinton couldn't seem to put away this game show host who was clearly running a joke of a campaign with no intention of winning.

It didn't help matters that all anybody wanted to talk about was whether "that gobshite Trump" was going to win. I spent a sizeable chunk of the trip assuring the fine people of the Republic of Ireland to have faith in America. We're slow to come around, but we're not suicidal.

•••

I would have many words to eat the next time I visited Ireland. In the early hours of the eleventh of November (or 11/9 as I'd refer to it as), the 2016 election was called in favor of

Donald Trump. I was three sheets to the wind, having spent the night steadily increasing my alcohol intake as results trickled in. The early part of the night involved copious amounts of talking off the ledge as progressive men and just about every woman I know was messaging me, demanding I calm their fears, given how certain I was of a Clinton victory.

Our party was to be held four days later.

Your party is going to be a disaster. Every one of your friends voted for Hillary. Everyone in your family voted for Hillary except Dad, who wrote YOU in. Half of your in-laws voted for Hillary. Nobody there is going to be happy. You're going to be a disaster.

The voice was right. I would be.

Early that morning, I didn't think Jay was moving fast enough to help get our home in order for the half-dozen friends who would stay there that night. Feeling myself tense up, it was time for Xanax #1.

In the middle of making round trips down the block to bring our beer and decorations to the Club House, one of Jay's relatives arrived four hours before the party. I hadn't even showered. I learned they rearranged who would stay at our house—Xanax #2.

I made a slideshow of Jay and me over the past forty years; its default picture was one of us taken on St. Patrick's Day in New York earlier that year. It was a selfie in which we both had our middle fingers extended, with the placard of the building behind us clearly visible: Trump Tower.

"Eddie, can you change that picture?" my mother-in-law asked.

Holy shit, I thought to myself. I can't handle this level of people-pleasing right now. I began the slideshow to get the pictures moving. The thing would end 20 minutes earlier since it had been timed out to play precisely twice over the four hours, but that no longer mattered to me. I had pictures and music set for specific periods to make the party as seamless as possible. But control was already slipping away.

I washed Xanax #2.5 down with Beer #4. The Ed Show was about to begin.

My last accurate recollection of the party was making a speech, thanking everyone for coming before apologizing for the obvious pall cast over the party by the tragic events of Election Day. From what I've been told, my mother and my father-in-law made beautiful toasts to us.

I was a colossal mess. And it was in front of everyone, including Dad, a shut-in who had just passed the five-year sober mark in August. Dr. Alex Urbiel was there too, my old college professor with whom I kept in just enough touch via the vast email decade of the Aughts before connecting on Facebook. All my friends—Mark, Doc, Ben, Walter, Hayes, Duce and their wives. Our aunts and uncles.

I fell on the stage, attempting to swap out speakers. I bumped into the bar frequently. Smoking a cigarette—my first in years as I transitioned to vaping in 2013—made me dizzy enough to fall into a bush and need help from my cousin to get out. Worst of all, I completely abandoned Jay to do all the hosting duties solo. I was useless on the cleanup. Someone had to drive me back to the house while everyone else walked.

This is Forty?

XXII

I made an immediate appointment with my physician to discuss alternatives to Xanax. I was feeling like I couldn't handle basic tasks without it, and my display at our fortieth was concrete evidence that I was developing a problem. Not once did I think that alcohol fueled that—quite the opposite. Alcohol was my constitutional right (look it up, the 21st Amendment!) Xanax imperiled that right and needed to be adjusted.

The doctor prescribed 10MG of Lexapro to take daily. I briefly saw a therapist to talk about "anger." For a near six-month stretch, I felt that my life was on track. Trump continued to be a ratings bonanza for *Reverb*. We had made some home renovations and booked another summer trip to Ireland. Maybe I was settling into middle age, and this was what it was like for normal people.

Wednesday morning, the 20th of June, 2018, was another day in the middle of another week in the middle of another month in the middle of another year. And it began as innocuous as most of them do. Got out of bed. Brewed a cup of coffee. Let the puppy out. Went to the bathroom, went through my morning reading routine: fantasy baseball score, MLB Standings, *Politico*, *New York Times*... and boom. Right there at the top of my screen:

> **American Cardinal Accused of Sexually Abusing Minor Is Removed From Ministry**
>
> *Cardinal Theodore E. McCarrick, the former archbishop of Washington and a prominent Roman Catholic voice in international and public policy, has been removed from ministry after an investigation found credible allegations that he sexually abused a teenager 47 years ago while serving as a priest in New York....*

Woe. Cardinal McCarrick. That Cardinal McCarrick. The one that I met multiple times as an altar boy. We were taught how to reverently address and approach this same guy. The guy in the funny yarmulke who—just by serving mass for him—turned me into a celebrity for a Sunday family dinner. He was a fucking molester, too.

I woke Jay up to tell her the news. I don't recall her reaction, but it wasn't one of great shock or disbelief. By this point, finding out that a member of the Catholic clergy was accused of sexually abusing minors or subordinates was about as shocking as finding out a senator was beholden to a lobbyist.

I made some wiseass remark on Facebook about having met him as a child and not being the least bit surprised. But in reality, it was less surprising than jolting. It all started coming back to me. It all came together. At that moment, I could smell the stale but sterile interior of the rectory. The smell was omnipresent throughout the building, regardless of the room. The lobby where Mrs. Forster worked. The pastor's office. The dining room where we had a post-mass coffee reception for the Archbishop. Father Gerry's bedroom—embedded in my memory with no context or revelation.

What was happening?

I called my mother to tell her the same—she met the news with a loud "You have GOT to be kidding me", before talking herself into the same reaction as Jay—a realization that there may be shock, but no genuine surprise.

•••

I moved on—or so I thought — and didn't really pay it much heed for the next few days. But that Sunday, the 23rd, was a game-changer.

Jay was staffing an event on the waterfront in Brooklyn. She had to be there at 6 AM, and I offered to drive her there. Gave me the chance to publish my Sunday *Reverb* work nice and early. An almost 3-hour round trip gave way to a hearty breakfast and an even heartier nap. I woke back up and figured it was a beautiful, sunny Sunday. What better way to enjoy it than to sit in a 95% empty, dark bar?

I've drunk "alone" at *Uncorked* plenty of times over the past few years. But it was almost always in the Happy Hour range or when there was an important ballgame on. When I knew there would be people there to converse with.

Not this Sunday.

Sunday summers at *Uncorked* were deader than disco. Didn't even have the regular staff. Something drew me there that day. I'm usually more inclined to have a few beers and listen to the Yankees game, or the Grateful Dead, on my deck or in my hammock. But not today.

I ordered up the first of many double IPAs and started reading the Sunday opinions in various publications. And then came the headline that turned my world upside down.

#MeToo Comes for the Archbishop by Ross Douthat. Top of the list in the *New York Times* "Sunday Review."

I was familiar with Mr. Douthat. He was often the token conservative thrown to the wolves on "Real Time with Bill Maher." And while I rarely—if ever–agreed with a thing he said, he presented himself with dignity and expressed compassion for humanity. Hey, that might sound like basic human decency, but in the Trump era, a very low bar exists for what makes up conservative decency.

Douthat dropped a bombshell in the first paragraph of his brilliant editorial about Theodore McCarrick—that he knew early in this millennium that there were rumors of McCarrick's indecent behavior. Douthat wrote:

> *"It was the early 2000s. I was attending some earnest panel on religion, and I was accosted by a type who haunts such events — gaunt, intense, with a litany of esoteric grievances. He was a traditionalist Catholic, a figure from the church's fringes, and he had a lot to say, as I tried to disentangle from him, about corruption in the Catholic clergy. The scandals in Boston had broken, so some of what he said was familiar, but he kept going, into a rant about Cardinal McCarrick: Did you know he makes seminarians sleep with him? Invites them to his beach house, gets in bed with them ..."*

And Mr. Douthat followed it all up with the sentence that jarred me into action:

> *"Now the question is whether the at-long-last coverage of McCarrick's sins will shake similar stories loose,"*

A torrent of memories flashed through my mind as if nothing in the last thirty years was as it seemed. I wasn't just some altar boy who was groped incidentally by a lone wolf. I was yet another pawn—one of god only knows how many throughout the 1700-year history of the Church—in their wicked, manipulative racket of giving aid, comfort, and protection to deviants who practice the most despicable and unmentionable crimes against the most precious and vulnerable people on earth: children.

It was almost an out-of-body experience. Yes, I had been aware for a few days now that McCarrick was accused of sexually abusing seminarians. But this connection? This spurred on a range of emotions I didn't think I could hold. That it was so well known within the Catholic hierarchy that an opinion columnist was aware of these rumors as far back as the "Spotlight" days. It flipped everything on its head. The Micro was now Macro and vice versa. I simultaneously felt like I was at ground zero of the sex abuse crisis while looking at it from 35,000 feet above. What the hell was happening?

•••

As I'm prone to do, my first instinct was to log on to Facebook and just drop the rant to end all rants. And as I ordered yet another heavy beer, I let my brain transmit to my fingertips with no regard for who may read it:

> *As I said a few days ago, Archbishop McCarrick was the grand Poobah when I was growing up in a Catholic parish. He is not the reason I am no longer a believer. But he IS the reason I find the Catholic Church to be less desirable than the Taliban, the Trump Organization, Al Qaeda and the Dallas Cowboys combined.*
>
> *"Uncle Ted" McCarrick took a priest accused of inappropriate behavior towards young boys and moved him to our parish. At the time that I was enrolled in the parish elementary school. And a member and eventual "president" of the altar boys.*
>
> *The Archdiocese Of Newark would eventually pay millions of dollars in settlements over the actions of that priest at not only our parish, but the other ones where he was deliberately placed, without any reporting to law enforcement.*
>
> *Part of that settlement involved an acknowledgment of the role he played in the death of a child in our parish.*
>
> *I didn't escape unscathed, but I know that so many kids were more damaged than I could imagine that I actually considered myself lucky. How sick is that?*
>
> *For a while, the closest people in my life had to put up with the ramifications of the simple fact that I was an altar boy at St. Francis of Assisi R.C. Church from 1986 to 1991. I'm better now than I have been*

> *in 25 years, but growing up a North Jersey Catholic is the gift that keeps on giving, because these stories keep coming out. And each time it gets a little easier to put the pieces together.*
>
> *The ghoul who placed the creep in my life was a creep himself. The demon who installed this pervert into a position of such esteem that he swam in my fucking family pool was himself a degenerative pervert beyond comprehension. Was the priest who infected our lovely little town a deviant because McCarrick made him so? I'll never know.*
>
> *What I know is that there is absolutely nothing in this world that will lead me back to the Catholic Church.*
>
> *I'm glad "Uncle Ted" is alive to get his comeuppance. I'm even happier that he'll be dead soon.*

To be clear, at the time that I wrote this, I had no evidence whatsoever that McCarrick was directly involved in Sudol's placement in St. Francis. The blind rage just instantly made that connection. Or perhaps I was simply searching for a logical explanation.

It temporarily felt like a load was lifted off my chest. Temporarily. Two of my closest friends from high school wrote of their love and support for the post. A bunch of strangers offered their sympathy and went on in various tangents about why they no longer go to church. But then a red circle with a white "1" in the middle showed up on my Messenger app.

•••

Marianne Dwyer was part of another large Irish-Catholic Ridgefield Park clan. I didn't quite know her personally, aside from knowing *who* she was. Her youngest son was a few years older than me. I believe we were in high school at the same time.

But through the magic of Facebook, we became friends. Like-minded people smell their own on social media. Marianne was unabashedly liberal, compassionate, and kind—just like me—maybe minus the kindness. Definitely minus the kindness. But I was happy to get to know her.

And while we had a lot in common—RP, Irish heritage, liberal politics, love of writing, and then some, it wasn't until I posted about McCarrick that I realized just how kindred our spirits were. That message icon that popped up while I was self-medicating at *Uncorked* was from Marianne. And what she told me comforted me in a sick and twisted way, as if it was the first time I truly—in the deepest recesses of my mind—felt that I wasn't crazy.

She messaged me to tell me she tried to vocalize to others in the church back in the late 80s, but nobody took her seriously. She said she had to distance herself from the only town and only parish she had ever known. She would not expose her children to what was happening in plain sight. She likened St. Francis to a cult.

Like a cult. So simple, yet so accurate. Gerry Sudol was a cult leader during his time at St. Francis. Especially while Fr. Francis was senile and Fr. Joe was not yet the pastor. He said jump, and the parish asked, "How high?" And Marianne couldn't have been more spot on when she called the situation "toxic." Looking back, I can't imagine how impotent the other priests—and the dozens of church elders, volunteers, nuns, teachers and other lay employees — must have felt.

I immediately thought of Mrs. Kennedy and her sudden resignation from running the altar boys. At 13, I couldn't understand why there was a power struggle between Sudol and herself. Weren't they all on the same team? God's team? But having long grown out of that naivety, it all made perfect sense.

She would not win a power struggle with a cult leader. He got every single goddamn thing he ever wanted from the parish. Adoration. Respect. The Youth Group. Unfettered access to the school day. Free labor. Running the altar boys was the crowning achievement of his takeover.

Marianne and I continued to chat about our remembrances of St. Francis at the dawn of the nineties and well into that decade. We talked about the tragedy of Willie's passing. She said, "It was a strange scene at Willie's funeral with everyone hugging Fr. Gerry," which almost made me throw up all over the bar at *Uncorked*.

I couldn't help but think of the ostracization we took part in with the non-altar boys in St. Francis. Or how even the public school students of our generation fought for his attention for the sacraments and rituals. He had the entire parish eating right out of his hands. How did I not explore the entire scope of his behavior at St. Francis until the McCarrick story jolted me?

I thought about the adults in the community back then. Most of them were roughly the age that I was in 2018. It's easy to say, "times are different". And it's true to an extent. But still. We were talking 1989, not 1589. Beyond that, our parents grew up post-Vatican II, when the church was allegedly trying to become less intimidating and more open. They lived through the sexual revolution, Woodstock, the Civil Rights struggle, Vietnam, and Watergate. They were supposed to have some healthy skepticism of authority.

However, Marianne hit the nail on the head when she said, "*They decided to silence those who had the integrity to challenge the dysfunction that's going on and cover it all up.*"

It would not take one parent. Or two. Or ten.

They were going up against the most powerful organization in the world. The planet's longest-running active government. What could they have done? I don't know.

And I still don't.

But did anyone else do anything?

XXIII

For a hot minute, I felt a little relieved. I got something off my chest, even if I was intentionally vague about my experience under McCarrick's Archdiocese of Newark. I don't know if people took what I had to say - *"didn't escape unscathed"* - to mean I was raped, molested, or simply witnessed bad things. And frankly, I didn't care. 2018, the #MeToo movement dominated the news cycle to that point.

At first, female celebrities recounted the harassment and sexual assault that they endured from creeps like Harvey Weinstein or Louis CK or Matt Lauer. Then every woman—Jay included—took to Facebook and Twitter to say "#MeToo" to show that they endured unwanted sexual advances in their lives as well. And like the stories coming out of Hollywood, women I knew lived through everything from inappropriate comments in the workplace to Class A Sexual Assault.

I sensed that, as Ross Douthat noted in his Op-Ed, #MeToo was eventually creeping into the sanctuaries of the American Catholic Church. What I posted that day after more than a few beers was intended to give a familiar face to the friends and readers I interact with daily. And maybe explain the overt hostility I've shown toward the church in my writings and rantings. I felt it was done.

And unfortunately, I *STILL* didn't think what I lived through was "bad enough." Even though I openly admitted it was sick that I felt "lucky," a big part of me did. I wasn't raped. I wasn't dead. Thousands of boys were. Psychologically, I was the guy who returned from war without his leg—not the one who returned in a body bag—and since the turn of the century, I continued to frame my entire existence through that prism.

For now, though, I was content to believe that I had said my peace, and that would be enough to finally put it all behind me: the anger, the sadness, the anxiety—all of it. Besides, Jay and I had much bigger things to think about. We were once again traveling to Europe in July.

This time, we would make stops in Dublin and Edinburgh and tacked Paris on for good measure. She had always wanted to see the city of lights for the same reasons everybody else does—the art, the architecture, the food, the wine, the culture. Me? I've wanted to visit Jim Morrison's grave since I was in eighth grade when The Doors transcended my understanding of—and relationship with—music. I still remember Sister Dianne telling me "Edward, Jim Morrison is NOT a positive role model" after I built a paper Mache statuette of the Lizard King in art class.

This time in Ireland, I finally got to knock an item off my bucket list: attending an Irish wedding.

I've heard the stories my whole life. They last all weekend long. You're constantly eating and drinking—and sometimes you sleep. I didn't think it could ever meet the expectations in my mind, but it ended up exceeding them.

Of course, there's a significant component to an Irish wedding that one must survive before spending the next 48 hours feasting on Guinness, potatoes, and every meat imaginable.

The church.

I'm well aware of my less-than-stellar track record for my behavior at weddings that take place in Catholic Churches. On top of that, I suffer a little more anxiety than usual overseas. From the moment I arrive at the airport until I pick my baggage up back in the States, I feel like I have no control. If something terrible were to happen, just the thought of the arduous task of getting back home is enough to make the back of my neck sweat and my heart race. Of course, being afraid of horrible things occurring while I have no control can easily be traced back to you-know-who, but I'd be lying if I said I was fully aware of that thought train throughout our cross-Atlantic jaunts. I just never stepped on cobblestones without at least one Xanax in my pocket.

I woke up that July morning in a Dublin hotel room thinking about how I couldn't afford to be a train wreck, how I couldn't do that to Jay in front of my mother's Irish family. These weren't people who watched me grow up drinking and built up a tolerance/expectation for how I could get.

Don't get me wrong; I shared many drinks with them in the States and the Emerald Isle. They saw me get sloppy. They saw me sing karaoke. They saw me go on a rant about Ronald Reagan or George W Bush or the Iraq War or the Vatican. But they've never seen me devolve into a total mess like most of the people I'm close with in America.

...

A taxi dropped us off at Aunt Rosie and Uncle Peter's house after we checked out of our hotel. They invited us to stay there the two nights before, but we've both been through enough wedding preparation mornings to know the drill. Especially at the home base of the bride, as their home was for my cousin.

The minute we crossed their threshold, we were home.

Uncle Peter immediately offered me a glass of Jameson. It might have been a bad idea, given my anxieties and knowing exactly where our next stop would be, but it felt right. And it *was* right.

And then I found out about our transportation method.

"You're riding with another man of God," Aunt Rosie told us jokingly, a reference to my online ordination years ago, that all family members still get a kick out of. "Your ma's cousin, Gerard."

Wait a minute. I'm taking an hour-long ride in a foreign country with "Father Gerry." What the actual fuck? I knew for a while that there was a priest in my Irish family. But really, I just assumed that was the case with every family in Ireland. I grew up with Father Horrigan at every family party. The concept of having the "family priest" wasn't foreign to me, even given how close Sudol got to us. Father Doyle, too. Still, "Father Gerry," my mother's cousin. The glass or two of Jameson was now playing with me. Father Fucking Gerry. You can't be serious.

Don't be a disaster.

Given my expectations, the church itself was underwhelming. I had seen a few old churches in Dublin proper, including where my grandfather was baptized. They were gorgeous, ornate, and almost but not quite gothic. The irony was never lost on me that these churches featured polished bronze, pure gold, and exceptional artwork, and many of them dated from a time when the few Irish who could scrounge up a few pounds were setting sail west to America to escape the unbearable poverty. But hey, isn't that religion everywhere?

Still, I was in an Irish church. Opinions and anxieties aside, I could—and did — appreciate the beauty of it all. I was in an establishment where other family members were married and baptized. And, at times, they had their shrouded caskets blessed. For better or for worse, my tribe had a connection to this structure. Jay and I were fortunate to be here for one of the most beautiful moments in our extended family's history. I would fight through any pre-existing feelings and cherish this wonderful event.

And I got through the ceremony without devolving or spiraling. It was a beautiful ceremony. Two wonderful families came together. It was everything true love was supposed to be. And I survived it.

And then, because, you know—blood pressure medication — I knew I had to take a piss before embarking on an hour-long car ride. So I asked a cousin if they knew where the men's room might be. "Sure," my cousin Richie—a big fella like myself said. "Just walk behind the altar; you'll see a doorway. Make a right."

It seemed simple enough. Walking through an altar for the first time in a while felt a little weird. But then I saw a sign, typed and taped to the wall next to the altar entrance (or exit):

"Nobody Under The Age of 18 is Permitted Beyond This Point Unless Accompanied by a Parent."

Wow!

They weren't even letting altar boys into the sacristy.

There it was—the reminder.

Ireland won't trust priests to even be alone with children. Ireland. Western Europe's bastion of Catholicism. The prominent homeland of many American Catholics. While American bishops argued over minor policy "reforms," this parish in Dublin County wouldn't even give a priest the benefit of the doubt.

It was encouraging, but unsettling. This shit was global. The worldwide opinion of the Roman Catholic Church felt it was at an all-time low. I should have taken some solace in that. Yet I didn't. I still didn't believe that the extent of this racket of abuse was anything close to revealed or publicized. Or dealt with.

But for now, an Irish prohibition on children being in the company of priests without a third party felt like a step in the right direction—well-deserved shame for a shameful organization.

However, it was time to spend an hour plus on the Irish motorway with new Father Gerry.

From witnessing the ceremony he just performed, I knew he had a sense of humor. I understand he came across as an open and genuine guy. And I know my family has a great bullshit detector, and he wouldn't be within a hundred miles of us if there were something amiss.

I quickly dismissed all those fears and concerns once we started our drive. After a minor talk about where we live, Gerry said, "I have to be honest. I'm not a big fan of your president. Not sure what you think of him, but from the news we get here…"

Say no more.

The following 75 minutes flew by as we traded jokes and anecdotes and shared a mutual disgust for the 45th President of the United States. We marveled at the American people's sheer ignorance of the significance of climate change and any attempt to offset it. We were kindred spirits.

And I was completely disarmed.

Getting that bit off my chest in that McCarrick post could have beneficial consequences. Maybe my shit was coming together. I felt more secure after spending a morning in an Irish Catholic Church than most days in my skin, regardless of where I was.

No internal voices were shaming me for my behavior, lot in life, accomplishments, or lack thereof. I drank like a fish for the rest of that wedding weekend—yes, it really was a weekend — and felt no remorse for humiliating behavior at all. I was genuinely relaxing with loved ones and didn't have a care in the world. It was the first sense of liberation I've ever had without the use of psychedelic mushrooms.

•••

Paris has topped her dream destinations for as long as I've known Jay. Within hours of our arrival, we were touring the banks of the Seine and marveling at the history of one of the most critical stretches of geography in Western civilization. Not long into our walk was the bridge to the Cathedral of Notre Dame.

"We should go now," she said. "We can cross it off the sightseeing list, and it's right here. The lines don't even look too long."

Ugh. A church.

But I could do this. No preparation. I can handle this. We spent very good money on this vacation, money that, frankly, any financial planner would have said STASH AWAY FOR RETIREMENT. So, it was a sunk cost. And it was—to the best of our knowledge—free.

Seeing the statuary tributes to Western civilization outside the cathedral was a once-in-a-lifetime marvel. I mean, you will not wander the streets of Harrisburg, Pennsylvania, see a bronze statue of Charlemagne on a horse, or read up on the Holy Roman Empire. No. This was the big-time baby. Religious connotations be damned!

I was going in.

The scene outside waiting to enter the cathedral reminded me of my first trip to the Statue of Liberty. You had school groups from all parts of the globe. Various middle-aged tourists. Locals who seemed like they did this annually. Overzealous amateur photographers. Oh, and the nuns. They were like flocks of geese. Uniformed. Following a leader. Walking single file. Even their uniforms portended to goslings following Mother Goose. There were nuns in every direction. Blue nuns. Gray nuns. Black nuns. White nuns. Light blue nuns. Holy shit, there were a lot of nuns.

The crowd was overstimulating, but not to where it distracted from the breathtaking detail of the architecture of this massive house of worship. Above the entrance, the most noticeable feature near eye level was a series of thirteen statuettes carved into the exterior wall. We both reached back into our religious upbringing and other related studies to guess what they represented. We gave it a good ninety seconds before deciding to Google it. I mean, hey, we're spending $10 a day on an international data plan, so we might as well take advantage of it. Turns out they represented the thirteen tribes of Israel.

We walked into the Cathedral and were both instantly overwhelmed. Without even thinking about the dark secrets of the Roman Catholic Church and the many sins committed while spreading their power across Western Europe, we stood there in awe. It's hard to comprehend at the moment just precisely where you're standing and what you're looking at. You can think about historical perspective beforehand and in the years after, but while you're surrounded by such magnificence, well, it would take a much stronger skeptic than me to dismiss the artificial beauty before me.

The entire interior of Notre Dame was like Catholicpalooza. There were multiple altars within the building; at one of them, an actual mass was being said. In enclaves along both sides were statues and other religious relics that people were praying in front of. The stained-glass windows were an attraction in and of themselves, particularly the focal circular window that would appear across Facebook a few years later when the Cathedral suffered an intense fire.

But beauty gave quick way to the mutual cynicism that's been a hallmark of our marriage. Jay nudged me on the elbow and said, "My god, look at the confessional sign!"

It appeared that you could get all seven sacraments, save for maybe last rites and holy orders—MAYBE—at Notre Dame. But they set up a dedicated section with a small army of priests ready to hear confession. Now, despite my upbringing, I saw nothing special about having your sins forgiven at one of the quintessential consecrated locations in all of Catholicism. I mean, your sins are forgiven whether you confess to a priest behind a screen in Guadalajara, Mexico, or if you're sitting on the Pope's lap while he takes his morning crap. Confess. Do prescribed penance. Soul wiped clean. Seemed pretty simple. But the crowds around the confession lines were the most concentrated of any feature.

But the sign Jay pointed to. My jaw dropped.

The typed words were in French—which neither of us read—but there were two columns: one with various flags and the other with a set of numbers. With our middle-aged eyes, we were positive they were exchange rates, as you see throughout any major city at home or abroad.

"They're charging for confession!" I said out loud.

"I guess it's really not that surprising," she replied.

I agreed. We walked closer. They weren't charging for confession. The left column was the language spoken by the attending priests, and the right column was their booths and time frames they'd be hearing about the sins of worldwide travelers. No currency exchanged at all.

Well, outside the many options for dumping your hard-earned money into a box.

I didn't drop a Euro on my way out; I gave the Church enough of my life. But I noted I was now two for two in healthily and safely spending time in churches since I spoke out about McCarrick.

•••

We had ample time to soak in Paris and her baguettes, wine, weird silver-painted human-robot street performers, the Eiffel Tower, etc. But one more metaphysical experience awaited: Jim Morrison's grave.

Jay has long since given up on trying to tone down my "histrionics" when I find myself in places I consider consequential or, dare I say, divine. (She's lucky she wasn't with me on my first three trips to Fenway Park). But for almost as long as she's known me, she's known that a particular plot of earth inside Paris' largest graveyard, Père Lachaise Cemetery, has consistently ranked among my dream visits — possibly more than any other coordinates on the planet.

I'm not ignorant of how pathetic that may sound to some people. Jim Morrison was not Elvis Presley, John Lennon, Frank Sinatra, or Louis Armstrong. The Doors didn't dramatically shift the paradigm of music. And for an American craving to see the resting place of an alcoholic millionaire who drank himself to death after reaching his creative apex at an age where I wasn't even thinking about buying a house, and then dropping dead before contemplating turning thirty—while Normandy was a half-day trip away—could be classified as disingenuous or a grossly miscalculated priorities for most people.

But I'm not like most people.

Père Lachaise was the only thing set in concrete for our second of four days in Paris. Per the usual GPS maps, it wasn't an unreasonable walk, maybe two miles from our hotel. But it was Hades hot and New Orleans humid. We were sore as hell from walking about six miles the day before. There was zero objection to an Uber. And it's a good thing we did because while I know nothing about the neighborhoods we drove past, I know from experience that they would have induced enough panic in me to swallow a double dose of Xanax. She would have crossed her fear threshold, where she automatically turns around about 15 blocks from the cemetery. (Hey, never dismiss the built-in phobia you have of graffiti when you grew up with New York City local news in the 1980s!)

The taxi dropped us off in a small cul-de-sac at the cemetery gate, and I could sense Jay was already getting fed up with my amazement. After about 10 minutes, we walked uphill around a bend on the cobblestone road and noticed a few people standing at the curb, keeping a respectful distance of 3 or so yards from a grave on the right. We were there.

I was there. It was time to soak it in. It was time to understand the gravity of where I was and what earthly relic was mere feet from where I stood. While it sounds ridiculous retrospectively, I'm fully cognizant of that, but I went into a trance. I instantly remembered everything. The Doors literally opened my "doors of perception" when I saw Oliver Stone's film. Sister Diane scolding me for the Morrison art project. The first time I smoked pot, listening to "The Crystal Ship." Dancing with who would eventually be my mother-in-law to "Touch Me" at her 40th birthday party. Picking Morrison as my American poet for an Honors

English III term paper, and my former Naval-Officer-during-the-Cuban-Missile-Crisis told me he was curious, but it better not be a love letter to him as he gave final approval. Unrolling and pinning up my "An American Poet" poster in my dorm room before I unpacked anything else. Buying their entire live catalog off eBay in the mid-aughts when people were unloading their CD collections after adding them to their iTunes library, and putting "Love Street" on our wedding favor-mixed disc.

But most of all, I reflected on how The Doors changed the direction of my identity, how the words of a man who died five years before I was born reached me at a point in my life where I needed reaching, perhaps more than any other moment in my forty-one years. I certainly didn't know it then, but I needed saving. I was walking a path of subservience, and this overtly dramatized version of events that Hollywood spit out to make a quick buck became my salvation.

I thought about all of this. I thought about the sheer physics of the bones below me, the organic material sharing this soil, and I realized that no matter how much I decried spirituality, religion, and especially the belief in the afterlife, something was happening at this site. There was some force more potent than me, something I couldn't understand, speaking to me. Maybe the hippies were right, after all.

But probably not.

Jay snapped my trance and said, "Ok, this is enough." Turns out I was there for fifteen minutes.

And as the universe would have it, this was "The End" of my life as I knew it.

XXIV

On Tuesday, August 13, 2018, I followed my usual routine of sipping coffee while the world awakened. It was my favorite time of year to have coffee on the deck before work; it aligned right around sunrise. Perusing the morning headlines was now referred to in common parlance as "doom scrolling," and this relatively cool morning was no different.

Facebook was first; nothing new there, just partisan bickering or reinforcement of preconceived beliefs. Then I opened the "New York Times," and one headline set a series of events in motion that would forever change my life, my health, my career, my sanity, my marriage, and above all else, my identity.

Pennsylvania Grand Jury Says Church Had a 'Playbook for Concealing the Truth'

This looked juicy, I thought as I read. How detailed was this playbook, and how widespread was it in the Commonwealth of Pennsylvania? The Times quoted directly from the Grand Jury report, which had identified over a thousand cases of clergy abuse over seventy years:

> "First, make sure to use euphemisms rather than real words to describe the sexual assaults in diocese documents. Never say 'rape'; say 'inappropriate contact' or 'boundary issues.'
>
> Second, don't conduct genuine investigations with properly trained personnel. Instead, assign fellow clergy members to ask inadequate questions and then make credibility determinations about the colleagues with whom they live and work."

This was reading like the summary of the settlement that the Archdiocese paid out to Willie Foster's family, where Father Gerry was one of the accused priests. There was no complex language in the settlement. There was no reference to "molestation" or even "abuse". The closest they came was the same sort of plausible deniability legalese.

The report continued:

> "Third, for an appearance of integrity, send priests for 'evaluation' at church-run psychiatric treatment centers. Allow these experts to 'diagnose' whether the priest was a pedophile, based largely on the priest's 'self-reports,' and regardless of whether the priest had actually engaged in sexual contact with a child.
>
> Fourth, when a priest does have to be removed, don't say why. Tell his parishioners that he is on 'sick leave' or suffering from 'nervous exhaustion.' Or say nothing at all."

Holy. Fucking. Shit!

That was, line for line, what happened with Sudol's removal back in 1994 when he abruptly left St. Francis. He was heading to a particular "hospital for priests," where doctors or church officials allegedly diagnosed him with "Nervous Exhaustion."

My head spun. I was having the physical reactions of a panic attack without the impending sense of doom. My entire life seemed to illuminate before my eyes. I had always known that the Roman Catholic Church shuffled problematic and abusive priests from parish to parish, but to see their "playbook" in the cold black and white of the New York Fucking Times brought it all back home.

My abuse did not happen in a vacuum at the hands of Father Gerry Sudol. Sudol abused me because the Catholic Church willfully fostered a safe environment for pedophiles to thrive.

•••

I stewed that entire morning commute, of which I was undoubtedly later than usual to work. I thought about the last part of the so-called playbook that the Grand Jury published and how it fit the Sudol experience to the letter:

> *Fifth, even if a priest is raping children, keep providing him housing and living expenses, although he may be using these resources to facilitate more sexual assaults.*
>
> *Sixth, if a predator's conduct becomes known to the community, don't remove him from the priesthood to ensure that no more children will be victimized. Instead, transfer him to a new location where no one will know he is a child abuser.*
>
> *Finally and above all, don't tell the police. Child sexual abuse, even short of actual penetration, is and has for all relevant times, been a crime. But don't treat it that way; handle it like a personnel matter, "in-house."*

I had to speak up. I had to say something. But how? There was no point in another cryptic McCarrick-like Facebook post. I had a growing platform with a regular Sunday column on *Reverb*. I would ask my editors if I could tell "my story."

Jay traveled that week; she called to check in while I was en route to work. I took the call off the car's Bluetooth and couldn't keep my thoughts straight. I fumbled, trying to tell her about the Grand Jury report. My mouth couldn't speak as fast as my brain was processing. I could finally say something like, "It was all one big conspiracy; I'm telling my fucking story."

I didn't stop to think about how it would impact her, to consider the potential microscope that I was going to be under. Nor did I consider how she would feel having me open myself up in the most vulnerable ways. All I knew was that I was putting pen to paper and saying, "Me Too."

The moment I logged into my workstation, I logged into the *Reverb* newsroom and shot a message to James Reader, my managing editor, and Ed Lynn—editor-in-chief:

> "Hey, fellas, sorry I've been MIA, but I owe you an explanation. The Grand Jury report about the Catholic Church came out (this morning). This is tough to say publicly, but I plan to: I'm a victim...But out of good comes bad. And I decided it was time to tell my story. I was wondering, with your permission, if I could share that story on RP this Sunday."

I told them I decided on a format—I would NOT use any real names; I wouldn't even use the name of the church. *Reverb* was a minor operation, and I wanted to assuage any worries about blowback. Honestly, my assumption was that the Church had an army of lawyers ready to pounce on anyone who dared speak out.

The editors were respectful in their questioning if I was sure I wanted to choose this platform. I couldn't think of any other way. I wanted more than another Facebook post and wouldn't "shop it around" to more prominent, widely-known publications. I knew myself: if I deviated from this plan I had just concocted about three hours earlier, I would never follow through.

James had the fire of a thousand suns in advocating to make this the biggest story in *Reverb's* history and sticking it to the powers that be in the Catholic Church. A warrior monk of the left, he had an innate knowledge of viral marketing and engagement building and getting the proper attention. Ed, who confessed he was a former altar boy, was more reserved and concerned that I could handle the coming storm.

I didn't think there would be a storm. I didn't know this story would resonate beyond Ridgefield Park folks, and even then, I didn't expect it to be more than a confirmation of what they already knew. They had to know, right?

Before I even got final approval, I typed furiously.

•••

Saturday, August 18th, would be a trial in compartmentalization, and I would fail miserably. The New York Yankees were celebrating the 25th Anniversary of their record-breaking 1998 World Series Championship Team. I watched every game of that World Series, save for one (a family wedding, where we needed to watch it in the facility manager's office), with my boys up in Ramapo way back when. That was a special team, and there were some memorable times.

None of us knew how a quarter century had flown by so rapidly. The players honored on that field were gray, balding, or both. And so were Walter, Duce, Sean, and myself when we purchased tickets and loaded into Walter's Jeep to pay our respects to the Boys of Autumn.

We arrived early enough to throw down beers on the top level of the Macombs Damn Parking Garage next to the colossal "New" Yankee Stadium, in its ninth season by now. This wasn't the Stadium of our youth. Nor was it the parking lot scene. Architects replicated the sights, the sounds enhanced, but you could never replace the smell. That was seventy-five years of spilled beer, missed toilets, every public iteration of smoking devices, and cooking oil. There wasn't enough hedge fund money in New York to transplant the Original Yankee Stadium scent scape across the street.

We were precisely everything Bruce Springsteen sang about in his 1984 epic "Glory Days" as we spent this morning in 2018 waxing nostalgic for all that was good in the late 1990s. All the while, the pit in my stomach was growing. Twenty-four hours from now, I had no idea what my life would look like; it was more unmoored than I had felt in some time.

I didn't over-indulge in the parking lot the way I usually do. Don't get me wrong, I had already drank enough that I wouldn't blow a legal .08 nine innings later, but I wasn't the walking, unsteady disaster I have been at Yankee outings in the past. Despite my relative temperance, I needed to find a bathroom as soon as we entered the ballpark.

Not to pee.

I had to throw up.

Nerves had never brought me to the point of vomit before in my life. And in the past, when I felt nerves getting the better of me, two or three sips of beer would soothe them. I had about a hundred times that this morning, and it did nothing.

After throwing up in an accessible stall of a Main Level bathroom, I washed my hands and face to the best of my ability to hide the flushness and glassy eyes that often accompany a heaving session before meeting the boys at the beer line.

They were easy to spot, as the four of us were wearing identical navy-blue "Thunder from Down Under" T-shirts in honor of '98 Yanks lefty reliever Graeme Lloyd—an unheralded but vital member of the squad whom we developed a cult following of in our Glory Days.

I couldn't bring myself to order a beer coming off that tumultuous evacuation of my stomach, so I requested a Vodka Tonic. It was going to be an expensive afternoon in the Bronx.

Sean and I left the game about an inning before Walter and Duce, who stayed behind to souvenir shop for their children. I had been quietly hoping for a chance to talk to him in private all morning, but likewise, I had the self-awareness not to attempt such a conversation during the game.

Unfortunately, $150 worth of stadium vodka had blunted the ability to have a deeper conversation beyond "I'm publishing my story about Father Gerry" tomorrow.

He wished me well, told me he always had my back and was proud of me. Then we talked about the Giants and the upcoming seson as we finished the final few beers floating around in the cooler back at the Jeep.

When the other two fellas returned, we agreed we don't get to hang out as often as we'd like, so the day has to continue. Our destination would be "Finks"—a barbecue joint that stood on the site where "Ireland's 32," host of my 21st birthday and the Y2K Scam Party, once did.

The excitement of an extended day with friends at one of my favorite establishments instantly overcame the anxiety and tension, causing my upset stomach to be so beer-resistant. About five minutes south of the George Washington Bridge over the Hudson River back to Jersey, I realized I should call Jay and let her know my plans.

"Fuck" I screamed from Walter's backseat.

I left my phone in the Bronx.

He offered to turn around, but I knew it was likely a lost cause. I told him to keep heading to Jersey and see if we could locate it on Sean's "Find My iPhone" app. It was already unfindable. I borrowed Sean's phone to do the responsible thing and call Jay, dreading the scolding I would get because of my irresponsibility with a thousand-dollar product.

She couldn't care less about the phone. She thanked me for letting her know and let me know what I should bring home from Fink's for dinner.

That was easier than it should have been. This is how low her expectations are, the inner dialogue said. *Just wait till the rest of the world laughs at you tomorrow.*

Fink's and friends are a quick way to silence the demons, though, and that began with Duce's suggestion that we start with a round of Jameson shots. The shot sent me directly to the stall, the same stall I threw up in for the first time this century. This time, I can't say alcohol didn't play a role in my body rejecting its contents. But I was a seasoned drinker by now. One shot of Jamo, an hour after my last drink, shouldn't send me running for the can.

I told the boys I couldn't hide it anymore and told them I was coming forward the next day. I had always been intentionally vague yet coy with my friends the way I was with my family ever since *The Globe's* report: Yes; I was impacted by the church sex scandal. No, it's not as bad as you're probably thinking. There was no rape.

To a man, they got up and hugged me. They reminded me they had my back, and we got back to drinking.

The rest of the world won't be so understanding—if they believe you at all.

When I got home, Jay was in tears. She needed to know why I could never be upfront with her, especially since I was comfortable enough to go public.

I confessed it all. I hadn't considered that I never got into the specifics of my abuse with her. She never demanded I did either. Yet if I could tell the world, why wasn't I able to say to the person I loved and trusted the most?

She hugged me. She told me she loved me. She wished I could have been comfortable enough sooner so I could have healed and we could have lived our best possible lives, not these clouded with anger and anxiety and overindulgence. She made me promise I would seek therapy as soon as possible. I agreed.

I passed out with no grasp of the impact that reading that Grand Jury report would have on the rest of my days.

XXV

On August 19, 2018, at 7:47 AM, I posted my truth to *Reverb Press* and its social media sites:

"The numbers from Tuesday's Grand Jury report on the Catholic Church in Pennsylvania's history of abusing minors popped off of computer screens across the globe like sparks hitting the unprotected eye of a steelworker. Seventy years. Over three hundred priests. Over one thousand victims. We've known for most of this century that there was a disgusting history of priests violating trust and sexually assaulting the children they were charged with spiritually fostering. We likewise knew that there was a deep conspiracy among the Church hierarchy to keep this abuse secret. Worst of all, we were aware that these clergymen accused of such horrific acts were often shuffled to new, unsuspecting parishes. Which meant nothing more than new, unsuspecting victims.

Still, the results of the investigation out of Harrisburg were jaw-dropping. Pennsylvania is only
24% Catholic, with approximately 3.2 million Pennsylvanians prescribing to the faith. The magnitude of the abuse was, for most people, beyond comprehension. But not for me.

It happened in my parish. It happened to me."

I wrote about the psychological impacts that I have lived with for thirty years and explained that I wouldn't be using the real names of anybody involved.

I provided the world with some background on the parish—dubbed not so subtly as "St. Lucifer's":

"That all changed, however, when we came back from summer vacation following fourth grade—1986. It was my class's first summer as Altar Boys.

While we were spending our days at the town pool, watching Peter Gabriel's "Sledgehammer" dominate MTV and Ferris Bueller play hooky on the big screen, St. Lucifer was undergoing a major administrative metamorphosis. The ancient school principal that ruled the roost with an iron fist was out. So were Sister Cruella (Sister Katherine, the original principle) and a few of her born-in-the-nineteenth- century cohorts. The new boss, Sister Eva, was only fifty-three years old. For St. Lucifer's School, that was practically adolescent.

It Seemed Normal At The Time"

I recounted how I learned about "The Birds and the Bees" from Father Gerry, with no parental notification, and I explained the foundations of the abuse...

"One of the 'perks' of being an altar boy was getting a special blessing from the priest who said mass, once the service concluded. We were trained to retreat to the sacristy—a sort of office/locker room hybrid set just off of the altar—turn around, kneel on one knee, and the

priest would literally bless us. *Father George* (Father Francis) *would just make a sign of the cross and that was it. Father Thelonious* (Father Vacarro) *would at least be verbal, saying something along the lines of May God the Father, Mary the Blessed Mother and blah blah blah blah blah Amen.*

It was a whole different ballgame with Father Damien. For starters, no more kneeling. He'd ask that we stand and then he would pull the two (on a weekday) or three (on a Sunday) of the altar boys in tight for a bear hug. And then he'd deliver his customized blessing.

I still remember the first two lines of it. I couldn't forget it if I tried. It's popped into my head while I've been at parties. I've heard it in my mind while trying to meditate.

It's even manifested while having sex.

Those 22 words seem simple and innocuous. Comforting, even if you just look at them at face value. But over three decades later, they still haunt the ever-loving shit out of me."

I followed these ghastly revelations by examining the community and generational attitudes:

"*Damien had this knack for hugging children. To many of the parents — the baby boomers— this was nothing odd. Quite the contrary. I'm only speculating, but I imagine that some of the more devout parents were thrilled to bits to see their children actually enjoying church. And we did.*

When he first arrived, he made it his mission to start a "Youth Group". My class was too young, but we anxiously awaited seventh grade when we could attend ourselves. Its immediate impact was obvious. Kids would call the parish rectory to find out which Sunday Mass he would be officiating. Attendance at his services were almost standing-room only, compared to the other four masses each Sunday which would be maybe 60% capacity, depending on how close you felt like sitting near other people (I preferred plenty of room to myself for the sole reason of not having to deal with strangers during the "sign of peace").

For all that you are, and for whatever your needs may be. Especially any needs that might make you worried, anxious or afraid...

Then Things Really Got Weird

But while the baby-boomers as a whole generally embraced what Father Damien brought to the parish, the older folks—the so-called Greatest Generation—weren't having any of what he was selling. His attempts to hug and kiss the senior citizens of the community were routinely rebuffed. I distinctly remember my grandfather, who wasn't a parishioner but occasionally joined us on special Sundays and holidays, saying something to the effect of there's something not right with that priest."

Damien's lifestyle was quite different. By the time we were in 5th grade, he acquired a few items that to this day remain unusual for a meager parish priest. He had a beach house down the Jersey Shore, a cottage out in the Pocono mountains of Pennsylvania, and a brand-new Chevy Astro Van. This priest now had twice the automobile seating capacity as my family of six did at the time.

It all became clear shortly after that, however, when he would routinely bring teenagers down the shore as we say in New Jersey. What fourteen or fifteen-year-old was going to pass up the chance to go to the beach for a few nights without their parents?

He had a special bond with the 7th and 8th graders when he first arrived. They were the first participants in his 'youth group', and his de facto beach buddies. But time marches on and soon those students would be out of that awkward pubescent period, out of St. Lucifer's and off to high school.

Which meant it was our turn for the extra attention."

For the first time, with an adult mindset, I confronted what we called "Gerrykisses":

"Somewhere around 6th grade, the post-mass altar boy blessing got weird. The bear hug remained the same, but it now included an encore. After he finished that goddamn For All That You Are schtick, he'd let go and then individually grab each altar boy. He'd look you in the eye, say 'Peace be with you Eddie' (or whatever your name was) and then give you a long, closed-mouth kiss. On the lips.

That was fucking strange.

Naturally, this was ridiculously confusing for 12-year-old boys in the waning years of the pre-politically correct world. I'm not proud of the language I used back then, but it didn't take long until we were all giggling on the basketball court about how Father Damien is a fag.

But the scary part is, none of us ever thought to complain to anyone. Not our parents. Not our teachers. Not Sister Eva. Not Father George. Nobody. On Wednesday night we'd be making jokes about him loving men (because we considered ourselves men, not boys) and on Thursday morning he'd be kissing us on the lips after the 7:00 mass.

Soon the kisses, with regularity, were open mouth. Not long after that, you'd feel his tongue licking your lips. I knew this wasn't right. My friends did too. We just never talked about it. I would use every kilowatt of energy in my body to keep my lips shut. It didn't matter.

Every time we served mass we were greeted with 30 seconds of pure hell."

I could not tell this tale without giving proper respect to the pure torture we put Matthew Baker through.

"I know kids can be cruel, but we were fucking vicious, man.

There was one student who came to our class in the 5th grade. Transferred from a nearby Catholic School. From what I recall, his parents were quite devout. (By this time, we knew the names and faces of every parishioner. The 'devout' ones made a scene of just how much they 'believed'. Singing loudly in church. Holding hands for the Lord's Prayer. Sitting as close to the altar as possible, and so on.) Father Damien took a liking to him too, but he wasn't "one of us".

We tortured the ever-loving shit out of this poor kid. I'm talking stuff that should have gotten us thrown in juvenile detention at times. We were continually lectured by the faculty, and Damien himself, about how we abused him. It was always written off as 'Well, he joined the class late, they're picking on the new kid.'

Bullshit. There's absolutely no doubt in my mind that we were projecting on him. And I know for sure because of the most common insult we would hurl his way.

'Fag'."

What followed was the most difficult thing I had ever written to that point in my life:

"One of those times fell in the summer between 7th and 8th grade. My childhood home had a large above-ground pool in the backyard. Father Damien was over for a BBQ one Sunday and he brought his extra-large trunks with him.

I have no idea how it happened, but I ended up in the pool alone with him. I don't know if my parents or siblings were in and eventually left, if he was in alone and I joined him, or vice versa. But there we were.

He said something about water being soothing, reminiscent of John the Baptist, and then asked me to float on my back and close my eyes. I did so instinctually, I guess. I don't recall putting up a fight at first. I was still a believer in 'the role of the Priest' and thought I was 'chosen' and 'going to heaven' and all that other fake news. He put one arm underneath my shoulder, the other underneath my upper thigh. It was reminiscent of the pose you often see of the Blessed Mother holding her son's lifeless body after he was taken down from the cross.

I seriously thought it was the start of some ritual.

He was talking about John the Baptist and then segued into our changing bodies. I'm paraphrasing the wording, but distinctly remember being asked:

Do you find that you now have to shower more often?
When you shower, do you notice you pay more attention to different areas and crevasses?
Are you noticing you now have hair in places you didn't before? Maybe on your legs. Maybe on your armpits ...

(TIME OUT: I'M IN THE FUCKING POOL WITH YOU, WEARING JUST A PAIR OF SHORTS. YOU CAN TELL IF I HAVE HAIR ON MY LEGS OR ARMPITS)

Maybe on your testicles? Maybe above your penis?

Playing '20 questions' about a 13-year-old's body was bad enough. But then I felt a minor rub against the back of ribs. And he began to thrust. The motherfucker was as hard as a rock, poking me in the back. In my own swimming pool. With my whole family home.

I made up a lie about having to pee (puke was more like it) and immediately put an end to it. And I told no one. And I continued going to church.

And I continued as an altar boy. And I went with Father Damien on group trips to his Pennsylvania cottage. ...

That's not the extent of what I know about Father Damien's reign of manipulation at St. Lucifer's. But it's all that I'm willing to share publicly at this point. And it's the extent of what happened to me personally."

In closing, I explained to my readers why I felt compelled to speak out now, and the lingering psychological effects:

"Following the Pennsylvania report and the public outcry, I felt that now was the time to tell my story. Not because I was stunned by the events in the Keystone State, but because I wasn't. Because I STILL don't think we've even scratched the surface of this scandal. However bad you think this is, believe me, it's worse. And it's nowhere near over. Father Damien is still a priest. And I'm willing to bet everything I have that he's not the only abuser that's still donning the vestments every Sunday.

Out of the 1,356 pages in the Grand Jury Report, there was one sentence that turned me whiter than a Trump rally. It was discussing the internal policies of the Archdioceses and how they should inform the public that a predator priest was removed:

By my junior year in (public) high school, I was still going to church every Sunday, but I was going through the motions. Going because it was what you were supposed to do. I came home from basketball practice one day and my mother says to me, 'Did you hear Father Damien left St. Lucifer's?'

I asked her why.

'Father Bob (the pastor who replaced Father George a few years prior) said 'nervous exhaustion' whatever that means'".

XXVI

Leaving my phone in the Bronx was the biggest blessing in disguise of my life.

Sean had informed my family that I had lost my device just a short distance from the Hanratty ancestral home on Anderson Avenue. By 8:15, Jay's phone was ringing, and I could tell by the sobbing on the other end—audible despite being pressed to Jay's ear—that it was Mom. I knew I wouldn't be able to run from this like a Facebook post from which I can hide notifications. Saturday's heavy drinking only made my morning anxiety worse, and I hadn't thought to have a Xanax—used almost only for hangovers at this point. But I couldn't ignore my mother's call, not this day.

Through tears heavier than any of life's losses and traumas that I've ever heard from her, she opened by saying, "I'm…so…sorry". And that's when I broke down, setting off Jay's tear ducts five feet away from me on the couch.

I assured her it was not her fault. The entire point of coming forward was to show how pervasive the whole ring of clergy abuse was within the Catholic Church. I didn't stand a chance as an altar boy, and she didn't stand a chance as a parent. The Catholic way of life was the only way of life.

I wasn't expecting a catharsis with my mother, but I was grateful for it. I felt as if we were finally on the same page and that the decision to tell my truth was a positive one. Any bitterness or resentment I had towards her for the mundane yet impactful decision to send me to St. Francis disappeared almost instantly. It was the first time I fully grasped how parents were victimized by the church as well, with the grossest violation of trust that can be committed, the trust to nurture and not harm a child.

Mom let me know Dad was sick to his stomach, and I said a silent "thank you" to the universe that he didn't want to—or couldn't bring himself to—speak to me. But Aunt Breda—who lived within the same complex where my parents had settled once life returned to normal following Dad's extended stay with us—was next.

There were even more tears as she expressed her genuine sorrow for what I experienced. It broke me even further. My godmother is the last person on earth who needs to apologize to anyone. One of the kindest spirits to walk the earth, she could pass for a nun with her gentile approach to life. But this morning, there was sorrowful anger in her voice. Hearing the pain and abuse from the warmest person I knew put the magnitude of this article into perspective.

I resisted the temptation to open my laptop and check whether there was any reaction on social media or how the story was being received via *Reverb's* internal analytics. I hadn't even finished my first cup of coffee. And before I did, Jay's phone rang again.

This time, it was Elizabeth, likewise amid significant crying. She apologized off the top, and I had to draw the line. Now, what the hell are you apologizing for? You're seven years younger than me. She explained she was sorry that I had to endure this and that she knew Sudol's actions had impacted my life. I appreciated that, more than she could know, an intellectual understanding of the lifelong psychological impacts of being an altar boy and how they manifest. She was younger than me but well into her thirties. She remembered the angry outbursts at the dinner table and my mocking digs about their school uniforms once I graduated from St. Francis.

Erin was the next call, and thankfully, there were no tears. She said the requisite "proud of you" and "sorry," but she complimented me on the writing itself, calling it "so professional." I didn't realize it then, but my baby sister managed me. She knew exactly what I needed, and having already had the tough emotional conversations with Mom, Aunt Breda, and Elizabeth, the last thing I wanted was another tearjerker.

Sean, however, spoke my language and understood my needs better than anyone. He shot an email I would read as soon as I opened the laptop. Yes! An Email. While coming forward about clergy abuse is reluctantly on the list of items I think are acceptable to call for, emails and texts will always be the preferred method of communication.

His message began by jokingly accusing me of intentionally leaving my phone at the Macombs Dam Parking Garage the day before. Then he recounted his feeling upset in his eighth-grade year (1994) when Sudol suddenly left with "Nervous Exhaustion." I shot him a sharp look and said something like, "Don't be upset; believe me, it's for the best," and how he ceased worrying after I reassured him.

I maintain no recollection of that conversation, but trauma likes to do that — suppress as much of it as your brain will allow. It would be the earliest example of a serious acknowledgment that Father Gerry was terrible news.

Sean's email was merely the tip of the iceberg, as I checked that before daring to open Facebook Messenger. When I did, it became apparent that my life had changed forever.

•••

A former St. Francis basketball player, a bit older than me and a name I hadn't heard in thirty years, reached out to call me "brave" and added that he did not doubt the accuracy of my article.

A man in his fifties messaged to apologize on behalf of the St. Francis community, of which he was a lifelong member. He said he remembered Gerry Sudol and was sad to learn that the long-standing rumors were true. I told the stranger that he knew me when he was the basketball coach of my 5th and 6th-grade teams at St. Francis. When he put two and two together, he was floored.

A woman who grew up around the corner from Jay, someone Jay babysat in the 1980s, told me that my wife was one of her earliest role models and that she felt heartbreak for both of us. I immediately informed Jay of that message, as I felt touched that somebody considered the impact on her.

She also echoed what more than a dozen other women who attended St. Francis during the Gerry years pointed out to me upon reading my article: It used to bother them immensely that Father Gerry never paid attention to the girls in St. Francis. The jealousy remains noticeable to this day. That's the thing about Rockstars: they burn so brightly that they reach beyond their intended audience.

One of the more popular athletes from RPHS during my tenure—an upperclassman I'd never have had the guts to approach in the mid-90s—shot me a Facebook message to say he made his son read my entire article so he could learn "How a real man acts" and that what I did took guts. That was an ego boost, as I had long feared the reaction of "alpha" type males, who command attention and fit a specific image.

No less than twenty former St. Francis altar boys contacted me to tell me there was no doubt in their minds. They remember the feelings of being trapped and trying to dodge the Gerrykisses. One fellow even pointed out the stubble, kicking up many awful memories.

I got messages from strangers, most beginning with "You don't know me but…" almost exclusively supportive, though there was the occasional radical Catholic that accused me of being a liar or an agent of Satan.

Among the most heartwarming wishes that came my way were from the parents of the 80s and 90s. The sorrow in their text was palpable, and I did my best to tell them what I had told my mom earlier that morning—this was so much bigger than one parish. There was nothing they could have done differently.

There were pings from all walks of my life: St. Francis students, RPHS friends, Ramapo friends, former co-workers, fellow bar-flies. All three of my regular bartenders at the time showed their support.

All of this happened before noon on Sunday. It overwhelmed me—in a good way, for once.

People believed me. I was wrong these years:

It WAS that bad.

•••

There was no mistaking the reality that 2018 was the peak of the #MeToo era based on the incoming messages I received from too many female friends, relatives, and strangers. Among the over 200 Facebook texts I got the first day my story ran were a shamefully high number of women who felt comfortable enough sharing their stories of unwanted sexual advances, sexual harassment, and rape. Date Rape in the 1990s and 2000s was significantly more widespread than I would have ever imagined–and shame on me for that.

These were the most challenging messages to read, but as I told myself, these readers not only took fifteen minutes to read your manifesto but likewise tracked you down on the internet and shared their most vulnerable experiences with you. You owe it to them. And I responded to every one of them—unwittingly getting addicted to being heralded as words my inner dialogue would never allow me to associate with myself: brave, heroic, remarkable.

I felt myself tighten with every survivor story I read, particularly the ones I could put a face to. Some of these women were significant parts of my life for four decades. Sometimes, I was a part of their lives as they were suffering these indignities at the hands of entitled abusers.

Nothing prepared me, however, for the healthy handful of people who reached out to tell me they've harbored grave concerns for their sons and brothers. I had no solace to offer. I knew who each boy they were referencing. I couldn't ease their fears; I'd be lying. Unless specifically told or disclosed in legal filings, I did not know of anyone else being abused at St. Francis. I felt powerless.

But nothing was as jarring as the men who said, "Me too."

Not all of them were related to Sudol, though many were.

Chris McLoughlin sent me a message later that night. He started out by saying I probably don't remember him (I did, I realized. I remembered every name from RP, especially the Irish ones.) He said he was one of the older altar boys and went on one of those Wildwood trips I mentioned in my story. He stated he had no recollection of specifics, but knew something wrong happened.

I knew precisely how he felt. It wasn't dissimilar to the toxic "Other people had it worse" thinking that clouded my judgment for as long as I could remember.

•••

When I caught my breath, I realized that my story's sudden virality in Ridgefield Park circles was traced back to Sara Graves, the daughter of Harry, the jack-of-all-tradesmen who saved a handful of altar boys from taking a sleep-deprived ride to a basketball game in 1991. Like many towns, RP has its fair share of town-related Facebook pages where old-timers share memories of how much better Main Street used to be and complain about the new generation of residents moving in.

In the days before my story's release, I told her I would have something to say about Gerry Sudol soon. We had begun a private chat after the McCarrick revelations. She has a memory like an eagle and recalled all the specifics—the celebratory masses, the events, etc. She may not have realized the magnitude of exactly what I'd have to say, but I didn't think a story that long would burn through local circles with that voracity.

Sara confirmed on a thread that Father Gerry Sudol was an active priest in ministry at Our Lady of Czestochowa in Jersey City, NJ—roughly 15 miles from RP. The parish had an elementary school on site, just like St. Francis.

The article was just the first step. The heavy lifting began Monday morning.

XXVII

Jay's work travels had kept her away from home for most Tuesdays, Wednesdays, and Thursdays throughout the summer. And our Friday nights, once the beacon of our week, were turning hostile. Tension bubbled each time she came home, as if there was an adverse psychological effect to the disruption of her consistently leaving and returning. Fortune favored us, however, the August 20, 2018, work week because she had no obligations that required her to leave the house.

She tracked down all pertinent phone numbers and email addresses for the Archdiocese and Our Lady of Czestochowa. She disseminated them on the various RP-based pages and all other Facebook platforms, where the story went viral.

Upon explaining to an official with the Archdiocese who she was, she was told that they would like her husband to make a formal statement on the record—again with that shit as if I'm the only one with the power to make you fire somebody FROM THEIR JOB (with cause, no less.)

I would draw a comparison—which I'd use repeatedly in the coming weeks—to a shoe salesperson at Macy's. If Macy's had to settle a seven-figure lawsuit in part because of the actions of the shoe salesman, they would replace him quicker than you can say, "Al Bundy." If there were dozens of further complaints and allegations against this guy, would Macy's truly need each one to lodge a formal complaint to realize that this fellow is a danger to customers and a liability to the company? I continue to have no tolerance for the notion that being a priest is anything different from being a lawyer, an accountant, or a shopping cart jockey.

Jay had my back fully. She remembered the aggressive tactics from 2003 to try to strong-arm me into going on the record with the Church. Having known me since 1982, dated me since 1994, and married to me since 2002, she had no reason to trust the Church either. She saw the manifestations more than anyone. She was my date for all of those weddings where I devolved into a sludge of drunkenness. She was my designated driver for all those family parties that I overdid to the point of embarrassment.

She had every reason to believe that, despite my holding this pain and this story so close to the vest for so long, this was the event that would provide my life and our relationship a U-Turn from the unspoken trauma that so often surfaced as hostility.

The answers from Our Lady of Czestochowa were laughable in their progression. Per their receptionist, throughout the workday Monday, the party line went from "This is the first we're hearing of it," to "We're aware of his past, but he's never been allowed to mingle with students," to "We don't know where he is at the moment, but he's not here."

Despite the severity of the issue, we laughed about the runaround we were getting and took great delight in speculating just how much we upset the Archdiocese's applecart. We had a commonality in a cause. We felt the wind at our back rather than the headwinds for the first time that we could remember.

I made no preparations for the storm that would follow the publication of my story because I was foolish and shortsighted and didn't think it was that big of a deal. On the other hand, Jay had no opportunity to prepare—she had no idea what to expect, not having heard the details until about twelve hours before the rest of the world and 48 hours after my editors did.

Nevertheless, she was thrust into the spotlight as my spouse and fellow warrior, and hundreds more people got to know "Ed and Jay" intimately. She exceeded her expectations in how aggressively she fought when the moment came and blew mine out of the water.

Little did I realize she had been preparing for this moment since the Grand Jury report became front-page news.

•••

Kerry Bannon, a genuine force to be reckoned with, graduated from RPHS three years before Jay and me. A true embodiment of the Gen X Jersey attitude, Kerry is the person you'd want in a foxhole—tenacious, fiercely loyal, and unyielding. Her ferocious fighting spirit extends beyond the battlefield of life, and her resilience has made her a standout among RPHS alumni. She took a keen interest in my story and was one of the most vocal critics of Sudol and St. Francis on RP's Facebook pages.

A three-way chat developed between Kerry, Jay, and me. I marveled as they recounted how many phone calls and emails they made or sent in the first few days following publication. It was like sitting in on a meeting between FDR and Winston Churchill in 1942. And they weren't the only ones—hundreds of predominantly women—from the St. Francis community were doing the same as Kerry and Jay. It wouldn't be long until pressure forced the Church's hand.

Kerry called the Hudson County Prosecutor's office to inform them that a sexual predator was living within feet of an elementary school in Jersey City. It led to me lodging a formal complaint with the Bergen County Special Victims Unit. However, the sympathetic detective was blunt in his assessment that since the abuse took before 1986, there were only a few select acts that would still be within the Statute of Limitations. Thankfully, for me, at least, my abuse wasn't enough to reach "Pre-1996 Class A" levels.

Kerry likewise opened up about the passing of her classmate, Phillip, three years earlier. I knew Phil—he was a St. Francis kid a few years ahead of me in Kerry's class. I completely forgot about him from the minute he graduated RPHS until we became passing friends on MySpace. During the Facebook era, however, we found a mutual interest in ragging on anything and everything related to St. Francis or the Catholic Church.

When we learned of his death, Jay and I were devastated. We took the ride down to Ridgefield Park to attend his wake. It was the first service I attended where the deceased was born after 1970—my birth decade, my generation.

Kerry told us he showed a crack in defense during an emotional conversation about a decade prior. He told her that Father Gerry wasn't the light everyone made him out to be and that he had made multiple advances towards him.

I knew exactly what she spoke of. There was an immense feeling of shame and guilt for even being in the same room with Sudol. You had the binary choice of succumbing to what we now knew was childhood sexual abuse—yes, even the Gerrykisses–or you could go against everything your developing brain was hard-wired to do: obey and respect the priest. That feeling alone could cause intense trauma.

I don't know what other, if any, baggage Phil was carrying when his life ended tragically in his early forties, but I knew that there was an enormous suitcase called Father Gerry among it. And Kerry firmly believed that her dear friend would still be here if it weren't for it.

That belief sparked her passion, making her among the more prominent "relentless bitches" as they dubbed themselves—the women from coast to coast with RP roots who were bombarding the parishes and Archdiocese.

That relentlessness led to Our Lady of Czestochowa confirming to Jay early Friday morning of that week that Father Gerry Sudol was no longer stationed at their parish.

My words made a difference. My words inspired action. The positive swell of emotion was a wholly foreign feeling. The internal demons did not counterattack.

•••

Although my *Reverb* editors had warned me about a potential media firestorm, I ultimately dismissed them. I was "another brick in the wall," so to speak. The Pennsylvania Grand Jury report was THE story, and I was just one of its countless thousand tributaries. That's why they were the editors and me, a mere head writer. They were right.

The first request came from a lifelong journo, Gerard DeMarco, who left the big paper business and formed a start-up focusing on hyper-local news. This is perfect for the click-and-share era of news consumption. Who won't read a story about their hometown or home area?

With an eternal ear to the ground in local Facebook groups it wasn't long after I logged into Facebook Wednesday morning at work—I was still without my iPhone—that Gerard reached out to me asking me if I'd be willing to go on record, basically repeating my story, for his publication "The Daily Voice."

I agreed immediately, bolstered by hundreds of messages and phone calls of support I had received over the last 72 hours. And then Gerard was blunt: "I know who the priest is that you're referencing, but you're going to have to name him."

I knew I couldn't take my story any further without doing so. I also didn't intend for the story to inspire much more than a "Ha! I knew it!" response. Giving no strong consideration to declining, however, I immediately agreed.

Hours later, under a close-up of myself taken above the River Liffey in Dublin that I supplied Gerard, was the headline:

"Ridgefield Park Native Hailed For Detailing Sexual Abuse At Hands of Popular Priest"

Directly below, in large print:

> *It was the summer before 8th grade when Ridgefield Park native Ed Hanratty said the worst sexual abuse he'd endured from a local priest happened—in his own backyard. Before then, the Rev. Gerald Sudol of St. Francis of Assisi Church had kissed him and other boys on the mouth, Hanratty said. But instead of telling their parents, the boys made jokes about his sexuality.*

The article continued in fascinating detail. Gerard coaxed a grand narrative about the arc of the silence for generations, and there was significantly more focus on the missed warning signs than even my article did. And it closed with a quote that I made while shooting from the hip at the end of our conversation:

> *"The community has always known. When we were kids, we laughed about it. When we were young adults, we ignored it," he said. "Now that we're older, we should be coming to grips with it."*

That was the first time I thought of the Sudol experience through a generational lens, but it was all coming together. There were distinct generational reactions to Father Gerry's arrival and tenure at St. Francis, and minimal overlap existed.

When he arrived, members of the so-called Greatest Generation—my grandparents' peers—avoided him like the plague (though many Americans would eventually show they couldn't care less about avoiding the plague). The Baby Boomers opened their hearts, doors, and wallets for him. Imagine the Beatles played Woodstock and gave everybody 100 shares of IBM—he was that much of a Boomer's wet dream. Gen X was basically told, "He's your daddy now; listen to him."

Thirty years later, there were few remaining members of the Greatest Generation. The Boomers were castigating themselves for missing the warning signs, and Gen X decided nobody else would fix it, so the responsibility fell to us.

•••

After the "Daily Voice" article spread through RP circles on social media like a brushfire, administrators of the multiple town-centered Facebook pages pushed back over the direction of the pages. Two distinct camps opened: the first, who believed these pages should be for sharing old high school pictures or getting nostalgic over the egg cream sodas you used to get at Ollerman's deli in 1966; and the second, who believed this was the biggest story to hit RP in decades, perhaps ever.

But this wasn't the fight worth having. Jay, Kerry, and I created a page to follow the story and share information. We called it "#RPStrong," following the format that Boston used after the Boston Marathon bombing and New Jersey used following the devastation of Hurricane Sandy.

We offered the mission statement.

> *1. Make sure Gerry Sudol is removed from his assignment that has so many children present, and see to it that the church makes sure he is never assigned near them again.*
>
> *2. Be here for everyone impacted. Not just the survivors, but as we see from posts - EVERYBODY in the community was affected by this. Spouses, friends, parents, siblings, teachers. Everyone. The only blame here lies with the Catholic Church and anyone who actually PROTECTED this monster. We've come together in such a beautiful, organic matter. You guys have been wonderful to me. Let's make sure that love and support are available for all who need it and seek it.*
>
> *3. Bring Gerry Sudol to justice. This is the long slog. We are a nation of laws and due process. As much as we'd all love to go throw him in the dungeon, it doesn't work that way. This is where we're going to have to help, assist, gather information, piece things together so if when any of us ever speak to investigators, we know who is able to corroborate what, who remembers what, who knows what, and so on and so forth. If he's ever going to be removed from society, it's going to take some teamwork.*

Almost instantaneously, it exceeded expectations as a depot for all pertinent information to the abuse at St. Francis and the greater Church Abuse scandal, which showed no signs of disappearing from the news cycle. By this point, even Pope Francis couldn't remain silent any longer. There was no longer any downplaying or denials.

One of the group's first messages was from Chris, who was coming forward to the rest of the group. He spent the morning meeting with the current St. Francis pastor, Father Larry.

Chris told the group,

> *"Wanted to let you know that I met with Fr. Larry this morning. I feel it was very productive (if only for myself). He's been in touch with the Diocese and the pastor of the Jersey City church where Gerry is in residence. He said he's a close friend of the pastor of OLC. Anyway, long story short, he took notes and documented my story and is sending it on to the diocese...*
>
> *Basically, he* (Sudol) *was acquitted because the person/people who received the settlement didn't show for his canonical trial. Which I guess is understandable with regards to their case being settled financially. I felt a weight lifted off my shoulders after meeting with him. And I was told that if I*

> seek counseling (which was obviously recommended, as I have no memory of the trip to wildwood and the Poconos) the parish will pay for it."

Father Larry—the current St. Francis pastor—failed to mention that the person who did not testify against Sudol in his canonical (Church) trial gave statements to the tribunal. They just didn't play ball with the church's dog and pony show.

Oversight aside, Chris's insight was illuminating. St. Francis knew it had a Sudol problem. There was no attempt to sweep anything under the rug or strong-arm survivors. Each person who came forward was informed that their report would be forwarded to the police—though there remained no evidence of a provable Class A felony within the Statutes of Limitation.

And #RPStrong was the first to remind everyone that this wasn't their first problem of this nature. The more people joined from town, the louder the allegations grew that Father David Ernst had a long list of skeletons in his closet from his time at St. Francis. The Baby Boomers on the site reflected on his youth group participation, sharing a beer with high school kids, and organizing camping trips, many of which ended with somebody being victimized by his advances.

It didn't take long to realize that Ernst was part of the same seven-figure settlement that named Sudol near the turn of the century.

•••

On the Friday morning of Revelation Week, I took great pride in posting to RP Strong:

> *One more update, and a potentially HUGE one: it has not been confirmed, but according to a priest who would know:*
>
> *Father Gerry "is not" at OLC as of today.*
>
> *As I said, not confirmed. And this is coming from a priest, make of that what you will.*
>
> *But if this is true, our first and most important goal has been met*

It was one of the first posts I made with my brand-new iPhone, which arrived after work on Thursday. I enjoyed the freedom to choose when to connect. However, it was eerily reminiscent of childhood—not being able to call your father on a whim, or look up precisely when Caligula reigned.

I don't know if I'd have survived that week if I was constantly drawn to the notifications and vibrations, which would have been nonstop. On my commutes alone, I would receive three dozen Facebook notifications. Staying wired at work and occasionally opening the laptop at home allowed me to remain disciplined in my reactions.

Sudol's removal—which became confirmed and official shortly after — was inevitable but still celebrated. I had just heard from Chris, who relayed intel from Father Larry. It was a fitting end to the most surreal week of my life.

The Friday night was cool and tolerable as we moved further away from mid-August's oppressive humidity. I was grabbing a case of beer out of the back of my Jeep—Mark, who lived locally now, would come down to the deck later and throw back some cold ones to cap it all off. It wasn't unusual for a Friday or Saturday night. He and his wife Debra were raising five-year-old twins. Our deck or *Uncorked* were often points for a quick rendezvous when one of them could get out of the house.

"Hey Ed, wait up," I heard from the driveway to my right. It was my neighbor Gary. I had been silently dreading confronting certain men after the story broke. The older generations, the guys who fit a more traditional vision of manhood. The warehouse workers at my job were the first hurdle I cleared; as to a man, they sought me out to compliment me on "the balls it took" or for "sticking it to those fucking bastards" (as more than one baptized Catholic told me).

Gary was a more significant hurdle. While we were very close with Gary and Jan, Gary handled almost every repair that went wrong in our money pit. I had developed the role of the guy who gets his tools from a bucket. And he'd make plenty of wisecracks about the incompetence in my handy work. Now he knew about my abuse, too.

He extended his hand to me for the first time since introducing himself 12 years earlier.

"That was a great fucking story, Ed," he said as he looked me in the eye. "That took some guts. I hope you bring these bastards to justice". He then went on one of his patented soliloquies where you couldn't walk away or get a word in, but I didn't mind. He grew up one of a dozen kids in a Polish Catholic household in the 70s. He knew what they were capable of.

Hours later, Mark was on the deck, offering his encouragement as we sucked down New England IPAs. All of my close friends had been super supportive. When I finally booted up the new phone, I was treated to a bundle of good wishes from Ben, Walter, Hayes, Doc, and many others—though I never doubted their backing or felt I could be viewed as less than around them. Any more so than my internal voices told me I already was, at least.

During our conversation, my phone illuminated with a new trial feature for every Verizon iPhone: non-contact caller ID, showing the name "Shawn Bello."

Jay and I looked at each other as if to say, "That can't be…"

Officer Shawn Bello was a sergeant with the RPPD in the 1980s and 1990s, probably a few years older than my parents. Well-known in town as an affable cop who would stop to chat with kids playing in the street or one of RP's many parks. It was hard to see Officer Bello as anything more than a devoted public servant. It's just a name I haven't considered in over twenty years.

I grabbed the phone and stormed away from the table. I have this thing about speaking on the phone around other people; the way I dart away probably makes me look like a creep, but the reality is I go absolutely batty if there are two distinct conversations going on.

I answered with a reserved "Hello?" as if I was answering an unidentified call.

"Eddie," the old cop began, using a name I'll only allow for people who knew me before I graduated RPHS, "I don't know if you remember me, Shawn Bello. I was a cop back in RP when you were growing up."

"Of Course, I remember you, Officer Bello; how have you been?"

After we exchanged pleasantries, Bello dove into the reason for the unsolicited phone call.

"Years ago, an older parishioner approached me to tell me he saw Gerry Sudol passionately kissing a boy as this man was leaving the side exit of the church, past the sacristy. He didn't know who the boy was, but said he was tall and skinny. I had always thought you were one possibility."

"I brought it upstairs," Bello continued, referring to police leadership. I was told that something would be said to St. Francis, but I don't know if anything was ever done. I was told, however, that this wasn't the first time at St. Francis. An older cop who was there through the late 60s and into the 90s told me they had a problem for years with Father Ernst.

"Nothing was done until the father in a prominent Irish Catholic family spoke to the then-Chief. Within days, the Archdiocese yanked Ernst after all those years."

You would think that "prominent Irish Catholic family" in Ridgefield Park would be specific, but it only narrowed it down to a couple of dozen heads of household. Still, if true, it was evidence that the Archdiocese of Newark knew that a problematic priest could survive over a decade at St. Francis.

I returned to the deck to Mark—fascinated by the quickly evolving developments — and Jay. I looked at her and said, "You ain't gonna believe this…"

XXVIII

Sunday was a day of reckoning in Catholic Churches across the state, if not the country. My in-laws called early that afternoon to tell us that Father Larry addressed the scandal head-on, acknowledging a story written by a former altar boy and that the Church failed us as children. The church was talking an excellent game in this iteration of their longstanding clergy abuse scandal.

The media also took notice as reporters began back-tracing the story and realized I was the genesis of the coverage in the New York City metropolitan area. About 6-10 local reporters wanted my reaction to the news that Sudol and another priest in nearby Westwood, NJ— Father Jim Weiner—were removed from their assignments because of new allegations.

I told each of them they could refer to my published story and my "Daily Voice" interview for background; I was not going to re-traumatize myself by recounting the pool incident in ten different ways, so ten different publications could claim me as a primary source over the same fact. All understood and wanted a quote or three about what motivated me and what I hoped to accomplish. That was fair enough and easy enough to customize and give each outlet a distinct quote without sounding like I'm reading off a press release (a major pet peeve I developed from 19 years in the news business).

Deena Yellin stood out from the other reporters, however. Deena, who covers "religion, faith, and values" for *The Record*—the dominant print/online outlet for northern New Jersey — wanted to know more than what I had already publicly stated. She wasn't looking to copy and paste another survivor story; she wanted to know how I felt.

What was it in the Grand Jury report that stood out to me?

How did I feel when I learned children were in close vicinity to Sudol?

What did justice look like?

What has the response been like?

Communicating with Deena was as easy as shooting the shit with Hayes about the NBA. The result was "RP Strong" being featured on the front page of *The Record* with the headline:

Two NJ priests step down as church investigates allegations.

Deena cited the group as part of the overwhelming response:

> *Hanratty, a freelance journalist, went public with his allegations and helped to start a Facebook group, RP Strong, to discuss abuse at St. Francis in Ridgefield Park and its "impact on the community we love, and most*

> importantly how we can share information and organize to ensure a happy ending to this dark chapter."

And unlike the other reports, she used more accurate terms to describe my emotions:

> Now Hanratty is angry.
>
> "I don't know why he was let back around children in the first place," he said. "Of all the parishes in the archdiocese, why was he sent to one with a school?"

•••

More often than not, television follows print, and my case was no exception. Tuesday morning, while at work, my iPhone—as I was back to being its indentured servant—buzzed with a Twitter Direct Message notification.

Those were rare. As much as I dove into Facebook, I rarely used Twitter for anything other than pushing out *Reverb* links and checking for breaking news. The DM came from WNBC News correspondent Ida Siegel asking if I was (a) the "Ed Hanratty of *Reverb Press*" and (b) whether I'd be willing to go on camera to do an interview.

The interview had to be shot before 3:00 to be broadcast on WNBC News at Five. I was in the office, which was better for Ida and her crew than meeting me at my home, which would have been too far a distance to cover and still have the report air on time. She asked if I was comfortable being interviewed at my office.

It would have been an ideal location; there were places inside and out that would have been perfect for stand-ups (stationary interviews) or walk-and-talks (tracking shot of the interview and reporter walking and speaking to each other). But the thought of the entire facility stopping to see the commotion that comes along with an interview was mortifying.

"I have a better idea," I told her on a follow-up phone call. "How about we do it at St. Francis?"

Ida loved the idea, realizing it was within a perfect travel radius, adding a significant backdrop to her story. I told her I could be there in thirty minutes and checked out of work.

The only problem was that I was dressed like a slob. KLJ Review's dress code was a step up from that of a nudist colony. I was in beat-up dusty cargo shorts and a too-large plain black pocket t-shirt. I ran to Target on my way to St. Francis, only to be disappointed by the lack of acceptable 3XL dress shirts and polos. I tried on a 2XL button-down, but it couldn't button sufficiently without making me look like a grilled sausage. However, I thought it might dress me up a bit if I wore it over the black shirt.

No deal. Too tight to get over the tent of a T-shirt.

I tucked that shirt in and kindly asked the cameraman to keep his angle "chest up." He obliged, save for the dreaded walk-and-talk, where I looked like Bluto from the Popeye cartoons waddling down Mount Vernon Street. In front of the primary sign announcing that this is St. Francis of Assisi church, I described the "touchy-feely" nature of Gerry Sudol's abuse — so much of it within the confines of that gothic structure in the background.

But there was my face, my voice, and my truth broadcast to the entire New York City metropolitan area beyond, prominently placed on the news division's website.

•••

Jay and I had a pre-planned getaway for Labor Day Weekend that went from luxury to necessity in the fortnight following my article's publication. We had won a lottery to have the first crack at tickets to see my generation's greatest living grunge band, Pearl Jam, play at Boston's charming and historic Fenway Park. While I loathe the Boston Red Sox, who call Fenway their home, the bandbox of a ballpark might be the most hallowed land in all American sports now that the original Yankee Stadium was grass and hot dog vendors.

The five-hour ride—Treehouse Brewery, on the route that always adds an hour to any New England getaway—flew by. Despite living together and having multiple phone conversations throughout the workday, we had gigabytes of information to share.

We had a more significant connection than at any point in our marriage to date. I felt, in a word, free (not to be mistaken for "healed")

We spent the hours before the concert on a personalized pub crawl covering the 1.5-mile hike from our hotel overlooking Boston Commons to the famous Fenway Park. We talked about the "generational moment" we appeared to be having. We were in the driver's seat for the first time, no longer beholden to the wishes of the Boomers nor limited by the internal shame of not being good enough.

It was time for us to lead.

The band played everything you'd want them to and more. "Alive" brought me back to the lockers of RPHS. "Yellow Ledbetter" to laughing at an early YouTube video mocking the inaudible lyrics with Ben, Hayes, Doc and Sean. The words front man Eddie Vedder sang off their debut album track "Release" resonated like never before:

> *I'll ride the wave*
>
> *Where it takes me*
>
> *I'll hold the pain*
>
> *Release me.*

Legendary musician Tom Petty passed away earlier that year. Vedder paid tribute by playing one of Petty's most iconic tunes on a guitar that Petty had once given him.

As the Fenway Faithful illuminated the flashlights on their cameras (o cigarette lighters, where art thou?) and he sang "I Won't Back Down," we looked at each other as if to say:

"Neither will we."

•••

In the cruelest twists of fate, *Reverb Press* began a steady decline in readership not long after my story went live. It likely started a little before. Swept up in the allegations of partisan bias being levied by politicians whose misdeeds social media would highlight regularly, Facebook's algorithms showed our work to our readers less and less until one Friday morning when we couldn't log in anymore. Facebook eliminated the *Reverb Press* page entirely, along with most of her sister sites. The URL was deplatformed.

I wanted to put out a follow-up piece, reporting on the many ways in which life had changed in three weeks, primarily for the better. Needing an outlet and having an unusual amount of confidence, I pitched my follow-up story to *Huff Post*, a left-leaning yet mainstream platform that pays writers per piece, not per view. Within hours, I heard from the *Huff Post* Personal editor, Noah Michelson, commending my bravery, extending his condolences for what happened, and asking for a full draft of my story.

I furiously typed the rest of my work shift and continued when I got home. I had a rough draft delivered to Noah before midnight. He liked what he saw and offered me $150 to run the story. *Are you kidding me? I thought to myself, I'm getting paid upfront. Wow!*

After some exchanges on editing, the editors published my story, with an accompanying feature image of my First Holy Communion portrait:

> **3 Weeks Ago I Revealed I Was Abused By A Priest. Here's How It Changed My Life.**
>
> *If I had known how much publicity I would receive, I might never have considered speaking out. But I'm glad I did.*
>
> **By Ed Hanratty, Guest Writer**

I wrote about my decision to come forward. How I remained singularly focused, and how the editors and *Reverb* treated me more like family than an employee. Jay's support. I wrote about the countless messages of support and the lack of shock from the wider community:

> It turns out, everybody remembered Father Gerry. Everyone knew something was amiss. Some people had very strong suspicions. Some had heard disturbing stories. Some were personally abused. Two families lost loved ones due to the aftermath of his abuse. But nobody ever said anything. And I understood why. Because it took me 30 years. Those who even hinted at impropriety back then were shunned. The parish engaged in victim-shaming. And our church was the cultural epicenter of the town — counting teachers, police officers, first responders, mayors and councilmen among its members.

I could finally give credit where it was due, since a particular term I'd use kept getting dropped from interviews:

> A group of women who dubbed themselves the "Relentless Bitches" led the charge to see this man removed from his position. They called the archdiocese. They called the county prosecutor. A detective from the county's special victims unit called me, seeking to verify my account before he confronted church authorities.

I closed with words that not a month prior would have seemed less believable than what was going on with American politics at the time:

> I've realized that I am not a victim, but a survivor. The alpha males who I once thought would mock me if they knew the truth have been among my biggest supporters. For the first time in my life, I feel like I've charted a course. Where exactly the final destination will turn out to be, I don't quite know. But seeing a community of people who haven't been in touch for decades suddenly rally as we came to grips with our not-so-secret secret has restored my faith in humanity in these often dystopian times.
>
> Channeling the anger I've harbored against the church into a productive and unyielding demand for full accountability and justice has turned out to be my lifelong mission — I just never knew it.
>
> I guess life really does begin at 40.

I memorialized my optimism for eternity, though I would look back at this moment more than once with scorn and regret.

• • •

What the *Reverb* story did locally, my *Huff Post* work did nationally. Suddenly, I was hearing from people—most of them survivors themselves—from all across America, even the world. I heard from people abused by priests. I heard from people abused by scout leaders, family members, and coaches. A fellow named Will, whom I developed a friendship with over my *Reverb* work, messaged me to say he was finally seeking help for the abuse he received in basic training from one of his commanding officers during the Vietnam War era. I heard from and struck a friendship with one of the brave survivors of the US Olympics and Michigan

State University deviant doctor Larry Nassar—a physician convicted of sexual abuse and serving life in prison after harming at least 265 young women.

But what struck me more than any of them was when I heard from another survivor—Ian Gminski—who told me he, too, was a survivor of Sudol's abuse. He told me it occurred in the early 1980s while Father Gerry served at Holy Family in Nutley. His abuses were in the same vein as mine, fitting Gerry's M.O. They only stopped when he left. And he only left when his mother lodged a complaint.

Boom! Firsthand evidence shows that formal complaints were lodged against Father Gerry Sudol before the Archdiocese transferred him to St. Francis, a parish that had proven a decade earlier that it will tolerate bothersome clergy.

This information—long assumed but finally corroborated straight from the horse's mouth—was brought to #RPStrong immediately. The outrage was palpable. Energy was now being directed towards emailing legislatures to encourage them to overturn the Civil Statute of Limitations for seeking recourse for sexual abuse. Few, if any, of Sudol's survivors had any legal recourse to seek justice or answers because the statutes had long expired.

That's when I got a phone call from an old parishioner whose name I had long forgotten. She told me she had tracked my phone number down through mutual friends and had something she wanted to get off her chest. She was there the night Sudol left St. Francis.

There was a meeting in the lower church one night in the fall of 1994. Parishioners gathered to plan one of the church's annual Spiritual Retreats for adults—weekends where you lock yourself away with no booze and pray (Sounds fucking fantastic!). Sudol and Joe Doyle were present, as it was a whole-parish affair.

Following the meeting, a parent approached Sudol and said that the family would appreciate it if he stopped kissing their son, as it makes the child uncomfortable. The parent mentioned that this was not the first time Sudol had to be asked to keep his paws off this altar boy.

Sudol confessed he couldn't stop kissing the altar boys. He turned flush, and as the parent drew closer, his nose started bleeding. Doyle sprung across the room and got between the two of them. He demanded Gerry return to the rectory and assured the parent that he was contacting the Archdiocese immediately.

Gerry would never be in ministry at St. Francis of Assisi ever again.

The archdiocese knew he was an abuser when he got there in 1986. They knew he was an abuser when he left in 1994. So did the pastor at St. Francis.

We needed to know more. What did the Church know, and when did they know it? We had the answers; we deserved to hear them.

Do you know how different life would have been for dozens, if not hundreds, of parishioners if they had been upfront and offered counseling on the spot? Thanks to their malfeasance, we'll never know.

I needed to find a lawyer.

XXIX

Greg Gianforcaro was dying to meet me.

A practicing attorney for decades, this short and stout middle-aged man possessed the ferocity of a pit bull with the affectionate charm of an Italian-New Jerseyan grandfather. He was already representing Jimmy Portersmith, another St. Francis altar boy abused by Sudol. I struck up a quick friendship with Jimmy—he was younger than me, perhaps Sean's age—but I only remembered him by name.

Jimmy called me four days after my story broke while I was shopping the meat aisle in my local ShopRite. I didn't have air buds or any sort of headphone device, so delicately conversing over sensitive topics was challenging. The people-pleaser in me insisted I take the phone call on that new device.

He explained that he always felt something was wrong with him but couldn't wrap his head around what until my story jarred the muscle memory to life. I encouraged him to seek whatever path he thought would get him the peace of mind he deserved and confessed to him I was planning to speak to a therapist when things calmed down so I could finally confront the demons that have been lying dormant since I hit "send" on the original essay.

Jimmy's path brought him to Greg, who, perhaps ironically, represented the Foster family in the lawsuit settled in earlier this century. When I publicly named him, he was already familiar with Sudol's reputation and behavior. When Jimmy got in contact with him, he asked if he could get me to speak with him.

Greg was not one of the half dozen attorneys who called me unsolicited in the days following. I wasn't looking for a lawyer, anyway. Money wasn't my motivation, and I had little interest in dragging this out for years.

Plus, we were finding out so much information on our own.

But because we were finding out so much information, its gravity was pointing towards a much bigger story than just one man's recounting of decades-old abuse. With that in mind, I took Jimmy up on an offer Greg made to meet for coffee at a Dunkin' in Morristown, New Jersey.

Jimmy and Greg were already there when I arrived, and Greg insisted on buying me a cup, asking me how I liked my coffee. I noticed a Dunkin protective case on his phone and chuckled at how many clients he likely netted doing just this.

After pleasantries, he thanked and praised me for having the courage to come forward. He used the word courage repeatedly.

He explained his history of fighting the Catholic Church, complete with a massive victory against a Holy Order of Priests at the Delbarton School, near to where we were caffeinating.

He told us he grew up with some of those boys and other victims of clergy abuse and he was aware of just how pervasive the problem was.

He was speaking my language. This is who I wanted in an attorney—not some ambulance chaser just interested in forcing a quick and lucrative settlement. I wanted somebody who could get answers. Maybe he could get the only answer I ever wanted: Why the hell was Sudol assigned to St. Francis in the first place?

•••

October 12th was the debut of seasonally appropriate weather in the fall of 2018. I woke up freezing without air conditioning for the first time since March. And, as had been the case of late, I woke up late (and with a bit of a wine hangover). My first instinct was to text the office and tell them I was *running behind*—something that had been happening too frequently. But then it quickly dawned on me I wouldn't work today, a personal day.

Unfortunately.

It was the day that I was scheduled to give my testimony to the Archbishop's Review Board at the Archdiocese of Newark's headquarters on their home turf.

The ARB was established—or reinvented — in the wake of the 2002 clergy abuse scandal. It was the first official step in removing a priest from ministry. It's also commonly called "defrocking" or "laicizing" him. Ultimately, they're just fancy words and terms for kicking him out of the priesthood and all the protections.

Survivors speak with a three-person subpanel, and those three folks are part of a larger fifteen-person panel that drafts a report, determines whether the accusations are credible, and makes a formal recommendation to the Archbishop whether the accused priest should remain a priest. Furthermore, all testimony is turned over to the prosecutor's office in the jurisdiction(s) where the abuse occurred.

The board invited me to testify in the unrest following the publication of my experience. When the Archdiocese finally returned Jay's phone call after a few days, they offered the invitation to me through her. My initial reaction was simple: *not a chance in bloody hell*.

I was not the only person to accuse Gerry Sudol of abuse. He was already named in that settlement over Willie's untimely death. Beyond that, the church showed its hand when they caved and removed him from Our Lady of Czestochowa within days of the *Reverb* story going viral. And I said on more than one occasion—anything I would tell the ARB I had already told everyone on the planet with an internet connection. If they wanted my accounting of what I experienced at the hands of Sudol, all they needed to do was google me.

My initial refusal wasn't based on fear, anxiety, or apprehension. It was based on principle.

I don't answer to the Catholic Church. The church has about as much authority over me as my fantasy football league has over them: zilch. From day one, I said I would gladly speak to law enforcement and tell them everything and anything they wanted to know. I am an American citizen and answer to the legislatures that make our laws and the judiciary that enforces them. If I wished for theocratic rule, I'd move to Iran.

Greg mostly agreed with me. Until he didn't.

Two weeks prior, he called me to inform me that the ARB had formally invited me to give my statement. They made the invitation through him shortly after he notified them he represented another St. Francis survivor and me. Despite my severe unwillingness to acknowledge even a hint of Archdiocesan authority, Greg made a compelling argument that not even I—in my never-ending disgust for this institution—could argue with.

He told me that, whether I liked it or not, I was a high-profile victim. My initial story spread across the internet like wildfire. I was featured in New Jersey's two most popular statewide news sites. I described my abuse on camera—in front of St. Francis — to over 20 million people in the New York City media market. *Huff Post* published me twice, the second article gaining even more traction because it linked my experience to that of the most divisive issue of 2018: the confirmation of Brett Kavanaugh to the Supreme Court (It was amazing how many people believed me instantly but then chastised Kavanaugh's accuser, Dr. Christine Blasey-Ford).

If I didn't do all I could to remove Gerry Sudol from the priesthood, I could appear self-serving or disingenuous. My arguments against testifying were quite nuanced, but my refusal to testify could be used against me and my reputation.

I couldn't disagree. Greg told me to sleep on it for a day, but I knew almost instantly that he was 100% correct. The primary reason I retained Greg's services is that no attorney in the state knows how the hierarchy of the Catholic Church operates better than he does.

Right after we hung up, I called Jay from the car. She interjected before I could finish Greg's reasoning and said, "Do it. It would be best to do it if you think you're comfortable enough. Don't give them anything to hold against you."

I immediately texted Greg and said, "Let's do this".

•••

Greg was unaware that another Sudol survivor—Chris—had already given his testimony to the ARB. A little more than a week before Greg reeled me in, Chris had messaged me while we were both living the Happy Hour life about 40 miles apart:

> *Hey Ed. I'm in the middle of a couple of Harpoon IPAs at the moment. I thought today may have been long and somewhat intimidating, but it wasn't. I thought about jumping back into the Uber that dropped me off. I couldn't. I figured I came this far, reported it through whatever channels, and now am on the record as someone who survived. I 100% understand your view of distrust and reluctance. I will share with you the letter I received from Newark, and I hope when you read it, you may consider*

reporting officially. Obviously, the part of the letter that bothers me, will bother you. That being said, the more who make an official complaint, the better chance he's out and hopefully prosecuted. I'll send a copy of the letter shortly if you want to see it. Thanks again, man.

I owed Chris to be forthright and open. Here's a man—one of the first to reach out to me after *Reverb* that was, to the best of my knowledge, just indeed coming to grips with his abuse while he was well into his forties. I certainly couldn't ignore his step, nor could I be inauthentic and give him some cheap reply full of platitudes about marching to the beat of different drums or what have you. Also, the clarity of India Pale Ale helped. I immediately got back to him.

> *Chris, thank you. Seriously. Thank you for stepping up and telling me what needs to be done, my brother. You're making a formal statement is an incredible action. I have the utmost respect for what you've done. It takes fucking BALLS, my friend. And you've got them. Part of me wishes I did, too. But since we've shared our secrets and are kindred spirits in an unfortunate-but-fortunate way, I owe you my full disclosure/opinion. I don't trust the church. I want nothing to do with the church. Frankly, I hold the church in such disgust that it's on par with the Ku Klux Klan or NAMBLA. But I'm jaded, and I realize that. I've spoken with prosecutors in Bergen and Hudson counties, and they assured me their reports will go to the Archdiocese. And believe me, if it means Gerry gets booted, I'll talk to the church. But honestly, man, I can't trust a single person in that organization.*

At least partially, I could help get Sudol booted from the ministry. I had come this far; turning my back on this opportunity would feel like a betrayal to myself and the thousands of people who had lent their support over the past six weeks. And if I could keep my composure, I could let the church know how much they had twice betrayed Ridgefield Park and the new information that had come to light within our discussions since the story broke. I could have the opportunity to tell them we were on to their "nervous exhaustion" conspiracy and just precisely how much—and how complicit—Joe Doyle was in the cover-up that followed Gerry's swift and mysterious 1994 dismissal that was literally, under the shroud of darkness.

After I confirmed to Greg that I would take this dreaded step, he informed me that Jimmy was also invited to give a statement. This would make three formal, detailed accounts about Sudol's actions from the survivors of his abuse — that I knew of. If this son of a bitch remained *in ministry* after this, it was going to be time to rethink the strategy. Like a Martin Luther-style rethinking.

•••

Before getting myself ready for the morning of my statement, I took my dog out to the yard so he could do his business while I contemplated mine over a cup of dark roast. I thought long and hard about popping a Xanax, weighing the pros and cons. The last thing I wanted to experience was a crippling panic attack. And while I had not yet suffered one since the revelation, I was getting proactive with the little yellow pills again.

I decided against it; however, in bargaining, I told myself I would bring two emergency pills in case of emergency.

When I made my way from the parking lot to the entrance to the main building, the wind was whipping past the cathedral and towards the administrative building. Jimmy and Greg were standing right in the doorway, waiting for me. Greg had a cup of Dunkin just the way I like it—straight black—waiting for me.

"Hey, Ed," he said as he led us both past the main door and into the lobby. "The panel is here. It's two gentlemen and a woman. I know this lady; she's a former nun. But believe me, she's on our side."

I bet she was. As the global focus grew on the decades—centuries, even—of systemic clergy abuse, nuns throughout Western society spoke up about the abuses and atrocities they, too, faced from priests or the greater church hierarchy.

"Jimmy's going to go first. I'll be with him as I will be with you. So, if you don't mind, you can make yourself comfortable in the reception area, and I'll come get you about a half hour after Jimmy wraps up."

In a flash, I was considering taking that Xanax. Thirty minutes alone in the Archdiocesan administrative center with my thoughts may as well have been 48 hours at that point. I didn't deal well with waiting on my best day, so I wasn't sure how I was going to handle this.

Still, I wanted to be at my sharpest for my testimony. I stepped outside to vape and scrolled through my phone in the howling winds of Newark. There was an email from Hayes, "RE: Week 6" (an ongoing weekly football chain):

"good luck, Ed!"

Simple. And it was motivating. I didn't need any Xanax.

When I sat in the waiting area, I couldn't resist eavesdropping on the collection of young senior citizens—men and women who appeared to be in their early sixties. They were awaiting a meeting with Archbishop Joe Tobin's personal secretary to discuss their annual golf outing fundraiser.

Typical, I said to myself. *I have to pour my heart out about abuse to a former nun and two volunteer randos, but the group discussing lavish fundraising experiences meets with the Archbishop's personal secretary.*

I then allowed my mind to wander in a different direction. I contemplated how, had Sudol never come to St. Francis, perhaps that could have been me, all clean-cut and straight-and-narrow, eager to plan an open-bar golf outing that also increased my chances of entry into heaven (assuming Alternate Ed was as vehemently Catholic as Reality Ed was Atheist.)

No. I couldn't see it, but it once again made me wonder how life would have looked had we never crossed paths. I don't know where I would be in that life, but I knew where I wouldn't be sitting presently.

•••

A visibly shaken Jimmy returned to the lobby about an hour later—double the half-hour we were told to expect. He reached out his fist for a fist bump and said, "Get'em, Ed," as life returned to face.

The three-person panel was disarming from the minute I walked in. They asked me if I needed anything and told me to make myself comfortable as I settled into one end of a long table, with Greg seated to my right.

At the other end, a generic-looking church elder sat on the left side, a near carbon copy of this gentleman sat across from him, and the former nun in the middle. They told me they read my "blog post," and while they admired what it took to publish that, I needed to recount it on the record with them in order for them to move to remove Sudol from the priesthood.

I took a deep breath and looked at Greg with an expression of "Last chance. Are you sure this is the right thing to do?". He nodded, and I began.

First, I went into detail about Gerry's arrival, a story that was all too familiar to them. I spoke of my family's immense trust in him, even mentioning how my dad would give him Yankee tickets to bring me and other altar boys. I talked about the grooming via the Gerrykisses, and they wanted me to explain more robustly how he would forcibly trap me into being kissed in such a manner.

I then recounted the pool experience, using more clinical terms than in my "blog post." When I described the post-Good Friday church transformation, the gentlemen on the left pushed for as many specifics as possible: where were his hands, how long did it last, and so on.

I was as bluntly honest as I could be. I told him my memories were not perfect, but I know I spent the day either being trapped or avoiding being trapped by him. The abuses were in line with everything else.

The firmness with which I answered appeared to put the panel at ease; the conversation was much more open and free-flowing from that point. They wanted to know—in detail—about the parish and if there was anyone who might have been told. I told them there was nobody I was comfortable reporting to, plus, once again, I thought nothing was necessarily "wrong" as much as it was "annoying." I believed it was merely part of the altar boy experience, as it happened to many altar boys before me.

The former nun spoke to conclude the hearing less than thirty minutes after it started, and she wanted to reiterate that my story was similar to many other stories she heard serving on this ARB. She believed me as she believed every other survivor who gave testimony, and she wanted me to leave the building understanding that they were on my side and wanted to see all abusers removed from their ranks.

That didn't change my mind that, unless the priests had some powerful labor union that I was unaware of, they had more than enough evidence to fire him decades ago. And if they believed me, believed Jimmy, thought Chris was credible, and who knows how many other people—why was Father Gerry still a priest?

He wouldn't be much longer.

After the Archbishop's Review Board investigation into the collective allegations against the Reverend Gerry Sudol, the board found the allegations to be credible enough to laicize him, permanently removing him from the Catholic Priesthood.

Another "Mission Accomplished," moment.

•••

Deena Yellin featured me in another article of *The Record* in the days following Thanksgiving. It was my first real interaction with the media since the ARB hearing. She was writing a feature on how survivors of clergy abuse were handling the holiday season following the revelations of the past year.

While most of the other subjects expressed sadness or regret, I told Deena that I had already suffered those painful holidays—I just never understood why. In 2018, the end of the year hit differently. I felt a sense of relief. I still experienced seasonal melancholia, but when I knew why, it became a little easier to cope with.

2018 was an excellent year.

The possibilities for 2019 enamored me.

XXX

If my decision to come forward created a blizzard in the latter half of 2018, the first part of 2019 was the ensuing avalanche.

The end of the holidays meant Jay would resume her travel-intense work schedule, albeit in a new position. Her travel would be more frequent but more localized, often limited to the Northeast, so the anxiety and sympathy for her frequent trips through airports would be eased.

But it meant 3-4 nights per week solo, just me and our dog. And whatever I felt like picking up from the beer store more often than not. If I was alone and I wasn't drinking, there was only one plausible explanation—I overdid it the night before and just wanted to go to sleep as early as possible. On those nights, I would usually let the pup out one more time at the witching hour of 7:30 (right after *Jeopardy!*) and head up to bed. Sure, I might smoke a bit of weed and play with my phone or watch a basketball game on the iPad for an hour or two, but I just wanted to be useless. I didn't WANT to be worthless, but my body wouldn't allow me to do anything else.

Somehow, this just became normal. That TANK email chain with Sean, Doc, and Hayes had almost become a daily happy hour. There was a little rhyme or reason, but mostly, somebody was usually drinking on weekdays, so there was a likelihood of virtual "company." Unless it was Wednesday. Because everybody was drinking on Wednesday, which we dubbed "Little Saturday." Something about communicating with your drinking buddies via email, text, or Twitter made it seem like you didn't have a problem, that you weren't getting shitfaced alone. And I still contend that it's not necessarily problematic.

Sean and Doc are dedicated, hardworking fathers who unwind with a few beers and a ballgame when the kids go to bed. Hayes is, well, Hayes. A guy capable of 4 martinis on a Tuesday that's up and at them before the sun comes up the next morning and can plow through the workday.

And we'd all joke about cracking a beer the minute we got home. And maybe they did. Hayes almost definitely did. But me? I couldn't even wait for home.

A great thing about of January in New Jersey is that you can buy cold beer on your lunch break, and when you leave work, it would be just as cold—if not colder. Without even giving it any thought, I developed this habit of putting two cold beers in the cupholder of my Jeep on days when I knew I was drinking. Of course, I thought my reasoning was brilliant—it's rush hour in the greater New York City area. There isn't any room for cops to pull a motorist over outside of some dramatically lousy driving. I mean, it's not like you can speed when three lanes of cars are coasting at 30 mph.

Somewhere in January, I ceased being productive. Those two beers in the car led to me coming home, throwing a load of laundry in the washing machine, and forgetting to toss it in the dryer (hence, needing to rewash it the next day). What used to be meal prep turned into ordering a pizza *AND* wings for one because when the girl on the phone said, "Will that be all?" I took it as a challenge.

And more often than not, I would spend the night in the slovenliest pose known to man. Lying on my stomach, on my couch, with the beer resting on the end table in front of me while I let the hours piss away bloviating on Facebook about how awful Trump was or posting a line from a song that I was blasting at an unreasonable decibel. *"Screen door slams, Mary's dress waves."*

I didn't realize it then, but I could no longer function properly in the analog world. If I got a phone call, I could choose not to answer (which I regularly did). If I got a text or a message from any of what seems like 100 apps where you can reach somebody personally, I could read and respond on time. If I didn't like what I was saying, I could backspace. It was communication on my terms and on my time.

On nights like this, I would text Jay rather frequently, only partially because I missed her. The primary reason was much more sinister. Unless I said something really stupid or out there, she wouldn't be able to tell just how drunk I was via text. When it came time for the goodnight call, I would try to say as little as possible, and try to Sherpa the conversation to a quick end. It rarely worked.

And there was no chance in hell that I was making it to work on time the following day.

This had become my new reality outside of the week between my birthday and the Super Bowl, when I was bedridden with the flu.

All the while, I was working overtime to convince myself that it was nothing out of the ordinary. I still had forward momentum. I was just in a lull in the fight.

•••

In recent years, Sean and I had started a new tradition of picking a day in mid-January to celebrate our birthdays, which bookend the month. For this year, we created a tour of lower New York State breweries, with Uber as our chauffeur.

Breweries became destinations for us. Sean and I traveled to Delaware to visit Dogfish Head and Massachusetts to wait in line for hours on a 25-degree day in January to get as many cans from Treehouse Brewing as management would allow us to buy.

The Uber dropped Jay and me off at an Irish pub in Pearl River, New York—a town that may as well be on Galway Bay. It was early—our first official stop, Defiant Brewing Company—but it didn't open for another 45 minutes. But that's never a problem in Pearl River. I don't know if these pubs ever close.

We sat and waited for Sean at this place under an ironically hung "No Irish Need Apply" sign. Jay ordered her default beverage from an Irish joint: Magner's cider and a glass of ice. I had Two Roads Brewing's "Road to Ruin" and another one.

The last thing I wanted to discuss was Sudol and how my life changed a few months ago. And I didn't. But boy, did I think about it—a lot. This was the first extended period where the entire case was on the back burner. The whirlwinds of August, September, and October gave way to the holidays, which were impossible to ignore.

But life was slowly returning to normal without my noticing. And I didn't know where it was taking me.

A few friends had given tepid commitments about meeting us on our tour. Such is life in your forties when all your friends have children of school/scout/dance/sports age. Most RSVPs are qualified with "if the game gets out on time" or "if we don't have a birthday party." But I knew that if they made it out, it was more than likely that the church wouldn't come up in conversation. I realized this was probably the first time I would go out with friends since that Yankee game the day before my *Reverb* story was published, where I would be "Ed" and not "Ed, the clergy abuse survivor and activist."

"I'll have another Two Roads," I tell the Irishman behind the bar.

Our birthday brewery tour of the lower Hudson Valley included a second location. And a third. And a fourth—where things got quite out of hand, for me at least. Well, only for me.

As we hit Defiant Brewing across the street from the Irish pub where we waited for Sean to meet us (and lubricate), Jay's Uncle John joined us. I fell in love with a new Double New England Style IPA called "Fake News." Jay and John spoke about his recent bout of illness, coming down with the flu two years after lymphoma treatments decimated his immune system. However, I was too "in the zone" to even pick up on the sensitivity of the issue, so I ordered them a plate of hot wings, even though John said multiple times he could not swallow because of his treatments.

John left as we closed out at Defiant and rode a few miles north to District 96 Brewing. This time, I ordered French fries for everyone because, hey, why not get more food? Ben showed up to partake in the fun—on his own because a 41-year-old should be able to meet friends for an hour or two without getting plastered.

Once again, we got somewhat segregated into two pairs—Ben and Jay discussed their hectic work lives, and Sean and I made it a mission to try every beer on tap and discuss Super Bowl bets we were considering.

In my mind, I wanted to be in on a real-life conversation with my wife and my groomsman. Ben had always had a vision of where he wanted to be at each point in his life—a road map of what had to be accomplished and by when. We used to knock him for it back in Ramapo. We'd be pulling bong hits in the dorm, and he would go on about having two kids, retiring at 65, and moving to a community on a golf course somewhere.

But goddamn it, the kid was on to something. Here they were, discussing the stresses of corporate management for their respective companies, Ben having just moved out of the starter home to a bigger one, as his kids were old enough where school districts mattered. And there I was. I was an overweight survivor of clergy abuse drowning myself in hops, figuring out how I was going to spend my $300 gambling balance on the Rams vs. Patriots and whether Gladys Knight would go over one minute and fifty seconds with her rendition of the National Anthem. We were far from watching Three's Company at 4 AM in Pine Hall.

But I was convincing myself I was in my glory.

When we left District 96, it was still daylight—a fact not lost on Sean or me. "Should I get the Uber?" I asked, forgetting if I had ordered the one that brought us here.

"I can fit us all," Ben said.

It was unfathomable to me at this point that somebody could drive to one brewery and drink responsibly enough to drive to another one. Completely foreign. From my perspective, there was a better chance of me flying to the moon and then off to Venus than moving from one craft brewery full of high-gravity beers to another.

Location #4 was an unmitigated disaster. I mean, the brewery itself was delightful. Like many brew-houses dotting the northeast landscape, Industrial Arts planted their flag in an abandoned warehouse district.

Walter was waiting for the four of us as we arrived. *Now we've got a party going on,* I thought to myself.

And everybody else may have been in a celebratory mood, but my idea of a party was slightly different.

A gentleman about my age, maybe a little older—and NOT wearing a MAGA hat — was enjoying a beer with his wife at a stand-alone table against the wall. I stammered and said, "Excuse me, do you support the president?" He said, "I do, thanks for asking, have a good night". And I started asking him why he supports death camps for Mexican children, taking his parents off of Medicare, ruining the lives of my gay friends, shitting on the sacrifice of POWs, raping women, and letting Russia run our government.

Walter drove Jay, Sean, and me to a BBQ joint about 20 minutes west, closer to home. While Sean took an Uber home, I couldn't get my app to work (it turns out I inadvertently turned off my cellular signal), so Walter graciously drove us home as snow fell—and heavily.

•••

After we got in, Jay asked if I wanted to go up to *Uncorked*. When have I ever said no to that?

So, with at least a dozen heavy-duty beers in my system and the snow falling at an inch an hour, I drove to our local.

It was only 8:00 PM when we walked in. The bartender offered us a nightcap but warned us they were closing because only an asshole would drive in this weather.

When I woke up the following day, I felt like shit. Not hungover shit where I need a greasy breakfast and some Advil (Well, yeah, I guess I felt *that* too). Shit, as in a shitty human being. It was bad enough I was spiraling to hell.

But I was taking Jay with me.

I've known her since before I could remember. She's the last person who would suggest driving to a bar in a snowstorm while both of us were probably four times (at least) the legal limit.

It's bad enough I was going out in a blaze of glory. Having her soul on my conscience was more than I could bear. She suffered enough with the ramifications of attending a Catholic School and falling in love with an altar boy. It's one thing if this was going to bring me down in my forties, it would be a whole different animal if it happened to this sweet, kind, dedicated angel.

The following day, after being chewed out for my display at Industrial Arts, I told her I would do better, that I was okay, and that she deserved my best.

•••

Martin Luther King Day is a perfectly placed holiday on the American calendar. While the man and his message deserve something more significant than a cold January Monday, it's a mile marker that workers can look to once the holidays are over and everyone settles back into their routine. If you can get through two full work weeks, your reward is a three-day weekend.

And coming off my deplorable behavior two days prior, it was needed and appreciated.

You're a waste; this is your second day of a hangover at your age. It's pathetic.

Jay was working from home that day, and some of her customers refused to acknowledge MLK's impact on our history. I was relatively productive. I did some morning food shopping and started some laundry. I even thought about going to the gym—which was a far cry from most mornings when contemplation never entered my mind. So that was a step in the right direction, I guess.

Going back to last August, I maintained casual, private contact with Jimmy Portersmith. I still don't know the specifics of how Sudol abused him, but given our prior talks and how shaken he appeared after the Archbishop's Review Board testimony, I assumed it was pretty goddamned awful.

I had last heard from Jimmy less than a week earlier, on January 16th. It was just a random check-in:

"Hey, my man, just checking in to see how you've been."

"I've had better days, dude, lol," he replied.

"I hear ya. Kinda spiraled a bit myself after the holidays."

"Same thing with me. I'm actually working in Ridgefield today,"

He sent me pictures of a bathroom remodel he was working on, and we talked about work and the brutally cold weather.

After a period of silence, he replied again, "Yeah, I've been really depressed lately."

"I hear ya, dude," I said. "I've been up and down. The downs have been pretty shitty, though. I gotta stop putting off therapy."

"Yeah, I've been doing the same thing; I haven't done shit with therapy."

"I've made two deadlines and chickened out each time," I told him. "I gave myself an end-of-January deadline now."

"That's funny. I've done the same thing; I didn't give myself a deadline."

"First I said Thanksgiving, then I said Xmas, and now I'm saying my birthday, lol," I responded.

"Yeah, I know the feeling. I get these (days) where I don't even want to get out of bed."

"Yup," I concurred. And that was the end of our conversation.

Until Martin Luther King Day.

At lunchtime, I picked up my phone, figuring I'd read MLB Trade Rumors or ESPN while I had some grub. But once I moved the device, there was a message from Jimmy staring at me on the home screen:

"I'm in St Clair's hospital." it read.

"Oh shit! Is everything ok?" I replied

"Not really. Did something stupid."

"What did you do?"

He didn't answer, and he didn't have to. I assumed the worst. My stomach dropped to the floor. Not again. Not another fucking tragic ending courtesy of the Reverend Gerry Sudol.

"Oh fuck, man. You getting the care you need?" I asked him.

"They're going to take my phone," he responded, as if a medical professional were approaching and planning to take the phone out of his hands. What the hell was I supposed to do with this information? Why did he reiterate which hospital he was in?

"Ok, brother. Follow the doctor's orders, get the help you need, and know I'm here if you need anything. Stay strong, my friend."

The conversation then went silent. I didn't even get the little checkmark saying my message was read.

Jay, who had dropped what she was doing and helped me through the conversation, said, "You have to call Greg."

She was right. What the hell was I going to do? Drive down to there and tell the psychiatric staff that Jimmy was a survivor of abuse. They've probably figured that out by now.

I called Greg right away and gave him all the details. He didn't violate Jimmy's confidentiality agreement at all, but he hinted that he was worried about Jimmy and had been having trouble getting in touch with him lately.

And I could understand that from Jimmy's perspective. I felt the same way from time to time when Greg's number would come up on my phone or when I received a text from him. Greg has been a warrior for victims' rights and church accountability. I was genuinely grateful for the guidance he had given me and looked forward to an eventual resolution where the good people of Ridgefield Park would get the answers they deserved. But every conversation with him—just as the requests for comments I would get from local media when a new church story broke—reminded me why I had relationships with these folks in the first place.

The "quiet part" of the ordeal was officially over. Jimmy's struggle clarified that there was no settling down. The ramifications of coming forward could manifest itself at any time.

For the first time since August, I questioned whether I had done the right thing in the first place. Would it have been better to let them sleeping dogs lie?

XXXI

Was I going to kill myself on the night of February 23, 2019?

Almost definitely not. But there was a greater-than-zero chance that it could be the last night of my life.

I stormed out of the house following an argument with Jay, which stemmed from her reaction to the 2018 Oscar-nominated film *A Star Is Born*. The movie depicted the booze-induced demise of fictional singer Jackson Maye (played brilliantly by Bradley Cooper), and she felt it hit a little too close to home. Those might have been her exact words.

I had been spiraling, and swiftly, since the end of the holidays, and the first few weeks of '19 found me in a tailspin.

The weekend coincided with a Vatican summit on the clergy abuse scandal, and the scope of the conspiracy was front and center in every major news outlet. The ironic thing about stories so vile and gut-wrenching, like clergy abuse, is that there is no political spin on it - It's just as likely to be vilified on Fox News as on MSNBC or *Huff Post*. It spurned investigations from blue-state attorneys general in New Jersey, New York, and California while also being investigated on a federal level by arguably the most conservative Attorney General in recent history, Jeff Sessions.

I finally found the motivation to get to the gym that fateful Saturday afternoon for the first time since late December, following those two hours watching "A Star Is Born." And it was a good workout—a fantastic one.

I got into that zone on the elliptical machine, where adrenaline and endorphins take over your body like a drug. Where you feel like your breathing and movement are in sync with something greater than yourself. You get a calming sense of clarity as you pound away at your exercise. You don't notice your sweat, the music in your headphones, or the college basketball game on the six-inch monitor on the machine you threw $10 on.

I walked out of that gym that afternoon feeling like a new man—like the ballooning slug I had been for over half a year was shedding its skin. I could taste and appreciate the mountain air in our cozy environs for the first time in a long time. I was sweating and stunk like someone threw a keg party in a White Castle dumpster, but I didn't care. I felt good again, pre-holidays good.

And I made the mistake of telling Jay just how good I felt.

"THAT'S what I've been missing for months," I exclaimed as I walked in the door, expecting to find her showered and getting ready to go out for a late lunch/early dinner at our favorite gastropub.

Instead, she was still in her pajamas, in the same spot on the couch when I left.

"Well, you still need to seek professional help," she replied.

My voice rose to a nasty, bellowing yell. "I KNOW! FOR THE LOVE OF FUCKING GOD, CAN I HAVE FIVE FUCKING MINUTES TO FEEL GOOD?!"

And it was all downhill from there.

She screamed back at me, accusing me of killing myself and reminding me I was about the same age that my father was when he began his slow, torturous descent into alcoholism that took just about everything he ever had.

She painstakingly recounted every incident I caused or created over the last six weeks. She said she was deathly concerned over how I would react to an upcoming *The Record* feature about how my parents handled my revelation about St. Francis. But I didn't hear concern. I didn't hear the desperate pleadings of the middle-aged woman who spent her life living with the ramifications of Gerry Sudol's impact on Ridgefield Park.

I heard someone trying to take away momentary euphoria—an oasis of clarity and calmness I hadn't felt since the initial reaction to coming forward.

Instantly, all clarity and peace left the building.

Like a poorly educated internet troll, I resorted to *whataboutism*, mentioning how she confronted me on more than one Friday night about how I had stopped writing and appeared stunted in a holding pattern.

"You have a few drinks and call me a failure!" I yelled.

"Maybe it's because I don't have the guts to say it sober!" she retorted.

And all I took from that was that my wife thinks I'm a failure. Not that she was concerned. Not that she was afraid that I was losing any motivation to move forward and better myself. I heard she thought I was a failure.

In a fit of rage, I yelled, "Fuck this! I'm out of here!"

"Don't come back," she said.

"Don't worry, I'm not fucking planning to. "

•••

I packed my CPAP machine, laptop, pajamas, and change of pants into a duffle bag and stormed out into the Jeep, up our hill, and to the left. I had no destination. I had my essentials and a credit card with roughly $800 still available after a very expensive December and January.

My first actual decision was when I got to the town center, a half mile away. Going left meant rural roads into upstate New York, while going right kept me straddling the New Jersey/New York border—a little closer to mass civilization. Like so many other times in my life, I veered left.

My next geographical choice was whether to head south towards New York City—closer to where I could duck in to see Erin, whom I leaned upon without intent organically. Or I could head north, but this time on the New York State Thruway, which could have me north of Albany in less than 2 hours or the Canadian border in under six. However, sans passport and a destination, Canada wasn't a realistic option.

South it would be. Closer to RP. Hell, maybe I'd get trashed at the Knights of Columbus. I could apologize for trashing their banner after my bachelor party fifteen years ago. I loosely thought of hotels in the lower Bergen County area—hotels near bars, if possible, as I merged onto New Jersey Route 17 South.

Then I saw the sign:

Ramapo College of New Jersey—Next Exit.

I veered two lanes over to ensure I didn't miss the turn. Right off the exit, at the intersection of Routes 17 and 22, was The Mason Jar—a restaurant and pub often frequented by campus faculty and staff, at least in my day. Their prices were too high for the students, definitely on purpose. I would pull in there and gather my thoughts on a road that felt like home.

The Mason Jar is between two budget motels—a Best Western and a Days Inn. Instantly, after ordering their highest-gravity beer, I scoped out potential reservations. Both had vacancies and rooms for not much more than a hundred bucks. I could get a room there, then text some folks I knew within a twenty-minute ride who might get me some cocaine. I'd order a thirty-pack from Drizzly when I left the bar. I'd write, drink, and snort until I had some sort of direction for my next writing focus, or I'd die trying.

But whatever darkness crept in with the new year had to go away. The turn was sudden and jolting. Two months into the weekend, I was celebrating the holidays and reflecting on all that my story accomplished. Now I was 2 miles north of campus, in the bar we could never afford, thinking about staying in a hotel room with a cheaper nightly rate than a 1999 bar tab, contemplating many bad things.

How the hell did this happen?

Instinctively, I texted the Ramapo friends' thread with a poster advertising a Grateful Dead cover band playing an upcoming Saturday at the Mason Jar, with the caption, "Airbnb a room in Pine Hall?"

Memory lane began. We reflected on the few times we were at the place and how other friends we knew got pinched for a DWI making the illegal left towards campus (when the right turn leads you onto the highway and a more roundabout way home—also by design).

Before long, we were laughing about a debunked urban legend that Canadians have Kermit the Frog but call him "Green Dennis."

Faith in myself was restored by the same people I could always count on.

I had two more beers, bringing my total to about $50's worth, and then ordered some food to go. I didn't think twice about driving home, despite being obviously over the limit and likely visibly intoxicated. I didn't care.

I came in and asked Jay to give me a work week and I would enroll in talk therapy.

...

I'm a professional avoider, and always have been. But the American healthcare system and the Roman Catholic Church really didn't make the already difficult step of beginning talk therapy easy. Greg handled the arrangements on my behalf, but getting their approval and reimbursements in a timely manner was cumbersome and lengthy.

Their preference was that I see one of their pre-approved counselors, to which my response was a big fat fucking "no." I'll find the shrink; you just leave the money on the nightstand. My first instinct was to shun the church completely, but our health insurance at the time was not conducive to low out-of-pocket-cost mental health.

I set a series of filters on Psychology Today to find who I hoped was the right therapist. I wanted the therapist to be female. I wasn't sure if I could be truly open about the details of my abuse with another man—a man who was, by society's standards, more accomplished (better) than me. Perhaps that was prejudicial thinking that cut me off from some of the best help possible, but it's what my mindset was during the therapy search. RP's "Relentless Bitches" likely had something to do with it.

I wanted the therapist to be at least halfway between work and home, if not closer to home. After 12 years of living in West Milford, I had really grown to hate my hour-each-way commute.

I selected three areas of focus: Trauma, Childhood Sexual Abuse, and Anger Management. The search Bot spits out a series of qualifying therapists; first among them was Dr. Jessica Grant.

Dr. Grant hit all the focal areas of my search, and her office was practically equidistant from work and home. After one initial consultation, I felt like it was a fit. It would take another month to get Archdiocese approval so they can reimburse me, as it would take them weeks to process the receipt I submitted. Despite the red tape, I could begin therapy with Doctor Grant.

After assessing me, Dr. Grant diagnosed me with Complex Post-Traumatic Stress Disorder, and while I always felt that would be the case, the diagnosis and description were illuminating. Dr. Grant spoke at length about the pillars and hallmarks of PTSD.

Negative self-talk? Check.

Inability to think clearly about the future? Check!

Inability to trust and a propensity for constructing walls? Check and check.

Lacking a true sense of self?

Checkmate.

The more Jessica spoke, the more I felt as if I was hearing the story of my life read back to me by a petite clinician a few years my junior. These early, frank discussions brought a sense of relief. All the negative feelings and emotions that had dictated how I carried myself since puberty now made sense. I wasn't "less than," and while I was clearly damaged, I wasn't defective, as I long felt I was.

The realizations are only part of the therapeutic process, however, and I became fixated on the fact that I was traumatized rather than diving into recovery and actively doing the work to live a healed life. In a perverse and twisted way, knowing why I behaved so poorly only justified those behaviors, creating a self-fueling cycle of trauma manifestations.

Jessica introduced me to the concept of "Radical Acceptance"—not trying to understand or excuse a circumstance, but to accept it—no matter how traumatizing; as a matter of fact. It sounds simple in theory, but it's much more difficult in practice.

There was no getting around the fact that my parish priest abused me. What I couldn't accept was the callous nature of the structural hierarchy and the willing populace that allowed it to happen. Until I could let go of that, healing was always going to be a pipe dream.

Jessica also informed me of the way the traumatized mind can shut down memories—at any age. Time has little to do with it. I'm haunted to this day why I know what Father Gerry's rectory bedroom looks like while having absolutely no recollection of why I was ever in it.

Dr. Grant was able to help me see that those negative voices that reverberated throughout my mind for as long as I could remember were the trapped cries of an unhealed child: *Angry Little Eddie.*

She asked me to commit to not drinking or smoking marijuana on the evenings that followed our sessions. I committed to not drinking but insisted for that to be successful, we'd have to switch from Thursdays because I drink on Thursdays.

Stubbornness aside, I was finally on the path to therapeutic healing.

XXXII

March 7, 2019, was a day not unlike that whipping-windy day the previous October when I testified before the Archbishop's Review Board. I woke up in a hotel room in Cherry Hill, New Jersey, on the opposite end of the state, having stayed at a Holiday Inn Express on an overnight business trip with Jay.

It was the day I was to testify before the New Jersey Senate Judiciary Committee at the State Capital in Trenton to urge the Senate to pass Bill S477—which would eliminate the civil statutes of limitation for a defined period for all older charges of sexual abuse.

Having limited myself to three Sam Adams Lagers from the hotel lobby the night before, I didn't have a hangover—and it was to my fortune. The hotel lobby breakfast was full of greasy meats, runny scrambled eggs, and everything a hungover stomach desires. On this morning, I would have only straight black coffee.

Jay and I arrived an hour before Greg told us to assemble. I thought it would be cool to tour the statehouse, one of America's oldest and in the capital's heart's historic district. As we pulled off the interstate and headed toward the Capital, it became clear that wouldn't happen.

We were told to follow signs for visitor parking, which was housed underneath an annex to the statehouse. After ten minutes in traffic two blocks away, we discovered it was already full. We had to find a pay lot five blocks from the building where we were told to assemble. As we approached the Capital, it seemed like every person or group we walked past was marveling at the turnout. Security guards openly admitted the crowds overwhelmed them at the entrance checkpoint.

The energy was noticeable throughout every hallway of the building. There would be no time for a tour as the demand to make public comments on Senate Bill 447 was so large that it had to be moved to a hearing room with double the capacity.

Survivors came out in droves.

Testimony began with two religious rights advocates warning that the bill would lead to frivolous lawsuits and prohibit the church from continuing its work of ridding the ministry of abusive priests.

The committee wasn't buying what they were selling.

Survivors started speaking a bit after 10:00 AM. Jay and I connected with Greg, who had an army of clients like myself ready to talk. We were told it could take an hour to get everyone to testify.

We sat there, hand in hand, for long stretches at a time, listening to testimony that sometimes seemed autobiographical. The testimony of a retired cop moved us–red in the face with a look that anyone who's ever spent severe time at a bar can identify—as he recounted the impact the abuse he suffered at the hands of his scout leader impacted his life. He spoke of finding refuge in alcohol and drugs, in overeating, and shutting people out. He mentioned how he was on prescription medication from an early age.

He was describing my life. So many survivors were.

•••

As the clock was banging up on 7:00 PM, I could finally offer my testimony. I stood at the witness table with four other survivors who, like me, raised their right hand and promised to tell the truth, the whole truth, and nothing but the truth, so help us God. We were on strict time limits, so I was forced to skip some of my prepared remarks. They were, however, submitted in full for the record:

Thank you for granting me the opportunity to address this body today.

"My name is Ed Hanratty. I have spent my entire life here, in my home state of New Jersey. I was born here. I was educated here. I have made lifelong friends here. I was married here. I bought a home here.

And I was sexually abused as a child here.

I don't pretend to speak for every victim of childhood sexual abuse, but for a great many of us, the current Statutes of Limitation deprive of us of two crucial steps that are necessary for our recovery and healing:

Accountability and closure.

I was routinely abused by my priest at St. Francis of Assisi in Ridgefield Park from the age of ten to fourteen. Yet I had no idea that it was abuse.

All childhood sexual abuse is tragic. But certain circumstances may dictate when a child even realizes that he or she is a victim of this trauma.

Hypothetically speaking—and heaven forbid—a child was abducted by a stranger or a casual acquaintance. That child would be keenly aware of the wrongdoing, and offered the full support of our communities, our law enforcement, our medical services and our schools.

And rightfully so.

However, in a case like mine—and those of too many survivors to calculate—when you are abused at a young age by somebody you are taught to trust; somebody whom your budding faith demands that you confess your sins to; how are you supposed to even know what you're experiencing is abuse? Especially at a pre-pubescent age.

For years, decades even, we laughed about or shrugged off the antics of my abuser. We grew up hearing tales from our parents about how the nuns used to beat them with rulers. The unintentional lesson learned was "this was just the price to pay for a Catholic education". They were hit by nuns. I was kissed and groped by a priest.

At 18—while only 25 minutes away from St. Francis, studying at Ramapo College of New Jersey — I still didn't think much of it. The same could be said at 21 or 22.

But I had ghosts. I had demons that were beginning to manifest.

I am an outgoing person. I've never been accused of being shy or reclusive, and certainly, nobody has ever accused me of being quiet.

Yet I struggled in situations where I was alone, one-on-one with an individual—teachers, professors, girlfriends, my buddies. By the time I graduated from Ramapo, I was only comfortable around people I loved and trusted if I could have a couple of beers or something stronger.

In the most intimate of situations, my anxiety would become even worse.

These trust and intimacy issues continue to plague me as I now sit before you in my early forties, though thankfully I have a greater understanding of them now and I'm finally getting the professional help I need.

But neither therapy nor the dangerous self-medication that I've sought at times will ever provide me with what I truly need and deserve:

Accountability and closure.

When I came forward with my story last August, I was approached by over 1,000 people who wanted to speak to me about what I had written. Most were strangers seeking to encourage and uplift me. A lot were people from Ridgefield Park, thanking me for confirming their 30-year-old suspicions.

But a select few—almost a dozen—were fellow victims and survivors of the same priest that abused me.

These are people with whom I haven't seen in person since before Seinfeld premiered. But when they opened up to me, their last three decades were plagued with many of the same issues that mine have been.

They deserve accountability and closure.

My parents just gave a heartbreaking interview to The Record in which they opened up about the guilt they felt for sending me to Catholic school. Think about that for a minute. They felt guilty for doing what their parents did, investing in their children's education. I had to read, in black and white, my father say "I failed my son".

They deserve accountability and closure.

My wife of almost seventeen years, who's seated in this room right now, grew up in St. Francis as well. We first met in kindergarten. She grew up amongst the dozens of boys who were exposed to this man's abuse. She has been living with the aftershock of it for as long as she can remember.

I want closure for her even more than I do for myself because of the responsibility I feel.

I know our time here is limited, but I have one more example of just how awful this situation was, and how it could have been so much different.

It didn't take too long for us to put the pieces together as to what happened at St. Francis that caused this priest to be removed. We learned that the pastor, in conjunction with the Archdiocese, whisked him away in the middle of the night, and told us he suffered from "Nervous Exhaustion".

How different would our lives be if they were upfront about this in 1994? If we could have sought the help immediately while we still had our whole lives in front of us?

But they didn't.

They just let us walk down self-destructive paths, left us to figure it out on their own.

No accountability. No closure.

In far too many cases, we can no longer see to it that these monsters and the men who covered up for them pay for the horrendous crimes that they have committed.

I beg of this committee, the Senate, the Assembly, and Governor Murphy to swiftly and judiciously reform the Statutes of Limitation for childhood sexual abuse.

Thank you for your time."

The bill passed the committee that night, with one lone holdout preventing a unanimous victory. It would then pass the full Senate and Assembly, and Governor Phil Murphy would sign it.

I would file a lawsuit against Gerry Sudol and the Archdiocese of Newark in the following weeks.

•••

The Boss would occasionally invite me out to a Mad-Men style lunch: four of five cocktails and a meal we'd pick at and each bring home for later. It was during one of these lunches in mid-April at Segovia—an old-school Spanish Tapas restaurant with a long, vintage bar that looked and smelled like it had many a story to tell—that I was on the receiving end of a call I couldn't ignore.

My phone buzzed on the bar top during my third Jameson on the rocks. "Greg Gianforcaro" appeared on the lock screen. "Gotta take this—lawyer," I said to The Boss as I grabbed the phone and darted outside.

Greg informed me that a national law firm that represents survivors of abuse, Jeff Andersen and Associates, based out of Minneapolis, wanted to use my case to test a somewhat novel theory, filing a public nuisance lawsuit to force the disclosure of documents. It was a not-subtle Trojan Horse to gain legal access to decades of church documentation. It was all I had ever wanted.

They needed me at the Newark Airport Ramada the following morning for a press conference to announce the filing of the lawsuit and the release of over 300 names of credibly accused priests in the State of New Jersey.

I agreed to do so, and less than 24 hours later, I was in a conference room at an airport hotel with a high-powered, smooth-talking lawyer from the Midwest.

The room was packed with fellow survivors, local media, and church attorneys. There were finger sandwiches. Dressed in a corduroy jacket that got dubbed my "Priest Fighting Jacket" by the friends in #RPStrong, I stood at the podium, reciting my story, what I had learned about my Parish, and why answers and accountability were non-negotiable to heal trauma.

The more questions I was asked—to be fair, mainly from Jeff Andersen himself—the more confident I felt I was doing the right thing. I only needed to look at the placards on my left and right easels. They were adorned with images of credibly accused priests in New Jersey, chief among them Gerry Sudol and David Ernst.

St. Francis was well represented on a list no parish ever wanted to find itself on.

I finally met Deena Yellin from *The Record* when the event concluded. I was so high on positive emotions that I broke all journalistic standards and gave this miniature woman a massive bear hug.

Before we even left the Ramada, I received a text from one of my friends saying that they just got choked up watching me on News 12 New Jersey, which was playing in their workplace cafeteria.

Making a difference was not unlike a drug.

XXXIII

You'll never drink alone if you befriend enough people at a local bar. So I wasn't technically alone on the Thursday before Memorial Day Weekend 2019 when I was sitting on a stool at *Uncorked* and received a call from the attorney Jeff Andersen. He was calling to thank me for my bravery in coming forward and filing the nuisance suit, but a judge just ruled I don't have standing to bring a public nuisance lawsuit.

They did not rule on or question the validity of my claims—which was all that I truly cared about. I studied the Supreme Court in great detail in college and have watched a cumulative 15,000 hours of Law & Order, so I'm well aware of terms like "standing" and other technicalities. The court merely disagreed with the avenue I pursued.

I called Jay to explain, and she took it in the same stride. Though she was a little perturbed by the public display over a lawsuit that the attorneys always considered a shot in the dark at best, she agreed that nobody challenged the heart of what I alleged.

Alerting my parents that this maneuver failed didn't go as smoothly. My mother—who still couldn't comprehend why authorities didn't arrest Gerry Sudol immediately following the revelations—bellowed, "You have GOT to be kidding me," expressing her dismay and disgust. I couldn't convince her that this was never a guarantee and that my lawsuit against Sudol and the Archdiocese was still being filed and moving through the system.

My father understood it slightly better but asked me for what had to be the fifteenth time if there was a way for them to sue the Archdiocese for what happened to them as parents.

Did he think any parent would be granted standing to sue for damages over their own adult decision to entrust their children to the Catholic Church? Kids don't have a choice. Adults do. The time for the Baby Boomers to act was during the Reagan/Bush years. They didn't, and it fell to Gen X to clean up the messes that we played no role in making other than just being there.

The next text I sent was to Scott Tooley, another of Sudol's survivors. Scott came forward to #RPStrong but watched the proceedings from a distance. He had reservations about going through the church process, and as someone who experienced those same emotions, I completely understood. I told him I would keep him abreast of the situation as it evolved forward, and if he wanted to inject himself into them at any point, I'd be happy to help make it happen.

Then, it was back to the business of kicking off Memorial Day Weekend.

Our friends Jason and Amanda (Jaymanda, for short) invited us to spend the weekend at their home. Along with Hayes and his wife Anna, or the Hayeses, the six of us slowly spent more of our free time together as we moved from our thirties into our forties.

As our other friends got down to the business of raising children, we nonparents would spend summers partying at Phish concerts or backyard barbecues despite living in three distinct and distant areas of Jersey—we were at the northern tip, the Hayeses were smack in the middle, and Jaymanda was right outside of Philadelphia.

We would spend Memorial Day weekend at Jaymanda's newly purchased large craftsman house. We loaded our Jeep with four cases of beer for the weekend, which surprisingly—despite near-daily text communication—would be the first time this crew had gotten together since my *Reverb* article the summer before.

I crushed an unhealthy number of those beers within the first three hours of our arrival. Jason announced he had acquired some psychedelic mushrooms for the evening, and after about six high-gravity beers, it felt like the only reasonable thing to do.

Their new home, which they dubbed "Club Oak" after their street name, was hyper-conducive to a psychedelic experience. Sitting on a fenced-in acre, their yard is vast and full of interesting nooks and crannies like a koi pond, a plant shack, and a greenhouse. It's stalked behind a chained link fence by a neighborly cat dubbed "Lasagna." Centuries-old weeping willows sway in the slightest breeze as they provide a natural barrier to the clearing that is their yard.

Our hosts strategically placed hammocks and air mattresses throughout the backyard so that trippers could find comfort wherever they wandered. Inside their beautiful home, bass reverberated from the various jam bands and electro-funk groups on rotation. There were black lights and beanbag chairs.

But once the psilocybin kicked in, I was drawn to a singular feature—their pool.

In my world, I began wading my arm through the water. In my head, I heard the childhood sounds of Sean, Elizabeth, Erin, and me splashing around. *I have to reclaim the water;* I thought to myself.

I had been the lone wanderer to this point, so I returned to the group. Jay was recapping her experience over the past ten months. It was overwhelmingly positive when we had the bull by the horns—when we were fighting to get Sudol removed, attending press conferences, testifying before the Senate, speaking to media outlets, and so on.

But it was extra dark when the lights were out. My sporadically and periodically displayed anger issues were now a feature. Friday nights after dinner—once the highlight of our week—now found me bitter and exuding tension.

There was no escaping it. This is who I am now, as I drifted the needle a smudge away from "Survivor" and back towards what I had been for most of my life:

"Victim."

•••

I awoke on the Fourth of July, 2019, with a basketball-sized anxiety pit in my stomach. It was the pinnacle of Ridgefield Park's year, her pride and joy—the Village Independence Day Parade. Jay and I would attend as we always did, viewing the marchers and revelers from the elevated corner of Main Street and Poplar Ave, three blocks from her parents' home and four blocks from St. Francis.

Seeing that it's the only village gathering we attend, it was to be the first one since I posted the *Reverb* Story eleven months earlier. Was I going to be stopped by random people? Would I be constantly speaking about the St. Francis affair? Would nobody say a word about it and whisper and stare at me?

My iPhone buzzed with a call as we were almost out the door. It was Scott Tooley. He had been up all night drinking, and he wasn't handling life well at the moment. He said he spiraled not long after we created #RPStrong, and he hasn't been able to get past his trauma.

I begged him to seek therapy. I told him how much better I felt having someone to speak with weekly while confessing that I'm still a work in progress. I told him to consider talking to Greg, who could get his appointments reimbursed as he did for me.

I could only hope I reached him as I reached the car after our conversation ended. But the image of this man struggling, miles away from any family, and unable to find the critical support that kept me functioning haunted me the entire 45-minute ride to RP.

Roughly half of the familiar faces we spoke with during the gathering mentioned the story, and all respectfully. I might not have been too happy with America on her birthday, as we learned of even more tales of sexual abuse at the hands of powerful men, but I remained proud of my hometown for the way they responded to the silence-breaking.

Back at my in-laws' cookout, it was a slightly different story. Relatives saw me for the first time since my televised press conference and wanted to catch up. What had we learned? What did we think we could learn?

One family friend stopped me multiple times to tell me she thinks what priests have been doing for ages to young boys is disgusting. She told me she was proud to tell her friends and congregation that she knew me. I was getting uncomfortable with the praise—if these people only knew how my trauma was manifesting they wouldn't be so proud.

This was, give or take, the twentieth 4th of July I spent all or part of at my in-law's house. It was a tradition that predated our marriage. And for those other nineteen, along with copious amounts of light beer and a fantastic spread of burgers, dogs, steak sandwiches, chicken, and whatever treats the guests bring, you would find engaging conversation. Sometimes, with people you text with every day. Other times, with the folks you only see at this event.

And those conversations were usually about the New York Giants' upcoming NFL Training Camp. Or the current Yankees' season and their lofty position in the standings, more often than not. There would be great tales of missed holes-in-one and massive exaggerations of everybody's golf game. There was always the potential for early fireworks in election years, but that tension never rose above a meager passive-aggressive comment.

In recent years, we would marvel at how much bigger each child of the next generation of RP 4th Party-goers got compared to last year, what sports the kids were playing, what ridiculous over-the-top helicopter parenting tactics were in vogue for the summer.

But not this year. This year, "Ed Hanratty, Noble Enemy of the Church" dominated at every turn in the conversation.

For better or worse, this was now my identity.

...

I'm not naturally inclined to "bring the fight" to someone else. Looking back at the original *Reverb* piece, I didn't name names. I waited until I had the overnight support of hundreds to identify Gerry Sudol and St. Francis of Assisi publicly. So, I spent the rest of the summer settling back into that morass of not knowing what to do or who I was.

I knew I could write. I was determined to write a book about my experiences with the church, but I had no straightforward end game. I sure didn't feel any better, and some days, I felt worse than before I made such a leap. But every time I recaptured my stories, I was documenting a slow descent into substance abuse, anger, and shame.

Shame. Dr. Grant warned me about that early in our initial session. Shame was the only genuine negative emotion, as I would learn. There are natural benefits to feeling sad, to feeling upset, to even feeling guilt. But shame? Shame is toxic and all-consuming. And while I fought like hell to convince myself otherwise on the exterior, I would go through stretches of a period where the only way to describe my feelings was "ashamed."

It was during a period such as this when I woke up on August 19, 2019, and acknowledged the anniversary on Facebook:

"I guess for the rest of my life, August 19th is going to be some sort of a 're-birthday' for me. It was one year ago that I finally decided to come forward about my experience growing up Catholic. An experience that we learn more and more every day was not as unique as it should be.

And here's the sad reality: I'm not 100% sure that if I had to do it all over again that I would have.

Don't get me wrong - there have been thousands of moments where I felt that it was the right thing to do. And even if there was only one, that moment made it all worth it: We got a known child abuser removed from a situation where he was living on the grounds of an elementary school. The four days that friends, relatives and strangers pounded the phone lines and email chains to the Archdiocese, law enforcement and the media will go down as the greatest thing I was ever a part of.

And there were many, many other highs. I've met more amazing people than I knew ever existed over the past 12 months - survivors from all corners of the globe. I was able to testify before the state senate to change the statute of limitations bill to hold the church accountable. I'm in the process of suing every Archdiocese in New Jersey for their records, demanding "What did the church know, and when did they know it?" Recently, we learned that the priest who terrorized our parish was accused of abuse at the church he served before he came to Ridgefield Park. Since I'm pot committed, that's only strengthened my resolve for the time being.

And the countless messages I've received from survivors speaking out for the first time made me feel like I wasn't alone, and gave me the sincere hope that they would begin their path to peace.

But these highs, man, you know what they bring. Lows.

Lots of time left with my thoughts. Therapy sessions where cans of worms I never knew I was carrying get opened up. Tunnel vision where I can't see the bigger picture. A propensity for dividing the world into good and evil. Blackouts. And an increased arsenal of medication, some prescribed, some not. Darkness. Self-blame. I've simultaneously felt that I was the most loved person on the planet while feeling stranded on a deserted island.

Please don't misinterpret this for a lack of gratitude. The way my long-time friends have had my back has been a heartwarming gift. The kindness expressed by new friends and strangers has restored my hope in humanity. And my family - all of them suddenly hurting because of my decision in one way or another - has been a rock. I love each and everyone of you.

I hope to complete the first draft of "Nervous Exhaustion" by Thanksgiving. My church-busting corduroy blazer is hanging in my closet, ready to be donned at a minute's notice. I can't afford to not move forward.

But it hasn't been easy. Here's hoping that by August 19, 2020, I feel more balanced and can unequivocally say that I did the right thing.

•••

The back half of 2019 was more of the same. Two steps forward, one step back. I thought I was absorbing therapy, but I was approaching it as if it was a seminar on Complex PTSD and not seeing the link between the tools I was learning and my responsibility to deploy them. For the first six months and more, I was more in awe of how the trauma impacted my life than what I could do to mitigate those impacts.

I had handled the holidays well. Maybe not as well as in 2018, but they went off with no hint of darkness, just my typical disdain for the pomp and circumstance associated with them (grooming, traveling, shopping, commercialism) Mark and his wife Debra hosted a holiday party for our close-knit group from Ramapo, now over twenty-five years since its inception. While the party wasn't as wild and raucous as our Pine Hall Christmas parties were, we still had more booze and cannabis than most would consider age-appropriate.

After some friends asked me if I wanted to smoke a bowl outside, I stepped into the fog of a misty December night, taking stock of where I had been and where I was going. The new year would likely be a resolution or direction to the lawsuits filed in droves against the Archdiocese.

But 2019 was not like 2018. Whereas '18 was an upward trajectory from publication forward, '19 was a series of peaks and valleys.

I couldn't help but wonder, what did 2020 have in store?

XXXIV

January 2020 was looking much like January 2019. Thanks to not one but two bouts with a virus that wasn't influenza but sure as hell fell like it, I had my longest stretch without therapy since I began eleven months earlier. The early-in-the-new-year estimate for when I could litigate my case against Gerry Sudol and the Archdiocese was overly optimistic. There was no movement in my case, as thousands of other survivors filed lawsuits after we successfully changed the law. Jay was traveling with more frequency again.

And on those few weeknights where I wasn't feeling sick and disgusting, I was once again getting too comfortable having a few too many beers by myself.

I wouldn't classify it as a spiral, though. I avoided getting completely out of hand—there were no blackout nights that left me with only hazy, dreadful, humiliating half-memories. In party situations, I could remain present, especially in situations where I had, in the past, made a complete and total fool of myself.

In my mind, the last Sunday in January is always a bit off, much like the two clock changes we get in March and November. There's no football scheduled, but the Super Bowl is still a week away. This completely changes the equilibrium of the day, but that doesn't exactly mean it's a bad thing.

I was motivated to cook a traditional Irish breakfast late in the morning since I hadn't got annihilated the night before and slept a whole night. When I cook something that looks good, I naturally post it to Facebook via Instagram, primarily to show the world that *I'm not this big just because I drink a lot of beer.*

It registered the usual number of likes and minor conversations and mainly engaged Chris McLoughlin, a Celtic cooking aficionado. We debated the merits of baking rashers (Irish bacon) versus skillet frying them (spoiler alert: there's no wrong answer), the best butchers in the tri-state area to buy authentic Irish pork, and our fondness for white pudding and Kerrygold butter.

Then I got a pop-up on my phone from Messenger. Chris shot me a text:

Hey Ed! It's excellent to discuss ways to cook the Breakfast of Champions with you. I would like to discuss something else with you at some point. I could bring some rasher samples to the table!

And I immediately knew what he meant.

•••

Chris was one of the first Sudol survivors to reach out to me in August of '18 when I published my story. He shared enough vague details—again, I didn't want to know the specifics of anybody else's experiences—that I had a good idea of what he had to deal with. He immediately took proactive steps, albeit down a different avenue than I did.

Chris received the same packet for review from the Victim's Compensation Fund as I got. Greg handled that seamlessly for me, with compassion and solemnity to meet the gravity of the situation. And the minute Chris told me he wanted to meet over a drink, I knew that meant he had received a settlement offer.

We settled on a day and location—The Cottage in Teaneck. It's a no-frills yet charming Irish pub with soccer on a dozen television sets all day. It seemed like the perfect spot for Hanratty to meet McLaughlin to discuss the Catholic Church.

Ironically, my therapist asked if I could reschedule that week's appointment for when I was supposed to catch up with Chris. I couldn't keep him waiting any longer, and if I'm being honest, I was eager to hear what he had to say. Not that I was expecting to hear anything that would change my mind about how I proceeded forward, but this was the first Sudol-related correspondent with the Archdiocese since New Jersey passed the S4177 and opened the window for survivors to seek answers from those responsible for their abuse.

It's difficult to quantify the impact of missing a therapy session. There may not be any immediate impact on the patient the way missing other medical treatments would. I've found that I could go a week or two without it and be just fine. Conversely, I could have a visit on Monday and be a basket-case by Thursday. But I grew to notice after 11 months that hitting three weeks without seeing the Doctor knocks me off my overall mental game.

But this couldn't wait.

•••

I had jitters leading up to our date that Thursday afternoon when I was about a block from the pub. I honestly couldn't remember the last time I saw Chris. We weren't even that close. Separated by two grades and enrolled in different schools? We might as well have lived on opposite coasts in the early eighties and nineties. Plus, anything I knew of him came via his mother's Irish Step Dancing classes, which performed at assemblies at St. Francis (which

Elizabeth was enrolled in), or his youngest sister, who was in our SF class for the last 3 or 4 grades.

Yet here we found ourselves on a cold, overcast winter afternoon: two middle-aged Irish Americans who'd spent a valuable number of hours on barstools on the precipice of perhaps the most impactful of those hours for both of us.

I walked into The Cottage a little before 3:30. There was no sign of Chris. Toward the end of the bar, two bartenders were going over some paperwork. One of them looked up to give me a welcoming nod. The darkness was perfect, not trying to compensate for the lack of natural light on a gloomy day. It may have been 3:30 AM.

Just as I pulled a stool from mid-bar, Chris walked out of the bathroom. It took me a split second to make sure he recognized me as well—we're relying on Facebook photos of each other. I extended my hand, saying, "Hey, Chris." He blew it off and gave me a firm hug.

That hug was among the most disarming gestures I have ever felt. I'm not ashamed to admit I got a little misty-eyed at it. If a picture is worth a thousand words, that embrace was worth every word in this book.

We collected ourselves, and I pulled my jacket over to the stool next to his. I asked him, "*So, how have you been?*". He said with a chuckle, "*About the same as you,*" and we both burst into hysterics. Ice broken.

We quickly got through the mandatory small talk—where are you living? How's work? How's your family? — but with the first noticeable break in the conversation, he got right down to the brass tacks.

"So, I finally heard from the Archdiocese about the paperwork I submitted to the compensation fund," he said with his unmistakable New York Irish accent. He went through great pains to convey that he was never interested in the money. I assured him I understood because that's been the case for me since my story went viral.

•••

We're not stupid. We know there's a loud minority of people in the message threads of church abuse articles on social media or publication websites that instantly resort to some foolish and uneducated comment about how survivors only come forward to reap financial benefits. In the days following my revelation, I parsed through these threads with a fine-toothed comb—often arguing with the internet trolls who have nothing better to do than share their misguided opinions as if they're the Gospel. Jay and Kerry frequently warned me against it and told me to ignore it because it ultimately did my well-being no good. And they were right.

These trolls don't deserve my anger or attention. If that's what they need to help them get through the day, so be it. They have absolutely zero influence over me or any other of the countless survivors of clergy abuse. If their initial instinct is to claim that any survivor of sexual abuse is in it for the money, then they have never suffered abuse themselves. There but for the Grace of whatever you believe in.

Or at least, that's what I would tell myself.

Once I gave Chris the abridged version of my evolution on the subject, he felt comfortable enough to give the cold, hard facts about his settlement offer letter.

He told me he found it low. By this point, reports about the first wave of settlement offers trickled out. According to local news sources, the average offer was approximately $185,000 in New Jersey. I made no assumptions about what I would consider fair. How *do* you put a price tag on the ramifications of abuse—especially when so many victims have already lived at least half of their life expectancy dealing with its ugly ramifications? Couple that with the fact that, in this case, the abusers were given aid, comfort, and permission to continue to terrorize children by the oldest government organization in the world. What *is* fair?

I don't know if $185,000 is fair or if $185 million would be fair, but at least the thought didn't immediately sicken me.

Unlike when Chris told me, *"They're offering 30 Grand"*.

Look, $30,000 is a lot of money—it's nothing to shrug off. Winning $30,000 on a lottery ticket would likely significantly improve your overall economic situation. But this isn't the state lottery commission that we're talking about. It's the Catholic Church. I would have been much more offended than Chris had let on.

On top of the insulting offer that Chris received, two stipulations came along with the agreement, should he choose to accept it. First, he had thirty days to decide to take—and find a lawyer to attest that he understood the agreement. Second, he was signing away from his right to seek anything more. A future financial settlement was obviously out of the question, but he would also waive his right to seek the truth. The Catholic Church will not volunteer incriminating evidence. That only comes by subpoena.

And we know Sudol had allegations before his appointment to St. Francis and that the parish (and, by extension, the Archdiocese) covered the circumstances of his removal up.

Once again, this is something a band of former students and altar servers pieced together via Facebook and text discussions. One can only imagine what was left to be discovered.

I told Chris that he needs to do what makes the most sense for himself, his recovery, and his loved ones. While I think the offer was ridiculously lowball, I would respect, appreciate, and love him regardless because everybody finds their path to closure—and I was patiently waiting for mine to present itself.

As we spoke more, it became apparent how similar the last thirty years have been for both of us. The pounds that were packed on. The medications that were prescribed. Trust issues.

Issues with opening up to the people closest to us. An inability to confront what happened to us. And the booze.

We joked about the stereotype about Irish alcoholism and how maybe people were looking past the obvious for all these centuries: we don't drink because we were born Irish.

We drink because we were raised Catholic.

PART 3

XXXV

I never thought I would live through a month as globally surreal as September 2001 again in my life (or at least, I hoped not to). Then March 2020 said, "Hold my $500 stockpile of beer". When it began, it was more of the same old slog I had been trying to work my way out of. I was trying to write, handle my adverse behaviors, drink a little less during the week when I was alone, and make plans for the upcoming "Holy Week" with Paddy's Day and the NCAA Tournament.

I mean, it was March. And it was shaping up to be a pretty spectacular one, too.

Jay and I were selected in a lottery for premium seats to see Pearl Jam at Madison Square Garden at the end of the month. We booked a Lower East Side hotel down the block from Katz's Delicatessen. Seeing Eddie Vedder and company is always a cherished opportunity and something I'd never take for granted. Still, visions of returning to the hotel after the show and bringing back a $30, 3 lb. pastrami sandwich were, no pun intended, my version of nirvana.

Doc had just settled into his new bachelor pad, taking the next step in separating from his wife. It was also the first time he—or any of us, for that matter—lived utterly alone. On the TANK email thread early that week, he invited Hayes, Sean, and me down for some Friday night shenanigans — checking out his local drinking establishments on March 6th. I had to decline; I committed to picking Jay up from Newark Airport. We were planning to go to *Uncorked* directly from Passenger Arrivals.

Hayes and Doc ended up drinking in Doc's barely furnished townhouse.

I ended up drinking alone in the living room with Jay, doom-scrolling her phone all night.

This "Corona Virus" was fucking serious.

Come Monday, there were reports of toilet paper flying off the shelves in Seattle. I logged into Amazon and ordered 64 rolls. I callously posted a pic on Instagram saying, "I have my priorities in order." I started a "My Corona" playlist featuring songs like "Aqualung" and "Down with Disease." Jay left for South Jersey work visits.

On Tuesday and Wednesday, the rumors of a New York area lockdown were all anybody could discuss. I already looked prophetic by ordering those 64 rolls. On both days, officials confirmed fresh cases in the county Jay was visiting.

Then came Thursday.

Before I was on the road, my boss called me and told me to bring my personal laptop in. I was being used as an emergency case study in remote connectivity to our office. By noon, my laptop had a new security feature installed by NBC Universal IT. It had a Cisco systems app that allowed me to log onto my work desktop from a unique device. My boss suggested I head home to test the remote capabilities from home. IT thought it was a brilliant idea. And why the hell would I object?

I planned a much larger-than-average Thursday shopping trip to stock up on food and drink. If I could get a three-hour head start on the rest of the anxious and confused public, I'd be a fool not to take it.

I ran into a local friend at one of the highway big-box liquor stores. He was looking for a bottle of wine for dinner. I had $350 worth of anesthetizing liquids in my shopping cart. He went to shake my hand. I extended my elbow out. He chuckled and said, "Oh, you're like that"? Years later, I'd realize what that interaction was foreshadowing.

As I was loading up on booze, Jay was being pulled from the field and told to return and remain home immediately.

At the close of business, NBC informed us we would be fully remote for at least the next two weeks. Everyone in the department was told to bring their laptops in on Friday. For me, it meant my "quarantine" had already begun. As I broke the seal on that $350 emotional survival kit, I contemplated how bizarre reality had become in such a short time. I posted to Facebook:

I'm home. For likely a long time. Today was spent making sure every person who had a personal laptop could work remotely. It was frustrating as heck over the last few days getting these abilities up and running, but it's done.

I've been in the same building for 20.5 years, almost to the date. Some people I crammed with to make this happen have been there just as long. We're on the back end of the news business. We've been through the disputed 2000 election, 9/11, Afghanistan, Iraq, The NYC Blackout, The Pacific Tsunami, The death of a Pope, Hurricane Katrina, The Great Recession, the election of Obama, Baltimore & Ferguson, Sandy Hook, Charleston, Parkland, Trump.

But nothing like today. Nothing like this new reality.

I don't know what life is going to look like when the office opens again. I just don't. Not my life, not the lives of the men and women who all exchanged a very heartfelt "stay safe" for all as they one by one got their VPN credentials and walked out the door this afternoon.

I look forward to virtually working with them for as long as this is our reality. And if normalcy makes a comeback, I'm going to make more of an effort to appreciate the parts of life I've taken for granted for so long.

Stay Safe my friends.

I would never set foot in that building again. And except for Hayes and two isolated lunch meet-ups, it would be the last time I'd see any of those familiar faces, which had been my routine for the entire 21st century.

•••

I've never seen a verb change meaning as quickly as the word "Zoom" did that first week of lockdown. It felt like every night, there was at least one video conference going on. And I'm not talking about work—that was a different animal. Friends, family. Friends of family. Friends of friends. Facebook strangers. Everything was a Zoom.

The Ramapo crowd established a solid string of Fridays together for the first time since the early millennium. It wasn't just the base crew; we went above and beyond. It felt like a runaway Pine Hall Christmas Party. Members of our old intramural hockey team, great friends, and even greater people who just drifted in different directions over the past two decades. Together again, we put our heads down and slog forward like only Gen X knows how to.

And it wouldn't be unusual for a smaller, satellite, virtual cocktail party to occur later. Those usually involved Ben and Sean at the bare minimum, with connections to live-dealer casinos, Venmo payments, and even more cocktails.

Dr Grant would often (because I don't learn) talk about the reason we're able to drink copious amounts of alcohol on vacation and not be completely bowled over the way we might if we get tuned up on a regular Sunday. Our minds are at rest, and our obligations are minimal. Our brains are not dreading the day-to-day routine. Covid—as it was widely known by now — was Permanent Vacation Drinking.

Everybody acknowledged it, nobody appeared to give a damn. I openly admitted on a work call that I was a few drinks deep at 3:15. I wouldn't think twice about scheduling an appointment to make the weekly contactless booze run at 11:00 AM on a Thursday. Jay was battling her insomnia by chugging costly bottles of whiskey got as gifts for our fortieth birthdays—the "special occasion whiskey."

All alcohol-related guardrails were void:

- **The commute was gone.** Drinking on a weeknight was often reined in by the sheer dread of an hour commute, an 8-hour day, and another hour commute. I was commuting to my guest bedroom, where I set up a workspace.
- **There was nothing to do tomorrow.** Like the commute, plans tempered many Fridays and Saturdays the next day. Especially if those plans didn't include drinking, where you had to do more than hang in till the first drink, but you couldn't make plans when you couldn't leave your house.
- **We were saving a significant amount of money.** Subtracting my daily commuting and at least half of Jay's business travel that wasn't reimbursable, we weren't spending almost $400 in gas per month. And those lofty liquor store bills still paled compared to one or two meals out per week, with two or three trips to *Uncorked*.
- **Everybody else was doing it!** When everyone you know is drinking their way through an apocalyptic trauma, you're not too concerned about being judged against their relative temperance when they're not exhibiting any.

For the first time in my drinking life, it was significantly more than beer. We were going through a handle of Tito's vodka per week. Our whiskey collection was taking a severe hit. And forget about the weed. It was a game changer once I realized I could toke during the workday and still do what needed to be done. New Jersey was decriminalizing marijuana, and opportunistic entrepreneurs were trying to fill the void between the black market and legitimate business with door-to-door delivery.

If there were an effortless way to get some cocaine, I would have been all over that as well. But an all-you-can-drink-and-smoke daily buffet was perfectly sufficient anesthetization.

...

Given the reliance on digital communication when you're being ordered to *remain at home*, it was no surprise that text or social media threads set off a cacophony of buzzes until we both completely silenced our alerts, realizing if you're constantly looking at your screen, you will not miss a text.

My primary, then as now, was what I've just come to call "The Guys Thread"—the Ramapo boys. My family at the time had two threads: "Siblings"—self-evident, including in-laws—and "The Family". Just add my folks and Aunt Breda. And while the Hanratty clan will never win awards for orderly organization, they were the only two threads made up of only Apple users, which was great because you could add or remove yourself at will. If only they were all like that.

Doc hopped on an enjoyable and booze-soaked sibling Zoom one weeknight during the second week of lockdown. He was an usher for Sean and me and was always around 208 as the girls grew up. If the Hanratty kids were the Beatles, he'd be Billy Preston. The Zoom gave way to a momentary text thread. Doc and I regressed to our younger selves the way we often do when we gather with hops and barley.

The Siblings + Doc thread quickly got whittled down to Doc, Jay, Erin, and me. So was born The Thread: four hurt people in various stages of denial over their hurt, adjusting to a strange new world where trauma and the unknown lurk as soon as you open your front door.

But while there was pain in the uncertainty, a sense of togetherness was ingrained in every Zoom, text, and socially distanced encounter. We lifted each other and respected the shared sacrifice. It felt like the mythical "shared sense of purpose" had returned for the first time since we lobbied in Trenton. Once again, there was moral clarity. There was no reason to mistrust. I don't think I felt that since the day before my *Huff Post* piece about Scott Kavanaugh ran live.

I tried to start each morning for the first few weeks by playing the Grateful Dead's *"Touch of Grey."* It's jampacked with inspirational lyrics for the moment: We will get by. We will survive. Every silver lining has a touch of grey.

I shared it relentlessly. Threads, texts, social media.

The Guys Thread was a remarkable blend of honest emotion, unique humor, and fatherly advice—which differs significantly from "professional advice," "family advice," and even "good advice."

You'd think I wouldn't have much to offer in that department, but keeping locked down kids became a paramount challenge to many parents, and my friends weren't any different. They entertained their kids each night by firing up a classic movie from our youth. It was a great escape to rattle off and even rewatch the old HBO classics — "Howard the Duck," "Clue," "Adventures in Baby Sitting," and dozens more.

On the home front, Jay and I were getting on very well. By the end of March, we had surpassed our record for the most continuous time spent together. Before the Stay At Home Order we'd joke about how I spent more time within 100 feet of Hayes than any other human on Earth—my immediate family included. But his record would fall over the next few years as eternity marched on.

April 12, 2020, was the first of the traditional family holidays that would have to be virtual that year. I suddenly didn't mind Easter as much as I usually do. Once the anxiety about holding it together—and let's be honest, the existential dread of commuting with a hangover the next day—was eliminated, the Resurrection ceased to be the significant trigger it had been since 1991. At least for one year.

Granted, the knowledge of and lead-up to Easter was always a contributing factor to the uncomfortable nature of that time of year. But when there's a deadly novel virus going around, there's not as much general chatter about plans for the holiday.

So I picked us up a ham and a couple of bottles of wine. We Zoomed with family. I even put on a suit for the video conference! It will be hard for any other Easter in the 21st century to top the first COVID Easter.

What we were willfully ignorant to, however, was the traumatic toll that isolation was already taking on us.

•••

Despite the slow roll towards what we still thought was an eventual reintegration, our social lives remained overwhelmingly digital. The TANK email thread never really missed a beat as we settled into our remote lives. Instead of chatting about which NBA playoff games to bet, it was about which Korean Pro-Baseball League games or horse races in Saudi Arabia. Instead of making potential summer concert plans, we spoke about what shows our favorite bands live-streamed last night. Instead of working out our lunch options with each other in the weird way we always did, we shared tips on survivalist cooking or praise for English Muffin Pizzas.

And boy, did we talk about drinking. We talked about it so much that we planned and executed a "50th Day of Lockdown," where we gathered on Zoom and chugged beers well into the night.

In many tribes, unity prevailed. But hostilities were showing signs of emerging with Jay and me on the home front, and these Zoom meetings were a proxy for most of the developing issues. My general behavior—which she would come to label "Alpha Asshole Asshole fratboy" antics—was cramping her space significantly. She was working on a West Coast schedule while I was finding "meetings" earlier and earlier each day, like some sort of anti-Alcoholics Anonymous.

We had long since surpassed our record for continuous time spent together, which we assumed was our honeymoon or a cross-Atlantic trip. It didn't matter by that point if it was 20 or 25 days when you're celebrating your 50th day of lockdown. Whereas most of our friends were still doing their mid-March drinking for seven weeks and counting, she had quietly made the conscientious decision to curtail her drinking not long after Easter. Let's just say I wasn't there yet.

Consumption was the only structure I had. The terror of the pandemic and America reverting to her regularly scheduled election-year division was palpable. But the lack of a commute felt like a gift from the heavens. Not showering with anything close to regularity was more enjoyable than I should probably admit. Having a workload that needed to be done rather than done between seven and three was quite a motivator.

But that motivator was to get *to the deck*. I created a narrative early on that we were forced to remain home so *the deck* would be my escape. The long, cold, lonely (late) winter was over, and spring was in the air. For Jay, however, that meant brutal allergies and an inability to enjoy *the Deck*.

My therapy with Dr Grant came to a sudden halt when a scheduling conflict led to a miscommunication. It contributed to the lack of structure I was settling into. Without therapy and a commute, without being expected to help with my family, with no children at home to worry about keeping socialized or educated, accountability was sorely lacking.

...

I celebrated St. Patrick's Day under the cover of shock that first week of quarantine. Not seeing humans for Easter and Mother's Day didn't bother me one bit. But as Memorial Day approached with no end in sight to the "*Two weeks to stop the spread*" that began the last week of March, melancholy finally settled in. There would not be a Memorial Day Weekend jam at Jaymanda's "Club Oak"

That acute seasonal depression would soon give way to anger and rage and lock in the most significant and most inflated anger narratives of my lifetime.

The fellas and I had always joked about how the Tuesday after Memorial Day was the worst day of the calendar year. Three days of (hopefully) pleasant weather, heavy quantities of food, and plenty of beer—and it all catches up with you when the alarm goes off on Tuesday at 4:50 AM. Oh, if only 2020s Tuesday problem was a hangover and Lincoln Tunnel traffic.

Not long after 11 AM that morning, I read an article on the NBC News website:

"Man dies after pleading 'I Can't Breathe' during arrest in Minneapolis,"

The tinderbox that had been sitting in the sun since before the virus came ashore was about to spark in ways that would change the way we discussed race in America forever.

When George Floyd cried out for his mama in the waning moments of his life, captured live and streamed a billion times over, many said that every mother in America heard that cry. I don't doubt that one bit. A powerless child being pinned back by an abusive figure of authority knows what it's like to make that cry as well.

These are the positions; these are the vocations that we're supposed to trust, regardless of our situation in life. I was far enough in my therapy to know my distrust of the police came from distrust of authority because of my childhood trauma, but not far enough along to work through it.

I hadn't fully processed my guttural reaction to the too-many-to-count high-profile police killings of unarmed young men of color throughout my life by now. I knew there was some obvious connection to authority abusing its power. Still, like most of my knowledge to this point, I knew fully in theory and nothing in practice or execution.

The student of history in me sees the pattern of racial abuse, and it angers me. The little fella inside of me sees the pattern of abusing the vulnerable, and it turns that anger into rage.

There was no chance I would handle the aftermath of Officer Derek Chauvin's knee well.

•••

Not all shared senses of purpose feel the same. The solidarity to hold Sudol and St. Francis accountable was inspiring. The unity we felt the first few weeks of lockdown was comforting. The "New Yorker" nod that was prevalent after 9/11 was reaffirming. And the social activity in the aftermath of the George Floyd murder was a shared sense of unspeakable wrath.

Unlike the other high-profile police-involved killings, there was very little defense of the offending officers. Sure, the Fox News Universe had a whisper campaign about drugs in Floyd's system or some dip-the-toe-in-the-water commentary about how you shouldn't use counterfeit $20 bills. But mostly, even the traditional "Back the Blue" folks were stunned at the eight minutes and twenty-six seconds that dominated our screens for weeks.

I know the friends Jay and I marched with were angry. I know from the Zoom calls how disgusted my tribes were. Despite our willingness to follow the science and sacrifice week after week for the greater good, we were frustrated with cabin fever, too. I loved having Mark and his family stop by the yard to drink beers 6 feet away. I loved it when my neighbor Dave came by, and we'd stream MSNBC on the deck. But we were pent up.

So, that reinforcement of every ugly stereotype about race in America rearing its head at this point wasn't a welcome turn of events. But I was taking it further.

I took no quarter on Facebook. I banged the drum every day, reminding my followers that the people who found Colin Kaepernick's knee to be so bloody offensive to what they believe America to be were conspicuously silent about the knee Officer Chauvin took on the throat of an unarmed, innocent man.

I left no wiggle room or space for reflection. The gray area and nuance I once prided myself on learning were gone. I had regressed to a raging adolescent.

•••

There was one noticeable tribe where discourse didn't revolve around the heinous nature of the murder or the broader picture about the mistakes America has made or the warning signs she ignored: Jay's family thread.

It would be disingenuous to claim hostility, but I've always worked to keep my opinions out of general family discussions on socio-political issues—both families. It's a place for pictures of everyone's kids or pets or celebrations and for coordinating plans. I have 8 or 9 other active chains in my messages where I can discuss the issues du jour. You can accurately say many negative things about me; being a troll isn't one of them.

At least once a day, a post that Jay or I made on social media would garner a retort from her family thread. Mind you, nobody else on that thread was an active Facebook poster. Most didn't even have an account. But that didn't stop her brothers from taking our words from that medium to the cozier confines of a family thread where you know you have the backing of mommy, daddy, brothers, and wives.

I would post "Take a Knee for Portland" on a social story, and within an hour, there would be a chime from the family thread—a predominantly Samsung user thread to boot—saying, "I'll stand for Portland or any city." I would post, "Trump costs the Big 10 a football season," and within the hour, boom! "I don't hold Trump responsible for the Big 10 canceling their season". Posts about the Biden/Harris ticket were met with "You mean Joe and the Ho'?"

Now, aside from Jay and me, nobody else had any context or fucking clue what was being said. The most frustrating part was Jay and I decided early on to treat them like over-tired toddlers who need to cry themselves to sleep. No responses, no engagement. Quite the opposite, Jay would try to nudge the chat back towards its original intent of casual discussions about our personal lives.

It didn't matter.

We initially found solidarity in the nonsense. Much like our battle for Survivor's Rights in Trenton two years prior, we were at our best when we agreed on right, wrong, and indifferent and were on the same page for execution.

A friend shared a meme of an overweight middle-aged woman with a mullet walking down a street, carrying an American flag with a "Trump 2020" flag being worn as a cape. The caption was simply "(Angry Mayonnaise Noises)".

From that point forward, we laughed off attempts to throw our words back at us as the "Mayo noises." And it worked for about ten days.

But then the internet responded adversely to socially conscious decisions—Uncle Ben removed the titular spokesman's character from its packaging. Aunt Jemima completely rebranded to shed the "Black Mammie" image we grew up with. Some random poster opined we should cancel "Paw Patrol" because it teaches children that cops are the good guys. It was entirely tongue-in-cheek. Nobody who can comprehend at a third-grade level believed that "Chase," the crime-fighting puppy from the popular kid's cartoon, was facing the same fate as Uncle Ben or Aunt Jemima. Or the General Lee before that.

Or, as I said on Facebook that Friday morning:

> *Some people are concerned that two dozen admirals and generals and six former Joint Chiefs of Staff have warned us about the madness of the commander in Chief, who's ordered live ammunition and chemical warfare on peaceful US demonstrators and international reporters.*
>
> *Others are getting their drawers twisted over what movies they've never seen are disappearing from a service they haven't subscribed to, or believing jokes about other shows and cartoons getting yanked from the air.*
>
> *Believe me, as one lone introspective voice: your children and/or grandchildren will read about this someday, and wonder where their parents or grandparents stood. And judge them on it.*

Take me at my word when I tell you that a post such as that settles into the Top 1% of "The least provocative things I've said on Facebook." Jay, who likewise posted something about the absurdity of believing a ridiculous rumor, was even less abrasive than me.

It didn't matter. We were both accused of targeting the family on social media as if they were the only ones in the Fox universe that were upset about pancake syrup and microwaveable rice.

I was boiling like a bag of Uncle Ben's. I knew why, but I couldn't execute or even devise a reasonable solution. I knew I was responding to being told by family that I was less than. I was responding to them making authoritative demands that I shut down social media accounts or make professional decisions based on their sensibilities. I was reacting to the most toxic statement that any human can ever make, per every therapist I've ever seen: "Nothing comes before family."

And that remained a tough thing to reconcile. I was a (ballooning) 300-pound, 43-year-old man stuck with the emotional responses of a scrawny twelve-year-old boy who couldn't make sense of the changing world around him.

XXXVI

In mid-June I got a call from Greg, the Lawyer that began with, "I hope you're sitting down."

Given his experience, it's understandable that Greg would consider every decision made by the Archdiocese to be adversarial and worthy of sitting down to receive. I told him to shoot; there's nothing that will shock me.

"The Archdiocese is cutting off your therapy reimbursements because you filed a claim," he said.

It didn't shock me. It was like pulling teeth to get reimbursements already. Now that the latest round of clergy abuse discussion has disappeared from the news cycle, so has their faux compassion for their victims. It's the same script they'd followed since the "Spotlight" days.

"The good news is, I got confirmation that your claim is in," he continued, "But in the interim, I'm sorry, Ed, this is the last month that they'll be covering counseling bills for anyone who files a claim against them."

Honestly, I didn't take it too personally. Or rather, seriously. I found it disgusting, yet typical. But I had gone months without therapy. I was surviving. The claim was submitted—it was behind me. Is the world shifting on its axis to where going outside can kill you? That has a way of re-prioritizing the traumas you're responding to. Or, at least, that is what an idiot would tell himself.

Which made the email request I got from Deena at *The Record* the next day even more surprising.

Deena was on top of every twist and turn in the Clergy Abuse scandal. Even when the spotlight was off the Archdiocese, she had her ear to the ground. That's why she wanted to interview me within hours of my finding out about the church's decision to yank therapy funding.

Deena conducted the interview over emails and a phone call. But the editors insisted they send a photographer for a photo shoot. They wanted images and videos to promote the story on their website, social media, and print. I couldn't argue with the promotion. I mean, that's the point of journalism, right? To reach as many people as possible with what we hoped was objective truth?

Internally, it was a different story.

It was one thing for Mark and his family, or my neighbor Dave, to swing by for outdoor drinks. Gary and Jan would meet us in our driveways for distanced Happy Hour. We had already met with Hayes and Ana twice for extended, socially distanced outdoor gatherings. But in those circumstances, I wore jeans and enough t-shirts and hoodies/flannels to layer up and down based on the temperature and the sunshine. But a stranger coming over?

That meant a shower. A shave. It was the first conscious decision on what to wear in months. Hard pants with belts. Shirts with collars. Did I even know where they were? We'd been living out of rotating hampers of clean t-shirts, sweats, gym shorts, socks, and underwear. I honestly didn't remember putting away the last load of "before times" clothes.

I found a button-down short-sleeved shirt and a pair of clean, unwrinkled jeans. I combed my hair and shaved my cheeks. I looked like a bored dad at an end-of-year pool party.

Deena assured me that the photographer would take all virus mitigation precautions and that the photo shoot would be outdoors. And it was. And it seemed to take forever.

The photographer kindly thanked me for my courage, to which muscle memory had me replying, "Thank you. It had to be done. For me, more than anyone else." But in my head, I'm thinking, "Oh yeah, the clergy abuse. Sorry, it's been a rough couple of months."

Then, it was Déjà vu.

I was Ed, Victim of Clergy Abuse all over again.

I polished off more than a twelve-pack of some high-gravity IPAs that night. It helped me forget. Did the trick. But the reminders were fast and fierce when I woke up. I was being shared on my socials, email, and text threads. My clean-ish shaven, angry-looking face was sitting on the swing porch on my deck, with big, bold letters:

Like Being Victimized All Over Again.

Fuck.

•••

Raising awareness about how the Archdiocese of Newark operates behind the scenes is always a benefit to putting myself out there, as I've said many times about what I believe my unique set of circumstances allows me to do. Another benefit to this interview and marketing push was that it reached its intended audience. Among those readers was Jessica Grant, my missing therapist.

By lunchtime that day, I had already received a text noting that it had been a while, asking if I would like to schedule a session. Within a week, my two-month therapy absence was over.

There was no acknowledgment that our meetings were interrupted. I don't know that either of us knew exactly how or when we stopped. It was a confusing time. That was the theme of our first session.

By the end of that appointment, I realized that what buttressed me through the last four months—the sudden shutdown, the economic panic, the massive shift in all biological habits (aside from food, drink, and sleep, it was around this time I started my "old man breaks"— taking a leak at 3 AM), the racial justice protests, the Angry Mayonnaise Noises was that I didn't have time to be stuck in my head. It wasn't a luxury anymore. Because time spent alone in my head is time spent being the victim. And my victim exterior was getting gruffier and more defensive.

...

The health upstairs was finally getting some attention, but I ignored my physical health. Ignoring may be too soft. I was waging war.

There never really was a draw-down from the March and April binge drinking. The hard stuff was downgraded as I regressed to my craft beer-drinking mean. But the starting time was still whenever I felt like it; the ending time was when I ran out or couldn't stand, and the quantity was higher than Willie Nelson on Earth Day. Oh, and yeah, I was smoking weed like I used to smoke cigarettes.

Once a week, there would be a drop-off from a weed courier. Flower, edibles, cartridges. Something was keeping me "right" just about all day long. Inevitably, I'd miss a dose of Lexapro, and the hangover depression would be worse, so I'd eat my feelings. I kept my work windows open on my MacBook while I did little to no actual work.

So, when I had a late summer physical with my primary care doctor, my anxiety was off the charts. And with good reason—I dreaded stepping on that scale as if I was getting my teeth extracted. I paired my clothing to the bare minimum—crocs, gym shorts, threadbare underwear, and a tank top. When the physician's assistant asked me to step on the scale, I slid out of the crocs and laid my phone and wallet on a supply stand beside it.

Like a high school wrestler, I was desperately trying "to make weight," only I didn't know what that weight was. Avoid 300? I would not feel great about 299.9, either. And I wasn't delusional enough to think something like 280 was possible.

Three Hundred Twelve Point Two.

I was disgusted as fuck. This naturally led to an uptick in anxiety, which is the last thing a patient with hypertension wants to deal with before getting their vitals taken during their annual checkup. But this wasn't my first rodeo. I had learned years prior that the only way to handle the anxiety of white-coat syndrome (where the patient's knowledge of the blood pressure being read causes the blood pressure to rise) was to attack it vigorously with medication. Two hours prior, I had taken two Beta Blockers, an ACE Inhibitor, and a Xanax and smoked a healthy bowl of Indica.

It worked, kind of. I got a normal reading that the Doc said: "was still a little elevated for someone under medication." Surely would not tell her I was presently "under medication. Plus."

A few weeks later, we hosted Dad's 70th birthday. Our home—West Milford–would always be a special place for the old man. He had just gotten diagnosed with lung cancer and was facing surgery the next month. We hadn't gathered as a family since the Christmas before, ten months prior.

We decided on a Yankees-themed party. Elizabeth found a bakery that made a beautiful fondant cake with pinstripes and the interlocking NY. Everyone wore navy, white, or gray. We lined my deck with Yankees pennants, and we set up a blue tent. The Yanks played that day, too, with Major League Baseball finally winding up a shortened season.

Joe DiMaggio famously said, "I'd like to thank the Good Lord for making me a Yankee." You could have easily manipulated the party's theme to be: "I'd like to thank our old dad for making me a Yankee fan."

The old man had the time of his life, surrounded by three generations of die-hard fans who could tie their fandom back to his childhood apartment on Andersen Avenue, looking down at the House that Ruth built. And in each of the couple dozen amazing photographs of the last complete family party I'd have at my home, I looked like a bloated, booze-filled, drug-fueled scruffy slob.

It was becoming clear that I wasn't okay.

...

One hundred thousand dollars.

That was the formal offer the Archdiocese made to me to compensate me for the harm caused to me as a child. Though, as they're prone to do, they clarified they weren't accepting responsibility because, of course, they weren't.

Minus the attorney's third that would go to Greg and Jeff Anderson Associates, I would take home $66,666.67. I had thirty days to accept or decline.

Accepting meant that the fight was over. I could remain vocal, active, and supportive for the next generation of survivors, but taking their deal meant I was surrendering my seat at the table—my hopes for an accurate and complete accounting of everything that happened at St. Francis.

Anderson's firm, along with other attorneys with skin in the game, had focused on those "heat maps" of credibly accused priests. Why did they exist? Why was St. Francis one of them? Did the relative quiet in which Ernst could operate—until a prominent Catholic family in town said something—the reason that Sudol was shifted to St. Francis in the first place?

Did any knowledge of Sudol's proclivities lead to McCarrick appointing Joe Doyle to monitor him? Why did it take almost four years from Doyle's arrival till Sudol came down with "Nervous Exhaustion"? Given the flood of lawsuits for which the Survivor's Bill of Rights law opened paths, there were hundreds of cases like Sudol's and St. Francis. Didn't we have the right to know?

Therein lies a significant problem, however.

There were hundreds of cases like Sudol's. There were over a dozen claims against him alone. Even without nefarious delay tactics, it would take years to get to a trial. All of which I had already been aware of and was still willing to entertain. But there was a new strategy the Church deployed, and it was a game changer in my mind: bankruptcy.

The Archdioceses of Camden in South Jersey, along with a few Archdioceses in the Northeast, were strategically filing for Chapter 11 bankruptcy to limit their liabilities and protect their assets. If the Archdiocese of Newark proceeded down that path, it was Game Over. And not just for monetary compensation; in all honesty, I still likely would have had a claim for a similar amount. But it removed the option for Discovery. You can't sue an entity for damages when the entity cannot make a right on those damages.

Finally, there was potential closure. I was so desperate for it. The latest interview made it clear to me it was time to move forward. However, it was a false hope that closure was imminent. Jay felt that my anger was escalating at this point. I didn't think it was, but not because I felt I was being docile. Quite the opposite—I felt my anger was in check because the entire world was angry; I had my finger on the pulse of the Zeitgeist.

I wasn't entirely wrong. The 2020 election was the election 2020 deserved. The country was burning hot, and I ran about 5 degrees hotter than most. The respective sides drew their proverbial battle lines. That gray area Jay would often get me to see was gone. Instead, I was coaxing out the black-and-white rigidity that childhood trauma thrusts upon people, was long gone.

It was No Retreat, No Surrender in my mind. The evidence was clear. We were losing over a thousand American lives per day; we had lost tens of millions of jobs. The president was downplaying the virus and putting real lives at risk. Who could want four more years of this shit?

A random right-wing troll or a middle-aged peer playing the dreaded and pathetic devil's advocate would occasionally reply to a post. My followers would swarm on their replies like the Tasmanian Devil. A gigantic cloud of notifications followed by the digital remains of someone I'd inevitably have to block for using racist or demeaning language.

In our respective corners, we believed we had the wind to our back. Polls were promising, but so were common sense and logic. The few MAGA-adjacent relatives and acquaintances I entered 2020 with had just about all let themselves out of my life by the peak of the racial justice demonstrations. We were absent the mayonnaise noises since Jay's last salvo had silenced the thread for the time being. We really had no exposure to anyone who could have possibly wanted this train wreck to continue.

The Macro level appeared to be gearing up for closure. Common sense was around the corner, and with it, a return to normalcy.

Against this backdrop, I decided that accepting the Church's offer was worth it for nothing more than the chance at closure. The dreams of fighting *until we're playing beer pong in the Sistine Chapel* were long extinguished. I had to ask myself what a legitimate end game looked like for this ordeal.

With the bombardment of last-minute lawsuits before the window to file closed, the Archdiocese could legitimately run the clock out for years. It was never about the money, but I didn't think fighting longer would have resulted in a significantly higher sum.

The election delivered the widely expected results, and the church provided a reasonably expected offer. The Macro and Micro were aligned for me to move on from. But I couldn't move on from either the Church or the MAGA movement. I had completely encapsulated myself in an anger bubble. There would be no closure; something in my subconscious wouldn't allow for it.

...

For the past few years, every December, I've thought about that feature in *The Record* about survivors struggling with the Holiday season following the tumult of the 2018 investigations, revelations, and allegations. I chuckle, thinking back to my naivety being on full display when I told Deena that I finally felt liberated, at peace, and able to celebrate the holidays.

It would have been a much different interview had it occurred during any subsequent holiday season. 2020 was no different. Except for the minor detail that 2020 was entirely different from any other holiday that anyone on Earth celebrated.

Early in November, the prevailing opinion was that Americans could celebrate intimate family holidays. It would be nothing like we may have been accustomed to—the house-hopping, expanded guest lists, etc.- but we felt there may be a chance to celebrate in person. And that chance remained distinct until the moment that the Delta variant of COVID-19 arrived.

This latest and most lethal variant yet ensured most families would have holidays with their immediate household only. Most people were genuinely upset. I was legitimately thrilled. I tried to temper the general disappointment by asking people if they'd like to set up a Zoom for Thanksgiving.

Jay's Uncle John was one of the first people I asked. He, along with my father, were the "near and dear" vulnerable people Jay and I reminded each other of every time we became fed up with the guidance of the rigamarole of the protections and mitigations. He said he was likely staying home because he didn't trust that everybody else was paying attention to the numbers the way we were. He said he'd be interested in a Zoom.

We got blitzed after we finished our grilled, bacon-wrapped turkey breasts, string bean casserole, broccoli, stuffing, cranberry sauce, and gravy. The Zoom never happened.

Complicated relationships with religious-based holidays aside, the one thing I always had to surrender was control to partake in them. It was always at somebody else's home; we never hosted. Often, it was a minimum of two homes, occasionally even three. I had no say over the menu—something that sounded like a blessing in my twenties, but chapped my hide as life went on. I was becoming more impressed with my culinary abilities.

Since leaving RP, we have stayed with Jay's family for most of our lives on holidays and following parties. Those days were over before the pandemic, since replaced by the impending sense of dread of an hour-long ride home, usually coming down from a pretty good drunk. And if we stayed, the next day was a total waste. And there were a half dozen frustrating steps to prepare the dog for such a visit.

It took away control. It caused anxiety. It disrupted internal peace.

But while this was nobody's problem or fault but my own, I could see a gleaming silver lining in having a homebound holiday season. Rather than savor the peace or make the most of a solemn situation, however, I acted out like a spoiled toddler who finally got his way.

I was whistling while I made breakfast. I showered and shaved and got right to prepping the Prime Rib. I made multiple declarations on my socials about "today is a good day." I completely ignored that Jay was heartbroken over missing people during the holiday, especially given the uncertainty we lived through all year.

I convinced myself I "won". I was victorious. Over what? Who the hell knows? Did I defeat Christmas? Was the virus suddenly going to go away? Did I defeat Christianity?

However, nine months of trauma permanently altered the divergence in my thinking. I was fully engulfed in an angry narrative that deemed anything I could make church-adjacent my enemy.

•••

My anger narrative on my micro life may have been contrived, but there was no way to overstate the tension and disdain in the macro world following the 2020 election. What appeared to the rest of the world as a close but relatively decisive election was rejected wholesale and frighteningly by the Republicans, who passionately supported the indisputable loser of the contest.

Every day, they were trotting out some two-bit ambulance chaser to claim the election was manipulated and stolen by only districts with large Black populations like Philly or Detroit or Atlanta. Rudy Giuliani mistook Four Seasons Total Landscaping for the Four Seasons Hotel and held a press conference between a crematorium and a sex toy shop. It was maddening. And it conjured up the feelings of being told what was happening in front of my eyes couldn't happen.

An average person would have shrugged this off, said, "What a bunch of silly geese," and went on with life, fully confident that cooler heads would prevail. And that's what most people did. The media loved painting the narrative of an evenly divided country, but there wasn't any objective evidence to suggest it was even. There was a loud and vocal minority acting in boorish ways that drove folks with issues similar to mine batty. But most of the country was moving on through the perilous holiday season, whether or not they liked it.

America's tension couldn't be higher despite the evidence presented daily in court challenges. And I was cracking.

My job was in complete auto-pilot by this point. I was a monk at the start of the pandemic compared to how hard I was partying when the holidays came around. My wake-up time was 4:50 before the lockdown began. It settled in around 6:00 a few weeks in. But by the holidays, I was pushing past 7:00, which was technically my start of shift, but nobody contacted me before 8:30—if they were to contact me at all.

Around 12:45 PM, I began taking naps. They started as 15-minute power naps to recharge. They soon became routine, so I had a 1:30 PM wake-up alarm set for every weekday. Then, I would bang out whatever bare minimum was left to do at work, send an email to make myself appear more engaged than I was, and repeat the cycle.

I wasn't drinking every day, but I was drinking every day that I felt good enough to drink. The only thing that held me back was the hangover from the night before. Or, as it became more frequent—the hangover from two nights ago that I couldn't kick. The whole time, I fixated on the irrational behavior of the MAGA movement and how the power infrastructure and feverish devotees were reminiscent of the Catholic Church I grew up in.

Through the haze of a black-and-white permanent fight-or-flight footing, I was beside myself. Externally, I was having some fun publicly mocking the "Stop the Steal movement." I mean, besides (a) giving that presser in front of a dildo shop, Giuliani also (b) made another media appearance with hair dye streaming down the side of his face and (c) was openly flatulent during a cockamamie desperate plea to the Michigan legislature not to certify their votes. It was effortless to poke fun at.

But internally, rage and confusion were building. This was supposed to be the end of the chaotic hell that was 2020. I approached it like an eleven-year-old: why is everybody so cruel? And just like that eleven-year-old searched for even more vulnerable people to lash out at, I was seeping back into familiar patterns.

It had been months since her family's chat was active. Our response to the Angry Mayonnaise Noises all but assured that. It didn't stop me from bitching about it to her every day, though. *"We're about to swear in the first Black Woman Vice President. You really think 'Joe and the Hoe' was appropriate?"*

But if I were contriving anger narratives out of offenses from multiple seasons ago, there would soon be a reason as legitimate as any. Or so I convinced myself.

By 3:00 PM on January 6, 2021, I was fully engaged in a text thread with the guys over what was unfolding before our eyes. A few Americans still didn't get the message that the election was over. As Congress met to certify the election results, they stormed the freaking Capitol to stop it. They were using mace. They were using any blunt object as a trajectory. There was ritualistic chanting. There was a dude in elk horns standing on the Senate leadership desk. It was right around this moment that the notion that MAGA as an entity had crossed the Rubicon from a political movement to a religious entity.

Reason, logic, and hard evidence no longer mattered. They organized so that their grievances became their *Mystery of Faith*. You couldn't logically tell them that Joe Biden won the election any more than you could tell the most devout of Christians that there's no way for a human to walk on water or to rise from the dead.

As far as Little Eddie was concerned, people engaging in spiritual organization threatened the safety and security of the vulnerable.

Especially when the church was halting the therapy of the vulnerable they abused.

I, too, had crossed a Rubicon.

XXXVII

"I'm digging a tunnel. Reception's terrible. Not good. About to undo the Treaty of 1482."

It was late on Saturday, January 9th, and Jay and I shared a rare moment—enjoying cocktails and music together, roaring in the living room. I couldn't help but chuckle at a text from Uncle John, his signature wit hitting its mark.

John was the lone practicing attorney we were close to while Doc was struggling in his preparations for the divorce. We feared Doc wasn't receiving adequate legal support—a prospect that worried us immensely. Beth was meticulously prepared, and the last thing we wanted was to witness Doc falter in court, losing everything and perhaps losing touch with his kids. I tried catching up with John earlier that day, but a poor connection cut the conversation short.

Later that night, he reached out to see what Jay and I were doing—not to make plans, but to check in. With the impending surge of COVID cases and colder temperatures driving us indoors, he sent a picture of a Moscow Mule he crafted in his basement—reminiscent of an Irish pub, albeit with a taupe carpet that you would never lay down where one pours a Guinness.

"Looks delicious! We're just hanging out, having some beers, and trying not to overthrow the Capitol", I quipped. Across the nation, most people remained incredulous at the events that unfolded at the Capitol earlier that week.

Less than two months later, we lost John to COVID-19. Our last conversation circled back to the moronic attempts at disrupting the peaceful transfer of power on January 6th. Not how Jay and I would finally take his recommendation on a Key West vacation. It's not about how his kids have it so much easier than we did growing up—especially regarding college cafeteria food. Not about golf, law, the Giants, health or life. January Fucking Sixth.

He passed away in the middle of the afternoon while we were driving back from a clinic, Jay having just received her first dose of the Moderna COVID-19 mRNA vaccine.

•••

Following a loss, it's not uncommon to wish, "I'd trade places with them if I could." Many echoed these sentiments after John's passing. I know I did. His life was purposeful and graceful, making his departure the cruelest twist of fate among those closest to us.

By February 2021, as we neared the first anniversary of the lockdown, no one foolishly believed, "This couldn't happen to my loved ones." But acceptance remained elusive.

The grieving process was brewing within our minds and hearts. *How could it be John? Wasn't he the one foremost in our thoughts when we advocated taking precautions for everyone's safety? With vaccinations underway, how did this happen? He had so much life left to live. What kind of country lets this happen?*

Therein lies the problem of convincing the masses that we are our brothers' keepers. When you put the onus on society to protect itself, the blame falls on society when there's a breakdown in that protection. Here came another emotional trigger that would jar the shit out of me for years—once again, the vulnerable and innocent among us fell prey to society's ignorance.

Didn't matter that as a severely immunocompromised individual, John was at extreme risk of not surviving a bout with the virus. Didn't matter that, due to preexisting conditions, the vaccine may not have been enough to save him. Didn't matter that over a million American families were experiencing the same sense of loss and grief. My hard-wired trauma response was already working overtime to make myself a victim of an international tragedy.

One of Jay's aunts drove down from New England to stay by us the night that he passed. We poured drinks. We shed tears. And while on speaker with another aunt; she broke a momentary pause in conversation to say what we had all been thinking:

"This only happened because of Donald Fucking Trump."

Unanimous and emphatic agreement from all involved on the call.

It may have been the passion of the moment and the instinctual need to blame something for a tragedy we can't understand. But for me, the equation was already being branded into the deepest of recesses of my mind:

(Ed + Gerry Sudol) = (John + Donald Trump) / Societal Indifference

...

I couldn't shed any actual tears since Lexapro makes you appear about as emotional as a German grandmother between the wars. But that doesn't mean that anger took root right away. The immediate focus was on celebrating a remarkable life extinguished too soon.

I insisted to Dr. Grant that I could handle attending his funeral in a Catholic Church—I had more anxiety about seeing my in-laws together for the first time since the Angry Mayonnaise Noises the following spring. There was going to be palpable tension. And while it wasn't at the forefront of my mind, I was working my way towards holding every Trump supporter responsible for losing a million Americans, just like John. I was constructing what I learned to be a Grievance Narrative—when we create a story in our mind that paints us as a victim, prohibiting us from seeing the bigger picture, processing, or healing. It's a hallmark of PTSD.

The services were among the saddest hours of anyone in attendance's life. Despite the apparent tension, there was still enough genuine love and understanding to help each other through two days of mourning.

After the priest gave the final blessing at John's eternal resting place in a beautiful North Jersey cemetery, it was time for the hard goodbyes. I turned to my youngest brother-in-law, masks down as we were outside in frigid temperatures, hugged him, and said, "Look, nobody should be judged by how they responded in 2020". I looked over at my older one and nodded, saying, "That goes for you, too," as I broke the first hug and started a second.

I can talk a great game, and The Grounded Me—as my therapy was encouraging to find—probably meant it. But the trauma train had already left the station. My grudges were going nowhere.

• • •

This most soul-crushing of events inspired a new, unhealthy activity, however. Spending like the world was ending tomorrow. Flush with settlement money - $66,666.67 to be exact after the lawyers got their cut for my story. Jay said that John's son was telling her he didn't know if he was going to keep the family's Giants tickets because he couldn't imagine going to the games without him. $3450 later, we were Giants season ticket holders.

John's favorite artist of all time was Elton John. Sir Elton was associated with John by those who knew him well more than most any other artist is associated with anyone. It just so happened that Elton John's "Farwell Yellow Brick Road" tour had to be canceled like every other 2020 tour, and his rescheduled appearance in Newark would be on what would have been John's next birthday. There was another grand spend. Floor seats for Jay and I. 100 levels for her parents and John's widow Diane.

John's family and others were already in the planning stages of a memorial golf outing in his honor. It would take place at the Seaview Golf Resort down the Jersey Shore, a little north of Atlantic City. It hosts an LPGA tournament, has stunning views of the AC skyline, and is one tough fucking course. I don't think I've ever seen John get frustrated with my lack of game the way he did one hungover 2014 morning as I was using two clubs too much to hack out of her thick rough.

I had still been using my "starter set" of golf clubs—a $199 purchase from 2009 that included every club plus a golf bag. They were a little too short for my build, but who cares? I could adjust my stance. But I needed proper clubs for John's memorial. So there went another $1200 on custom-extended wedges and irons, grips, and, for good measure, a pair of Footjoy "Saddle Shoe" golf cleats reminiscent of the pair John always wore.

Drunken sailors had nothing on a trauma-shocked basket of grief and anxiety with sixty grand in his pocket.

• • •

The first time her family gathered after John's passing was Easter weekend, a month later. Jay's Uncle Fred just received some heady medical news. Diane and the kids would be there. For me, it was a chance to put my money where my mouth was—I broke the ice to break the tension and this was going to be the first test whether I was capable or I was just being aspirational.

Easter was always a trigger, and I knew that. 2020 was a one-off reprieve. Regardless of how long I've been aware that my resistance to Easter was, however, I still insist on carrying through. Worse, I made no genuine attempts to reconcile with it. That leaves little room for growth and acceptance.

The superficial arguments I've had about Easter remain true—what's the point of a holiday on a Sunday when you have work the next day, the absurdity of the Resurrection, that you got two more family holidays coming down the turnpike makes it redundant, etc.—I hold those to this day. But they were merely a mask for the pain I was avoiding.

What made this approach dangerous was that it reinforced the memories of the Holy Saturday abuse by keeping it constantly in my thoughts. I couldn't hear "Easter" without thinking of dodging the groping. Hell, there's a line in one of my favorite Doors songs ever, "Cancel my subscription to the Resurrection". It wasn't unusual for that lyric alone to send my mind drifting back to St. Francis.

Against that backdrop, I agreed to go to the first family gathering since John's funeral. And it went about as well as I was probably expecting it to go deep down inside.

There was no tension. There were no passive-aggressive comments about anything remotely political, controversial, or topical. Even if there were, I wouldn't have remembered because I got piss drunk. I know I brought a six-pack of some high-ABV% IPA's, and I know within 90 minutes, I was in my mother-in-law's liquor cabinet, making myself heavy-handed vodka tonics. At one point, our four-year-old niece tugged on my sister-in-law's shirt to say, "That big guy just spilled funny water on me."

From my vantage point in their backyard, I was looking at the attempts to hide the pain in the faces of every adult seated there that afternoon. Behind them, across the street, rising above their hedges and the blooming maple trees that dot their street, was the roof, steeple, and bell-tower of St. Francis of Assisi.

It wasn't our youth anymore. Everybody else had grown up, had responsibilities, and felt the need to comport themselves. But not Little Eddie.

And not on Easter weekend.

•••

Professionals say one of the most effective ways to process grief is to find something productive to pour your energy into. It was a piece of advice I could follow. As we were struggling with the loss of John, vaccines were slowly but surely working their way to market. And demand was through the roof.

I couldn't understand why it wouldn't be. Everyone had lived through the same twelve months I just did, right? This was the first significant breakthrough against a global scourge that was killing 15 million humans worldwide in 2020 and '21. The rollout of the vaccines was confusing—and understandably so. This was one of the greatest accomplishments in drug production in the history of medicine. The United States was its most significant driver and was in the transition between two administrations. To monitor the success of these shots in virus mitigation (eradication may have still been the goal at that point), meticulous records needed to be kept.

This wasn't the release of Special Edition Air Jordans.

The way the Centers for Disease Control and Prevention determined the rollout would work would be in phases. Medical professionals and first responders would be the first to have access, somewhere in mid-December '20—no arguing. The next group to be eligible was Americans with an underlying condition that put them at high risk for hospitalization or death. Likewise, it makes sense.

I had read about this and immediately sent a message to my primary care doctor and asked if I could get a PDF of a letter stating I have high blood pressure (Hypertension was a pre-existing condition that made you eligible.) She was happy to oblige and told "Whom it May Concern" that I had been diagnosed with hypertension. And pre-diabetes, morbid obesity, and tobacco use. She all but said *inoculate this dude pronto.*

I'd soon find out it was an unnecessary humiliation. Outside of clicking a box that says you met one criterion, there were absolutely no attempts to validate accuracy. Your personal identifiers: name, identification photo, birthday—had to match on shot day. But you could have weighed 105 lbs and claimed obesity; they didn't care.

Once this became known, everybody was racing to get their jab.

It took me about 4 hours to get an appointment for my vaccine the first day they were available. The shot was scheduled for two weeks later. Once that was secured, I got Jay one. Then Elizabeth got one for Mom and Dad. Then I got one for Aunt Breda, Erin, and Sean. Then his wife.

I then reached out to my close and personals and told them I was getting rather adept at pulling reservations. I learned tricks like "CVS releases slots at 4:55 AM" or "The mass vaccine sites release the next available day not long after the current day ends." Before I knew it, I had booked for my neighbor Dave and his wife, Ben and his wife, Mark, and Doc. The shared sense of sacrifice, the common vision, that dopamine-related rush I get from helping people was returning after a long, cold, lonely winter full of hostility and loss.

As others did, I went public on Facebook, volunteering my time and know-how to make vaccine reservations for anyone who wanted one. How couldn't I? The most remarkable man I ever knew just fell victim to this awful disease. Nobody should have to live with that pain if we slay this demon for good. It takes all of us. (And it also helped that I could do much of it on company time.)

By the time May arrived, securing appointments was becoming more accessible. My services were no longer needed. I booked approximately 75 vaccine appointments. For the first time since we lobbied in Trenton, I felt valuable and purposeful.

•••

By the first week in May, our Party People—The Hayeses and Jaymanda — were all fully vaccinated by CDC Standards. We got together for three of the five weekends that month. We hosted an Independence Day party that ranked among our best. The six of us would cap off the "Hot Vaxxed Summer" with a four-day escape down the Shore to Wildwood—the first return for Jay and me since 1996. While the past year's tragedies, particularly the most recent ones, remained heavy on our hearts, there was a sense of survival, a feeling like "we made it."

I hugged like I never hugged before. Having close contact with friends—and the ability to go indoors, speak indoors, eat indoors was a feeling I had no idea how much I had missed by this point. The titular line from John Lennon's epic holiday tune played repeatedly in my head—"War is Over."

Gathering with friends felt like winning a war, though. The six of us had intimate and expressive discussions throughout the pandemic in ways that made me appreciate our relationship's maturity. Family threads were what they were for everyone. The guy's thread is always particular because of my longstanding love and admiration for those men. But the six of us had life experiences, mores, trauma bonds, and circumstances that were unique but relatable to each other. To hug these sons of bitches challenged Lexapro so much that my eyes did well up when I pulled Hayes in on our "bro-hug."

It felt terrific to get celebratory shit-faced as opposed to coping-annihilated.

Beneath the surface, however, the darkness was still lurking.

When the vax-bookings were over, I was back in the prison of my headspace.

•••

From Jay's perspective, I was already at a point where outside help, if not intervention, was needed. My drinking hadn't increased—I was close to my maximum capacity anyway since the lockdown began over a year ago: drink today, recover tomorrow, repeat. But my anger and general demeanor had turned dark once the shock of John's passing wore off, and I was left alone with my thoughts.

Before school was over for the year, the vaccines were now widely available to anyone who wanted one. The days of waking up at 4:30 to book an appointment for a stranger in rural Pennsylvania at a Rite-Aid 40 miles west of her home were over. You wanted a shot; you got one.

However, the only people who wanted the shot were those willing to hand over most of their personal information to whom they prayed was a well-intentioned stranger on the internet. Fox News and conservative media were in the middle of a not-so-low-key campaign to question the efficacy of the vaccine and the push to get as many people vaccinated as possible.

It wouldn't have been as bothersome if DONALD FUCKING TRUMP WASN'T THE PRESIDENT WHO AUTHORIZED THE RECORD-BREAKING APPROVAL FOR THE VAX. For real! Folks were virtually worshipping the lifts in his shoes over separating children from mothers, mocking the disabled, instituting a Muslim ban, and pledging to punish women who seek an abortion, but with the greater good and public health, you're suddenly skeptical?

It wouldn't compute. It couldn't compute.

…

Mark was the first person Jay contacted to snap me out of it. His family stopped by the deck after dinner on a summer Friday. By this point, Fridays start at 2:00 at the latest. She pulled him aside when I was chatting with his wife, Debra, and their twins. Moments later, Mark put his arm around me, grabbed me by the back of my neck, and hugged me, telling me he wanted me to know I could reach out to him at any point. He's got my back. He's in my corner. He loves me. I can let it all go.

"Something was up with Mark," I told Jay after they had left.

"What do you mean?"

"I think he thinks I'm gay, and he might be too," I replied

"Why the fuck would you say something like that?" she asked with a look of shock and disgust.

"He was all touchy-feely and telling me he loves me and I can be myself around him."

"You're an asshole. I told him you were struggling, and I was struggling to reach you. I told him you could use emotional support right now, and it has to come from someone beyond me."

"Ah," I said with a huge, drunken sigh of relief. "that makes sense. Don't do that again."

She didn't. At least not behind my back.

But "Hot Vaxxed Summer" was over.

Weeks later, I still objected to the idea that I was in any crisis or spiral. *I get up, I go to work, I have my opinions, but they're not harming anybody. I only get angry when people get angry with me.* We had a somewhat contentious fight in the morning that inspired her to call my mother. Yes, at 44 years old, I was having my mommy called on me.

Naturally, "Mom" showed up on my phone screen. I knew if I ignored it, she'd keep calling. I don't know why I expected her to lash out at me with the fire of a thousand suns, but I postured myself as if that was coming.

"Hey ma, look...."

"Honey, please calm down. Please listen. Now, can your father and I come up and speak with you?"

What? Kindness? Warmth? Who would dare provide this to me?

"Sure ma, come on up. I ain't going anywhere."

Less than an hour later, Mom, Dad, Jay, and I sat around the deck talking about my anger. I still didn't understand the depths of what they were speaking of. In my mind, there was some tension between the two of us because we had been stuck inside together for about 15 months—fifteen months of anxiety, trauma, confusion, and loss.

My parents spoke about knowing I've always been angry and that it would mean the world to them if I sought more help. *But I'm seeing Dr. Grant regularly; what the fuck more do you want from me?*

I didn't bother pre-gaming their visit with beer; I knew that would be viewed as a slap in the face to all three of them—even though it's long been my pre-company ritual. I like to crack a beer roughly 20 minutes before guests arrive, so I'm only one deep. Like any fully adjusted middle-aged man.

But once things were comfortable and peaceful at the table—rather, once I believed they'd remain so since nobody came with any hostility, purely love, and concern—I asked Mom if she'd like a glass of wine. A guaranteed yes, and a guaranteed start to my Saturday evening drinking experience.

Mom's compassion and understanding were what I needed. I didn't realize how much I craved that level of calm. And Dad, man, he delivered. He showed a brilliant combination of fatherly psychology and tough love that I never knew he had in him. He started by praising me, which, I guess, they know better than most is effective.

In a drawn-out classic Bronx reserved voice, "Look. You know your history better than me. Look at what your grandparents faced with the Depression, the War..."

He teetered out with that, as I held my breath, praying he wouldn't add "and the neighborhoods changing" as older Boomers are prone to do. Then he "Dad'ed Up."

"You had it tough too, and this has been tough. This is very tough on all of us. But we have to work our therapies."

BOOM! That was some man-to-man shit right there. AA folks use "Work the program," the way bartenders use "Cheers," or Smurfs use "Smurf." But he knew the rigidity of AA, primarily the higher power part, would always be a non-starter for me. But he knew I took my therapy seriously, even if it wasn't coming together the way I desperately so wanted it to.

I mean, it couldn't be working if I was spending a Saturday night on my deck with my wife and parents, slowly getting drunk and wondering why I'm so off the rails when I have a roof over my head, a wife who loves me, a family that has my back, a job, and my health.

I cried to Jay that night. Told her that was the first time I remember Dad being a father like that since Uncle Bob died.

Little Eddie was pacified.

XXXVIII

The only thing keeping me somewhat in check by the fall of '21 was an ongoing attempt to build a new department at work from the ground up. My job remained the half-serious measure it devolved into a dozen years prior when corporate allegedly slashed our operating budget in half. However, a new opportunity had been percolating that could add a sense of pride and urgency to my career and significantly increase my income.

I had spent most of my working time over the previous ten months planning, testing, projecting, and researching every avenue to secure this contract. The Boss had all but checked out, and I was running all negotiations with client management. Taking phone calls at all hours. Jay got a kick out of it when we were out to dinner, and Walter got the same chuckle on the golf course. Here's laid-back professional Ed taking work calls like a functioning adult!

So when I got a phone call from NBC Universal Burbank around the close of business one day in early September, I was expecting a resolution on how we would move forward and how much my job was about to change. What I didn't expect was that my job was about to end.

"Hi Ed, I just wanted to inform you we will go in an entirely different direction. We've reviewed the Statement of Work Order and believe we need only give thirty days' notice, but we're giving forty out of respect for the long-time relationship between KLJ Review and NBC News."

October 15 would be KLJ's last day of existence.

I told Jay right away I didn't even have time to concoct some story about how it wasn't definitive or anything like that. I said it straight out, "I'm so fucked".

I had to call The Boss. I shouldn't have fallen to an employee who hadn't gotten a raise since the first year of the Obama administration to tell the man who founded the company thirty years ago that his business was dead, but that's the position I had wedged my life into. I was ready for many adverse reactions, but what I wasn't ready for was being told to "keep it to myself. We don't want everyone burning their time off." Now I was supposed to be part of scumbaggery and fucking with people about to experience vulnerability like never in their lives? I couldn't abide by that.

I immediately called Hayes and told him the job we worked together every day since January 2002 was ending—with a reminder that we're legally entitled to unused vacation time. The Boss was going to pay the staff, regardless. But the next series of phone calls reflected my biggest fears. One by one, I called Sean, Elizabeth, and Erin. I'm about a six-pack deep at this point because that's precisely where I ran the minute I got off the phone with Burbank.

I told each of them almost verbatim the same thing: I lost my job in my mid-forties, I'm processing loss, to begin with, I'm awful with money, I'm kind of drunk at 5:30 on a Wednesday, but I will not end up like Dad.

I cringe reading that now. If you have any experience with cognitive-behavioral therapy, you're probably cringing as well. With trauma as jarring as a sudden job loss, my mind went directly to losing everything the way my dad did.

I had to say it wouldn't be me because I knew how easy it could be.

...

Financial planners will never tell you that the best thing to do when you suddenly lose half your household income is to fly first class to California, rent a Mustang convertible, and shack up at a resort on Catalina Island for four nights. But it's what the universe had in store.

Earlier in the year, Phish announced their return to the road with a series of outdoor shows throughout 2021. Jay wasn't able to get tickets to their shows in New York, Philadelphia, or even Boston, but she could get them for Chula Vista, California. The American Airlines credit card we had tied to Amazon throughout the pandemic had earned us an embarrassing and irresponsibly large number of miles—so many that we could book First Class, JFK to LAX, Round Trip.

Was it the smart thing to do? To make it our first post-pandemic air travel vacation? No, and the cost had the least to do with it.

We were snapping back from a pretty awful stretch. My internal and external triggers were being worked overtime, and my trauma responses were not performing up to acceptable standards. We attempted to realign because it just wasn't working. I had no idea why. As far as I could tell, we were a couple married nineteen years, who'd been in each other's space nonstop for almost a year and a half.

She disagreed. She saw the darkness in me that was showing up more frequently. I took that perception as an attempt to keep me as a perpetual victim, to remind me daily that I'm less than because the clergy abused me.

As the departure for California drew closer, so did the pressure to prove to myself that I had my shit together. I was convincing myself that every time I acted out, Gerry Sudol was harming me all over again. I just had no idea how and when it was going to manifest.

But I knew I had to make California great. It had to make up for everything else my behaviors had allegedly ruined—whether or not I believed I destroyed them. I would convince myself that we deserved this—that I earned this: first class, luxury resort, convertible, West Coast Phish tickets.

Jay worked her ass off to be in this position. Whereas my pandemic work — for the twenty months I was employed—had been even more of a zombie walk than my in-person work was. I was going to Shop Rite whenever I felt like it. I didn't hesitate to schedule midweek golf with anyone who could get away. I got really high in the middle of the day.

It wasn't the same for her. She was constantly told her job was on the line, only to be told she was vital to the company's operation and slowly gained more territory and responsibility. She deserved all that this trip offered and then some.

But checking into the flight and all the perks of first-class travel reminded me of how much of a fraud I was.

I was not collecting a regular paycheck for the first time since a brief respite in 1999. I had no idea how much settlement money I had left; some was in a stock market account, and the rest went into our regular bank account. I knew plenty of money was available for our usual daily expectations. Vacations? Not so much.

Because I had no interest in figuring out exactly where we stood financially, I just opened up a line of credit, used it to move a couple of thousand bucks onto the American Airlines card that was banging up on its limit, and we'd have plenty of money for the trip.

Besides, I would find an even better job soon, and all would be ok.

On our first full day, we set out to hit the many incredible microbreweries in San Diego. It was reminiscent of the Before Times, when we'd explore places like Boston or Denver or Philly or New Orleans. We laughed about memories. We compared tasting opinions on the beers. We avoided homeless encampments.

We had a great lunch at a brewery across from where the San Diego Padres played—then walked to the adjoined team store, where I was overrun with nostalgia for the poop-brown and mustard-yellow Padres logos and uniform of my youth. We had already picked up T-shirts from two of the breweries we hit, so we might as well throw another $100 of merch on the card.

I got into a conversation with the guy behind the counter. I'm trashed and rambling about the old 1984 Topps cards of Padres All-Stars Tony Gwynn and Kevin McReynolds, and he's loving every minute. We got so lost in conversation that I left the day's souvenirs on the counter when our Uber back to Catalina Island arrived.

A great day out like that was an excellent foundation for ensuring the concert succeeded. Phish has always been significantly more important to Jay than me, and a positive Phish experience can buttress her forward for months. All ex-Catholics need some form of spiritual nourishment.

I ordered some pre-rolled joints for the hotel room. We left for the show with a handful of beers in a plastic bag. West Coast Phish was happening, and it would be a blast.

The parking lot scene was everything I imagined and then some. Known in the jam band communities as "Shakedown Street"—a nod to a classic Grateful Dead tune from the mid-70s—it's a place where you can find everything from veggie burritos to tie-dye shirts to balloons full of nitrous oxide (laughing gas).

And I made myself at home. The last thing I remember in the parking lot was firing up one of those pre-rolled joints that was so kindly delivered to my room. The next thing I know, all 300+ lbs. of me is looking up at two arena staffers trying to help me up from the metal detector I knocked over when I barreled into it during gate entry.

Jay was off to the side, in tears, begging security to let me in. She told them this was our first trip since the pandemic, and she came from Jersey. Whatever she said about me seemed to work because I dusted myself up, got up, and we were off to our seats.

But she wasn't pleased. I ruined West Coast Phish before the band played a single note.

...

I never knew how that bit of structure at KLJ kept my entire life together. In the before times, I could show up in my pajamas. I took as many smoke breaks as I wanted until I quit smoking. Then I vaped at my desk. People had to know. Nobody said shit.

Never tracked my time off. In the rare event that I showed up on time by 7, I rewarded myself by leaving before 3. If there were a holiday on Monday, I'd be out by 10 in the morning the Friday before "to beat the holiday traffic."

All of this was rewarded with the title of General Manager and about 35% more pay than the staff members who had their time tracked, output monitored, and policies enforced.

Yet, it was enough glue to keep me projecting myself as a fully formed human to the world. It appeared the remote lifestyle challenged that structure, but compared to what would become of days when the company fully closed, I had the discipline of a West Point cadet.

Had the job ended during the in-person days, there would have been goodbyes, a final commute, and a massive disruption to my schedule. But a year and a half of homebound life made the transition negligible. I was still waking up around seven most days, drinking every other day, and doing nothing productive in between. The only difference is I wasn't getting a check for $1100 in the mail each week.

None of this was registering, however, because I created the greatest grievance narrative of my life to that point: nobody deserved Thanksgiving this year because America failed her vulnerable. With the holiday rapidly approaching, I knew I had to get myself right before sitting down with Jay's family for dinner. I rearranged my therapy schedule to meet with Dr. Grant as late as she'd see me before the holiday. If she offered "right after the Macy's Parade," I'd have jumped on it.

One should always be emotionally honest with their therapist. But it's something many of us struggle with. And something I've often been hesitant to do. But I was unusually frank during that discussion. I said I worked to believe there was any authenticity behind Thanksgiving this year, that there was nothing to be grateful for. I confessed I was so nervous that one of my in-laws would make a passive-aggressive (or worse, blatantly obvious) political comment that would set me off or put me in an awkward spot.

She tried to get me to see that I was projecting my fears onto everyone else. She asked if I thought that anyone in our families hosted holiday dinners intending to harm a loved one or make them uncomfortable. I sarcastically replied that I couldn't think of any other reason they would if not to make it awkward, but her point was taken.

The day went relatively well. There was no hostility as we prepared for the day, at least not outside the usual tension that occurs when two neurodivergent people have to go out into the wild and socialize.

The conversation was respectful. There was still a pall cast over the holiday. We were six months removed from burying a universally adored loved one; it was hard not to have that front and center in our thoughts. Of course, with alcohol being abundant, coping mechanisms existed.

I had the best intentions. I brought a four pack of Industrial Arts Torque Wrench. It's a pretty heavy beer that packs a punch. They were gone by dinner. And dinner involved wine. And dessert was a vodka tonic because I was way too full to drink Uncle Fred's Budweiser.

After dinner, I moved to the living room to resume watching a football game that my unemployed ass wagered too much money on it. Watching football with my father-in-law has always been one of my greatest pleasures. A former All-County safety from St Cecilia's High School, the man could have seriously been a defensive coordinator in the NFL—or higher—if he chose that career path.

It was all feeling like a relaxing Thanksgiving reminiscent of the Before Times.

"You know, it was Iran's money in the first place, but we shouldn't have given them all $6 Billion on those pallets.", he said from out of nowhere. I could have finished his sentence but allowed him to go ahead.

"What we have to do is tell them, 'Look, we know you were responsible for the IED explosions that killed our soldiers in Iraq, so we're going to withhold money to pay their relatives.'"

I wasn't pissed that he was telling me his idea for peace with Iran for the twenty-eighth time. I wasn't even pissed that it was wholly inaccurate and implausible. It took no responsibility for the long-established reality that the USA was the invading and conquering force. They don't get to complain about the messages local people send them to get out.

Jay caught my eye to the motion that it was time to leave. There's no motion; it's always been a simple glance. Seeing it is one of the best feelings in the world, we agree it's finally time to hit the road. We said our goodbyes, and on the way to the car, she asked if I had had a lovely time.

With a chuckle, I said, "It was a perfect day until your dad started talking about the Iran nuclear deal again."

"Ah, the one where he says they should withhold money for IED victims?"

"That very one."

Seven short Ridgefield Park blocks later, she believed I ran a stop sign on the approach to Route 80. She gave a jarring "STOP SIGN" that rattled the fuck out of me. I saw it, and even if I didn't, I spent the summer of '93 painting every sign pole in town. I know where all the RP stop signs are.

I had an awkward roll through the Stop, then punched it towards the entrance ramp onto Route 80.

"Are you ok to drive?" she asked.

I unloaded on her. How dare she ask me if I was alright to drive? How dare I have to listen to the Iran Nuclear Deal speech for the 25th time? How dare anyone think they have a right to Thanksgiving this year? All of it.

I'm not ready to celebrate Thanksgiving, so nobody should be.

I unloaded because she was right. I was writing checks my body couldn't cash by agreeing to drive home—and had been for some time. Back in the day, Ben and I were known and often needled for our complex yet firm refusal to drive drunk. Mind you, we'd never offer to drive—but we were militant about not drinking and driving.

I started getting comfortable with a short, two-turn/third-of-a-mile ride home from *Uncorked* about a decade earlier. I rarely strayed from local roads if I'd had too much to drink. Now I was driving on Route 80, obviously impaired, and screaming about how Thanksgiving is a fraud.

Pass the turnips.

XXXIX

I spent Easter 2022 at my favorite Irish pub!

No, I didn't shun our families to do Easter in a way that satisfies my "it's a holiday" criteria. My favorite Irish pub—*The Cottage Bar,* where I had those therapeutic drinks with Chris before the world changed forever — was a block north of the hospital where I was born. Good old Holy Name. It's also the hospital where my mother was recovering from surgery to remove a mass we would soon learn was Stage IV cancer.

It was not quite a week earlier that I got an early Monday morning phone call from my old man.

"Did you hear from Mom? She's in the hospital."

Being the so-called healthy parent wasn't his strong suit. A few days and some relentless follow-ups later, the news rattled our world. No matter what kind of delivery, encouragement, or statistics you they give you, your mind only forges one path forward when you hear "Stage Four Cancer": The End.

In one of my first therapy sessions, while learning the intricacies of what trauma is, Dr. Grant told me that sexual abuse was at the top of the list. Just ahead of the loss of a parent and loss of a job. Fantastic! John's passing and the ever-growing vocational morass I found myself in were all the evidence I needed to know my trauma responses left much to be desired.

The intrusive thoughts were working overtime that Holy Week. We had always had a joke-fear (one of those things you're worried about, so you minimize it) about what would happen if Mom went before Dad. His condition wasn't getting any better. He had already played his last round of golf without knowing it. And he depended utterly on her for just about everything outside of ordering crap online.

How would he function? Who would shoulder the responsibility? He wouldn't be able to be left alone for long periods. And forget about getting him together for anything related to a farewell. It sounds petty, but it was suddenly a genuine possibility.

Compounding the stressors, this was the first time I've ever had to confront my feelings about my mother and St. Francis, honestly. There was no denying the underlying fact—I was abused under her care at the school she insisted I attend. In a faith that she raised me in.

I wasn't being disingenuous when I came forward and told the mothers of Ridgefield Park that there was nothing they could have reasonably done to stop Sudol in his tracks. Not back then, regardless of how strong the suspicions may have been. They couldn't. By now, we know the scope was much more enormous than Sudol. It's so much bigger than St. Francis and Ridgefield Park. So much bigger than me or my mother.

Once I spoke my truth, I comforted and consoled my family members. I felt guilt for their guilt, but I harbored no ill will toward them for my circumstances. I was more concerned with their accepting that there was nothing for me to forgive because it was, in fact, so much bigger than me. Practically speaking, I was right. But I never asked myself if I held them responsible. Did I really forgive them? Or was it more important to me they weren't upset?

I danced around this issue many times over the decades, but the situation on the ground was such that I couldn't avoid it anymore. I had to overcome my feelings about my parents during my upbringing.

And I was upset when I was honest with myself. My mother was among the most overprotective mothers in St. Francis. How could she miss that? What made her so militant in insisting I attend Catholic school? Had she not heard horror stories about abusive priests by the time she was thirty?

I was the victim, damnit! She should have known better. She never should have let him into the house. She shouldn't have been so obsessed with her perception and reputation and being one of the "in" mothers in the parish. She was so impulsive that she ditched Father Horrigan for Sudol to baptize Erin. Didn't think twice about sending me away to his cabin—multiple times.

Then a daunting thought invaded my head. I could ask these same questions of her parents—and of their parents. People-pleasing was so important to me that I insisted on getting married in St. Francis. The only reason I'm not asking this question of myself is that I have no children to be spiritually accountable for. Who was I to judge? This wasn't isolated, it was institutional. All blame lies on the shoulders of the institution.

The thought trains were conflicting, but I knew which one was healthy and which one was going to keep me stewing in toxicity.

•••

Mom got sick right around the time I was quietly quitting on Plan A for the next phase of my professional life. After KLJ went belly-up, I convinced myself that being an independent writer would be my pathway to a livelihood. I had settlement money, and starting early in the year, I was eligible for quite-generous-thank-you-blue-state New Jersey unemployment insurance. I would use those 26 weeks to build an audience with regular columns and insight and breaking news analysis. It's a combination of my entire internet publishing history.

I was going to analyze modern events through the lens of history. After all, we were in a period of history on steroids, a far cry from that ignorance of youth yearning to experience instability back in Pine Hall. The failed January 6 coup anniversary was a great time to talk about the War of 1812. The early Biden economic agenda was comparable to the debates surrounding FDR's New Deal legislation. This was something I could excel in.

I would live the life of a writer. I'd throw grooming to the wind (all that meant was not shaving anymore, instead of trimming my beard once a week). I'd keep unique hours centered on my creative peak (5:10 AM). I would leverage my social media experience for a multimedia experience. I would tease a podcast and gauge the response.

And I did all of it! Reception from friends, followers, and newcomers alike was positive. Engagement was steadily building. For three weeks before Little Eddie started speaking his truth.

Fancy yourself a writer? You're a former middle management desk jockey who blogs from time to time. You think you'll make a living doing this? You won't. It's too much work. You've been doing this for a month, and how many publications are banging on your door? You think picking up one subscriber per post is sustainable? Those 300 subscribers you have now are all out of pity. They follow you because you got molested, you freak. Everybody loves a train wreck. Your friends are laughing at you.

Somewhere around this point in time, I disassociated from reality. Instead of colorfully exaggerating ways in which I was doing fine and earning a living while I figured shit out, I just started outright lying.

I got an online tutoring gig. It made me feel pretty damn good, too; I had a pupil named Andy, a sophomore AP Government student. Once a week, I got to talk about the Federalist Papers. It only paid $15 per hour, but I told people it was between $35 and $50. *I can't be seen as less than.*

I continued lying to Jay about money, and she took me at my word. Disturbingly, I began lying to Dr Grant.

I started feeling like I was letting her down by not being healed yet, by being constantly hostile, by having exactly nothing in my life going right. So I lied to HER about how much money I was making, how much beer I was drinking, how many fights we were having, and just about everything else. It didn't matter that Jay reached out to her when I would get completely unhinged.

The more it was apparent that things were slipping away, the more I tried to convince her it was getting better. I was self-sabotaging on a completely new level.

•••

We had a busy couple of weeks—our most firm commitments since the Before Times—and they were bookended by arguably the two most anticipated events of the calendar year: Memorial Day Weekend at Jaymanda's along with The Hayeses and then the Wildwood Crest week down the Jersey Shore.

I was shell-shocked for the entire month of May—the worst hair trigger of my life to that point. I was amid two major life traumas at 45 without knowing what to do. The advice was coming in fast and furious; I was hearing but not listening to a damn thing. I had that feeling on the mound, being coached by Dad about pitching from the stretch and blacking out as he gave me a crash course as Little Ferry was running wild around the bases. Only this wasn't a lousy inning; it was a terrible month.

It came to a head in the long car ride down to Jaymanda's. I screamed through all my greatest hits. I was yelling about the Angry Mayonnaise noises and how fucked up they were. *I had trust ripped out from me by the people I was most vulnerable with. How the fuck was that ever okay? Over fucking Trump? The cocksucker who killed a million Americans mismanaging the virus and tried to overthrow the government?!?!?!?*

Utterly unhinged, I drove down the New Jersey Turnpike. I was borderline frothing as we turned off the local main drag onto their block. And then, the minute I parked, I was magically back to myself again. I was safe. I was in my happy place. With my tribe. Out of the confined space of a car.

Because we're awesome people, we dressed up like vintage WWF superstars. Jay did a phenomenal job dressing up as Ric Flair. The Hayeses were Captain Lou Albano and Cindi Lauper. Jaymanda was Randy "Macho Man" Savage and "Rowdy Roddy Piper." I found a one-size-fits-all black singlet and called myself Andre the Giant. The darkness of the prior weeks, months, and years seemed to disappear completely.

The safest and most secure I had felt in a long time was wearing nothing but an over-the-shoulder Speedo.

I couldn't even comprehend being on a defensive footing, and the psychedelic mushrooms we took undoubtedly helped. In that version of Jay, I saw the partner I wanted to spend the rest of my life with, nary a hint of hostility. In that version of me, Tripping Ed, I had conquered my demons.

I was a seasoned veteran of psychedelic and hallucinogenic drugs by now. I knew long before I ate that fungus that it would not be a big fun social party, that I'd spend a lot more time in my head than sober me would ever be comfortable with. But something had to give, and I had to embrace that it's just how it has to be. After a social hour around the firepit where we all waited for the shrooms to kick in, it turned just into that: a party of one, location: Ed's head.

Every time I trip, I risk Little Eddie will pirate the voyage. It was now three years since I had that mushroom experience at the same home, in front of the pool, where I reclaimed water. But that night, I couldn't think about anything other than how far I had devolved over three years.

You're on your way to being a statistic. Your marriage is falling apart. You have no job. You have no idea how to get a job. You're finally being exposed as the fraud you've always been. And you haven't admitted it yet, but that front tooth of yours is loose.

All of which is typical Little Eddie banter. But on trippy drugs, he gets more meta....

What about Willie and Phil? They didn't get the gift of 45 years of life. They suffered in silence until the silence became deafening. They didn't have the resources available to you. Their mothers are witnessing your decline on Facebook.

You're re-traumatizing them.

You're re-traumatizing yourself.

•••

Jay couldn't have been more accepting of my status among the unemployed. She fully supported my attempts to make "Rearview Mirror" a thing, let alone a living. She knew better than anyone, outside of maybe Hayes, how unbelievably unchallenging KLJ was and how stunting that could be. So, she encouraged me to take my time and find a purpose and not just a job.

I was beating myself up daily, not for collecting unemployment—it's a system I paid into for this reason every week since I was sixteen, save for some off-the-books work in high school. But for not having a direction. Managing staff at KLJ wasn't exactly like being a teacher, electrician, or quarterback. There's no subcategory on Career Builder for "Jack of all Windows-Based Trades, Master of None."

A year ago, our trip to the Jersey shore with Jaymanda and the Hayeses was everything we needed to emerge from the morass of COVID-19. Even though KLJ was hardly challenging, they still earned vacation days. I emailed declaring them as such. You don't have to email the Secretary of Labor to request vacation time when you're unemployed. The state paid the same $804.00 per week, whether looking for work, sleeping off a hangover, self-sabotaging, or going down the shore.

If Wildwood 2021 was Woodstock, Wildwood 2022 was Woodstock '99. The location was the same; the vibe couldn't be more different.

We had a surprisingly pleasant car ride, likely because we were in a brand new loaner car from the dealership (One of the few perks of a global supply chain disruption was how long you could end up in a loaner). Seeing everybody and having those first hotel drinks before unpacking was everything I expected it to be. The entire first day was great.

It was so great that Jay had a little too much fun. As is often the case when one of us overdoes it, the other wants little to do with it once we're safely wherever our heads lie. Now, ninety-five percent of the time, I'm the one who went overboard, but night one of Vacation '22 was part of that minuscule 5%.

She kept asking why I was yet to heal. She was reminding me she loved me, that the people around me loved me. That she loved me. That she missed me. That she needed me back. Then she said whatever I was doing wasn't working.

The "working" part set me off.

I don't know if it was because she was the drunk one, and I felt sympathy towards her, but I acted out by using my tools to the extreme. I didn't yell or scream. I wasn't animated. I stormed out of bed, grabbed my nicotine and THC pens, and went into the bathroom. I took five. I chilled. I puffed the shit out of the pens, looking in the mirror and telling myself that I had to remain calm. That I can't ruin this trip on the first night. I took one more THC hit, exhaled, and went back into the room.

To the sound of Jay snoring. (So I ordered a pizza.)

•••

The next day began with an unsettling call from Erin. Dad was hospitalized again. Doctors feared that his lung cancer had returned. They didn't believe he could handle a traditional biopsy. They were considering hospice.

"HOSPICE?!" I said out loud, waking Jay up.

I called Erin, then my mother, and got the complete story. It was accurate up to the traditional biopsy part, but nobody said anything about "hospice." What they said was in the absence of the ability to biopsy, it has to be managed and monitored and that the goal was to keep him pain-free in the interim.

I tried to shift my focus and use my tools, but I didn't try hard enough. My brain was a volley between Jay yelling, "Doesn't work," and "Dad's in Hospice." Neither was true. Jay wasn't speaking of my unemployment but my tools, and Dad was still pursuing his medical treatments; he just could not undergo a test. It didn't matter because I checked out of the hotel room around that time, and Little Eddie checked in.

We went out to a brewery for a group dinner that night. Everybody was already a little intoxicated in their way. I was thoroughly trashed. Without even thinking, I finished a 12-pack of IPAs in the afternoon and a vodka mule while showering and almost definitely had less than 400 calories of non-potato chip food for the day.

I don't remember dinner at the brewery, but the pictures looked nice. And I didn't remember the infamous "second location," a boardwalk bar until I was throwing up in the bathroom and subsequently being asked to leave when I returned to our table and started vaping. Night ruined for everyone.

We spent most of the next two days on the beach. Except I would take long trips back to the hotel room to "refill" for everyone. Some of them were over an hour long. Jay told me my absences were noticeable. I had no answer for her beyond, "I don't want to bring people down; I'm still really rattled by the hospice call."

She bought it. I guess the other four did, too. But it was a load of shit.

I had long ago come to peace with my father's mortality, or so I thought I did at that point. Truth is, it was jarring but forgotten with the first sip of Industrial Arts Wrench New England Style India Pale Ale that morning. I was habitually retreating until I was too drunk to give a fuck all vacation because I was trying to keep Little Eddie away from everyone else's hard-earned vacation.

Because you sure as shit didn't deserve it, did you, fraud? Drinking, smoking, bitching, and whining your life away. Those people down there, they pity you. They don't want to spend time with you; they HAVE to spend time with you. You're the guy who admitted a priest diddled him and then collapsed for everyone to see. These are the last people on earth who have any tolerance for you and your shit. You think they didn't notice the awkward way you were eating wings because of that dangling tooth?

It's not good enough even when you use your tools like you're doing now. They're talking about you.

Everybody's talking about you, you unemployed piece of shit. The only people who still love you are your parents, and they'll both be dead soon.

XLV

Northern New Jersey's Route 23 was once the gateway to the state's highlands region, an area where you'll find West Milford, among other rural/mountain communities. Beginning less than 35 miles from midtown Manhattan, the area was ideal for the sweet spot in leisure travel between the postwar automobile boom and the expansion of air conditioning and commercial air travel. Like its more famous fellow city escape, the Catskills, the Jersey highlands offered an array of mom-and-pop resorts and motels for families looking to get away from the concrete heatwaves and seek comfort in its lakes, tree shade, and mountain breeze.

The Regency was likely one such resort. I hadn't visited the property until the summer of 2001, though, when Jay, her mother, and I toured the facilities while searching for a wedding venue. By that point, it was owned by the Best Western hospitality chain. Its charm was more kitsch. A Kentucky Fried Chicken, strip malls, and the heavy traffic that comes with being a 6-mile artery between Interstate 80 and Interstate 287 disturbed its serenity. Despite my excitement over a groomsman suite with a fully tended bar and an ashtray, the general feeling was that it was more suited for a *Dirty Dancing* reboot than the festival we planned to host.

Twenty-one years later, I found myself back at the property. By then, it was sold again; now it was under the Baymont Hotels banner—and there was no ambiguity about the state of the hotel: it was a shit hole. Jay and I had separated two days after we returned from the shore, and we were alternating between Jay traveling for work and me crashing with Doc, Erin, or in cheap hotels.

And the Baymont was the cheapest of the cheap.

New Jersey banned indoor smoking at all businesses, including hotels, in 2006. For the next five years, it wasn't unusual to have a lingering tobacco stench in bars, restaurants, lodging, and other venues where you used to light up at will. Eventually, establishments were repainted, rebuilt, or aired out, and remnants of an unhealthier age went the way of spittoons and pay phones (Though, come to think of it, I believe the Baymont still had both spittoons and payphones). But in July 2022, I swore I was standing in the middle of a cigar-rolling factory.

The elaborate ballroom and bar where I temporarily imagined dancing my wedding night away were shuttered. A sign above the front desk reminded monthly guests that, for legal reasons, they must check out every 28 days and check back in.

Oh, and prostitutes. Monthly guests need love, too.

But the most obvious sign that the resort was eons away from its golden era was the decrepit state of the in-ground pool, once the place's crown jewel.

It wasn't hard to imagine an upper-middle-class family hanging poolside during the Kennedy administration. Mom - a scarf over her hair and oversized sunglasses. Sipping on a gin and tonic, reading "Payton's Place". Dad, in a fishing cap and a relaxed chino button-down shirt, is perusing the *Wall Street Journal* as he enjoys a Manhattan. The kids partaking in dangerous horseplay in the pool so out-of-place today that they would get an NC-17 rating.

But today? The pool was bone dry. Mold stains surrounded the drains and onetime filter pumps. The few remnants of last autumn that hadn't decomposed yet littered the cracked concrete bottom. The "No Diving" stenciled warnings were nearly opaque.

And I was standing it over it, a little after sundown on a typically humid summer night, wondering if I got enough of a running start, would my 300-pound, piss-drunk ass definitely die if I got enough of a running start to jump into its deep end? Or would I only end up with an even more miserable experience? One where I could not walk, breathe, piss, eat, drink, fart, or fuck under my power—but I'd still be able to think.

I'd still be able to remember the trauma from my childhood in the 1980s.

I'd still be able to remember the denial that begot the silent suffering that I spent nearly thirty years living with.

I'd still be able to remember the regrettable behaviors I exhibited when I had no idea the root cause was that very trauma. How I assumed I was just inherently bad, broken, and damaged.

I'd still be able to remember the long, torturous, but fruitful journey toward sharing my story.

I'd still be able to remember the feeling of immense justice, satisfaction, and worth when my story inspired a community to create enough outrage that Gerry Sudol would be hastily removed from a parish that shared a parcel of land with an elementary school. And that he would ultimately be removed from the ministry.

I'd still be able to remember the amateur detective work that we did to uncover how we believe our small town in North Jersey became an intentional landing spot for known child abusers.

I'd still be able to remember having my essay featured in the top spot on Yahoo! News and the *Huff Post* or being in the A-Block of New York City network news.

I'd still be able to remember my testimony before the New Jersey Senate Judiciary Committee, advocating for eliminating the Statutes of Limitations for survivors of childhood sexual abuse to seek answers and justice.

Worst of all, I would still remember the darkness inside of me that confronting this abuse unlocked in me not long after the lights, reporters, and attention went away.

I just wouldn't be able to heal.

I'd love to say that my decision to walk back to my room that night was because of a profound desire to get better, live my best life, reconcile with my then-estranged wife, finally get my mind, and body in shape and make the second half of my life everything I didn't let the first half be. But the reality of my parent's spiraling health gave me substantial pause. I can be selfish. I can be stubborn. I, unfortunately, can be downright cruel.

But lucky for me, I still had a shred of empathy left. I'll remember the depths of that conversation with myself for as long as my brain functions. It wasn't the first time the thought had crossed my mind since I came forward, and it wouldn't be the last.

It was, however, the most attention I've ever given the act. I felt like I had all the reasons in the world to sprint and leap, and very few reasons not to that pertained to my feelings and not the reaction of others.

Complex post-traumatic stress disorder, that's how. And it's a series of trials and tribulations I wouldn't wish on my worst enemy.

Not even Gerry Sudol.

...

My contemplation of whether it was all worth it, set against the backdrop of a drained-out in-ground pool, began a fortnight earlier on our deck—July 2, 2021. The nation was still grappling with the repercussions of the Dobbs v Jackson Supreme Court decision, a seismic shift that overturned Roe v Wade, stripping away a woman's guaranteed right to make her own reproductive decisions. Few topics stir my passions as intensely as abortion. The thread connecting conservative authoritarian religious intrusions into personal lives, clear in both the anti-choice movement and the environment that fostered clergy abuse for so long, is easy to trace.

At least it's not in my mind. Or on my Facebook page, where I posted:

"I have an honest, two-part question for MAGA mothers and grandmothers out there.

1. Do you realize that your daughter's granddaughters will learn that you were a MAGA Republican?

2. Do you realize you are gonna be passed down through family history as the forced birth extremist? Especially now they we have social media and 23andMe and your great great great nephew will he able to learn of your anti-woman views with the click of a button

3. At long last, have you no decency?"

That was my mindset and footing for "Independence Day." Still a little perturbed by "not working" in Wildwood the week prior. My cause du jour was not attending my in-laws' annual 4th of July party. Almost six months ago, I was watching criminals waving American flags use those flags to preserve the presidency of a badly defeated candidate. I made a concrete grievance narrative that anytime a crowd of overwhelmingly white, older people gathered with lots of American flags, it was an endorsement of the Capitol Siege.

How the fuck don't people see this? We had an election. America won, and fascism lost. Then they tried to stop it violently! They're silencing the voices of the vulnerable to preserve their defeated vision of America. Let them have July 4th; We have January 6th, our very own "VT Day." In our world, in our country, women have autonomy. In our country, being pro-choice isn't "vile"; stripping away women's rights is.

But it wasn't enough that I endorsed my grievance narrative. I was growing increasingly livid with Jay for not seeing the same thing.

Whose side are you really on, Jay?

I'm unsure how the argument started, but I raged on the deck. I was screaming. I got animated, waving my arms around. I activated a "big bear posture" in a way I never had prior. Full of fury, I apparently told Jay that all of my behaviors resulted from her actions. I have no recollection of saying it, but it struck such a nerve that I don't doubt its authenticity.

She packed up and left. She headed straight for Erin's. I had no idea that I would discover the severity of a critical pillar of C-PTSD: Fear of abandonment.

•••

That tooth abandoned me that night. I woke up the following day with a different feel in my mouth, and when I ripped my CPAP off and got a grip of my surroundings was that front tooth resting right above the indent where my head just was, like some reverse-tooth-fairy experience where middle age leaves your former tooth on your pillow as a reward for the unhealthy decisions of your life's first nine holes.

I assumed Jay and I were retreating to our respective corners. *Let her go fiddle while Rome burns; I'm going to see those precious nieces who are oblivious to what just happened to them.*

This narrative had an awful lot of external support. My Family Chat was livid following the decision. Everyone but Dad (who only responds to congratulate loved ones or wish them Happy Birthday) had some reaction to *Dobbs*. Jay, Jason, and I walked the Wildwood boardwalk a week ago wearing pro-Roe t-shirts. If I didn't ruin the trip with my depression, I likely would have ruined it with my post-*Dobbs* anger.

Supported or not, justified or not, it was still a grievance narrative. About ten minutes after I woke up, I took an Uber to Sean's house, where my family was gathering. I was careful not to classify it as anything other than getting together because of a day off from work. At least, that's what I told myself, despite not working.

I had a coffee, ran to the liquor store to get a twelve-pack of Coors Light, came home, opened one, and showered. I texted Erin to get the lay of the land; Jay was going to her family as expected; I would see Erin at Sean's place.

I came in hot. I arrived sweaty and a beer or three deep, carrying an opened 12-pack of shitty light beer. Eager to rip off the Band-Aid, I showed everyone my new and devolved smile.

It's not bad enough that your parents spent thousands of dollars on your education only to have you end up unemployed at 46, but now you have to rub it in their faces that they wasted all that money on braces.

Erin arrived about twenty minutes later, tears streaming down her face, ostensibly over something unrelated to Jay staying at her place the night before. Amid her emotional distress, I overheard her saying, "I'm just tired of being stuck in the middle."

That snippet was all I needed to conclude that she expressed the challenge of being caught between Jay and me. With strides longer than my attempts at the triple jump in '93, I crossed Sean's living room to reach her, emphatically reassuring her she no longer had to feel stuck between us. Mom attempted to intervene, but I brushed her off.

Turning back to the group sheltered in the air-conditioned space, I proclaimed that if they loved my wife so much, they could "fucking have her" and I stormed out. During my lap around Sean's complex, beer in one hand and THC pen in the other, I encountered Aunt Breda. It later transpired that the issue Erin was lamenting was an internal matter between Mom and Aunt Breda. I had exploded over a misinterpretation.

It's as if I had convinced myself that an explosion was inevitable and only a matter of finding the trigger.

There was always a tacit adult understanding between Aunt Breda and me regarding trauma, therapy, and acceptance. Unlike the parent-child dynamic within my family, there was no guilt or shame associated with her, even if she carried guilt for my experience. She could ease my turmoil in moments of heightened emotion, grabbing my wrist and emphatically expressing her understanding of my pain.

Why did it have to be so challenging?

•••

The following week was full of tension, pain, and hostility. Jay said she wanted to separate for three months and get her own place to reassess our position. We were so misaligned that she had no idea how financially implausible it would be at that point to have two domiciles while I was coming toward the end of my unemployment insurance.

I agreed to give her space around her work schedule; we would alternate nights at home depending on her schedule. She was in Virginia on Tuesday, Wednesday, and Thursday that week. I would find somewhere to lay my head for the weekend.

Come Friday, I was completely immersing myself in this "trial separation." Doc and Erin were pulling overtime to keep us as sane as possible. It would be unfair for either of us to downplay their efforts; they were a vivid reminder that you can't navigate life without a solid support system. Years after helping Erin escape a toxic relationship with her daughter's father or being a sounding board for the worst of Doc's reactions to his divorce, it was our turn. The Ridgefield Park bond runs deep.

Doc generously extended the hospitality of his bachelor pad, a space I had yet to visit, courtesy of the first invitation coinciding with the initial weekend of March 2020. Stepping into his place was a stark emotional contrast. The moment his door swung open, I felt a sense of familiarity in a location I had never set foot in.

To kick off our evening, we shared a moon rock joint—you know; the kind dipped in hash oil. Within an hour, we emptied his kids' spare change jar, attempting to guess the minting year of each coin based on its weathered appearance. Surprisingly, we didn't even make a dent in the case of the Industrial Arts Wrench.

I had expected a heartfelt "talk it out" session, a chance to compare notes on the unraveling of his marriage to where Jay and I currently found ourselves. However, there was almost none of that. Brian, a seasoned veteran of such situations, instinctively knew precisely what I needed.

The next evening didn't go as well.

•••

Ben, being another Ride-or-Die, recognized I needed to be in a better place and extended an invitation for a BBQ with his family, along with Sean, his wife, and daughter. It was your typical sweltering New Jersey July Saturday: hotter than hell and humid as shit. After leaving Doc's that morning, I knew I needed a shower, but home wasn't an option. I had agreed to stay "out" until Jay headed out for business on Monday morning.

For a fleeting moment, the idea of depleting all our available funds in the early weeks of this separation crossed my mind—a sort of "Fuck Around and Find Out" statement. I contemplated staying at posh hotels, indulging in elaborate meals, maybe even heading down to Atlantic City for some reckless debauchery. I knew that such a spree would inflict as much long-term damage on me as it would on Jay, but long-term considerations were nowhere on my mental radar. *When you ain't got nothin', you got nothin' to lose.*

In a cruel twist of fate, I settled on the Baymont Motor Lodge because something inside me whispered, "Keep it cheap, just in case." A Tarheel Blue Columbia insulated backpack cooler became my trusty travel companion during my displacement from home—my version of Wilson the Volleyball. Before I embraced my role as the husband checking into a budget motel for the weekend, I made a pit stop at Bottle King to ensure the cooler was fully stocked. Just one step away from the Bachelor Arms Garden Apartments.

My room was massive—party-hosting levels of space. Other guests clearly knew this and were hosting them. The unmistakable scent of smoke hung in the air. I felt no trepidation about indulging in some pot, unlike the usual caution exercised in hotels where getting caught could cost a couple of hundred bucks.

To my delight, the air conditioner worked like a charm, swiftly chilling the room to a crisp 60 degrees. I cracked open a beer, settled on the bed while scrolling through my socials, had another brew during my shower, and summoned an Uber for the short two-mile jaunt to Ben's.

Everything went smoothly until I spotted the kids joyfully splashing around in the pool, including my niece. While there might have been a lingering pool trigger from my childhood, it wasn't the primary source of the emotions that suddenly took a sharp turn.

You're an embarrassment, someone people don't want around their kids. Jay is right; you're a disaster. Look at this innocent fun—you'll never experience the joy in their faces again. No one will ever want you within a zip code of their children.

I didn't outwardly explode. Instead, I retreated to a shaded corner of Ben's yard, fired off a text to The Family Chat, and, with a touch of venom, demanded they disown me if they were going to believe the rumors circulating about me behind my back. It wasn't accusatory, but it was undoubtedly nasty.

Returning my phone to my pocket, I rejoined the party. A beer or two later, I crossed paths with Sean's wife on my way to the bathroom.

"Hey Ed, what inspired that text you just sent?" she asked calmly and friendly.

"Oh, um"... Damn, I completely forgot I had sent that text barely 15 minutes ago. Her question snapped me back to reality. I can't recall exactly what I told her, but once in the bathroom, I hurriedly summoned an Uber. It was time to grab Wilson the Cooler and return to the Baymont.

Roughly five hours later, I wondered if it was all worth it as I stared into the emptiness of that in-ground pool.

No wife. No job. No family. No friends. No hope. No tooth.

XLVI

There was a shift in the way I handled shame following that dance with drunken stupidity, and it was noticeable the following day. To that point in time, anytime that I overdid it with alcohol to the point of mortifying behavior (and my antics at Ben's and in the vacant pool space met that threshold with ease), I would wake up with unspeakable feelings of shame and guilt. But not that morning.

I wasn't crippled by shame the way I absolutely should have been. Instead, I woke up to an almost fully formed, brand-new grievance:

Everybody has turned on you. Your wife won't stop triggering you at home. Her family still hates you because you reject MAGA. She's convinced your family that you're crazy. Everyone is talking behind your back. Nobody else gives a shit about how badly we all failed to protect the vulnerable. Everyone wants to pretend it didn't happen.

You might as well keep taking it as it comes; this is all you'll ever be, so you might as well let life happen to you. You're not a survivor; you're a victim, and you'll always be a victim.

I genuinely convinced myself there was a semblance of nobility, or perhaps misguided machismo, in embracing a day-to-day existence. If the end were to arrive, so be it.

But by intertwining Jay with my family's perceived disappointment in me, I unconsciously turned them into adversaries. Over the years, I had subconsciously established a "trinity of support" in my adult life. When life threw challenges my way, I would inevitably turn to and confide in Jay, extended family, or friends. Now, I had alienated two-thirds of that vital support system.

Therapy should have been a support, but I solidified the walls I put up during our sessions. It felt like the movie *Ground Hog Day*. I would recap my week at almost the same time for each appointment:

"Some good, some bad. Still have episodes of rage. Drank a little (more or less, depending on the week) than last week. Accepted that this is not who I want to be."

It did not matter that I convinced myself that I was rocking my therapy, getting better every day, and advocating that everybody find a therapist to take care of their heads. I was projecting my fantasy. After over four years of cognitive-behavioral therapy, I was worse off than when I started by every metric possible.

Jay had been suggesting couples therapy for about a year by now, but I remained resistant. *Why should you have to go through your entire life all over again with a new therapist? You can't talk about your marriage without talking about how you fucked it all up by coming forward about being diddled.*

But when we both live out of suitcases, there's a compelling argument that outside help may be the course of action.

•••

As the pandemic unfolded, mental health in America was in a rough patch. Amid the surge of therapy apps and websites, Talkspace stood out, boasting a user-friendly interface (a crucial factor when Jay and I weren't sharing the same space) and positive reviews. Our designated therapist was "Lance."

Now, Lance, a middle-aged dude conducting sessions from his leather recliner, was a sight. His camera seemed to have no fixed perch; he held his phone like a Facetime call. Not one to judge appearances—I've attended sessions in last night's sleepwear—but this guy rocked T-shirts and gym shorts.

After delving into our disputes, particularly those at Jaymanda's or on our travels, Lance dropped a revelation with a straight face: "It's clear that Ed's main trigger is other motorists. Consider soothing music or podcasts while driving."

I might not have had my act together, but I knew my trigger wasn't just the folks on the road. Sure, most of them suck, but let's be serious, Lance.

Despite my skepticism, this sweatpants-clad couch therapist would unwittingly referee a more significant debate between Jay and me: whether I'd attend Uncle John's memorial golf outing at the end of the month.

The second annual memorial at Seaview Golf Resort in Galloway, New Jersey, was approaching. It was John's favorite course, one I'd enjoyed with him in the glorious times before Covid, before Trump, before I came forward.

The inaugural event in 2021 was emotionally charged, a lovely affair marred by grief six months after John's passing. Tears flowed, and Jay and I fought the entire time and all the way home.

Despite our current predicament, I felt entitled to accept the invitation extended months ago. Jay, however, disagreed, thinking I should stay home.

Little Eddie wasn't having it.

How fucking dare you? You're going to keep me away from a Memorial? The fuck ever happened to "sickness and health". When he was battling cancer, I was bringing his family meals. My phone is full of text messages where he's thanking me for including his son in golf, baseball, hoops, even drinking! I did everything to ensure that the vulnerable among us were protected, and you're gonna keep me from a memorial? That's fucking rich.

In July 2022, I still carried every trauma since my decision to come forward, and few were heavier than John's passing. Eighteen months later, it made no sense. One Saturday, we're joking about the clowns trying to overthrow the government; the next, he's in a hospital, and now it's his second annual memorial. And here I am, uninvited.

In the presence of Lance and his recliner, I reluctantly agreed to stay away, aiming to ease Jay's fears that I'd "ruin it" with my toxicity. Inside, I was stewing throughout the separation. It was the first time I suspected my diagnosis extended beyond C-PTSD. I couldn't comprehend why this was happening to me. All I knew for sure was that she banned me from a memorial outing, and my wife had left me, providing a seamless excuse for hitting up dive bars and liquor stores just about every day.

I surrendered.

"I will not go, Jay," I said on the three-way call with my wife and our therapist's big Facetime head, "I don't want you to have any more anxiety. Give everyone my best."

•••

The week between that therapy session and the outing felt like a month. I had to vacate the premises in the days leading up to the trip because Jay was home and preparing for it. This time, I found an Extended Stay America that was as cheap as the Baymont but less suicidal. It still had prostitutes, but it didn't smell like smoke, and all the guests were friendly. And I could tell by observing which folks were there for the same reason I was. (I overheard two guests at check-in provide the 201 area code as their contact number, the same area code in which the Extended Stay lies. You don't run away for a night to practice self-care at the Ikea of hotel chains.)

Our paths crossed at home on the morning she was set to leave. My checkout was 11; she had planned to be on the road shortly before noon. She was almost ready to leave when I walked in. And I walked in, intending to go directly to the bedroom to fuck around on PlayStation until she left. And then I saw her golf bag.

Sticking out of the top was a 1996 Taylor Made driver—a club that a drinking acquaintance once gave me. I loved the club, but it was never my primary driver. Jay found a natural swing with the club being longer and heavier than her ladies' driver, but not as bulky and awkward as she found contemporary woods to be.

I walked over to her bag and removed the driver, a putter, and three other sticks she used from my original starter set.

"These are my fucking clubs. You have no right to them if you're keeping me from the outing."

She called me petty, and Little Eddie reached for his Big Bear defense.

"Oh, you think I'm petty? Well, I'll show up and check into the hotel booked in MY name and arrive at the first tee tomorrow morning with the invitation I received, and I'll hit the balls I designed and sit in that FedEx box you have packed."

And I was ready to.

"Go ahead; I'll have the Galloway Police waiting for you."

Did she just threaten you with the cops? The fucking cops? She's trying to get your goat again. Threatening you with the cops while she's about to leave for a memorial outing that she banned you from!

She left for her parents' house. After her car pulled out, I went to my car and texted her, "See you in RP," and followed her route.

"Look in your rearview," I texted again as I pulled onto Macopin Road, the residential county road parallel to Route 23 in West Milford.

She immediately called and told me she would have her parents and the Ridgefield Park Police waiting if I followed her.

"Great! Let the RPPD strike me down in the shadow of St. Francis. How fucking poetic would that be?" I said.

A momentary flash of reason told me to stop following her. Either that or I knew the Vreeland House Tavern I was about to pass was about to open. Either way, I ducked into the tavern's parking lot but continued texting as if I were still following her.

It went back and forth, primarily her talk-texting about how unhinged I was and my replies proving her right. But after a half hour, I surrendered. I parked my ass on a bar stool at the tavern and kicked off ten hours of pity-drinking.

As that often does, it gave way that crushing feelings of guilt and shame the following day—for the first time in a while; I had drank enough while getting angry enough to cause such a deficit that I couldn't get out of bed. It's usually one or the other, and I can begrudgingly function the day after. While what I now considered "my former family" was honoring one of the most extraordinary men I had ever known, I was sleeping off a five-star hangover and doing nothing with my life.

It would be surprising if I got up from bed five times that day. My bedroom had devolved into a cave. It wasn't even "our" bedroom. It was a guest bedroom when the pandemic began. Then, it became my home office. By now, it was where I spent 85% of my time at home. The mountains' low angle blocks the sun from shining directly through its east-facing windows. Heavy curtains handle the rest. I can make the sunniest of days feel like a dreary February dusk.

I had smoked enough pot and popped a Xanax to keep me anesthetized for most of the day. It kept me feeling rather fine for somebody whose greatest accomplishment for the day was picking up the DoorDash order left at the front door. Perhaps greasy Italian food was just as responsible as the benzos and grass.

Late that night, as I was drifting in and out of consciousness, a text from Jay came up on my lock screen. I debated ignoring and continuing off to sleep, but curiosity got the best of me. I unlocked the phone to read about 100 words about how much she missed me and wished I could have been there. I appreciated the concern and allowed myself to think that maybe things would work out just fine, that this would be the conclusion of "The Tension."

As I was contemplating a reply, another communication from Jay came through. It was a picture sent to a WhatsApp friend chat. She was with family, decked out in glow-in-the-dark bracelets and necklaces. The caption was "Have glowies, will travel"—a reference to the party favors prevalent at Phish concerts. This was a thread of friends we regularly went to Phish shows with.

As the "likes" from friends came in, I stewed. They all received the picture as intended. Little Eddie, however, saw it as football spiking.

Look at that; she's teasing you by telling you how much you're missed and how badly she wishes you could have been there today. Then she shows you how she really feels in that picture, with the people who started The Tension with the Angry Mayonnaise noises smiling along with her. She's rubbing it in your face that you weren't good enough to go to a goddamn Covid memorial!

•••

Jay didn't return home as much as she decided not to leave again once she returned from a business trip that followed Seaview. As was often the case with our biggest fights, they have a crescendo at peak anger that often drains us to the point of surrender. Nothing gets resolved, and my anger over what I would soon consistently refer to as *"The Banning"* was no exception.

I learned early in therapy, when I was being educated about PTSD, that abandonment could trigger strong negative reactions and emotions. As ridiculous as it sounds, I never connected "abandonment" to Jay leaving until well after the fact. I surrendered the conversation to Little Eddie, believing that this was part of her grand plan to grind me into a *stump of a man*.

Maybe she harbored resentment towards me for the way I came forward four years ago. Maybe she was pissed that I wasn't working. Maybe she was the one who was mentally ill and I don't stand a chance. Perhaps it was all the above.

I didn't know what it was, but I didn't think it was abandonment. Which is a funny concept for a Gen X kid, isn't it? Our entire experience is driven by the engine rooted in our own upbringing.

In memes, we celebrate it nostalgically, like staying out until the streetlights went on or drinking from a garden hose, or sarcastically, like being nurtured back to health when sick by Bob Barker, Doritos, and ginger ale, or how after-school care prepared us for the Covid lockdowns.

All these are humorous or satirical ways of expressing that we abandoned ourselves, learned things the hard way, taught not to trust at an early age, and taught to trust the wrong people even earlier.

XLII

"Happy New Year, Fam. Here's to a great '23. It will either be my best year or my last one."

That text, exuding a mix of fatal optimism and optimistic fatality, marked the start of 2023 in "The Thread" with Jay, Doc, and Erin. The latter half of '22 carried as much tension and trauma as the first. I had gone more than a year without steady employment, and my life seemed caught in a downward spiral. Denial, however, remained my steadfast companion.

From my perspective, firmly grounded in a defensive posture, I would consistently pat myself on the back for avoiding self-pity, all the while questioning why nothing seemed to change. I told Dr. Grant my belief was that everything would turn around at any moment; I just had to find a job.

But the reality on the ground needed to be more conducive to employment or any positive change. It seemed more aligned with a slow disassociation from everything and everyone that once brought me joy, including my house.

Even in the days when I still held a job, the cabin cried out for a paint job. Jay persistently inquired about hiring contractors, but to Little Eddie, it felt like nagging. *Could she not take a hint? There's no money to paint it!* By 2023, the signs of neglect were undeniable — streaks from the air conditioners each summer, peeling support beams, and cracking logs.

The interior needed attention, less in terms of money but care.

A wooden step on the way down to the garage, the last one, gave out a few weeks into lockdown. Propping it up with two cans of baked beans on the concrete floor, it slanted and instilled fear in Jay, making her think she wouldn't walk down that step again.

A hasty application of ceiling paint to cover water damage seemed reasonable enough. Leaving folded laundry on the dining room table was good enough. Letting dishes soak was good enough. Neglecting to put toilet paper on the roll was good enough; bringing the whole six-pack of it into the bathroom and using it as needed was good enough. Leaving Amazon deliveries outside until they were required was good enough.

While one might have deemed everything good enough, the reality fell far short of being good. I replaced my tooth with a pop-in veneer. It was a glorified mouthguard, more suitable for a running back than for the daily grind of life. Before long, the set was collecting dust on my nightstand as I surrendered to the toothlessness. I hadn't cut my hair in about fifteen months. I walked my days with a shaggy, unkempt, graying, thinning mop—and facial hair to match, as I had all but surrendered to nature with my beard. And my weight stabilized at "Still Too Fat."

As another tepid winter gave way to another extremely pollinated spring, the past-due notices piled up. I needed to catch up with my landscaper, skipped an energy payment or two, and ceased paying some personal loans for the time being. It turns out that "take a loan now, pay it back when you get a job" is something you must see all the way through for it to succeed.

As Memorial Day Weekend loomed, tensions escalated. Jay opted out of our traditional summer kickoff at Jaymanda's, citing an inability to "wear a mask" while my demons persisted and my circumstances remained stagnant. Despite the discord, I was determined not to miss it.

Reality, however, had other plans.

I attended solo, immersing myself in the festivities. The first night involved mushrooms, a venture into the recesses of my mind. Amidst the euphoria, I enjoyed beers in the yard with Hayes and Jason and fixated on an intricately detailed Phish lithograph. Eventually, I retreated to my weekend abode, lingering in my thoughts long after sunrise.

Only slept a few hours. I woke up and began drinking again as Hayes was already in the pool, enjoying a pre-noon beer. The day took a turn when a barrage of texts from Jay delivered the sobering news of a week's worth of late notices in the mail—representing nearly every account we held.

She had no idea how dire the situation was. She didn't know that the settlement money was all gone. I couldn't hide it anymore.

...

She was patient with me. She gave me time to collect myself and then the totality of our financial outlook. Every time she asked, however, became the proverbial "another brick in the wall:" I became more defensive and equally confused about why I was acting as such.

I knew I yearned for help in all parts of my life, but the economic sector could use extra love and care. But I wouldn't budge. I was speaking and begging as if I understood the gravity. Still, I refused to change any thought patterns internally, which assured me that destructive behaviors would continue.

Not long after Father's Day, I realized there was no way we would make the most basic of bills for June — the essentials, like the mortgage and car insurance. I didn't know where to turn. Defaulting on loans I took out when I believed unemployment was a temporary setback had shot my credit, cutting off that avenue.

I sent Walter and Ben individual texts, feeling lower than I may have ever felt, begging for $400 to help me skate through the end of the month, and then unemployment would start again in July—based on the final calendar year that I worked at KLJ—and I'd get them back as soon as I could. I went to make a cup of coffee. I came back to two separate Venmo notifications of $400 payments sent.

I did what I've found so difficult to do since doctors increased my Lexapro dosage: cry.

My initial emotions reeked of victimhood, as Little Eddie's responses are always outsized and attention-seeking. *Why me? The three of us started in the same place; they seemed so put together that they could honor this request at a whim, moving no money around or no deliberation. I've never been in that position outside of a handful of weeks. Where did I go wrong?*

But the warmth and understanding that these two chosen brothers displayed towards me silenced that little shit. I realized that while it sucked to be in the position I was in, they still had my back. All of those intrusive thoughts about everybody looking at me with a blend of pity or disgust were just that — bullshit intrusions that distracted me from the reality that I'm worthy of being loved by some pretty awesome people.

I told myself this was an investment in me by the people who know me the best. It was a vote of confidence from people I always aspired to be. I wish I believed what I was saying.

A few mornings later, Jay asked about gaining access to all of our financial accounts. I immediately tensed up. I was doing well; I maintained balance. We weren't fighting. I wasn't hung up on perceived slights from months earlier. I had the belief of my brothers.

And I failed.

I went from zero to 9 on the anger scale in no time flat. I started screaming about the Mayonnaise noises. I told her it was a disgrace that she kept me from Seaview and the golf outing. I reiterated my belief that MAGA was escaping the culpability their ignorance brought upon the most vulnerable. Every trauma of the last three years crafted a grievance narrative, and I placed the blame for every previous infraction at her feet.

Using facts, albeit somewhat hostilely, she highlighted that I had been unemployed for a year and a half, that I fixated on matters beyond my control, and that my daily yelling about it often made her the target. I turned purple before I used my tools. I extracted, grabbed the car keys, and took off, going on a ten-minute drive around the neighborhood. Passing the mishmash of cabins and ranch houses with Pinecliff Lake glimmering behind them, I turned on Spa Radio and started boxed breathing for the first time since I worked in person.

After circling a second time, I made the right down my block and went home. I walked through the door and heard Mom on speaker saying, in her angry Irish voice, "He needs to hit rock bottom!" Jay concurred.

Big Bear replaced the calm and rational version of myself that used tools and extricated in a flash.

"Hang up the phone!" I screamed. Then, I went into a haze. The next thing I knew, I was sitting on a stool—a bud and a shot of fireball deep - at the only bar in the area open at 10:45 in the morning—Murphy's Tavern, a townie bar known for its wings and 10:30 AM first call.

I opened the Notes app on my iPhone and began drafting a message for my family. Enough was enough. And it ended up being a doozy:

"This morning, I overheard my wife and my mother screaming about how I need to hit rock bottom. While this infuriated me, I also had to find the irony. I'm almost 300 lbs. I'm losing my teeth. I haven't been able to find a job in a year and a half. Blew the fruits of our hard work. I only eat, drink, and smoke things that are proven to take years away, not extend them. Probably diabetic. Can't bring laundry upstairs without losing breath.

If it can get lower than this, I'm legitimately curious what that looks like. The only Savior who did anything for me wrote, "When you ain't got nothing, you got nothing to lose."

Got no job, got no money, got no tooth, got no dignity, no living room door, nobody who understands the obvious: this is who I am and who I've always been. Fuck, even my dog tried to run away from me the other night.

The temper that was so cute because I was a "younger Billy Reilly" wasn't cute. It ate me alive, and it wasn't Grandpa; it was you know fucking who.

Before I go any further, I'm not some clueless, down-on-his-luck "drop-dead drunk" who's unaware of patterns and stages. I'm not crying out for help; ships have sailed, and toothpaste is out of the tube.

For as long as I can remember, any issues I've ever caused or have been at the epicenter of have been met with either a cold shoulder, an attempt to excuse away my actions, or the nastiest attitudes and deep-cutting words.

I have tried every outlet possible to be heard about "why I am the way I am". I've confessed with tears in my eyes, I screamed it in the most disgusting ways. I published a memoir essay that was viewed by at least 25,000 people on every continent but Antarctica.

Every step of progress has been met by "Why aren't you well yet?" This is a legitimate question but one completely antithetical to recovery.

I was on a roll. I was sidebar chatting with Jay, telling her I completely surrendered and that she should proceed without me in every venture. I told her I wouldn't be coming home this afternoon for anything other than my laptop and CPAP.

I told her I'd find a homeless shelter with an internet connection and an electrical outlet.

By now, it was past noon, which meant the Irish Whisper Public House, just across the street—I didn't even have to move my car—was now open. I settled my tab at Murphy's, threw my phone in my pocket, and strolled across the block to the Whisper—a more cozy environment for where my head was.

"The Whisper," as it's known, is a throwback to the dive bars of my youth that any 80s kid remembers from their dads taking them in for a quick pop during parenting duties on a Saturday afternoon. Aged wood-paneled walls surround a weathered oak bar. Dusty plaques and pennants adorn the beat-up walls. The air carries a scent of decades of shots, pints, cocktails, and bottles.

Once I settled in, I got right back to The Eldest Child's Manifesto:

"While I have learned to accept that you can't control what other people say or think about you, a combined eight decades of institutional knowledge of both of my families leads me to one of two conclusions: I was the sole individual engaging in eviscerating talk behind someone's back, or I've got a medieval arsenal of swords in my back.

So I am begging every one of you. If you love me, let me go. I am a net negative in your life, as has been made clear to me on multiple occasions.

I cause apprehension around my nieces and nephews when I'm even allowed around them, and I understand why I'm not. You may think I haven't picked up on all the times we've been nudged to leave, but I'm not oblivious.

But that's not who I ever intended to be.

The irony is that last week, I started schooling for the first time since Monica Lewinsky banged her head on the bottom of the Resolute Desk. I made the mistake of thinking I had it in me to rebound from this.

It became increasingly clear that I didn't.

I'm not sure where I'm going from here. Writing a farewell to a family letter from a Chili's bar at 11:30 on a Thursday isn't something I had on my Bingo card.

I have a lot to sort out logistically, especially for Jay. But once the big-ticket stuff is done, I'll send you guys access to my "Ed" folder on OneDrive.

There, you'll find a folder called "Back Nine," which is a project I was working on about how two dozen rounds of golf between 2013 and 2016 fortified and redefined my relationship with Dad. That's about 20,000 words.

The other is "Nervous Exhaustion," about 50k words on my life with the church and its tentacles. I've been working on that since I heard Obama mention "non-believers" in his first inaugural address in 2009.

And while it's macabre, you'll find some eulogy drafts.

From the bottom of my heart, I love every one of you with my fullest capacity to love. Unfortunately, as pointed out multiple times, that's not much of a capacity. But it's to capacity.

Since I have nothing of value to leave anyone, I will drop this wish here; feel free to ignore it.

One of the most principled actions ever carried out in American history, a lesson way too many "liberals" have forgotten, was what General George Marshall, upon the discovery of the death camps throughout central Europe at the end of the war, ordered every German citizen in the area to dig graves for the victims of right-wing fanaticism. Because "there's no plausible way they didn't realize what they let happen."

Along the same line, I would like a Rite of Christian Burial at St. Francis of Assisi, Ridgefield Park. Preferably officiated by the same criminal that married us.

Because there's no plausible way he - or the rest of St. Francis - didn't know what was happening. Shit, 4 days after I came forward Officer Bello called me to tell me some old parishioner saw a boy WHO MATCHED MY DESCRIPTION being abused in the sacristy.

Above all else, I am sincerely sorry that my toxicity has spilled into your lives. The only people who have never been burned by loving me are tavern owners."

I immediately sent it to Erin with a message that I was having a drink, hitting the pen, and then sending it to the family. I was fed up with the paranoia, the innuendo, and the assumption that everyone was disgusted with me when they had heard nothing from my mouth. She replied with three words that paused me from pulling the pin on a massive grenade:

"Ed please don't,"

Even after seven or eight drinks by 12:30 PM, I was powerless to ignore Erin's plea. It wasn't condescending, jovial, or condescending. She didn't make me feel bad or downplay my situation's severity. She listened.

A call from Aunt Breda interrupted my drinking and debating. She never called just to see how I was doing; this had to be necessary. I answered.

"Eddie, listen, I'm here with your mother. She thinks you're mad at her for speaking with Jaime this morning, and she—"

Little Eddie cut her off right there. *"Are you serious? She's worried about whether I'm mad at her. I'm amid a breakdown and have no idea where I'm even sleeping tonight. My marriage is over, my life is basically over, and she's concerned about me still stewing over her speaking to my wife. She needs to get a fucking grip."*

I hung up the phone and then immediately texted Aunt Breda. And I included "The Note".

"So sorry for the abrupt end. Here's how I'm feeling."

As expected, she called me right back.

"Listen, Eddie, I will go through the fires of hell to find Gerry Sudol and confront him if that's what it will take. I know you're hurting. I know it weighs on you. Whatever you think will help, I will do it."

I had already grabbed my drink and moved to the empty outdoor patio because this conversation was heading in directions not suitable for public consumption (Public being the bartender and two other people whose lives brought them to a dive bar drinking at noon on a Tuesday). I could feel tears, buoyed by whiskey and beer, fighting through the Lexapro.

"Aunt Breda, I'm in so much pain," I whaled as the tears flowed.

•••

I never sent "The Note" to the family. I sent it only to Erin, Aunt Breda, and Jay-who sent it to Dr. Grant. She called it "a goodbye" and wanted to explore my words, but we went nowhere with it. My time with her felt as if it was drawing to a close.

I spent the next few hours steadily getting even more drunk and engaging in any text or social message that showed up on my phone. As dinner time approached, I reached out to Jay to say I was coming home but not driving home. She actually offered to pick me up.

I actually had the gall to accept.

•••

The shadow of what I had disdainfully labeled as Groundhog Day cast a gloom over the approaching summer of 2023, mirroring the disastrous events of the previous year, albeit with significantly less financial cushion. Uncle John's third annual memorial loomed ahead, and I remained entangled in the unresolved issues stemming from The Banning of the previous summer.

Each day, I oscillated between aggressive confrontations with Jay, emphasizing *"the stunt she pulled"* the prior July, and moments of calm rationality where I busied myself designing balls for the upcoming event and politely asking Jay if she had time to get to a driving range to shake off the rust.

There was no apparent contradiction—both facets were merely different expressions of myself. I felt justified in my bouts of rage, attributing them to my response to trauma, while during my rational phases, I saw myself as the person I had always believed I was. A subconscious mechanism allowed me to disassociate adverse behaviors as "not me," shielding me from the consequences. For the longest time, I suspected Lexapro might cause my lucidity to be temporary at best—frequently shielding me from internal repercussions and dismissing external ones the rest of the time.

We spent the month entangled in disputes over my alleged ability to turn any event into a disaster, and, true to form, I lived up to my reputation at the memorial golf outing. I gravitated towards the younger kids, friends of John's son, and evaded my in-laws, opting to spend time with John's friends from Ridgefield Park in the 70s and 80s. Jay, wary of my potential for embarrassment, stayed in the hotel room for the night.

Predictably, we found ourselves in another heated argument on the journey home. As we arrived, the looming specter of financial ruin, fueled by my prolonged unemployment and distorted trauma responses, became increasingly difficult to evade.

An email from the Commander-By-the-Sea Motel in Wildwood served as a stark reminder of impending financial challenges. Failure to immediately settle the 50% deposit would jeopardize our reservation for the annual trip with The Hayeses and Jaymanda. The impending 100% due in two weeks only added to my mounting concerns.

Simultaneously, an email from the New York Football Giants demanded the final deposit for the 2023 season tickets. Panic set in as I grappled with the pressing question of where I would procure the funds.

Choosing to evade the issue, I immersed myself in a weekend of drinking. Eventually, I had to come clean with Jay—I wouldn't be joining the vacation, and I had mishandled the hotel reservation. I urged her to go ahead without me, emphasizing the need for me to stay home and intensify my job search. The expenses associated with my vacation habits were unjustifiable.

I disclosed my decision only after Jay had embarked on the Jersey Turnpike. I effectively ghosted an entire vacation, disregarding what was supposed to be a week of rejuvenation and celebration of sustaining friendships. In my eyes, I wasn't worthy, and I felt undeserving of such an experience.

You? Taking a vacation? A vacation from what, you stupid drunk? Day drinking and ordering pizza? For everyone else, that's a vacation; for you, that's called a Wednesday. These people work for a living; they deserve it. You tried this last year and stayed trapped in your head. Remember? Jay left the same week you got back.

Something had to change. Dramatically. And immediately.

XLIII

"You're not getting the help you need," Jay screamed at me one beautiful September morning. I was staring out the window at the first hints of hardened leaves—not entirely turned but dead nonetheless—that fell from the maples that separate our home from Gary's next door, inside the abode, Groundhog Day continued with Jay repeating that sentence that had all but become a mantra at this point.

But for once, I agreed. I had just completed my yearly physical, and I maintained the status quo—neither improving nor worsening, just riding the medicated plateau. In the casual chat with my doctor about the non-physical aspects of life, I zeroed in on the persistent focus struggles. In a blink, I left with a prescription for Strattera, a Ritalin alternative tailored to accommodate my pre-existing hypertension management.

For that keeping score at home, I brought my list of medications at 46 to Metoprolol, Benicar HTC, Xanax, Crestor, Cialis, Lexapro, and Strattera.

The side effect of Straterra was an increase in rage. I wasn't drinking any more or less than before. I was a tad more productive because of the rise in focus, but my rage was quicker to come, longer to stay, and louder to listen to. And I was becoming increasingly more animated — hands flailing, ceiling beams pounded, heart rate rapidly rising.

Compounding this, no firm appointment with Dr. Grant was on the horizon. Her vacation coincided with our next regularly scheduled session, and the subsequent week, as I tried to log onto the video conferencing platform, there was nothing to click on. While I could have immediately reached out, casually expressing my belief that we were meeting that day and assuring her it wasn't an issue—I'd happily adapt to her earliest convenience—I hesitated. This scenario had unfolded many times over the past four years, prompting me to adjust our plans several times.

This time, though, I chose not to.

I thought back to one of our earliest discussions during our very first session. She had asked about my history with talk therapy, and I informed her she was my third therapist. After telling her I never really felt like either put me on a path to behaving better, she replied, "most times, I fault the therapist for that, not the patient."

As cringeworthy as it is, I asked the same question that made a man like Ronald Reagan president once upon a time: Are you better off now than you were four years ago? No aspect of my life has been better since I began cognitive-behavioral therapy.

- I was beyond questioning my decision to come forward; I had advanced to outright regretting it.
- My marriage had endured one separation, and things actually got worse afterward.

- I was unemployed and had no idea how to find a suitable job I believed I could handle.
- My family looked at me with pity and concern.
- I couldn't face my friends, having to cancel the RFFL Draft, once the pinnacle of my calendar year, and leaving every offer to meet for a drink open-ended, hoping there would be no follow-through—there rarely was.
- My house was physically and metaphorically crumbling to shit.

The laundry list of traumas in that same period was just as lengthy. It was a three-year period marred by illness, loss, and death. However, I was under the care of the same therapist for these traumas.

I confided to Jay that I agreed; I needed an alternative path of help. She began rattling off a litany of them, from the non-starters (inpatient therapy) to the ineffective (rebooting with Dr. Grant). But somewhere in between was a word that caught my attention: ketamine.

The surge in popularity of Spravato, a nasal spray containing ketamine, as a treatment for depression and PTSD, was a paradigm shift in mental health care over the last half-decade. This novel approach billed itself as hope for individuals resistant to traditional antidepressants. I knew it as "Special K"—a horse tranquilizer I once took in college after playing ten straight beer pong games that knocked me out and made me piss myself.

The last I had heard about it being used therapeutically—probably right before the pandemic—was an expensive out-of-pocket treatment offered in some sporadic states. In reality, there was a clinic eighteen miles away that administered the drug and accepted my medical insurance.

Intrigued, but more importantly, motivated, I propelled forward. I don't know if a hallucinogenic therapy or the relative ease inspired me at which I could get started—probably a combination of the two. All that was needed was a psychiatrist's recommendation, and I was on my way. Conveniently, they provided the psychiatrist—which is like giving someone with anxiety a $500 winning scratch off. They would do the hard part? Jackpot.

Of course, they would do the hard part; they only cared about getting me on their books. However, my primary care physician had put in a request for a psychiatrist to contact me two weeks ago during my annual. I hadn't heard back, and this ketamine organization will take the baton.

I was committed.

•••

The only real guidance they gave me before my first Spravato treatment was that I could not drive home. I understood why, but I had my suspicions that after a treatment or two, I'd know how my body responds, and I'll be able to bullshit the staff and drive myself home.

I toyed with the idea of fucking around and finding out, but I took an Uber instead. Jay agreed to pick me up.

Walking into the Keta Center was a mind-fuck.

I couldn't shake the feeling of its fading glory, a relic of in-person working times, when occupied offices of miserable workers filled every floor. The lingering remnants of the remote work revolution were clear, with vacancy signs hanging in windows and messy wires in the hallway. *Were they cooking ketamine here?*

As I entered, they greeted me with an offer of snacks before anything else. *Okay, these people know their tripping priorities.* After exchanging the most basic information, I obliged, and they ushered me into a room.

The room was clinical to a fault. Devoid of any warmth or natural light. It resembled a setting from a medical drama, complete with a fully reclining electric chair, a lifeless fake potted fern, and a generic painting attempting to inject a semblance of aesthetic appeal. The stucco ceilings loomed overhead, while a small desk for the physician's assistant served as the nerve center of this medical theater.

The assistant took my vitals and provided a clinical prelude to the procedure. She showed me an inhaler, not unlike a sinus pump such as Flonase, and how I was supposed to cover one nostril while I inhaled through the other like I was banging a rail of cocaine.

She handed me a tester spray, one with saline mist. I passed the test, took the ketamine pump, and was off to the races.

The assistant left, promising to return to check my vitals about thirty minutes later. There was no guided therapy or meditation—just six total pumps of Special K, an eye mask, a recliner, and my earbuds.

I immediately felt my senses heighten. The bass in my AirPods reverberated at a pace that I married to my pulse. The berrylicious notes from the complimentary *Gushers* I snacked on while awaiting instructions returned. Both of my nostrils were wide open. The initial burst of euphoria encompassed me from head to toe.

And then my mind opened up completely. I looked at myself from an elevated plane as if I were an outside observer. I wandered through my head as if it were an attic and saw the tools I needed to supply my life with confidence, integrity, and love. I saw my traumas as empty, turned-over boxes: job loss, my parent's health, John's passing, The Pandemic, and the impact of all of this on my marriage. And the most oversized box of all: Sudol.

I needed the tools on that attic floor: extraction, meditation, structure, and radical acceptance. But what cluttered the entire floor were the contents of those boxes. The excess baggage of trauma was stopping me from using my tools to live with a purpose.

After two hours, driving home was impossible, damnit. Looks like I'll be booking more Uber than I like.

•••

Two days later, back in the same chair for the second treatment, the larger dose by 33% intensified the effects significantly.

The drug has a way of precisely identifying what you need to work on. Even if I entered intending to listen to the Marine Corps Marching Band and watching World War II movies, I'd likely return to St. Francis. And that happened when I was thinking about ways to be a more present uncle during the second session. I thought about those beautiful nieces and nephews, and suddenly, I was having visions of myself at those same ages.

I saw potential, swagger, kindness, and compassion—the kid who loved everybody. That pre-braces buck front tooth, currently on my nightstand, not in my mouth, reminded me he's still alive somewhere.

Realizing I came into this world as that carefree spirit, some of Dr. Grant's earliest words echoed: the best way to believe we can do something is to know that we've done it before.

I spent the weekend following the second session telling anyone who would listen how great Ketamine was, how much more apparent it was making things, and how I believed it was the missing piece. I also spent the weekend displaying rage and getting shorter around the house. The internal belief needed to be aligned with external actions.

•••

In 1992, Reebok concocted a track and field rivalry between two completely unknown athletes: Dan O'Brien and Dave Johnson. The Summer Olympics would take place in Barcelona that summer, and their goal was to make these two athletes the stars of the show (which also included the men's basketball "Dream Team"). "Dan vs Dave" blared across our television screens, magazine advertisements, billboards, etc. I'm pretty sure there were T-shirts. The hype was working, and people were paying attention, making it more embarrassing when Dan failed to qualify for the trip to Spain.

That was my third session.

My expectations were high for a continued expansion of my consciousness. I was on the path to recovery, and I believed it, thanks to this onetime designer drug. Instead, I ended up having the proverbial bad trip. It wasn't a scary experience like you may have heard about or lived through yourself. I wasn't cowering, scared, or hoping for the effects to wear off. But my mind guided me down a perilous staircase.

I saw an exaggerated state of myself. A glutton who can't stop eating. A drunk who can't stop drinking. A writer who can't start writing. A husband who can't hold up his end of the bargain. A son so damaged that he had to tell his mother he wouldn't be in contact for six weeks due to therapy. A friend who doesn't show up for vacation. A Giants fan that can't afford his season tickets.

A Fraud.

There was a darkness that followed me between the third and fourth sessions. Jay picked up on it as well and fortified her defenses. I went out that Saturday around noon and got completely blitzed watching college football. I drove home like an idiot, stopping to get a twelve-pack of Budweiser—the beer I drink when I'm not feeling great about myself. I purchased a bag of ice, intending to keep the beer in a cooler in the garage — avoiding passive-aggressive snickers from Jay every time I opened the fridge door.

It didn't matter. She remained stoic and steadfast in tuning me out, finally content enough to let me do my worst to myself because she was all out of ideas.

⋯

During the Uber ride to the fourth session, I pondered the sheer absurdity of the old D.A.R.E. program and the broader concept of "The War on Drugs." Like the ineffective "Stranger Danger" campaign, these initiatives often produced results opposite their intended goals. Did the decision-makers in the mid-1980s genuinely believe that educating kids, who inherently think they're invincible, about the details of drugs, their costs, and where to buy them would effectively "Keep kids off drugs"?

Consider the countless therapies like ketamine, which could be transformative or even life-saving, facing delays or never coming to fruition because of the global stigma associated with recreational drug use. All the while, these very stakeholders were laying the groundwork for the opioid crisis, surpassing any drug abuse epidemic seen during the "Just Say No" era.

Much like The War on Drugs, the war on my demons needed to be rethought entirely, and that was what I got out of the fourth session. There were enough platitudes to fill a mall kiosk with motivational kitchen signs: Figure out who you want to be. One day at a time. Forgiveness is for you, not for them. Live intentionally. Be true to yourself.

All sound great in theory, but they could have been more effectively implemented. I needed to take a leaf blower up to the attic and blow out all the obstructions and impediments to progress. What needed to stay could be re-boxed and properly stored once processed. I had to say goodbye to everything else.

Somewhere in the space between my decision to come forward in 2018 and the tumultuous events of 2020, my identity underwent a profound transformation. I unwittingly morphed into a mere avatar, embodying everything I despised about myself and the world around me. I filtered every action I took through this veneer of self-disdain. Trauma responses tainted even my attempts to do what was right, replacing my usual instincts with the distorted lens of past wounds.

At long last, a perspective finally emerged that comprehends the impact of Sudol's abuse on my life without permitting it to serve as an excuse or casting me solely as a victim. While the concept might seem straightforward in theory, the reality of implementing it was intricately challenging. I grappled with the realization that whenever I encountered situations that triggered feelings of threat, insecurity, or challenged safety, my reactions were rooted in the deep well of that initial trauma. Confronting such moments meant facing them with the limited tools of a twelve-year-old altar boy.

I had long embraced the fact that my childhood experiences shaped my response to trauma. It manifested early on and grew more apparent as my understanding of Complex PTSD deepened. However, the 'why' remained elusive, and without grasping it, acceptance seemed an elusive path.

The immediate subsequent realization acknowledged that my fits and false starts weren't mere shortcomings, as embarrassing as they might be, but integral components of the healing journey. Changing the fact that I frequently succumbed to my demons was beyond my control; all I could do was acknowledge it. Until I confronted and forgave myself, breaking free from the cycle of unraveling without understanding would remain an unattainable goal. These destructive behaviors will persist.

Still had no idea how to forgive myself, but at least I saw a path.

•••

Session five seamlessly continued the trajectory set by the previous appointment, diving into the intricate path to forgiveness. Mastering self-forgiveness was the linchpin for unlocking boundless possibilities — extending compassion to my parents, my community, the adversaries concocted in my mind, the Church, and perhaps even the MAGA contingent (though, even in the K-induced haze, I recognized specific delusions were of the grandeur variety). Yet, what did forgiveness indeed entail?

True forgiveness demanded acknowledging that the acts occurred, a process intricately linked with Radical Acceptance. This meant confronting the harsh reality that I was a victim of abuse, absolving myself of blame, acknowledging the subsequent adverse behaviors that tinted thirty-five years of existence, and acknowledging the stark reality of the abuse.

Crucially, it involved recognizing that armed with this newfound knowledge, yesterday's news — the false starts, the Groundhog Day-like cycles — were agonizing but had to become relics of the past.

•••

I had no idea that session six would be my final ketamine treatment.

It started as clinical as the others. I was becoming adept at taking large handfuls of Gushers as my frame blocked the reception table (calling it a desk would be generous) and stuffing my hoodie's pouch with them. There was no limitation on how many you could take, but a Hanratty is at his best when he thinks he's pulling something over on someone.

After the third infusion and liftoff, I zeroed in on the age-old problem that has haunted me for as far back as memory allows: who do I aspire to be?

To my surprise, I knew the answer all along. "The easiest way to do something is to realize you've done it before." The essence of who I yearn to become has been an intrinsic part of me—even when latent, overshadowed only when I succumbed to the darkness.

My aspiration is clear — to embody a man of unwavering integrity capable of standing independently, a respected writer with a resonant voice committed to safeguarding and shedding light on society's most vulnerable. I yearn to be the person who stands by loved ones in times of need, viewing indulgence not as a lifestyle but as a recreational respite. My quest is to rediscover and mold that version of myself envisioned when I first ventured from Ridgefield Park to college.

And I knew I could do this because I had done it all before.

The believed-resounding success of this treatment made what followed even more confusing and disturbing. Jay picked me up, as she had for the previous five. She had done her research to keep me comfortable—kept the car cool, had Grateful Dead radio on at a noticeable but lower volume, and shied away from asking pressing questions.

I volunteered I spoke with an intake nurse at a group therapy center for patients with PTSD. Although my actual quote coming down off of K was probably something like "Called PTSD group nurse intake conversation PTSD."

She asked if they accepted our insurance, and I told her they would file against our deductible on our behalf.

"Ok. I'm just wondering how we're going to afford it," she answered calmly.

The tranquility of her statement didn't matter. I began to disassociate and lose control of my entire body. It was as if I was a spirit that left my body, looking down on my reaction, and it wasn't pretty.

I began screaming incoherently—not understanding what I was saying or what the content was even related to. My arms started flailing, restrained only by the seatbelt. My flying hand ended up making contact with the side of her head. She went into a state of shock.

"We're going to the cops, or we're going to a hospital, but you are not coming home."

I'm regaining consciousness, and my mind is returning to my corporal being, but I'm still elevated way beyond comfort. *"I'm not going to no pigs, and I'm not going to no laugh factory! You don't want me home. Take me to the fucking Whisper,"* I yelled.

"I'm not bringing you to a bar!" she yelled back as the car's Bluetooth turned on. I heard a dial tone, and the LED flashed, "Calling Erin Hanratty."

Of course she is! This is what she always does: get everyone else involved in your business and try to turn your family against you the way her family has already turned against you. The demons persist because she insists on making them persist.

"Erin, he can't come home! He's screaming, and he just hit my face."

"*I did no such thing, kiddo,*" I yell back.

"Ed, do you want to come stay here?" Erin calmly asked.

"Nope, if I'm not going to my house, I'm going to the Irish Whisper."

"Do you really think going to a bar is a good idea?"

"*Absolutely not, but I'm not going to no loony bin and just wait and see what happens if the fucking cops get involved.*"

With that, I hit the end call button, and as fate would have it, we were rounding the corner toward the Ringwood Police Department. Jay hooked a quick right into the vast municipal lot and threw the car into park. She stared out from the dashboard into the abyss, contemplating whether to go inside and report me as unsafe. She weighed the consequences, turned the car off, and gently left the vehicle, heading towards the police barracks.

XLIV

Jay never went into the police department. She called both the ketamine center and my psychiatrist as she paced the parking lot. Both of them said I needed to feel safe to come down and that a hospital was the best opportunity. But she knew there wasn't a chance in hell that I would accept voluntarily going to a hospital. If she held firm to her belief that I could not go home, there were only two viable options: cops or Whisper.

The Irish Whisper had few people in it on that cool, late October evening that I meandered in, still coming down off the effects of a ketamine trip and the explosive outbursts of the last ninety minutes. I immediately called Erin to let her know I was okay.

"I don't think it was the best decision to go to a bar," she said with a chuckle, "but at least you're somewhere you feel safe."

She was right, unfortunately. The Whisper had inadvertently become a refuge for me during times of stress at home, an escape that I, unfortunately, found too easy to choose. Its ambiance is reminiscent of my dad's and grandfather's basements.

However, it was never as comfortable for me as that night. Erin was correct; I was secure. So safe, so secure, that I stayed for four hours. I befriended a lovely young man who had a fancy THC-heated pen. I told him I was coming from a ketamine treatment, and it was the greatest thing in the world, a miracle. It was healing my PTSD and easing my depression.

"PTSD? I'm sorry to hear that. Where did you serve?"

"St Francis of Assisi Altar Boys, Class of '91," I smirked. He got the joke immediately as a look of mortification set over his face.

•••

My jaw locked up as the Lyft dropped me off at home.

Getting ready to walk through an un-weeded walkway, passing a lawn untouched since Labor Day, using the back door because of a jammed front lock I ignored, I proceeded past my wife, currently untrustworthy in my altered mind. And I managed it. But as I settled in around 11:00, knowing that something had to radically change because, you know, that's the fucking point of ketamine therapy—I knew there was only one contact in my phone, one guaranteed answer out of all of those names collected over the years.

"Dad—Cell,"

I dialed it. There was no answer. I exhaled.

But then my phone lit up.

"Dad—Cell"

I had no icebreakers. There's nothing to talk about the Yanks or Giants or Rangers. He called me back right before midnight on a Tuesday. We both knew what this conversation was going to be. He was more prepared for it than I ever could be.

"Hey, Dad, I didn't mean to wake you; I'll talk to you tomorrow."

"Nah, Ed, you didn't wake me. What's up?"

I didn't think twice. I welled up like he did in that god-awful brown Uncle Bob robe back in the day.

"Dad, I want to let you know how proud I am of tackling your demons because I'm having a hell of a time tackling mine."

It was almost insulting how quickly he turned into My Father. I know it was his AA training to save me at any minute, and he did—even if it wasn't in the almost twelve-step way he may have hoped.

I bawled my eyes out, Lexapro be damned, asking him when he learned his demons were controlling him, and he bluntly and without hesitation or even stutter, said: "till it was too late."

I told him about the ketamine treatment—and how it opened pathways. Without missing a beat, he says "like LSD then"—not as a question but as a confirmation that he knows what I'm speaking about. And while ketamine and LSD are Obama/Cheney cousins at best, I got that he was trying to understand me and put things into a perspective he could grasp.

See, Dad would tell me (and eventually Jay, Brian, John, Ben, and maybe a random drinking buddy I took home back in the Teaneck Road days) this story about how he and his buddy dropped acid one night in 1970 and he ran into a girl on the subway platform that rattled him. He would always add to the tale that it was "during 'Nam'." He never spent a day in boot camp, but as I started putting things into "before the pandemic" terms, I realized it wasn't a sense of self-aggrandizement. It was a point of personal reference during a memorable social trauma.

His broken-record story went on to how he didn't recognize this girl in the subway who knew him by name. In the romanticized version, he was some twenty-year-old stud who danced with the devil, lived to tell the tale, and passed on sage knowledge. But I was a twenty-year-old Hanratty once, too. I know that shame.

And that generational perception divide was a little starker when I asked him the question I've wanted to most of my adult life — "Did your dad drink like, you know, me and you?"

"Ahhhhh, yes and no,"—the typical Big Ed answer to a yes or no question. He said, "You have to understand. It was a different time back then. There were clubs, and when you went to those clubs, people expected it to be that way."

I'm sobering up by the second as his lack of irony splashes me in the face.

"Like Dad had a club, it was more of a cop bar up in High Bridge. Sometimes Aunt Butch would watch us. Sometimes, he'd take Mom. But they had their thing on Sundays, which was just expected."

I spoke up and said, "Well, Dad, you had the Knights; I had every outlet I could find, too."

And in true Big Ed fashion, he wasn't condescending but dropped the "Yeah, but when you were a cop in those years, and after the war…"

That was a flashpoint where I realized I was getting back to myself. The demons clearly would have preferred I manipulated the conversation towards the brute force that the NYPD responded to Johnson's Great Society with Bronx cops in particular…but they didn't. I listened to him talk about his life and how drinking was just always a part of it till it wasn't, till I realized he was a hurt boy who never had a chance. He wasn't expected to survive childbirth and was constantly reminded of that fact.

While nice and lubricated, I figured I'd ask that one question that never made sense: How was Grandpa Eddie in both the Battle of the Bulge AND Okinawa? It's something that had been chewing at my history mainframe for decades. And the answer was deflating.

It turns out Staff Sergeant Hanratty reenlisted after D-Day. Not Pearl Harbor. He laced up his boots after Hitler's days were numbered. There was domestic pressure for non-disabled men at home to relieve the boys who gave us democracy for three generations. He got to Belgium, the Little Fascist swallowed his Lugar in a bunker, and Grandpa was put on a ship to the Pacific. Somewhere between then and August of 45, the US dropped two nuclear bombs. He got to come home and make progenies, and that's a small part of why you're reading this.

I never got the chance to meet my grandfather. I bear his name, and I hold his pain and his failures as my father did. But that late Thursday night conversation was the closest I ever came to knowing the man as anything more than a mythical patriarch.

It was also the closest I had felt to my father since Gerry Sudol came into my life.

Dad was always the white whale on this voyage. He possessed a lifetime of experience with depression and addiction. Jay and I played a vital, pivotal role in his recovery and his new lease on life. And he was there for the entire Sudol saga. But I would never even consider using him as a resource in that way. For most of my life, that idea sounded laughable.

Ketamine had somehow made me realize how important of a linchpin he was, however. For all the talk about my mother—all the mothers of Ridgefield Park—I held resentment towards the old man for parts of five decades.

He was just as keen to have Gerry over the house as my mom was. He was the one who gave Gerry his company's Yankee tickets and money for Sizzler to bring me and a few altar boys. He was the one who went into a grief spiral after his twin died and insisted on buying a new set of cassocks for altar boys to last a generation. He fostered the environment just as much as any mother could have.

All these years, I felt the distance between us—the lack of handshakes, the struggle to meet eyes—was because I disappointed him by not reaching some perceived potential, never considering it was because he disappointed me.

Now, at seventy-three years old and on the precipice of hospice care, it was not the time to let him know that. Just putting the pieces together was an overwhelming sense of healing.

His listening was his acknowledgment, his lack of judgment was his apology, and his fighting every cell in his body and pill in his system to remain lucid and engage in the conversation was his love.

Despite her health maladies, my mother remained sharp as a tack. We've had countless conversations about Sudol, the Church, the 80s and 90s, and little more needs to be said. Anything related to St. Francis that I had with my mother was long settled.

But I never thought I needed closure with—or the need to forgive Dad until it happened.

...

I woke up to one of the most paradoxical days of my journey. The sun streamed through the crease of my blackout curtains, and I confronted my early morning anxiety. Ketamine, my newfound companion in self-discovery, had been offering profound insights into the tangled recesses of my mind. It was like peeling back layers of long-buried memories, unraveling the complex web of emotions that had defined my existence.

But then there are the violent and frightening side effects. That's not who I want to be by any stretch. It's not who I ever was. I still remember the incident from a third person/witness point of view rather than the first person/participant I was. The overwhelming sense of rage that had consumed me was something I never wanted to feel again.

Amidst the internal struggle, my psychiatrist reached out, sensing the turmoil through the invisible threads of our connection. In a candid conversation, I laid bare my fears, exposing the raw vulnerability that Ketamine had both unearthed and exacerbated. She was very sympathetic and recommended halting the treatment until discussing further with the ketamine center.

Within an hour of that conversation, "KETA CENTER" appeared as an incoming call on my iPhone. In a decisive moment, I refused to answer the center's call. The looming specter of peril overshadowed the potential advantages I saw in Ketamine's therapeutic effects. The crossroads had arrived, and I couldn't risk revisiting the darkness manifesting that strongly.

For all the tangible progress, I couldn't risk putting Jay in the position to bring me to a police station again.

But I had to maintain the progress somehow. I had to accept that ketamine provided me with radical insights and guidance, but significant problems require big solutions, and sometimes, they carry enormous risks. I couldn't afford to have another incident like that again.

•••

Knowing I needed to do more and doing more are two different things. I would love to say that I got right back on the horse, and my recovery was a straight trajectory forward after that cathartic discussion with Dad. But that's not how it works.

The holidays of 2023 were the worst in our marriage. I spent Thanksgiving sitting at my desk pounding IPAs and Fireball shots. Jay spent Christmas on the couch while I got loaded for two days at Erin's apartment.

But as the year ended, I couldn't help but think about the first text I sent in it, almost three hundred sixty-five days to the date. "It's going to be my best year or my last one."

All bluster. Here you are, Ground Hog Day.

But it wasn't bluster. I was a mere hour away from passing into 2024, so it wasn't my last. However, if I kept following my true north and seeking answers and understanding, I would be miles ahead of where I was coming into '23—or any other year of my life for that part.

In the early days of the new year, I summoned the strength to pull myself together and muster just enough confidence to embark on a quest for a new therapist and a reliable psychiatrist. Through a series of evaluations and candid discussions, I laid bare the essence of my journey: the roots of the original trauma, its insidious manifestations throughout my life, the therapeutic odyssey I had undertaken, and the disturbing behaviors that became my unwelcome companions in the aftermath of my story's publication and the subsequent lockdown.

After scrutiny, my newfound care team (and yes, it felt oddly comforting to have one) reached a decisive diagnosis: Bipolar Depression stemming from Complex Post-Traumatic Stress Disorder. The revelation felt like the missing puzzle piece that had eluded me all along.

The profound impact of the trauma had led to my medical diagnosis now, in a way, recognizing *Angry Little Eddie*, a persona I reluctantly acknowledged over a year earlier. It was a revelation that explained the times when I spiraled into a different version of myself, akin to a binge-drinking middle-aged Teen Wolf. Negotiating with this alter ego required acknowledging the fundamental truth: this wasn't the real me; it wasn't how I intended to react.

The existing medication regimen, which began with the long-standing but insufficient Lexapro, was inadequate for this new diagnosis. The doctor prescribed Abilify and Lamictal to me. Once I worked them into my routine, the outbursts declined dramatically.

That son of a bitch in a collar may have permanently altered my brain chemistry, but I was finally giving my head the factory reset it so desperately deserved.

If I had known that a conversation with my old man would have inspired this aggressive path to better myself, I would have done so before I graduated high school.

XLV

Every episode of the 1980s "GI Joe" cartoon concluded with a Joe aiding a child or imparting lessons on safety, always culminating in the mantra "Knowing is Half the Battle." A similar sentiment echoed when I became aware of my bipolar depression. I couldn't permit my mind to once more fall prey to the illusion that mere awareness suffices.

Now armed with the understanding, I not only comprehended the why, but, more crucially, I embraced the belief that I (finally) possessed the clarity necessary for healing. However, the path forward remained uncertain. Nearly five cumulative years of therapy equipped me with an arsenal of tools to confront the issues fueling my rage. While ketamine worked wonders in purging the excess and revealing my toolkit, the challenge lay in figuring out where to begin.

But there's a line from a Grateful Dead tune—Scarlet Begonias, off the *Mars Hotel* album — that would play in the background in the early Pine Hall days while Ben and I would burn dirt weed out of a plastic bong:

Once in a while, you get shown the light

In the strangest of places, if you look at it right

As fate would have it, the strangest of places was an innocuous text conversation with that same former roommate towards the end of the holidays. He was asking about how my treatment was going; I clued him in on the ups and extreme downs of ketamine and how I'm floating through the swamp right now, knowing I need more but struggling to get on the track.

He shared with me a tool he found helpful in dealing with a personal, professional crisis of his own recently—writing letters to either yourself or the aggrieving party, if only to get it out of your head.

I replied I had been in therapy long enough that I'd heard all the tools, including letter-writing, many times and had terabytes of letters on my MacBook.

Why are you bullshitting him, you fraud? Sure, you've been told about letter writing dozens of times, but like almost every other tool, you've used it sporadically or not at all.

For once, Little Eddie was right. I was bullshitting one of my best friends. Dismissing his caring advice and lying about what I've attempted or accomplished during therapy. And the only way to do right by him—and to be authentic to me — was to get busy writing.

So, I got to work on three letters I needed to write to close this ugly, multi-decade chapter and get on a true healing path.

...

Dear Gerry,

I guess I can't call you Father Gerry anymore. Sorry, not sorry. Boy, did I make your golden years rough, or what? Believe me when I say it wasn't my intention, but I couldn't care less about any disruptions to the comfort you were enjoying, believing you got away with abusing so many of us in our youth while we suffered in silence. While I suffered in silence.

You had no right to my body, Gerry. There was never any time, in any culture, where it was okay to swap spit through open-mouth-tongue kissing with ten, eleven, and twelve-year-old boys. None. It was never OK to lay your massive hands on my shoulders, my ass, or my legs. It was never acceptable to thrust up against me on my parents' property.

You exploited their kindness and, worse, their faith.

For decades, I convinced myself that what you did to me was no big deal. Because of your chosen vocation's stellar reputation, the occasional grab-ass was dismissed as "oh, one of those quirky priests." But as bad as engaging in that type of horseplay with minors is, you went significantly further, and you know it.

I've read the depositions, big guy. What you did to me would get you locked up for twenty-five years if it happened today. What you did to some other boys would get you strapped to a gurney in some states.

Your actions prevented Willie Forster from ever seeing the 21st century. Your abuse robbed Phil of the Parish reckoning he deserved to witness. Your transfer to Saint Francis in the fateful year of 1986 brought me to the precipice of suicide on two separate occasions. Not adding to your body count was a motivating factor in stopping me.

In the long void between when I last saw you crossing the street and our movement getting you removed from the ministry, I often wondered if you had any sleepless nights wondering if someone would expose you. *Spotlight* had to scare the shit out of you, no? Or did you think when the Church wrote a check to Willie's survivors that you were in the clear?

Regardless of *your fears and emotions or any thoughts that might make you worried, anxious, or afraid*—I'm not writing this because I want to spike a football or rub anything in your face. I'm writing this to say I Forgive You.

The practical person in me firmly believes that you were likely abused similarly. I know this because your abuse turned me into someone who would display abusive behaviors when he would alter his brain chemistry because of trauma (thanks again for that). Hurt people hurt people. I never once considered stealing the innocence of children, but I believe someone nurtured you to become a child sex abuser. I don't think you intended to become one. I

How can I forgive something so many decent, God-fearing people find unforgivable? Not forgiving has been unbearable. Harboring has made life near impossible.

You abused me regularly. You altered my neurochemistry for good. And I forgive you.

May God have mercy on your soul,

Eddie Hanratty (SF, Class of '91)

•••

To the Parents, Teachers, and Staff of St Francis:

When I first came forward in 2018, I assured you I did not harbor any ill will. I was lying. I was lying to myself—I wanted to believe I did. But I was lying to you as well.

The more I learned, the more I couldn't help but ask, how could nobody have known what was happening right under their noses? Let's be frank for a minute here. Sudol was never shy about how much he loved kids. He was never shy about hugging kids—which isn't necessarily a harbinger of nefarious intention. But he was never shy about kissing them right out in the middle of Mt. Vernon Street.

He wasn't Father Guido Sarducci of SNL fame, fresh off the boat from Sicily, giving every man, woman, and child a peck on each cheek. He was only kissing the boys like that.

I understand your excitement about your children's desire to spend time at the church, but did you ever stop to realize how strange that was? In the age of Duck Hunt, Double Dare, and Transformers, we shouldn't have wanted to hang out at the church. There were after-school specials and "Very Special Episodes" about this.

I know some people knew right away. I don't fault them for not speaking up, though so many sent smoke signals that Doyle had to come "clean up". But those brave few weren't ready or capable of handling the inevitable blowback that would have followed.

Which is why it fell on everyone, and everyone failed.

But the failures were inevitable. Denied a fair chance from the start. What this odyssey taught me is that the Catholic Church wielded salvation like a perennially elusive carrot for centuries, and the healing of generational traumas isn't an overnight affair. You were merely sculpting us and navigating parish life the only way you knew — mirroring the approach your parents likely instilled in you.

You could not have done better because you didn't know how to do better, just as your parents didn't know how to do better when Father Ernst was terrorizing the town and parish a generation earlier. The failures that led to the abuse in the 80s did not differ from any of the preceding decades and centuries. You didn't have the tools to stand up and tell the church this couldn't happen anymore, not in the shadow of your parents.

That was a job for Generation X.

With all of my gratitude for your unyielding support,

Ed

XLVI

I used my therapy as a crutch, and that was a painful reality to digest as I began my ascent from the long and ugly spiral. It was early in January 2024—a year after I declared '23 my "best" or "last" year. In years past, I would view the fact that 2023 was not my best year—and may arguably have been my worst—as a failure. But not this time. I framed it as a gift. One year ago, I felt I only had two options: thrive or die.

I know better now.

The fresh therapeutic start allowed me to focus on the bigger picture, not the minute details of life between sessions that became the norm between Dr. Grant and me. At long last, I was prepared to tackle the elusive "Radical Acceptance," a concept that I could not accept in my care to this point.

With a clearer mind than before the 2018 revelations about Cardinal McCarrick, I was ready to assess everything I needed to radically accept.

The harshest reality to accept is that I was a bitter, broken, and confused man—nearly 47 years of age—who needed to relearn how to function all over again, this time knowing that I suffer from complex post-traumatic stress disorder. I have to treat and respect that the way I would any other damaged body part.

When I golf, my pregame routine involves grabbing my driver and using it for leverage as I stretch out my back, shoulders, knees, and hips. It's preventative care, so I don't cripple myself with a pulled hamstring or a thrown-out back over the next four hours. I needed to radically accept that similar exercises are required for my emotional being to do things I thought I used to do with ease.

It's up to me to avoid my triggers. If that means I can't trust myself to be somewhere or do something where I can't fully trust my capabilities, I have to either do the work or decline to take part.

The success of this required radical acceptance that, while "Trump Derangement Syndrome" was concocted on right-wing message boards, it is a genuine phenomenon, and I was not immune to it. I've precisely explained why I have such a guttural reaction to The Celebrity Apprentice; I can't speak to anyone else. However, I suspect so many of them have reasons similar to mine. I believe he was the worst officeholder in the history of the United States—a nation with officeholders like Jefferson Davis and Joe McCarthy—and I believe I let him live rent-free in my head for years; both things can be true.

You'll never convince me otherwise that this country would have taken it on the chin the way it did during the COVID-19 pandemic had Hillary Clinton won or had it been the second term of a Mitt Romney administration. Likewise, don't bother telling me that the jury that found him culpable of sexual assault got it wrong. But every second I spend railing about why I and others find him and his movement so off-putting is one where I'm avoiding the root causes of my anger.

I was angry long before he ever dreamed of hosting a game show.

Once I came to this conclusion, my time spent on Facebook plummeted, itself a tremendous mental health improvement.

I can no longer let macro events trigger a spiral in me because they are not intended to harm me. There is a line between empathy and obsession, and I spent most of my life heading straight for obsession, with a primal need to see the wronged or abused achieve justice at the expense of common sense and sanity.

And that cost me my empathy. I could not see how much pain and sorrow my descent had caused my wife, my family, and my close friends. As I moved farther from the darkness, I noticed all of their efforts over the last three years to keep me engaged, to check in on me, or to find other ways to show their concern.

It cost me empathy for Jay—locked indoors with me alone for three years as I fell further and further into darkness. She bore an overwhelming brunt of my trauma manifestations that got worse with every trauma: coming forward, the lockdown, John's passing, my father's long decline, my mother's cancer diagnosis, my job loss, and the absolute drain on our finances my inability to find work during the longest stretch of record-low unemployment in recorded history.

It's impossible to stress how much pain living with me through the spiral had caused.

The responsibility to accept all of this does not belong to the Holy Catholic and Apostolic Church, Defrocked Cardinal Theodore McCarrick, the Archdiocese of Newark, St. Francis, or Gerry Sudol.

It lies with me.

Just as it lies with me to manage what substances I put in my body and what my intentions with them are. I realized I had walked a delicate dance between drinking for fun and drinking to medicate my entire life. Often, those lines would blur. But beginning with the Stay-at-Home orders in the early days of the pandemic, there was no longer a line because there was no longer an alternative: I was self-medicating and nothing else.

Despite seeing my father's success with Alcoholics Anonymous, the avenue never appealed to me. Too much of the program's success depends on submission and surrendering to a higher power. There's an avenue of personal accountability that doesn't exist within this framework, and that's the power we have inside ourselves to heal without the aid of a so-called higher power.

I've had it explained to me that a "higher power" doesn't mean God, but having attended some meetings supporting my old man, that's merely lip service. Meetings end with the Lord's Prayer, not The Higher Power's one. This is not something I can succumb to.

A funny thing happened once I began to radically accept, though. I drank like a responsible adult. Two cocktails over four hours on the golf course. One beer with lunch. With no extra booze brought home to "continue the party" by myself. I have enough respect for alcohol to know I can't ever say I have a total handle on it—or any substance, for that matter. Radical acceptance means accepting your limitations as well. But I'm no longer consumed with, or beating myself up over, my drinking habits anymore.

If circumstances dictate that I eventually swear off the booze at some point, so be it. But I'm not letting the people, places, and things that caused me harm impact my ability to have some drinks while socializing with friends, hitting a tiny little white ball up and down a park, or catching the Yanks on a sunny Bronx afternoon.

So much of this, when spilled out in black and white, seems elementary to the point of absurdity. Yet it was a long and painful slog to get to those points of acceptance. And I still may have been confronting them if I hadn't dramatically changed my approach to mental healthcare following the ketamine treatment.

•••

My ordeal with the church also required acceptance of this magnitude. I didn't want to admit it, but I felt resentment at the way my case was handled. When I first announced my truth, the primary issue centered on how Sudol ever ended up at St. Francis. I was not alone in assuming that the natural progression of events would lead to a team of lawyers and clerks pouring through documents during the discovery phase of a lawsuit.

Nowhere did I think the system would group me in as one of thousands, that the church and survivors would flood the courts with lawsuits. Perhaps I should have.

Nor did I ever assume that it would be because of the testimony that survivors gave to the State Senate and Assembly. I've allowed that intrusive thought—my efforts directly contributed to my inability to get the closure that St. Francis deserved — to enter my mind. But these thoughts don't grip me like a vice anymore.

I no longer need the Archdiocese to come clean about what they knew about Gerry Sudol and what they knew about St. Francis in 1986. While it would have been something special to see a "You can't handle the truth" moment play out in a courtroom, the odds were always stacked heavily against that happening. The church is quite adept at playing the long game and waiting for media attention to evaporate.

I don't need them to come clean because I, and now you, know the truth about what happened. A parent credibly accused Sudol of sexual abuse at his stop prior to St. Francis. St. Francis housed David Ernst for a decade despite the cloud of suspicion that hovered over him. They assigned Sudol to St. Francis. The Archdiocese sent Joe Doyle to get the parish back on track, ostensibly meaning monitoring Gerry. A parent confronted Gerry about his behaviors with children, and officials shuffled him away under the cover of darkness with no explanation given to the parish beyond "nervous exhaustion."

I have radically accepted that this knowledge is enough. This is what emotional justice and peace of mind look like to me.

Sometimes, knowing is *all* the battle.

•••

Not all of these realizations and acceptances were negative. I owed myself a lot of positive self-talk, which was part of the healing process I couldn't grasp until I could accept it.

I was never loving when giving myself assessments or pep talks. I would always see my life through the prism of what I didn't have—kids, a more stable job, a balanced checkbook, my 1995 svelte physique; over what I did—a loving wife, two concerned and loving families, a roof over my head, plenty of food in my gut, and a fantastic circle of friends that any guy would be fortunate to have in his corner.

Similarly, I had allowed all that I accomplished—all that the community achieved—to dim into the background before completely fading away as darkness crept in. I wrestled excessively with my decision to come forward, often pinpointing it as my life's turning point and harboring resentment for what can't be unsaid or undone. I have thought about my truth every day since coming forward. If I continue to do so, I owe it to myself to focus on the fantastic things born out of the decision.

Thanks to my decision to come forward and the chain reaction set in motion, authorities removed abusive priests from the ministry. I was a spark in the inferno that led to the changing of New Jersey's Statutes of Limitation. I played a part in that, and I had to radically accept that I can do good things—the right things—and make a difference. That I am capable.

That I am good enough.

•••

Once I stopped obsessing over who I was, I began to find my identity again. Jay, Dr. Grant, and my parents asked at different (and multiple) times, "Who do you want to be? Who are you?" I had not realized how much shame had caused me to run away from my most significant truth: my being. I don't know who I am fully, but that's okay, too.

Throughout the pandemic and the subsequent years, I transformed from a man who would stop at nothing to bring accountability to the church into a man who felt bitter, angry, and betrayed by his world being ripped out from under him just as he was finding his footing. Coming off that one-on-one cathartic meeting with Chris and then being jolted into a panic where the only thing that mattered was surviving in a world where the air can kill you was among the worst things that could have ever happened to my psychological well-being.

But that didn't have to change my identity, and it no longer has.

I'm looking forward to getting to know the new me, as I believe he maintains so many of the outstanding characteristics I displayed before the darkness seeped in. The guy who gives a shit is still alive and looking to make a comeback. He needs to get his feet back underneath him.

I fully identify as a survivor now, but a survivor educated enough to know that he will always toe a fine line with Victimhood.

And therein lies the ultimate key to recovering from trauma: "will always."

I will always have to manage my triggers. I will always need to maintain my mental health with professionals the way I would (and should) a cardiologist. Given that there is no shame tied to my trauma, that will not be a hard thing to accept.

Friends I hold dear will always have an elevated concern for me; instead of finding humiliation or that dreaded s-word, I take solace in having such a fantastic support system. My lockdown descent drove every one of them mad, yet to this day, I'm the recipient of appreciative check-ins and included in conversations as if I'm still the same guy I've always been—only better.

...

The best advice I can give to anyone whose loved one is suffering from PTSD is to make them feel safe. Even when it looks like they don't love you, even when they're a completely different person. And believe me, IT WILL appear that they don't love you. But know that they do.

It will be frustrating. It will seem like a fool's errand. And it will hurt.

When you finally get them to seek therapy, the hurt is only beginning. Shit will get unpacked, and that will drive them mad. It's, unfortunately, part of the process—though if I could do it all over again, I would start with the dual psychologist/psychiatrist track.

Understand the difference between their external manifestation of these traumas and the moments of clarity where you get glimpses of the kinder, peaceful version of themselves. More often than not, the latter is who they intend to be. Getting to who they want to be, however, is the hardest journey they'll likely ever endure.

And to those who suffer from the condition, I never believed it, but you are not alone. You may think that your trauma was so unique to you that nobody else can understand, but that's not true. There are resources—both in your personal life and in the mental health community—to help you heal your trauma. The sooner, the better.

You are not a bad person, a failure, or a disappointment to all you hold dear. I know this because I have radically accepted that I am not a bad person, a failure, or a disappointment. You deserve to live the richest life possible. You are so much more than the events that traumatized you. As much as anyone else, you deserve to wake up happy and go to bed feeling the same way. You matter, and you are loved.

I know this because I matter and because I'm loved.

I'm never going to change the fact that Father Gerry Sudol routinely abused me at St. Francis. It will be an integral part of my life for the rest of my days. I don't know if I will ever get to where I can go an entire day without at least one passing thought about him and how he impacted my life.

But it no longer consumes me.

I am at peace with my decisions. I have forgiven myself for a lifetime of negative emotions. I can often identify when *Angry Little Eddie* is trying to manifest, and I usually shut him down before he consumes me.

And sometimes, I don't succeed. My key to understanding healing is to stop chasing the mythical "healed" declaration. Healing is a lifelong process; there's never going to be that "Eureka" moment when you realize your baggage is a thing of the past. I was healing yesterday, I'm healing at the moment, and I will be healing tomorrow.

And that was the key to recovering all along. Radically accepting that healing lasts forever. And that it doesn't have to be intimidating—quite the contrary. Healing feels every bit as relieving as the initial trauma felt debilitating. But only if you're honest with yourself every step of the way.

•••

There was one more letter I knew I had to write following Ben's eye-opening recommendation. A letter I wasn't willing to pen until I was ready to sincerely say goodbye.

Dear Little Eddie,

It wasn't your fault. What happened with Father Gerry was not your fault, and it wasn't normal. You had every right to feel awkward and alone.

You were a wonderful, very smart kid. You had the kindest soul, and you would drop everything to help anyone with anything. Everyone adored you, and for good reason.

You lost that glow somewhere in sixth grade, and it's okay. Once again, it's not your fault. You had to stop being "little" Eddie and grow up quickly—faster than anyone around you knew. There was nothing wrong with you. Let that sink in. There was nothing wrong with you. Your responses were completely normal for a child who was enduring what you were enduring.

But here's the deal, my skinny little goofball friend—I need you to heal. See, I'm forty-seven years of age now, and I can't heal until you heal. I know it sounds ridiculous, especially since you're probably learning in "Science" right now that psychiatry is witchcraft. But it's true.

The last thirty-five years since we last saw each other were pretty damn turbulent. There's a lot that I truly wish had gone differently. But I'm here to tell the story, so don't stop believing in happy endings like you just did Santa Claus.

Our happy ending isn't possible until I heal you, though, partner. And that means I have to stop listening to you every time I get upset, uncomfortable, or anxious. I need to stop yelling because it was not your fault.

This isn't the end, though, not by a mile. Little Eddie will live on in my heart as the 2nd baseman for Bill Casey's Autobody in Farm League, or the kid who took a wiffle ball bat to a Prince LP because Prince's eye scared your little brother.

The only shame I ever want Little Eddie to feel is shame over begging for and receiving that Mets satin jacket for Christmas of '86.

Disregard all that you have been taught about the confessional and reconciliation. Real forgiveness starts inside of you, and it's time for us to forgive ourselves.

Forever Grateful,

You

AUTHOR'S NOTE & ACKNOWLEDGEMENTS

Days after I finished this original manuscript, my father's long and courageous battle with cancer came to an end. He was a constant source of encouragement for this book from when I told him I was starting it while we were on the Preakness East golf course in Wayne, NJ, in the fall of 2018. It was no less of a trauma than any mentioned within the pages of this memoir and the first one I faced with a full arsenal of understanding, tools, and emotional cognizance.

I want to think I handled it as well as anyone could have, despite its many challenges, pitfalls, and landmines that dot any family trauma. I didn't drink my way through this loss the way I did for all earlier ones. If Dad's spirit is in the universe, I believe he'd be inclined to be proud of how I navigated his passing. Still, bringing this book to publication without him here to read it has been bittersweet.

Rest well, Big Ed.

From the moment I sat down to write my story, I have been extremely cautious and conscious of the sensitive subject matter and the highly personal nature of all it entails. For that reason alone, an overwhelming number of names have been altered. This is my story and my perspective, and I've used extreme caution to protect the identities of all involved in this journey. When possible, dates and locations have been changed as well, though it's hard to separate this story from many of the places wherein.

The genesis of my decision to speak my truth was obviously the "Reverb Press" article published in August of 2018. I would not have been able to get that off the ground without the guidance, compassion, and expertise of my editors there, James Reader and Ed Lynn.

I decided to self-publish after hearing feedback from those who had experience with the process. I never would have gotten this off the ground without the suggestions and guidance of friends, particularly Eric Couillard, Haitham Naba, and Samara Lynn.

Publishing independently meant being responsible for every aspect of this presentation. While the cover art is a personal original, I had to find a keen photographer for the official author portrait. I found a miracle worker in David Stewart Brown Photography. Aside from being an amazing anchor of support on my journey, Dave Brown is as talented a visual artist as I've ever met—I don't look nearly as presentable and together as his work suggests IRL.

Since I'm stubborn, frugal, and above all else, "learning to fly" again, I had a very unconditional editing process for this work. And it would not have come to fruition without two incredible, professional, and observant beta readers; Kim Johnson and Colleen Sabo.

I wasn't able to focus fully on *Nervous Exhaustion* until I possessed enough clarity to do so. Getting to that point, as you have read by now, was long and arduous. It wasn't possible to acknowledge every person who helped along the way. It still isn't, but I'd like to try.

The support from Ridgefield Park was overwhelming when I first came forward. Former parents, classmates, altar boys, and people I never met offered me familial-level support. I cherished every note of encouragement. Among those who were offering them repeatedly in public and private were Sara Graves, Kerry Milnes, Jen Wicoff, Maryanne Foster, John Tymon, Hugh Coffey, Anne Snead, Janet Terry, JP Moloughney, Dianne Saccoccia, Pam Feehan, Bernadette Choflet, David DeCarlo, Michael Coviello, Laura Casatelli, Theresa Calleja, Lydia McLean, Pat Morrone, and Koren Montalbano.

My longtime friends, as noted throughout these pages, were rocks. I wouldn't be able to reach this point without the love and backing of the Sprengel family, the Johnson family, the Peterson family, the Woods family, the Hipp family, the Burmeister family, the Kilgore family, Richard Cutrona, Professor Jay, Brian Thompson, Greg Peterson, Alex Urbiel, Lara Holden, Carol Grauman, Amanda Grove, Shamara Ijames, Beth Miller, Sara Vanhouten, and Leslie Cruz.

The entire ordeal, from my decision to come forward to the publication of this book and all of the coverage and attention, was not always easy on—or comfortable for—my family and in-laws. Faith is deeply personal, and the lines between faith and religion are often blurred. My truth struck at the heart of this deeply personal belief. But if it caused them any consternation, they never let me know. They loved me through my worst and backed me through my best. My heartfelt gratitude to the Hanratty and Reap families and to "extended ones" the Tuite family, the Hutchinson family, the Averys, and the Gordons.

More people than I can name reached out with concern for me while I was in the deepest of valleys. Many of them folks I've never met in person. But something in my outward behavior struck them as cries for help, and even the most basic of check-ins meant the world to me and—no hyperbole—often saved me. Most of you likely have no idea those "keep your head up" prompts kept my head above water. We truly are our brothers' keepers. I was helped out of the darkness by Scott O'Neill, Dev Chastain, Patty Votta, Jennifer Sullivan, Ajene Simmons, Noel Sweeney, Dan Hanratty, Tara Misplay, Lorri Davis, Jeff Goulbourne, Tony Lord, Mark Palmieri, Jeanette Taibi, and Jo Conrath.

Finally, none of this would be possible without the love and support—in so many ways—of my wife, Jaime. From the moment she saw me hand-writing a high-school drama in 1995 to the tough love act of buying me a writing desk, she's been my loudest cheerleader and never wavered in her belief that I would finish this work.
(Ok, maybe she rightly wavered at the worst of times.) Above all else, she shouldered the financial, emotional, practical, and mental burdens of our marriage almost exclusively on her own throughout my collapse and recovery while I was unable to get out of my own way or string together enough good days to ease the pain and concern.

If the world saw the tip of my iceberg when I came forward and saw me as brave and heroic, Jay witnessed the danger below the water's surface. This book does not do enough justice to her sacrifice, tolerance, and strength through the darkest hours. And it never would have been written without her.

ABOUT THE AUTHOR

Photo Credit: David Stewart Brown Photography

Ed Hanratty is a seasoned writer with over 20 years of experience in the news media industry. A lifelong resident of New Jersey, Ed lives with his wife Jaime and their dog Yogi along the northern border of the state. His career in journalism began in 2002, and since then, he has made a name for himself as a freelance writer, contributing to renowned outlets such as NBC News, Reverb Press, HuffPost, and Yahoo! News.

When he's not immersed in his writing, Ed enjoys a variety of pastimes that keep him grounded and inspired. He admits to golfing poorly but finds joy in the game nonetheless. His love for music is a constant companion, and he never misses an opportunity to watch a good ballgame.

"Nervous Exhaustion" is Ed Hanratty's debut memoir, where he courageously shares his personal journey through childhood abuse, survival, and advocacy. This deeply moving book not only exposes the harrowing experiences he endured but also serves as a testament to his resilience and dedication to helping others. Ed is already hard at work on his next project, a reimagining of what a Father's Day book can be, promising more heartfelt and impactful storytelling to come.

Printed in the USA
CPSIA information can be obtained
at www.ICGtesting.com
CBHW030825070724
11194CB00002B/50